LIBRARY IN A BOOK

ECOTERRORISM

Douglas Long

☑®
Facts On File, Inc.

ECOTERRORISM

Facts On File, Inc.
132 West 31st Street
New York NY 10001

Library of Congress Cataloging-in-Publication Data
Long, Douglas, 1967-
   Ecoterrorism / Douglas Long.
      p. cm.—(Library in a book)
Includes bibliographical references and index.
   ISBN 0-8160-5525-4
   1. Environmentalism—United States—History. 2. Ecoterrorism—United States—History. I. Title. II. Series.
   GE197.L66 2004
   303.6′25–dc22
         2003024721

Facts On File books are available at special discounts when purchased in bulk quantities for businesses, associations, institutions, or sales promotions. Please call our Special Sales Department in New York at (212) 967-8800 or (800) 322-8755.

You can find Facts On File on the World Wide Web at http://www.factsonfile.com

Printed in the United States of America

MP Hermitage 10 9 8 7 6 5 4 3 2 1

This book is printed on acid-free paper.

CONTENTS

PART I
OVERVIEW OF THE TOPIC

Chapter 1
Issues in Ecoterrorism   **3**

Chapter 2
The Law and Ecoterrorism   **61**

Chapter 3
Chronology   **88**

Chapter 4
Biographical Listing   **127**

Chapter 5
Glossary   **148**

PART II
GUIDE TO FURTHER RESEARCH

Chapter 6
How to Research Ecoterrorism   **159**

Chapter 7
Annotated Bibliography   **170**

Chapter 8
Organizations and Agencies   **238**

PART III
APPENDICES

Appendix A
Statement of James F. Jarboe, February 12, 2002   **257**

Appendix B
Written Testimony of Craig Rosebraugh, February 7, 2002   **264**

Appendix C
Testimony of Ron Arnold, June 9, 1998   **279**

Appendix D
Testimony of Barry R. Clausen, June 9, 1998   **282**

Appendix E
Excerpts from the "Unabomber Manifesto,"
September 19, 1995   **285**

Index   **289**

PART I

OVERVIEW OF THE TOPIC

CHAPTER 1

ISSUES IN ECOTERRORISM

Before October 18, 1998, few people in the United States had heard of the Earth Liberation Front (ELF). On that night, arsonists set a series of fires at a Vail, Colorado, ski facility, in which four ski lifts, a restaurant, a picnic facility, and a utility building were destroyed. Damage exceeded $12 million, making it the most expensive act of destruction in the name of environmentalism in U.S. history at the time. On October 21, Colorado Public Radio and the *Vail Trail* newspaper received a communiqué from the ELF that explained,

> *On behalf of the lynx, 5 [The communiqué claimed five buildings, but only three were actually destroyed] buildings and four ski lifts at Vail were reduced to ashes on the night of Sunday, October 18th. Vail, Inc. is already the largest ski operation in North America and now wants to expand it even further. The 12 miles of roads and 885 acres of clear cuts will ruin the last, best lynx habitat in the state. Putting profits ahead of Colorado's wildlife will not be tolerated. This action is just a warning. We will be back if this greedy corporation continues to trespass into wild and unroaded areas. For your safety and convenience, we strongly advise skiers to choose other destinations until Vail cancels its inexcusable plans for expansion.[1]*

The Federal Bureau of Investigation (FBI) estimates that between 1996 and 2002, the ELF and an affiliated organization, the Animal Liberation Front (ALF), committed more than 600 criminal acts in the United States, resulting in damages in excess of $43 million. Much of this was caused by the use of arson against animal research laboratories, U.S. Forest Service equipment, new housing developments, genetic research facilities, and sport utility vehicles (SUVs).

The FBI categorizes ELF/ALF attacks as acts of "ecoterrorism," which it defines as "the use or threatened use of violence of a criminal nature against innocent victims or property by an environmentally oriented, subnational

3

group for environmental-political reasons, or aimed at an audience beyond the target, often of a symbolic nature." According to the U.S. government, ecoterrorism falls within the category of special interest extremism, which can be distinguished from traditional right-wing and left-wing extremism in that proponents seek to resolve specific issues (in this case slowing destruction of the environment) rather than to effect widespread political change. Some special interest extremists, the FBI has noted, have turned increasingly toward vandalism and terrorist activity in attempts to further their causes. Among these extremists are anti-abortion activists, animal rights activists, and radical environmentalists.

The ELF/ALF are not the first groups to eschew the use of political lobbies, petitions, and letter-writing campaigns in favor of more extreme means to further environmental causes. The early 1970s saw a spate of isolated acts of environmental sabotage across the United States, from a campaign against polluting corporations in Illinois led by an anonymous man known as the Fox to the destruction of mining equipment on Black Mesa in the desert Southwest by the Arizona Phantom. Also around this time, the environmental organization Greenpeace, taking its cues from Indian pacifist Mohandas K. Gandhi and the U.S. Civil Rights movement, began using nonviolent civil disobedience to protest nuclear testing and whaling on the open seas. In 1977, founding member Paul Watson, believing that nonviolent tactics did not go far enough to protect animal life in the world's oceans, split from Greenpeace to form the Sea Shepherd Conservation Society (SSCS). This new organization took activism on the high seas to a new level by using such methods of destruction as cutting drift nets and ramming whaling ships to attack commercial fishing operations. In 1980, Dave Foreman and four other environmental activists formed Earth First!, which condoned the use of "monkeywrenching" to destroy offensive billboards, sabotage construction equipment, and drive spikes into trees to prevent logging. Most ominously, in 1978 Theodore Kaczynski (the Unabomber) began an 18-year bombing campaign that targeted scientists and businessmen he felt were responsible for perpetuating the environmentally destructive "industrial-technological" system. Before he was caught by the FBI in 1996, Kaczynski had killed three people and injured 23.

This list represents a wide variety of radical environmental tactics and philosophies, all of which have been labeled as "terrorist activity" at one time or another. Many radical environmentalists argue that, with the exception of Kaczynski's clearly terroristic bombing campaign, such a label is unfair. Even the ELF, they point out, takes great care to avoid harming both humans and animals even while destroying private property. Is it reasonable, ELF supporters ask, to compare the crime of burning down an empty building to the more heinous act of hijacking commercial airliners and flying them into the World Trade Center towers? Given the increased zeal with which federal authorities have sought to arrest terrorists since September 11, 2001, answers to questions concerning the point at which political expression crosses the line from peaceful civil disobedience to acts of violence and, beyond that, into the realm of terrorism have become vitally important.

CIVIL DISOBEDIENCE, SABOTAGE, AND TERRORISM

Although the scale of violence used by the ELF/ALF is tiny compared to that perpetrated by political terrorists, the fact remains that these activists have chosen to work outside the democratic system, using illegal acts of destruction in order to bring attention to their agenda. These militant environmentalists have argued that their campaign against inanimate objects is a struggle for liberation akin to such all-American revolutionary acts of property destruction as the Boston Tea Party. Critics maintain that ecoterrorists operate under the assumption that nature is good and humans are bad, a dangerous philosophy that will ultimately lead the most radical among them to emulate the murderous tactics of the Unabomber.

Radical environmental groups generally share the belief that human destruction of the Earth has reached a critical stage, leaving no time for compromise or to work within the established legal system. They also agree that "fundamental alterations in values or social, political, and economic structures are needed to bring humans into harmony with nature."[2] On a tactical level, these groups rely on the use of "direct action," which involves abandoning "symbolic" protest action (such as lobbying politicians to change their policies) in favor of taking action to achieve an immediate result in an area of concern. Direct action against logging, for example, can include planting trees to replace those that have been cut, taking up long-term residence in a tree (a tactic known as "tree sitting"), or hammering metal spikes into a stand of trees ("tree spiking"). Tree sitting and tree spiking are both used to prevent trees from being cut down, but each represents a distinct form of direct action.

Tree sitting falls within the realm of "civil disobedience," a form of protest that involves breaking the law to register discontent about laws or policies that activists deem unjust or unethical. Such actions, usually nonviolent and nondestructive, are not intended to subvert the government but rather to persuade authorities to change the law to rectify the perceived injustice. Participants in civil disobedience are usually willing to accept the consequences of their actions by not resisting arrest and by accepting legal penalties imposed on them. Tree spiking, on the other hand, is a form of "sabotage" that involves the threat of property damage: If a spiked tree is cut and run through a saw mill, the mill's blade may be damaged or destroyed when it hits the metal spike. Sabotage committed for the purpose of protecting the environment is known variously as monkeywrenching, ecotage, or ecosabotage. Other forms of monkeywrenching include destroying construction and logging equipment, removing survey stakes, defacing or destroying billboards, slashing the tires of off-road vehicles, and setting fire to new homes under construction. Unlike those who participate in civil disobedience, monkeywrenchers tend to operate anonymously and in secret to avoid getting caught.

These distinctions are extremely important to the study of ecoterrorism. Some attempts have been made to equate the actions of nonviolent activists, such as Greenpeace, with those of saboteurs like the ELF/ALF. Among those who have pressed federal authorities to lump bombing and sabotage with civil disobedience is Ron Arnold, founder of the anti-environmental wise use movement. Arnold believes that civil disobedience that involves "imposing physical impediments preventing persons from going where they ordinarily have a right to go," far from being peaceful, constitutes "an act of physical coercion, an act of violence against another, regardless of how passively performed." Although he acknowledges "a tradition of civil disobedience in America, seminally expressed in Henry David Thoreau's *On the Duty of Civil Disobedience*," he says that "there is no right to civil disobedience."[3] At a 1998 hearing on ecoterrorism before the House of Representatives Subcommittee on Crime, Arnold stated that "the range of ecoterror crimes ranges from the most violent felonies of attempted murder to misdemeanor offenses such as criminal trespass."

One danger in accepting this point of view, political activists point out, is illustrated by Arnold's acknowledgment of Thoreau as a proponent of civil disobedience. There is a long tradition of support for civil disobedience in the United States, dating back to its use by American colonists in the 18th century against the English colonial government. Thoreau and Martin Luther King, Jr., advocated its use as a means to combat injustice in society, and civil disobedience has been "used by both ordinary citizens and political dissenters to protest unfair taxes, death penalty, racism, war, militarism, sexism, nuclear testing, abortion, restrictions on women's rights, animal testing, AIDS policies of the federal government, and environmental issues such as whaling, sealing, and logging."[4] To broaden the definition of terrorism to include criminal trespass and other acts of passive resistance would mean placing civil disobedience advocates Thoreau, Mohandas K. Gandhi, Martin Luther King, Jr., and the founders of Greenpeace alongside Osama bin Laden in the pantheon of terrorist masterminds, an extremist position that the vast majority of Americans would clearly find unacceptable.

Issues in Ecoterrorism

More difficult is the question of whether sabotage should be considered an act of terrorism. Gandhi believed that the destruction of property is an act of violence, as does Greenpeace. This view lies at the root of Greenpeace's decision to expel member Paul Watson for being a violent "vigilante" after he tossed a sealer's club into the water during a 1977 protest. Watson, who once wrote that "few changes on this planet have taken place solely because of nonviolent action" and that "to remain nonviolent totally is to allow the perpetuation of violence against people, animals, and the environment," formed the more radical Sea Shepherd Conservation Society (SSCS) immediately after his expulsion.[5] FBI Domestic Terrorism Section Chief James F. Jarboe has identified the formation of SSCS as the genesis of ecoterrorism, even though the group has maintained strict guidelines against harming humans or animals in its actions. Based on this designation and the U.S. Department of Justice's belief that the ELF/ALF are dangerous domestic terrorist organizations, it is clear that federal authorities hold the view that destruction of property is a violent act and that destruction of property for political ends is a terrorist act.

Not everyone agrees. Earth First! cofounder Dave Foreman argues that monkeywrenching is "nonviolent resistance to the destruction of natural diversity and wilderness" that is

> *never directed toward human beings or other forms of life. It is aimed at inanimate machines and tools that are destroying life. Care is always taken to minimize any possible threat to people, including the monkeywrenchers themselves.*[6]

Edward Abbey, a radical environmentalist and anarchist who helped inspire the formation of Earth First!, believed there was a clear difference between terrorism and sabotage, the first being a form of deadly violence directed against people and other living things, the second being the use of force against inanimate objects. He once defined terrorism as "deadly violence—for a political and/or economic purpose—carried out against people and other living things, [that] is usually conducted by governments against their own citizens . . . or by corporate entities . . . against the land and all creatures that depend upon the land for life and livelihood."[7] Likewise, the ELF claims its actions are guided by a nonviolent, nonterrorist ideology whose aim is to "protect all life on planet earth."[8]

In the midst of this wrangling over terms and tactics, what remains clear is that the democratic form of government upon which the political system in the United States is based generally favors social change using peaceful means and nonviolent resistance rather than more extreme methods. The use of blatantly criminal tactics, including the destruction of property, is difficult to justify ethically and is usually thought to lack political credibility. The burden, therefore, is on groups like the ELF/ALF to defend their choice of tactics.

What is also clear is that continuing worries over terrorist attacks in the United States since 9/11 have facilitated attempts to broaden the definition of *terrorism*. On September 11, 2003, following a drive-by shooting that killed two teenagers at a bus stop, Los Angeles police chief William J. Bratton compared that crime to the terrorist attacks on New York and Washington, D.C., that had occurred exactly two years before. "The reality is we are facing two forms of terrorism," he stated at a press conference, "that from across the waters and the terrorism here at home."[9] This growing tendency to equate common, albeit tragic, crimes with acts of terrorism is particularly distressing to civil libertarians following passage of the USA PATRIOT Act of 2001, which expanded the FBI's powers of search and surveillance and also legalized the indefinite detention of both citizens and noncitizens without formal charges in the course of terrorism investigations. In the absence of clear consensus on the parameters of terrorism, many civil libertarians worry that questionable use of search and seizure, even in investigations of ordinary citizens or nonviolent political activists, can be justified by federal authorities.

Again, this debate over terminology has serious repercussions for radical environmentalists. At a February 12, 2002, congressional hearing on ecoterrorism, Richard Berman, executive director of the Center for Consumer Freedom, suggested that the FBI seek out ELF/ALF activists with the "same vengeance" that they pursue supporters of al-Qaeda.[10] Representative Scott McInnis of Colorado asked, "If you're going to tolerate [ecoterrorism], then why not tolerate al-Qaeda?" He urged lawmakers and law enforcement personnel to "take away the Robin Hood mystique from these terrorists, which is what they are."[11] Others have enumerated the parallels between al-Qaeda and the ELF/ALF, claiming that both believe "they are the sole proprietor of truth and righteousness," both believe they "have the right to impose their concepts of truth and righteousness on society," and both "attack people who they think have violated nature's or God's law."[12]

This attempt to equate al-Qaeda and ecoterrorism has drawn its share of criticism, even from those who do not support the ELF's tactics. Many people question the idea that destructive but nonlethal arsons committed by the ELF/ALF are of the same caliber as the September 11 attacks by al-Qaeda that killed thousands of people. One writer suggested that using the word *terrorist* to describe ELF/ALF activists only served to diminish the term, pointing out that while incidences of property destruction are not uncommon in American culture, "the wholesale slaughter of thousands of innocent civilians is a horror unique in its barbarity."[13]

In a democratic culture that tends not to accept extremist tactics as a legitimate form of political expression and that is still recovering from the shock of 9/11, consensus among mainstream environmentalists is that groups like the ELF/ALF may prove to be a liability to the environmental movement as a whole. In the long run, property destruction, whether one views it as an act of terrorism or not, threatens to be counterproductive because it makes all environmentalists seem irrational and dangerous. Perhaps more important, environmentalists say, it creates an atmosphere of public acceptance for the harassment and persecution of nonviolent activists who have nothing to do with terrorism.

THE U.S. ENVIRONMENTAL MOVEMENT

Radical environmentalism did not, of course, appear out of thin air. It is therefore important to survey the development of the American environmental movement and discuss the ideas and trends that gave birth to the philosophies and tactics of the more militant environmentalists of the 1970s and beyond.

PRECURSORS TO ENVIRONMENTALISM

The emergence of environmentalism in the United States is generally seen as a backlash against a long tradition of viewing nature as an infinite resource to be conquered and tamed for use by humans. From the first successful English settlement at Jamestown, Virginia, in 1607, colonists coveted land ownership and considered any tract not occupied by Europeans to be available for the taking. Land ownership usually involved cutting down trees and transforming the parcel from forestland to farmland.

During the 17th century, these settlers, many of whom had sailed to the Americas to escape religious persecution, believed, according to writer Benjamin Kline, that they had a God-given right to subdue both nature and the "heathen" Native Americans, and that efforts to bring European civilization to the Americas were a fulfillment of God's will. By the 19th century, views of the relationship between humanity and nature were also influenced by the philosophies of the Enlightenment and the scientific revolution, which saw the conquest of nature as necessary to ensure the continued progress of humanity. Technological advancement was praised as a means to increase the rate at which nature could be exploited to supply humanity's needs and raise the standard of living.

During the 1840s, a melding of both the religious and Enlightenment justifications for conquering the environment resulted in the concept of

Ecoterrorism

Manifest Destiny, the belief that God had ordained Americans to spread their civilization and culture across the continent. Americans pursued this idea with such zeal that by 1860 the United States had become the fourth-ranked industrial nation in the world. During this time, the rate of urbanization rapidly increased, railroads expanded, logging of forests quickened, hunting brought North American bison and many predator species close to extinction, and domesticated farm animals began replacing native species.

Following the Civil War, when westward expansion became official government policy, the pace of these changes further increased. The federal government enacted a series of laws designed to induce pioneers to face the hardships of the frontier. The Homestead Act of 1862 granted settlers 160 acres if they lived on and developed the land for five years. The Timber Culture Act of 1873, an effort to improve land in dry areas, granted homesteaders an additional 160 acres if they grew trees on 40 of them. The Desert Land Act of 1877 offered 640 acres at $1.25 each in states with little rainfall, provided the owner irrigated part of it within three years. The Timber and Stone Act of 1878 sold 160 acres of forestland for $2.50 each. Although intended to benefit individuals and families, these loosely regulated laws were often exploited by speculators, timber companies, and cattle ranchers seeking to increase investments and profits. Meanwhile, the Industrial Revolution fueled rapid urbanization in the East, replacing nature with the artificial surroundings of cities.

In the midst of this frenzy of expansion and development, a small number of individuals began rejecting the mechanical, authoritarian view of the universe popularized during the Enlightenment. The American and European Romantic cultural movements, lasting roughly from 1770 to 1830, had already called for an appreciation of personal freedom, individualism, imagination, and intuition. This rejection of cold scientific rationality led many proponents of Romanticism to cultivate a love of wilderness and the mysteries of nature.

During the 1840s and 1850s, the American transcendental movement, taking its cue from the Romantics, denounced the materialism of industrial culture and exalted nature and Native American and Asian philosophies. Transcendental writers Ralph Waldo Emerson and Henry David Thoreau developed the philosophy of the Oversoul, a divine moral force that flowed through and existed within every living thing. Humans were seen as just one component of a diverse natural system, while the Earth was considered to be an organic entity possessing a body and imbued with a spirit of its own. This emphasis on the interconnectedness of all life would later become an important component of deep ecology and other philosophies that inspired radical environmentalism.

Thoreau, in fact, presaged the development of the environmental movement in several respects, and his deep reverence for nature laid the foundation for contemporary environmental ethics. He is considered to be among the first American writers to challenge the destruction of nature on moral grounds and to criticize the federal government and industrialists for their belief that natural resources were inexhaustible. He once protested when local farmers cut down trees and cleared underbrush, writing, "If some are prosecuted for abusing children, others deserve to be prosecuted for maltreating the face of nature committed to their care."[14]

In 1845, Thoreau moved to a cabin at Walden Pond near Concord, Massachusetts, to write, live a simple life, and carefully observe his surroundings. The resulting book, *Walden, or Life in the Woods,* revealed the author's view that nature, far from being a wasteland to be conquered in the name of human progress, deserved to be preserved for the spiritual benefit of all humans. Such a project, he believed, would be more rewarding than the endless pursuit of material gain.

Thoreau was also well known for his willingness to take action in support of social issues. He spoke frequently at abolitionist meetings, and in 1846, in protest of the Mexican War, he was jailed for refusing to pay the poll tax. Three years later, he presented his theory of social action in the long essay "Civil Disobedience," which continues to influence activists who use passive resistance as a means to protest perceived injustices. In another book, *A Week on the Concord and Merrimack Rivers* (1849), Thoreau wrote of his willingness to at least entertain actions that went beyond mere passive resistance. Worried that a dam under construction on the Concord River would interrupt shad spawning runs, he wrote, "Who hears the fishes when they cry? I for one am with thee, and who knows what may avail a crowbar against Billerica dam."[15] Such acts of sabotage would become the hallmark of Earth First! during the 1980s.

CONSERVATION AND PRESERVATION

The basic principles of conservation were first presented by George Perkins Marsh in the book *Man and Nature* (1864), which argued, against popular consensus, that many past civilizations had crumbled because they had wasted natural resources. Marsh counseled that humanity's "power to transform the natural world should entail a commensurate sense of responsibility."[16] These radical ideas fueled a backlash against the perceived ravages of the Industrial Revolution that began to bear fruit in 1872 when the federal government designated Yellowstone as the first national park in the world. Around the same time, U.S. Interior Secretary Carl Schurz began lobbying for the protection of federally owned forests. In 1891, Congress authorized

11

the president to designate public lands as forest reserves (later called national forests), a power used by presidents Benjamin Harrison and Grover Cleveland in the 1890s to protect more than 35 million acres of forestland.

Also influential in the creation of new national parks and forest reserves was naturalist John Muir, credited by many environmentalists as the first activist to develop a conscious environmental ethic. In the 1870s, he began publishing articles on the natural wonders of California's Sierra Nevada that helped raise public support for the designation of Yosemite Valley as a national park in 1890. Two years later, Muir founded the Sierra Club with the goal of enlisting government and popular support for safeguarding the natural features of the Sierra Nevada from development. Success in the Yosemite Valley campaign inspired Muir to spend the 1890s pressuring the federal government to establish a system of forest reserves in the surrounding region.

In 1901, Theodore Roosevelt became the first president of the Progressive Era, which was characterized by efforts to increase government regulation in order to limit the excesses of large corporations and rectify problems that had arisen from the unrestricted growth that occurred during the Industrial Revolution. Upon taking office, Roosevelt declared that conservation would be one of his administration's top priorities. True to his word, the president expanded the national forest system from 42 million acres to 172 million acres, urged Congress to create six new national parks and 51 national wildlife refuges, and promoted passage of the Lacey Antiquities Act of 1906, which gave him the power to create 18 national monuments in the western United States.

In 1905, Roosevelt also created the U.S. Forest Service (USFS) to manage the national forest system. The agency's first head was Gifford Pinchot, whose approach to forestry was based on a utilitarian ideal that viewed nature as a depository of natural resources for human use. This policy, which continues to shape USFS management practices to this day, found its ultimate expression at Roosevelt's 1908 Conservation Conference at the White House. Roosevelt and Pinchot convinced state officials in attendance that the main goal of conservation was to protect human health, an idea that remains a strong argument in favor of regulating the use of natural resources.

Conspicuously absent from the Conservation Conference was John Muir, whom Pinchot had intentionally failed to invite. Pinchot and Muir were the lead proponents of two different, and often opposing, approaches to wilderness management. Pinchot was the driving force behind conservation, the view that undeveloped forests and grasslands should be managed with the aim of ensuring that future generations would have an adequate supply of the natural resources harvested from these areas. This philosophy has resulted in USFS management practices based on multiple use, which involves keeping national forests open to a wide range of activities, such as mining, logging, hunting, and recreation. Muir, on the other hand, had developed the philosophy of "preservation," which held that undeveloped natural areas had intrinsic value and deserved to exist for their own sake rather than as depositories of natural resources for human use. Muir and his supporters argued that Pinchot's policies would eventually lead to commercial misuse of nature.

Pinchot's refusal to invite Muir to the 1908 conference was an early shot in an ongoing battle between conservationists and preservationists that came to a climax in 1913, when officials from the city of San Francisco sought to build a dam in Yosemite National Park that would flood picturesque Hetch Hetchy Valley. Muir fought to stop construction because he believed the project would undermine the integrity of the park system and because the reservoir would destroy the beauty of the valley. Pinchot and Roosevelt both supported the dam, which San Francisco officials said would solve the city's water problems and provide a source of hydroelectricity. Although Congress eventually passed a bill that allowed the dam to be built, handing a victory to conservationists, Muir's campaign to stop the project widened public support for the idea of preservation.

Not long after the 1908 Conservation Conference, Arizona USFS employee Aldo Leopold began questioning the conservationist view when he shot a wolf as part of a federal program to rid the Southwest of predators so there would be more deer for hunters. Leopold wrote that seeing the "fierce fire dying" in the animal's eyes led him to conclude that "neither the wolf nor the mountain agreed" with USFS policies.[17] He became an advocate of wolf protection, was instrumental in establishing the first official wilderness area in a national forest (a preservationist-oriented designation that disallowed development and resource extraction), and cofounded the preservationist Wilderness Society. In the 1940s, Leopold wrote *A Sand County Almanac*, a compendium of notes and journal entries that provided insight into the preservationist philosophy. Most influential was the section titled "The Land Ethic," in which Leopold suggested extending ethics beyond human-to-human and human-to-society relations to include "man's relation to the land and to the animals and plants which grow upon it." In this section he wrote, "A thing is right when it tends to preserve the integrity, stability, and beauty of the biotic community. It is wrong when it tends otherwise."[18] This ethic was a precursor of deep ecology, an environmental philosophy developed in the 1970s that had a profound influence on radical environmentalism.

Efforts to slow the destruction of the environment lost impetus in the 1920s under the administration of President William Howard Taft, who was more interested in economic development, but conservation again became an issue during the New Deal administration of President Franklin Roosevelt in the 1930s. Although Roosevelt was forced to give priority to the pressing economic concerns of the Great Depression, he was sympathetic to conservation issues and believed that managing the environment was a huge and complex task that required the power and money of the federal government. During this time, Interior Secretary Harold L. Ickes helped expand the national park system, while Robert Marshall, chief of the USFS Division of Recreation and Lands, helped steer the USFS, at least temporarily, toward preservation policies. In 1935, he founded the Wilderness Society with Aldo Leopold. The Roosevelt administration also outlawed the killing of predators in national parks and formed the U.S. Fish and Wildlife Service (FWS), which immediately established 160 new wildlife refuges.

This push toward environmental protection was interrupted by the outbreak of World War II; the cold war and economic prosperity of the postwar era continued to divert attention away from environmental concerns. The resulting atomic age also helped spur renewed belief in scientific supremacy and the idea that science could be used to control nature and fix humanity's problems. Clues that all was not well, however, occasionally bubbled up from beneath the veneer of widespread prosperity. Most notorious was the blanket of industrial smog that settled over the valley of the steel-mill town of Donora, Pennsylvania, in October 1947. By the time the smog lifted several days later, 20 people were dead and 6,000 more had fallen ill.

ENVIRONMENTALISM AS A MASS MOVEMENT

Despite a general lack of interest in environmental issues throughout the 1950s, Sierra Club executive director David Brower spent the decade widening the organization's focus beyond the Sierra Nevada and developing more aggressive means to confront environmental degradation. Using a variety of unprecedented lobbying strategies, he succeeded in stopping federal efforts to build dams in Colorado's Dinosaur National Monument. As part of a compromise, however, Brower agreed not to oppose construction of Arizona's Glen Canyon Dam, later seen by radical environmentalists as a symbol of federal environmental policies run amok.

The impetus toward the development of environmentalism as a mass movement began after the 1962 publication of Rachel Carson's book *Silent Spring*, which presented scientific evidence that widespread use of pesticides and herbicides was harmful to humans and to wildlife, especially birds. Representatives of the agriculture and pesticide industries charged that Carson's book was part of a communist plot to ruin American agriculture, while some politicians tried to trivialize the book because Carson was a woman. Despite the opposition, Carson's book led President John F. Kennedy to establish the President's Science Advisory Committee to investigate the effects of pesticide use. By the end of 1962, 40 bills regulating the use of pesticides had been introduced in state legislatures across the country.

More legislation followed. The Clean Air Act of 1963 appropriated funds to deal with air pollution. The Wilderness Act of 1964, seen as a turning point for the U.S. environmental movement, gave legislative protection to 9 million acres of wilderness and included mechanisms for designating more acreage in the future. The U.S. Park Service, U.S. Forest Service, and U.S. Fish and Wildlife Service were given the task of reviewing holdings for potential wilderness designation, and the Federal Land Policy and Management Act of 1976 expanded the 1964 act to include the Bureau of Land Management. The Wilderness Act was a rare victory for preservation over conservation: Lands under its protection were closed to development, and opportunities for resource extraction were seriously curtailed.

Meanwhile, environmentalism began taking hold of the popular imagination, both as a result of the work of organized environmental groups and as an expression of growing anger among the public over a series of environmental disasters, including the 1969 Santa Barbara, California, oil spill and the time the Cuyahoga River in Ohio caught fire. Large numbers of people became concerned about extinction of species, pollution of water and air, destruction of forests, and squandering of natural resources. Under the guidance of David Brower, the Sierra Club grew sevenfold during the 1960s, from 16,066 members in 1960 to 114,336 in 1970, and scored important victories in stopping the construction of a series of dams in the Grand Canyon. The movement built toward Earth Day in 1970, which "marked the birth of environmentalism as a social movement with broad public support."[19]

The idea for Earth Day began when a group of students organized an environmental "teach-in" at the University of Michigan. With promotion from Wisconsin senator Gaylord Nelson, this small gathering was transformed into a national event. In an article for *Reader's Digest*, Nelson wrote, "Whether they are burning billboards, burying an internal combustion engine or giving out 'dishonor awards' ('Smokestack of the Month'), students everywhere have shown a flair for spotlighting the issue." Earth Day coordinator Denis Hayes, a Harvard pre-law student, called on Earth Day participants to "bypass the traditional political process." Both of these comments acknowledged the growing importance of protests based on direct action and presaged Earth First!'s use of both sabotage and guerrilla theater.[20]

Earth Day itself, held April 22, 1970, was considered by many to be a resounding success. Twenty million people participated in events at 1,500 campuses and 10,000 schools across the nation; 250,000 people gathered in Washington, D.C., where both houses of Congress recessed to allow members to take part in the day's events; and 100,000 people walked down Fifth Avenue in Manhattan, which was closed to traffic for two hours. Not everyone was enthralled with the growing environmental movement. Interior Secretary Walter Hickel chose Earth Day to announce plans for an 800-mile oil pipeline across the Arctic tundra in Alaska, while on the same day the U.S. Department of Commerce granted a permit for a major oil refinery outside Honolulu, Hawaii. Meanwhile, many leftists who had been involved in the 1960s counterculture saw Earth Day as a distraction from the antiwar and black power movements. Students for a Democratic Society (SDS) and many African-American militants boycotted events.

Nevertheless, broad public support for Earth Day gave added impetus to the drive for environmental legislation on the federal level. In his 1970 State of the Union address, President Richard Nixon said that the 1970s "absolutely must be the years when America pays its debt to the past by reclaiming the purity of its air, its water. . . . It is literally now or never."[21] Signing the National Environmental Policy Act (NEPA) on January 1, 1970, was his first official act of what he called the new "environmental decade."[22] The legislation, which required environmental impact statements for federally funded construction projects and led to the establishment of the Environmental Protection Agency (EPA) to enforce new statutes, was followed by the revised Clean Air Act of 1970, which identified 189 smog-causing pollutants, established standards to regulate their emission, and required installation of anti-pollution technology in factories. The Clean Water Act of 1972 regulated the release of pollutants into waterways and mandated steps to restore polluted waters for recreational use, while the Endangered Species Act of 1973 allowed species to be listed as endangered or threatened without considering the economic consequences.

RADICAL ENVIRONMENTALISM

The years following Earth Day saw a dramatic increase in membership among mainstream environmental organizations, such as the Sierra Club and the Wilderness Society, which continued to focus on legislation, lawsuits, regulatory action, and the electorate. New groups also formed, many of which were inspired by changing social values that had emerged during the 1960s to radicalize their views. By Earth Day, the term *revolution* had become a common part of environmental rhetoric, even among leaders of mainstream groups. For many, revolution merely meant significant changes in personal lifestyles, while others condoned wholesale alterations of values and attitudes toward nature. Some radicals, however, called for extensive changes in legal and economic institutions, and the most extreme indicated a willingness to fight for the outright overthrow of the U.S. political system.

Issues in Ecoterrorism

EARLY MILITANT ACTIONS

In January 1970, even as President Nixon was signing NEPA into law and mainstream environmentalists were gearing up for Earth Day, San Francisco–based Bay Area Institute codirector Barry Weisberg argued that an "authentic environmental movement" would develop only when "something very basic and very revolutionary is done about the continued destruction of our life support system." Militant actions against "corporate despoilers," including sabotage, would be part of this movement, which he believed was imminent.[23]

The following year, a group of Earth Day organizers formed Environmental Action to focus public concerns on solutions to ecological problems. The group published *Earth Tool Kit* (1971), which urged environmentalists to undertake direct action "without any intermediate steps and with a specific objective in mind." Such actions could be violent or nonviolent, the authors wrote, but "must be carefully planned to avoid confusion and to generate the right results and sympathies among a larger group of people." The goal was to get the public to apply "social pressures to corporations and other institutions that are polluting, exploiting or otherwise acting as bad citizens."[24]

In 1972, Environmental Action published a second book, this one called *Ecotage!* The title marked the coining of the term *ecotage* (a combination of *ecology* and *sabotage*), which the authors chose over *sabotology* (*sabotage* plus *ecology*) because it emphasized the ecological aspects of their actions.[25] The book was born out of a "national contest" in which Environmental Action called on activists to send in ideas for individual and collective action, the best of which they promised to publish. The authors called the result a "collection of ideas . . . on how the individual can apply social pressures to corporations and other institutions that are polluting, exploiting, or otherwise acting as bad citizens." The contest prompted the U.S. Chamber of Commerce to issue a warning to its members that businesses might be the "target of sabotage done in the name of ecology."[26]

Most of the suggestions published in *Ecotage!* were mainstream, such as organizing letter-writing campaigns and boycotts. A few, however, touched on tactics that would later be espoused by Earth First! Among these were destroying billboards, putting sugar in gas tanks, removing survey stakes, mailing the carcasses of coyotes killed by federal poisoning campaigns to the U.S. Fish and Wildlife Service, destroying equipment at construction sites, and wrecking highway construction projects by "turning over tractors and bulldozers and tearing up the already laid concrete with pick-axes."[27]

Such actions did not occur only in the minds of the contributors. In fact, Environmental Action's contest had been inspired by the exploits of an

17

anonymous eco-saboteur known as the Fox, who conducted a campaign against polluting corporations in Chicago in the early 1970s. He plugged polluting drains at a soap manufacturing plant with bales of straw, rocks, and logs; installed a cap on the chimney of an aluminum processing company; and walked into the Chicago office of a vice president of U.S. Steel and dumped a container of sewage he had collected from the company's drains in Gary, Indiana.

Chicago Daily News columnist Mike Royko, who scored a secret interview with the Fox, described the "antipollution 'Zorro'" as "an ordinary soft-spoken citizen" who is "approaching middle age, has a respectable job, a family, and has never before gone outside the law." When asked why he started his sabotage campaign, the Fox said simply, "I've always lived in Kane County and I remember how beautiful it was."[28] These actions were covered by the national media and struck a chord with average Americans. A commissioner of the Federal Water Quality Administration in the Interior Department, speaking before the American Society of Civil Engineers, acknowledged, "'The Fox,' by his deeds, challenges us all with the question: 'Do we, as individuals in a technological society, have the will to control and prevent the degradation of our environment?'"[29]

Other activists in the Midwest sought to have a similar impact. Around the same time of the Fox's campaign, a group known as the Billboard Bandits used chain saws to cut down billboards across Michigan. During the mid-1970s, a group of Minnesota farmers calling themselves the Bolt Weevils registered their anger over the installation of high-voltage power lines across their land by using wrenches to topple at least 15 steel towers. They were concerned about health problems caused by the power lines, which were part of an energy project involving several coal-fired power plants in the region. Over the course of nearly two years, thousands of farmers protested, and 140 were arrested for various acts of sabotage and civil disobedience. The state of Minnesota called in more than 200 state troopers, as well as FBI and private security agents. The protest ended in 1978.

Activists willing to use direct action appeared in other regions of the United States as well. A group called Eco-Commando Force '70 was active for a brief time in the Miami, Florida, area. Claiming to be a five-member "clandestine guerrilla organization," the group used yellow dye and sealed bottles to track and publicize the extent to which sewage affected the Atlantic Ocean and the water systems of Miami and nearby communities.

The Southwest saw radical activity as early as 1958, when Edward Abbey and some friends used saws to cut down more than 10 billboards in New Mexico. In 1968, Abbey documented earlier efforts to waylay a National Park Service road-building project by pulling up survey stakes. For two years in the early 1970s, an anonymous activist known as the Arizona Phantom sabotaged coal mining operations at Black Mesa, Arizona, by tearing up railroad tracks and repeatedly damaging heavy equipment. The Phantom, who was also credited with an unsuccessful attempt to blow up a coal slurry line, ended his campaign as mysteriously as he began it, and no one ever found out his identity. Many people suspected that the sabotage was the work of the Black Mesa Defense Fund, an organization founded by Marc Gaede and Jack Loeffler that used lawsuits and lobbying efforts in an attempt to close the strip mine. Eventual Earth First! cofounder Dave Foreman volunteered with the group during this time, but he was still years away from his transformation from a mainstream environmentalist into a militant.

Arizona also had its own billboard bandits. In summer 1971, a group known as the Tucson Eco-Raiders began cutting down billboards, pouring lead into the locks of developers' houses, pulling up survey stakes from housing developments, ripping electrical and plumbing fixtures out of unsold houses, and sabotaging bulldozers. One member told a reporter that they bore "a grudge against developers who go in and flatten out everything. In general, if we see a nice area of the desert being destroyed, we'll do something about it." The group once left a pile of thousands of discarded cans and bottles at the doorstep of soft-drink bottler Kalil Company with a note reading, "A little non-returnable glass: Kalil makes it Tucson's problem. We make it Kalil's problem.—Eco-Raiders." By 1973, the Eco-Raiders had torn down hundreds of billboards. Succumbing to pressure from developers, county officials allocated the resources necessary to catch the activists, who turned out to be five college-age boys "fed up with rampant development in Arizona."[30]

RADICAL ENVIRONMENTAL PHILOSOPHIES

Most of the actions of the first half of the 1970s represented isolated incidents whose tactics were inspired by the counterculture of the 1960s rather than a coherent radical environmental movement. During this same time, however, a number of key environmentalists developed philosophies that inspired later radicals and gave activists a common purpose. Although these theories did not always logically imply radical tactics, they did inspire and stimulate radical activists to "pursue direct action tactics with more vigor and commitment." They also "provided personal justification for behavior in the face of social criticism of tactics."[31]

Just as use of direct action by environmentalists was an outgrowth of tactics used by anti–Vietnam War protesters, these philosophies were inspired by intellectual trends that had come to the forefront of American consciousness during the youth rebellions of the 1960s. Among these were Marxism, socialism, feminism, and Eastern religion. The ascendance of these ideas among radical environmentalists was based on the belief that capitalism, patriarchal society, and the Judeo-Christian tradition were responsible for the despoliation of nature. Most important among these new environmental philosophies were deep ecology, ecofeminism, social ecology, and bioregionalism.

Deep Ecology

The basic ideas of deep ecology were introduced by Norwegian philosopher Arne Naess in an article published in the philosophical journal *Inquiry* in 1973. He spent the next several years refining his thoughts in books, articles, and lectures, finally publishing a full discussion of the philosophy in *Ecology, Community and Lifestyle: Outline of an Ecosophy* (1990). Although Naess was considered the founder of the movement, American academics Bill Devall and George Sessions also worked on formulating the philosophy and interpreting its finer points for audiences in the United States.

Naess used the term *deep ecology* to distinguish his form of environmentalism from "shallow ecology," which he defined as the mainstream environmental movement that emphasized the "fight against pollution and resource depletion" and whose central objective was maintaining "the health and affluence of people in developed countries."[32] Deep ecology, on the other hand, is characterized by a more holistic approach to nature exemplified by the preservation ethic and the writings of Aldo Leopold and Rachel Carson. Naess called for a fundamental change in human consciousness that acknowledged the intrinsic value of all natural things, the biocentric equality of all species, and the "submergence of human self in a larger natural self" reminiscent of Thoreau's Oversoul.[33] This requires rejecting an anthropocentric view of the world and acknowledging that humans are not the center of life on Earth but only part of it and that all living things, human and otherwise, have "the equal right to live and blossom." The long-standing attempt to ignore both the interconnectedness of all living organisms and the dependence of humans on nature "has contributed to the alienation of man from himself."[34]

Naess believed that anyone who subscribed to this biocentric view of the world had an obligation to implement necessary changes to basic economic, technological, and ideological structures. This process began on a personal, spiritual level with ceasing to see oneself as an isolated, competitive ego and beginning to identify with other humans and species, an idea similar to and inspired by the Eastern concept of self-realization. This personal transformation, Naess believed, would lead to social and political, and therefore economic and technological, transformation. On a practical level, widespread "self-realization" would allow humans to dwell in a classless, decentralized society based on small, autonomous communities where people would live simple lives and have minimal impact on nature. Such a society would facilitate increased use of renewable energy resources and reduce the "number of links in hierarchical chains of decisions." It would also replace diversity based on exploitation and suppression (in which the exploiter lives differently from the suppressed) with a more egalitarian form of diversity based on differences in attitudes and behavior. The latter type of diversity, Naess believed, increased adaptability and thus heightened the chance of survival and of developing new modes of life. Survival of the fittest, deep ecologists believed, "should mean coexisting and cooperating in complex relationships rather than killing, exploiting, suppressing." The key was "appreciating *life quality* (dwelling in situations of inherent value) rather than adhering to an increasingly higher standard of living."[35]

Deep ecologists have been widely criticized for valuing animals above humans. Ron Arnold described the philosophy as "an ultimate expression of hate for the industrial system."[36] Supporters argue that rather than valuing all life above humans, they value all life above forms of human behavior that are destructive to life, both human and nonhuman, on the planet. Radicals who believe that the global crisis is so bad that there is no time for the gradual tactics used by mainstream organizations say they are prepared to take up the cause of nonhumans and elevate their interests over at least some of the commercial interests of humans. Dave Foremen and others involved in the formation of Earth First! shared this view.

Ecofeminism

Ecofeminism was developed in the 1970s from the synthesis of a diverse collection of feminist and environmental philosophies and tactical ideas. The term *ecofeminisme* was coined in 1974 by French writer Françoise d'Eaubonne to "represent women's potential for bringing about an ecological revolution to ensure human survival on the planet."[37] This effort was based on analysis of environmental problems from the perspective of the feminist critique of patriarchal systems, as well as on attempts to offer alternative systems intended to liberate both women and nature from oppression.

The basis of ecofeminism is the belief that there is an ideological connection between the oppression of nature and the oppression of women in patriarchal societies. It is therefore necessary to view the rape of a woman as stemming from the same impulse that leads corporations and governments to "rape" the wilderness by destroying it. The goal of ecofeminists is to reform patriarchal society, which they believe will simultaneously empower women and end wanton destruction of the Earth. Ecofeminists are often critical of deep ecology, which they say ignores "major causes of nature

21

oppression" and has "falsely assumed that the earth could be saved without undermining patriarchal structures."[38]

Among the more important ecofeminist theorists are Ynestra King, Karen J. Warren, Carolyn Merchant, and Elizabeth Dodson Gray. Merchant's book *The Death of Nature* (1980) shows how the scientific revolution of 16th- and 17th-century Europe rejected the previous view of the cosmos as an organism and replaced it with a hierarchical, machine-based model. This facilitated the eventual domination of both nature and women. Merchant believed that environmentalism and women's movements thus shared an interest in rejecting many of the values imposed by the modern scientific view of the world. Gray's *Green Paradise Lost* (1981) is an interdisciplinary study of feminism, ecology, philosophy, religion, and psychology that calls for a rejection of alienation of humans from one another and from the Earth. This is to be replaced by an Edenic society based on harmony, wholeness, diversity, and interconnection.

Social Ecology

This philosophy is primarily the invention of Murray Bookchin, an anarchist philosopher who founded the Institute for Social Ecology in Vermont and was one of the first thinkers in the United States to provide a radical critique of society based on ecology.

Inspired by Peter Kropotkin and other nonviolent anarchists, Bookchin concluded that environmental problems could not be solved in a free-market capitalist society because such hierarchical and authoritarian social, economic, and political structures allow humans to dominate others and nature. Bookchin argued that humans should emulate nature, which is characterized by a form of cooperation among organisms that furthers evolutionary goals. Social ecologists therefore counsel decentralizing social and economic relationships to allow the creation of new forms of democratic community, economic production, and "appropriate technology" (small-scale, renewable, and sustainable energy sources) that are more modest in scale and less consumptive. Although this sounds similar to deep ecology's project of creating a classless, decentralized society, Bookchin has criticized deep ecology as a form of "antihumanist" and "eco-brutalist" environmentalism that is hopelessly naïve about the need for widespread social change and ending human oppression.

Bioregionalism

Bioregionalism—a synthesis of such countercultural philosophies as back-to-the-land communalism, appropriate technology, social anarchism, and feminism—is considered by many proponents to be a means through which

Bookchin's theory of social ecology can be implemented. Bioregionalists often think of themselves as having moved beyond environmentalism and general philosophizing into the realm of developing practical ideas about building and living in human social communities that are compatible with ecological systems.

Bioregionalists commit to living an ecologically sustainable, stable, and self-sufficient lifestyle in a small community developed in close accordance with the natural patterns of the specific ecological region in which it exists. Poet Gary Snyder referred to this as "showing solidarity with a region."[39] Theorist Jim Dodge called it "ecology with a vengeance" because it meant "refusing to destroy the environment as the dominant culture does and preventing others from doing so by any nonviolent means necessary."[40] He suggested developing specific, individualized social programs for cities, suburbs, rural areas, and wilderness areas based on analysis of local conditions, then growing these outward toward the entire bioregion. Political groups in various bioregions of the continent would then cooperate in larger bioregional congresses.

Author Peter C. List considers bioregionalism to be compatible with ecofeminism because "notions of community and home tie together feminist attitudes about social relationships with ecological attitudes about the right forms of harmonious environmental living."[41] Judith Plant has even said that she considers the concept of bioregionalism to be incomplete without ecofeminism: Since feminism emphasizes the value of personal relationships and rejection of oppression, it "supplies important perspectives on how domestic life should be revalued in local places."[42]

GREENPEACE

Isolated incidents of sabotage aside, the first well-organized and highly visible radical activist environmental group was Greenpeace. This organization rejected sabotage and other acts that could destroy property or cause harm to humans in favor of Gandhian tenets of nonviolent passive resistance and civil disobedience. These tactics were originally used in attempts to bring media and public attention to nuclear testing, a project later expanded to include protests against whaling, oil drilling, seal hunting, and genetic engineering. Although many mainstream environmental groups considered these tactics too extreme, List writes that film footage of Greenpeace actions generated such widespread sympathy for the plight of sea mammals that "public attitudes about the ethical character of these actions softened, and acceptance of the need for unconventional environmental tactics blossomed."[43]

Greenpeace also promoted a morality that made harm to both humans and nonhumans ethically wrong. This idea was detailed in the organization's

1976 "Declaration of Interdependence," in which members claimed they were "patriots, not of any one nation, state or military alliance, but of the entire earth." The declaration also stated that humans had "arrived at a place in history where decisive action must be taken to avoid a general environmental disaster" and that there could be "no further delay or our children will be denied their future." The document also revealed Greenpeace's affinity with the philosophy of deep ecology and its belief that humans are not the center of life on Earth, a view enumerated in the Three Laws of Ecology: "that all forms of life are interdependent," "that the stability (unity, security, harmony, togetherness) of ecosystems is dependent on their diversity (complexity)," and "that all resources (food, water, air, minerals, energy) are finite and there are limits to the growth of all living systems."[44]

Greenpeace evolved from the Don't Make a Wave Committee, formed in 1969 by Canadian environmentalists in Vancouver to protest underwater nuclear tests being conducted in Alaska's Aleutian Islands by the U.S. Atomic Energy Commission. Although three tests had already occurred at Amchitka Island, activists worried about warnings from geologists that additional tests being planned could trigger earthquakes and tsunamis in the seismically active region. In September 1970, about 6,000 protestors blockaded the U.S.-Canada border at Blaine, Washington, to protest the nuclear tests. On September 15, 1971, 12 volunteer activists set sail from Vancouver on the 80-foot halibut boat *Greenpeace* and headed for Amchitka Island. The 42-day voyage, which was endorsed by large numbers of British Columbians and Prime Minister Pierre Elliot Trudeau of Canada, was undermined by delays in the nuclear test program, worsening autumn weather, and an arrest by the U.S. Coast Guard based on a seldom-used tariff regulation, all of which conspired to force the battered boat back to Vancouver.

A replacement ship was quickly found, a 120-foot converted mine sweeper named *Greenpeace Too* and manned by skipper Hank Johansen and 29 volunteers. Faced with 70-mile-per-hour winds, the ship was still 700 miles away from Amchitka when the nuclear tests took place on November 4. However, the Don't Make a Wave Committee's efforts had garnered enough negative publicity to force the U.S. Supreme Court to determine whether the Amchitka test should be cancelled on environmental grounds. Although the justices decided, by a margin of one vote, to let the test continue, the Atomic Energy Commission cancelled plans for additional nuclear activity in the area and quietly turned the test site into a bird sanctuary in spring 1972.

In 1972 the Don't Make a Wave Committee folded and reformed as the Greenpeace Foundation, consisting of activists who had sailed on *Greenpeace* and *Greenpeace Too*. The Amchitka Island action was only the first in an ongoing series of ocean-based protests by the group, all of which were characterized by strict adherence to nonviolent civil disobedience. Greenpeace itself, however, was subject to a number of violent attacks. In summer 1972, the vessel *Greenpeace III* was rammed by a French military ship during a protest of that nation's nuclear tests over Mururoa Atoll in the South Pacific. The following year, *Greenpeace III* returned to the atoll, where it was boarded by French commandoes who beat captain David McTaggart and navigator Nigel Ingram with rubber truncheons. McTaggart suffered partial loss of vision in his left eye as a result. Most notoriously, in 1985, French government agents used explosives to sink the Greenpeace ship *Rainbow Warrior* in the harbor of Auckland, New Zealand, killing photographer Fernando Pereira in the process.

Greenpeace's membership subsequently grew, peaking around 1991. Interest declined during the 1990s. In the United States, this decline occurred partly because the administration of President Bill Clinton was popularly perceived as posing little threat to the environment and partly because internal discord led to the resignation of Greenpeace USA's entire board of directors. The organization was revitalized by new executive director John Passacantando and by a resurgence in membership prompted by what many view as President George W. Bush's anti-environmental politics.

Greenpeace has continued to use nonviolent direct action tactics but has also moved closer to the mainstream over the years by increasing its use of lobbying and public relations efforts. These new efforts have included calling on leaders of *Fortune* 100 companies to clarify their position on the Kyoto Protocol, using the Internet to recruit members with business expertise, commissioning financial studies, collecting advice from sympathetic investment bankers, and poaching talent from the corporate world. In 2000, Greenpeace purchased 140,000 shares in Shell Oil Company to help persuade it to invest in a large-scale solar panel factory. The group also united 100 BP Amoco shareholders with a total of more than 150,000 shares to oppose the company's controversial Northstar oil pipeline project in the Arctic Ocean. During the 1990s, Greenpeace added genetically engineered (GE) foods to its list of protest targets, arguing that these products pose unknown risks to human health and the global environment and accusing the companies that produce them of a new form of "biological pollution" that is alive, that reproduces, and that moves through the environment.

SEA SHEPHERD CONSERVATION SOCIETY

In his statement before the 2002 congressional hearing on the threat of ecoterrorism, FBI Domestic Terrorism Section chief James F. Jarboe effectively exonerated Greenpeace from any accusations of violence when he said that acts of ecoterrorism have occurred around the globe "[s]ince 1977, when disaffected members of the ecological preservation group Greenpeace formed the Sea Shepherd Conservation Society and attacked commercial fishing operations by cutting drift nets."[45] Sea Shepherd Conservation Society (SSCS) founder Paul Watson had taken part in Greenpeace expeditions against whaling and harp seal hunting, but he was expelled in 1977 for "vigilante" actions after he picked up a sealer's club and tossed it into the water during a protest.

Watson believed that Greenpeace's brand of nonviolent direct action had its place but also thought that activists had to develop new practices that would cripple machinery used to destroy nature. He believed that respect for animal life should take precedence "over respect for property which is used to take lives" but maintained a clear distinction between attacking machines and harming individuals.[46] Toward respecting life in all SSCS protests, Watson drafted a set of five rules for direct action in the field:

1. No explosives.
2. No utilization of weapons.
3. No action taken that even has a remote possibility of causing injury to a living thing. Respect for life must always be our primary consideration.
4. If apprehended, do not resist arrest in a violent manner.
5. Be prepared to accept full responsibility and suffer the possible consequences for your actions.[47]

Following the formation of SSCS, Watson bought an ocean-going boat with donations from Cleveland Amory's Fund for Animals and immediately set out with volunteers to make a project out of harassing ships engaged in whaling, sealing, and drift-net fishing. By the early 1980s, the SSCS had become known as the naval arm of Earth First! Despite his militancy, Watson gained a measure of support among the public and minor celebrities. When arrested in 1983 for interfering with Canada's seal hunt, his $10,000 bail was posted by actor Mike Farrell of the television show *M*A*S*H*. Maxwell Gail of *Barney Miller* taped a commercial seeking donations for SSCS that aired on local stations in California. Actor Harvey Korman raised money for Watson on a quiz show that donated the winnings of its celebrity players to environmental and animal rights groups.

Watson increased his anti-whaling efforts in 1986 after the International Whaling Commission (IWC) announced a moratorium on commercial whaling. Iceland and Norway asked for permits to kill whales for scientific research purposes, a request that was rejected by the IWC's scientific committee with the comment that the petitioning nations were "seeking to prostitute science in an attempt to mask a commercial venture."[48] Despite the moratorium, the Soviet Union, Japan, Iceland, Norway, and South Korea continued their whale hunts.

Watson, in his own mind at least, was suddenly able to take the moral high ground, arguing that his interference with whaling operations was merely an attempt to enforce international law. One of the SSCS's most destructive actions in this regard occurred on November 8, 1986, when two activists broke into a whale processing plant near Reykjavík, Iceland, and spent eight hours smashing refrigeration machinery, diesel engines, pumps, engine parts, laboratory equipment, and computers. The damage was later estimated to be about $1.8 million. The activists then boarded two docked whaling ships and removed bolts from the salt water sea valve flange, causing them to sink within 40 minutes. Damage for the two ships was estimated at $2.8 million. One of the saboteurs was Rod Coronado, who later, in the early 1990s, served as the media spokesperson for the ALF and later spent time in jail for firebombing a research laboratory at Michigan State University.

The SSCS remains active despite ongoing attempts to bring legal action against Watson for his confrontational actions. The group made headlines in October 1998, when members vowed to disrupt the revival of a whale-hunting ritual by the Makah Indians of Neah Bay, Washington. Granted the right, based on a provision in an 1855 government treaty, to circumvent the global whaling ban, the Makah set out on their first hunting expedition in 70 years while the SSCS conducted boat patrols and broadcast underwater orca sounds to keep the gray whales far offshore. At one point, angry tribal members threw rocks at the SSCS vessel, *Sirenian*, injuring two crew members and damaging the group's Zodiac raft. Three society members were briefly detained by tribal police. As a result, the SSCS agreed not to land on Makah territory but vowed to continue efforts to disrupt the hunt.

EDWARD ABBEY

In 1968, western novelist and essayist Edward Abbey published *Desert Solitaire*, an account of his stint as a seasonal park ranger in Utah's Arches National Monument in the late 1950s. Well known for its moving descriptions of the power and beauty of the desert landscape, the book also presaged Abbey's commitment, in both deed and thought, to the type of activity that would later come to be known as monkeywrenching. His account of pulling up survey stakes placed by a National Park Service crew planning on building a paved road through the park has already been mentioned. The chapter "Down the River" describes a rafting trip on the Colorado River through Glen Canyon, soon to be submerged by construction of the Glen Canyon Dam. While admiring the doomed landscape, Abbey daydreams about an "unknown hero with a rucksack full of dynamite" who will blow up the dam, creating "the loveliest explosion ever seen by man, reducing the great dam to a heap of rubble in the path of the river." Abbey suggests naming the "splendid new rapids thus created" the Floyd E. Dominy Falls, in honor of the chief of the Reclamation Bureau, the federal agency responsible for the dam's construction.[49] The idea of destroying the dam was an ongoing obsession of Abbey's, and it became the central theme of his 1975 novel, *The Monkey Wrench Gang*.

Abbey made a career out of defending the American West from what he saw as "the idiocies and dangers of modern technology and the authoritarian industrial state."[50] He considered himself a nonviolent anarchist, arguing in his University of New Mexico master's thesis that anarchism was a positive philosophy rooted in the Jeffersonian ideal of a civil society based on absolute individual liberty. It was, he believed, "democracy taken seriously," and the true patriot's task was to defend his or her beloved country against the government.[51] He once wrote, "Representative government in the USA represents money, not people, and therefore has forfeited our allegiance and moral support."[52] To Abbey, anarchism meant maximum democracy: Federal structures, all of which had been corrupted by power, should be replaced by "decentralized, equally distributed, fairly shared" power arrangements.[53]

While Abbey gained a large following and later became a living inspiration for Earth First!, he was also denounced in some quarters as a racist and a misanthrope. The charges of racism were based on Abbey's anti-immigration stance and his suggestion that illegal immigrants from Latin America be met at the border, given firearms and ammunition, and sent back to Mexico to clean up the problems that prompted them to leave their homes in the first place. "The people," he wrote of Mexican citizens, "know who their enemies are."[54] As with deep ecologists, Abbey was accused of misanthropy because he was thought by many to value animals above humans. His claim in *Desert Solitaire* that as a humanist he would "rather kill a *man* than a snake" is often used as evidence for this contention, but defenders point out that the comment, based on a humorous inversion of the definition of "humanist," is not to be taken literally.[55] Likewise, the suggestion to arm Mexicans and foment rebellion south of the border has been defended as a rhetorical device intended to point out the failings of a government whose citizens feel they must look to another nation for relief from poverty. Attempts to settle arguments about these and other comments have long been confounded by an inability to determine "where the disgruntled romantic idealism leaves off and the leg-pulling mischief starts" in Abbey's writing.[56]

Similar debates have surrounded Abbey's novel *The Monkey Wrench Gang*, labeled by critics a blueprint for a methodical campaign of ecoterrorism and defended by Abbey as a mere "novel, a work of fiction, and—I like to think—a work of art." He maintained that it would be "naïve to read it as a tract, a program for action, or a manifesto."[57] Despite this denial, the novel clearly became a model for Earth First! activists. In 1981, Dave Foreman went so far as to acknowledge that one of the original purposes of Earth First! was "to inspire others to carry out activities straight from the pages of *The Monkey Wrench Gang* even though Earth First!, we agreed, would itself be ostensibly law-abiding."[58] The effectiveness of this project was apparent in the comments of one Arizona rancher who said that although he had never wished a man dead in his whole life, he would make an exception for Edward Abbey. "Because of those damned books of his," the rancher complained, "people are cutting barbed wire and messing with ranchers all over the place."[59]

The Monkey Wrench Gang follows the exploits of four disgruntled activists who use sabotage as a means to halt the destruction of wilderness in the Southwest. Their ultimate aim is to dynamite the Glen Canyon Dam and allow the Colorado River to flow unimpeded. The saboteurs' first act is a raid on a road-building project in Utah. Considering the loving care with which Abbey describes the characters pulling up survey stakes and "decommissioning" heavy equipment, it is difficult not to imagine that the author intended the chapter as a how-to guide. Likewise, these suspicions can apply to the spree that follows, which involves the destruction of more road-building equipment, a drill rig, barbed wire fences, and logging equipment, as well as a railroad bridge at the Peabody Coal Company strip mine at Black Mesa, Arizona.

The importance of Abbey's influence on Earth First! is unmistakable. At one point in *The Monkey Wrench Gang*, one of the saboteurs decides that any ideology held by the group should be made up as they go along. This concept of allowing "practice [to] form . . . doctrine, thus assuring precise theoretical coherence"[60] was reflected in Foreman's later comment that Earth First! activists should "let our actions set the finer points of our philosophy."[61] In another scene, the activists imagine a disorganized movement involving small groups of people, none knowing anything about the other groups, committing acts of sabotage all across the nation. This vision was later adopted by both Earth First! and the ELF/ALF.

EARTH FIRST!

Emulation of *The Monkey Wrench Gang* was not, of course, the sole reason for the formation of Earth First! Following the 1980 presidential election, activists became concerned about President Ronald Reagan's anti-environmental policies. Upon moving into the White House, Reagan immediately and symbolically removed the solar panels President Jimmy Carter had installed on the roof. His attitude toward environmental issues was also apparent in his choice of cabinet members: Energy Secretary Donald Hodel gained notoriety for suggesting that the best way to combat ozone depletion was to apply stronger suntan lotion, and Environmental Protection Agency (EPA) head Ann Gorsuch Burford spent the majority of her tenure rendering the agency ineffective by reducing its budget by $200 million and its staff by 23 percent. Interior Secretary James Watt supported selling public land to resource extraction industries, an idea so alarming to environmentalists that they began a "Dump Watt" petition drive that collected nearly 1 million signatures.

Perhaps the most important factor in the formation of Earth First! was the 1979 Roadless Area Review and Evaluation (RARE II). The Wilderness Act of 1964 and later amendments had called on the U.S. Forest Service (USFS), National Park Service (NPS), Bureau of Land Management (BLM), and Fish and Wildlife Service (FWS) to evaluate their holdings to determine what areas were eligible for the act's strict federal protections. During its first review (RARE) in 1971, the USFS studied nearly 1,500 roadless areas totaling 55.9 million acres, held 300 public meetings, and received 50,000 comments from the public. However, the agency's refusal to include the impacts of logging and mining in its review led to a widespread threat of lawsuits by environmental groups, forcing a re-evaluation in the late 1970s.

The second evaluation (RARE II) recommended 10 million acres of land in the lower 48 states and 5 million acres in Alaska for wilderness protection, while 36 million acres were opened for development and 11 million were set aside for further study. Mainstream environmental groups, including the Sierra Club and the Wilderness Society, declared victory, while an increasingly radical minority charged that the environmental impact statements for areas to be developed were biased in favor of industry and that the original figure of 62 million acres grossly underestimated the amount of land that should have been eligible for wilderness designation. The Sierra Club and Wilderness Society tried to dissuade angry environmentalists from challenging RARE II in court, fearing that such a move would succeed and create an anti-environmental backlash among politicians.

Origins and Ideas

Included in the ranks of environmentalists whose anger over RARE II prompted them to abandon mainstream efforts were Wilderness Society activists Dave Foreman and Bart Koehler; Sierra Club member Ron Kezar; and Wyoming environmentalists Mike Roselle and Howie Wolke. In April 1980, these five men went camping in Mexico's Pinacate Desert. On the way home, while driving through Arizona, they decided that the environmental movement needed a direct action group willing to do more than lobby politicians. Foreman was credited with coining the name Earth First! because it "succinctly summed up the one thing on which we could all agree: that in *any* decision, consideration for the health of the Earth must come first."[62] Roselle designed the group's logo, a green fist in a circle, while they all decided that the motto would be "No compromise in defense of Mother Earth." The movement, in the beginning at least, would inaugurate a new chapter in the struggle between conservation and preservation, with Earth First! activists focusing on the preservationist ideal of maximizing the amount of acreage in national forests closed to development and resource extraction.

A few weeks after returning from Mexico, Foreman quietly began the campaign of guerrilla theater tactics that would soon become a hallmark of Earth First! He and a group of friends hiked to the ghost town of Cooney in New Mexico's Gila Wilderness, where they erected a plaque honoring the Apache for raiding the mining camp in 1880 and for striving to "protect these mountains from mining and other destructive activities of the white race."[63] The group went public on March 21 (spring equinox) of the following year, when 75 protestors rallied at the despised Glen Canyon Dam and held signs with such slogans as "Damn Watt, Not Rivers," "Free the Colorado," and "Let It Flow." In a blatant nod to *The Monkey Wrench Gang*, five activists broke away from the rest and unfurled 300 feet of black plastic down the front of the dam, creating the impression of a growing crack. Edward Abbey himself spoke from the back of a pickup truck, telling those gathered to "oppose the destruction of our homeland" by politicians and industrialists. He added that "if opposition is not enough, we must resist. And if resistance is not enough, then subvert."[64]

It was clear that Earth First! was following Abbey in his hatred of Glen Canyon Dam, which Foreman agreed was "the symbol of the destruction of the wilderness, of the technological rape of the West,"[65] but the new movement offered more than mere fantasies of destruction based on a work of fiction. Foreman was an apolitical radical who believed that social and political life should center on the preservation and restoration of nature, a philosophy he described as "wilderness fundamentalism." He believed that the use of direct action would lead to an ecologically sustainable, stable, and self-sufficient lifestyle that integrated small social communities with local ecosystems. In Foreman, the philosophy of deep ecology found its most militant expression.

This commitment to nature over traditional leftist issues fueled the ongoing debate between deep ecologists and social ecologists, the latter of whom thought it was a mistake to assume that changes in attitudes toward nature could occur without revolutionizing capitalist economic systems and tackling such problems as racism, poverty, militarism, and sexism. Foreman brushed off these criticisms, claiming that Earth First! was "big enough to contain street poets and cowboy bar bouncers, agnostics and pagans, vegetarians and raw steak eaters, pacifists and those who think that turning the other cheek is a good way to get a sore face."[66] He considered it possible for the movement to focus on nature even while finding common ground with feminist, Indian rights, anti-nuclear, peace, civil rights, and civil liberties groups.

A more specific agenda was offered in the pages of the *Earth First! Newsletter*, later renamed the *Earth First! Journal*. Within one year the newsletter had 1,500 subscribers, a number that grew to more than 5,000 by the end of the 1980s. With Earth First! offering no formal organization, leaders, officers, bylaws, incorporation, or tax status, subscribers were the closest the movement came to a membership list. The periodical published photographs, editorials, accounts of protest actions, poetry, and how-to advice for monkeywrenchers. The staff also sold T-shirts and bumper stickers with slogans that revealed an Abbeyesque sense of humor and patriotism, including "American Wilderness: Love It or Leave It Alone," "Earth: Love It or Leave It," and "God Bless America—Let's Save Some of It."

The first issue of the newsletter introduced the Earth First! national wilderness proposal, which called for a system of "ecological preserves" within which "the developments of man will be obliterated." This included no permanent human habitation (with the exception of indigenous people with traditional lifestyles); no use of mechanical equipment or vehicles; no roads; no logging, mining, or grazing; no suppression of wildfires; and no aircraft overflights. It called for mechanisms to facilitate restoration ecology, including the removal of exotic species, reintroduction of extirpated species (such as grizzly bears), and dismantling of dams, roads, and power lines. What it did not call for was the dismantling of civilization. Of urban areas Foreman wrote, "Keep Cleveland, Los Angeles. Contain them. Try to make them habitable. But identify areas—big areas—that can be restored to a semblance of natural conditions."[67]

As with deep ecologists before them, the founding members of Earth First! faced charges of misanthropy and of valuing animals above humans. Much of this criticism is not surprising given the often controversial content of the *Earth First! Journal*. In a 1989 article called "Love Your Mother—Don't Become One," Leslie Lyon wrote, "The best day of my life . . . was the day I decided never to have children."[68] More notoriously, the May 1, 1987, issue ran an article in which Christopher Manes, writing under the pseudonym Miss Ann Thropy, suggested that acquired immunodeficiency syndrome (AIDS) was nature's way of protecting the planet from excess population. "I take it as axiomatic that the only real hope for the continuation of diverse ecosystems on this planet is an enormous decline in population," he wrote. "If the AIDS epidemic didn't exist, radical environmentalists would have to invent one."[69] Concerning widespread famine in Ethiopia, Foreman himself once remarked that "the best thing would be to let nature seek its own balance" and let the people there starve.[70] These comments and others set off firestorms of debate both inside and outside the ranks of Earth First!, illustrating one drawback of the movement's lack of formal organization and its attempts to remain diverse: Anyone could present any point of view at any time. The ensuing controversy often reflected badly on the entire movement.

Monkeywrenching

These controversies were ultimately overshadowed by the debates that sprang up around Earth First!'s use of sabotage. Although monkeywrenching was part of the movement's repertoire from the beginning, the practice was formalized in 1985 when Foreman published *Ecodefense: A Field Guide to Monkeywrenching*. The book described in great detail a variety of tactics for radical environmentalists, from letter writing and political lobbying to guerrilla theater demonstrations at government resource agency offices, from civil disobedience (blockading logging roads and sitting in trees) to sabotage (pulling survey stakes, spiking trees, trashing billboards, and destroying heavy construction equipment). In the introduction, Abbey compared monkeywrenching to a form a self-defense against the rapacious practices of governments and corporations. The book was self-published as a "Ned Ludd Book," a homage to the 19th-century British fabric weaver who provoked his coworkers to destroy machines and equipment over fears that new mechanized looms would cost them their jobs.

All philosophizing aside, this type of direct action lay at the core of the movement from the outset. Foreman believed that expressing rage at wilderness destruction by taking action was more important than sitting around refining ideology. He described his brand of direct action as nonviolent and ethical, to be used not by everyone, but by those who "hold biological diversity and life in higher regard than they do inanimate private property."[71] The point of sabotage was to thwart, at least temporarily, the forces of industrialism:

> *Maybe a species will be saved or a forest will go uncut or a dam will be torn down. Maybe not. A monkey wrench thrown into the gears of the machine may not stop it. But it might delay it. Make it cost more. And it feels good to put it there.*[72]

Even while promoting property destruction, Foreman condemned "mindless, erratic vandalism" as "counterproductive as well as unethical."[73] He and other environmental radicals saw themselves as breaking the law out of opposition to a moral wrong, as belonging to a long line of American dissidents that included the Revolutionary War patriots responsible for the Boston Tea Party and the pre–Civil War abolitionists who ran the Underground Railroad. According to Foreman, he and others "do not engage in radical action because we are primarily motivated by opposition to authority . . . but because we are *for* something—the beauty, wisdom, and abundance of this living planet."[74]

The most controversial form of monkeywrenching was tree spiking, which involved hammering long nails into the trunks of old-growth trees slated to be logged on public land. Proper protocol, as spelled out in *Ecodefense*, demanded that activists warn logging companies and the U.S. Forest Service that an area had been spiked, forcing corporations to decide whether the cost of removing thousands of metal rods was worth the profit to be made. The hope among radical environmentalists was that if the cost of spike removal was too high, the cut would not be made, or that a decreased profit margin would discourage logging in areas where environmental radicals were known to be active.

The first Earth First! tree spiking campaign began in October 1984, when activists mailed a letter to the *Register-Guard* newspaper in Eugene, Oregon, claiming that about 1,000 spikes had been nailed into trees that were part of a proposed timber sale in Oregon's Hardesty Mountain roadless area. The USFS spent thousands of dollars removing them. Earth First! supporters cite at least two cases, one in Washington's Wenatchee National Forest and one on Virginia's George Washington National Forest, where tree spiking caused timber sales to be lost because the USFS could not guarantee potential buyers that all the spikes had been removed.

Critics argue that the spikes are capable of shattering chain-saw blades, putting loggers in danger of injury or even death. This fear was realized on May 13, 1987, when a spike shattered a band saw in a Louisiana-Pacific lumber mill in Cloverdale, California. Millworker George Alexander was seriously injured, and Louisiana-Pacific held a press conference in which a spokesperson blamed Earth First! for the deed. Radical environmentalists denied the accusation, claiming that tree spikers inform timber companies about their activities, the point being to prevent logging, not harm workers. Also, the tree in question was a second-growth redwood, not virgin timber of the type Earth First! normally sought to protect. The Mendocino County Sheriff's Department later identified a man named William Joseph Ervin as a suspect. Ervin was a radical libertarian unaffiliated with Earth First! who lived in the area and was known to have spiked several trees on his own property to deter timber thieves. Lacking enough evidence, however, the local district attorney's office never brought charges against him or anyone else.

Tree spiking raised enough hackles in states with significant logging operations that in 1988, congressional delegates from the Pacific Northwest, led by Idaho senator James McClure and Oregon senator Mark Hatfield, successfully attached a rider to the Drug Act of 1988 making tree spiking a felony. Oregon representative Robert Smith, who supported the bill, said that "tree spiking is a radical environmentalist's version of razor blades in Halloween candy."[75] Dave Pease, editor of *Forest Industries* magazine, wrote, "As for spikers, if I could warp logic and law to my own notions like they do, I would shoot them down . . . like the yellow curs they are." Harry Merlo, president of Louisiana-Pacific, added, "Terrorism is the name of the game for radical environmental goals."[76]

Earth First! cofounder Mike Roselle attempted to answer these accusations by claiming that using the word *terrorism* in relation to tree spiking is to render the term meaningless. Tree spiking, he said, was intended to prevent logging, not hurt people, whereas terrorism should be defined as a willful attack on innocent people. Roselle also condemned the timber industry, which he said had the worst safety record of any enterprise in the United States. Concerns over safety had led to frequent disputes between management and workers, he said, but "risk to humans hasn't stopped the timber industry from cutting old growth." Society, he complained, was willing to risk injury to humans for economic reasons but not to preserve the natural world.[77]

The Arizona Five

The FBI, unimpressed by such arguments, had been watching Earth First! since its formation in 1980. In May 1986, however, a group of activists cut electrical power lines leading to the Palo Verde nuclear power plant in Arizona, giving the FBI cause to begin a more thorough investigation based on fears that such activities could cause a nuclear meltdown. The FBI classified Earth First! as a "soft-core" terrorist group to distinguish it from "hard-core" terrorists who killed humans. (This distinction has been lost since 9/11.) Attorney General Edwin Meese gave the agency the go-ahead to launch an elaborate campaign involving wiretaps, body wires, and infiltrators, the first time such tactics were used against an environmental group. During 1988 and 1989, the FBI spent $2 million and dedicated 50 agents to the investigation.

Federal investigators focused their surveillance on activities in Arizona, even though hundreds of protests and acts of sabotage were being committed all across the West. Their goal, it turned out, was to arrest Tucson resident Dave Foreman, and their method was to implicate him in the activities of an Earth First! cell facetiously calling itself the Evan Mecham Eco Terrorist International Conspiracy (EMETIC; Evan Mecham was Arizona's governor at the time). On October 5, 1987, the group (consisting of activists Mark Davis and Peg Millett) used a propane cutting torch to damage the main cable chairlift at the Fairfield ski resort in Arizona, protesting the resort's planned expansion onto sacred Indian land. On September 25, 1988, Davis and Millett, again operating under the name EMETIC, were joined by Ilse Asplund when they toppled power line poles leading to a uranium mine near the Grand Canyon in Arizona. One month later, they struck Fairfield again, this time severing the chairlift's main support pylon.

In the meantime, a special agent of the Phoenix office of the FBI, Mike Fain, had infiltrated the group under the name Mike Tait. Although by this point internal bickering within Earth First! had caused Foreman to begin distancing himself from the movement, Fain and other agents made every effort to drag him back in and implicate him in the activities of EMETIC. Part of this plan was an unsuccessful attempt by infiltrators to push Earth First! activists into using thermite to topple a power line so the government could cast Foreman as a terrorist who made use of explosives.

On the night of May 30, 1989, Earth First! saboteurs Millett, Davis, and Marc Baker, accompanied by Mike "Fain," set out to knock over an electrical transmission tower near Wenden, Arizona. Just as the cutting was about to begin, a flare illuminated the scene, and 50 FBI agents swooped in and arrested Davis and Baker. Millett, somehow evading a search that involved bloodhounds and two helicopters, hiked through the desert and then hitchhiked back to her home in Prescott, 60 miles away. She was arrested the next day, as was Dave Foreman, who was roused from his bed at 7 A.M. by gun-wielding federal agents. Although he was not at the scene of the sabotage, he was arrested on charges that he had supplied $580 and two copies of his book *Ecodefense* to the other activists. In December, the Arizona Four became the Arizona Five when FBI agents arrested Ilse Asplund for her affiliation with EMETIC.

The FBI alleged that EMETIC's activities, particularly the attempt to cut the electrical transmission tower near Wenden, were dry runs for a larger conspiracy to damage power lines leading to nuclear facilities in Arizona, California, and Colorado. The trial lasted through summer 1991, and all the defendants negotiated plea bargains. Asplund was sentenced to one year in federal prison, five years probation, a $2,000 fine, and 100 hours of community service; Baker was sentenced to one year in federal prison, five months probation, a $5,000 fine, and 100 hours of community service; and Millet served three years in federal prison without parole and was ordered to pay restitution to Fairfield in the amount of $19,821. The harshest sentence was reserved for Davis, who spent six years in federal prison and was also ordered to pay $19,821 to Fairfield.

Foreman's defense team, which included famed attorney Gerry Spence, successfully separated the Earth First! cofounder from the other defendants on the grounds that he had not taken a direct role in EMETIC's monkey-wrenching spree. Spence argued that the FBI investigation was "one of the most 'blatant, unlawful' entrapment schemes in U.S. history,"[78] an accusation supported by a statement made and inadvertently recorded by Mike Fain on his own FBI body tap: "[Foreman] isn't really the guy we need to pop . . . in terms of the actual perpetrator. . . . This is the guy we need to pop to send a message, and that's all we're really doing. . . . If we don't nail this guy . . . we're not sending a message."[79] Foreman pointed to the tape as proof that the FBI's goal was to "intimidate the entire environmental and social-action movement in this country."[80] In the end, he escaped jail by pleading guilty to a felony conspiracy charge for distributing copies of *Ecodefense*. He was placed on probation for five years.

Earth First! After Foreman

Even before the arrest of the Arizona Five, Earth First! had been split by internal disputes between deep ecologists who wanted to concentrate on wilderness and environmental issues (Foreman among them) and social ecologists who stressed the need to tie these issues to problems of social justice and change. Mike Roselle had already given up monkeywrenching and joined Greenpeace. He later cofounded the Ruckus Society, dedicated to training social activists in nonviolent protest tactics. Foreman, after several years of slowly divorcing himself from the movement and beginning work on other projects, formally quit Earth First! following the Arizona Five trial.

In his farewell essay, Foreman acknowledged that Earth First! had become divided and that the annual gatherings were attracting increasing numbers of leftists more interested in "storming the barricades of capitalism" than defending the wilderness. He wrote that he would "continue to applaud the courageous actions of those operating with the Earth First! name" but complained that the movement had become "muddied by haphazard vandalism" and "kiddie stunts like flag burnings and shopping mall puke-ins." Although he renounced the use of sabotage for himself, he counseled that "wise monkeywrenchers can more safely practice their midnight art by not drawing attention to themselves as known activists with any group." Meanwhile, those like himself who were more interested in conservation biology and "big wilderness" than social issues would "promote their ideas under a name other than Earth First!"[81]

Longtime *Earth First! Journal* editor John Davis also left the movement, echoing Foreman's sentiments when he wrote, "Many of us who still want to focus on wilderness and biodiversity issues, and to leave social issues to other groups, have therefore decided to let the EF! movement go where it will and continue our work under different banners."[82] Foreman and Davis started a new journal called *Wild Earth* and began work on the Wildlands Project (TWP), an ambitious plan to "re-wild" America by making 50 percent of the land off-limits to human occupation.

Earth First!, meanwhile, continued on without Foreman. A new direction in the movement was spearheaded by Judi Bari, who organized the 1990 Redwood Summer campaign to protest logging in Northern California. Bari had initially been wary of the "no compromise" direct action group, which she felt had been founded by macho, beer-drinking men, but was eventually won over by the fact that Earth First! activists "were the only people willing to put their bodies in front of the bulldozers and chain saws to save the trees."[83] The loose structure and diverse nature of Earth First! allowed her to eschew the sabotage tactics advocated by Earth First!'s founders in favor of a more explicit nonviolence code based on the Civil Rights movement and on finding common ground with loggers. This included forming an alliance with the radical labor group Industrial Workers of the World (IWW) and vowing that activists would give up the practice of tree spiking.

Redwood Summer brought thousands of activists from across the country to Northern California to confront the logging practices of Maxxam/Pacific Lumber Company. Just as Bari intended, the protests focused less on monkeywrenching and more on civil disobedience, including marches, occupations of threatened groves, tree sits, blockades, and rallies. Despite this, a number of confrontations between environmentalists and loggers resulted in violence. The most tragic event, however, occurred just as the campaign was getting started.

On May 24, 1990, a bomb exploded in the car of activists Bari and Darryl Cherney. Bari was sent to the hospital with a shattered pelvis and broken back; Cherney suffered cuts, bruises, and temporary deafness. The FBI and the Oakland Police Department immediately arrested them on suspicion of possessing explosives. Earth First! activists claimed that the bomb had been planted by anti-environmentalists or even by law enforcement officials. An investigation by the FBI and the Oakland Police Department was eventually dropped before charges were filed, and no attempt was made to find the bomber.

Bari and Cherney refused to let the matter end there. They filed suit against the FBI and the Oakland police, claiming they had been slandered and falsely linked to domestic terrorism. Bari videotaped her testimony in 1997, just weeks before she died of cancer. Among her complaints was the accusation that several weeks before the bombing, four of the local FBI agents who investigated the explosion (including lead investigator Frank Doyle) attended a training course in which the federal agency blew up cars with pipe bombs and practiced responding, thus creating virtually the same crime scene that was about to happen in Oakland. During the trial, which occurred in 2002, additional evidence was presented that the FBI fed the Oakland police two false theories about the explosion—that the bomb had been hidden in Bari's guitar and that bags of nails matching those in the bomb had been found in the car—that were later used to obtain search warrants. The jury found that the FBI had willfully lied about both theories in order to obtain illegal warrants and make false arrests.

Investigator Doyle and other agents denied that attempts had been made by the FBI to connect Bari or Cherney with terrorist activity. Under oath, the agents said they had never heard of Bari or Cherney before the bombing and that they were not investigating Earth First! An FBI field report written minutes after the bomb exploded, however, stated that Bari and Cherney were "the subjects of an FBI investigation in the terrorist department."[84] The jury subsequently found that six of the seven defendants had violated Bari and Cherney's First and Fourth Amendment rights by arresting the activists, searching their homes, and carrying out a smear campaign in the press by calling Earth First! a terrorist organization and calling the activists bombers. Jurists awarded a total of $4.4 million to Cherney and the estate of Judi Bari.

Bari's denouncement of spiking and her emphasis on nonviolent protest actions during Redwood Summer signaled a general, but not absolute, move away from monkeywrenching and toward civil disobedience for Earth First! In 1993, activists gathered in Idaho to protest road building and logging in the Cove Mallard area of Nez Perce National Forest. Although the campaign mostly involved tree sitting and human blockades to stop road building, the specter of monkeywrenching emerged when someone disabled a Caterpillar tractor by putting sand in its fuel tank, smashing its gauges, and cutting the fuel and hydraulic lines. During the course of the protest, USFS and law enforcement officials made more than 50 arrests, issued more than 100 citations, and searched the Earth First! camp in an unsuccessful attempt to find evidence that the group had monkeywrenched heavy equipment. Locals who saw the new logging road as a boon to the economy were less than thrilled by the presence of the radical environmentalists: The owners of the nearby Lodgepole Pine Inn put a sign in the window reading, "We reserve the right to refuse service to all Earth First!ers and their associates," while a poster at one end of the closest town sported a drawing of an activist with a bullet hole in his forehead. Like many Earth First! campaigns, this one ended in failure, and the road was eventually built.

The 1990 Redwood Summer campaign, meanwhile, grew into a decade-long struggle between environmentalists and loggers with its share of drama and tragedy. Much of the activity focused on redwood trees in the Headwaters Forest region of Northern California. Plans to clear cut the area by Maxxam/Pacific Lumber Company prompted protesters to embark on long-term tree sits, the most famous of which was a two-year marathon conducted by Julia Butterfly Hill from December 10, 1997, to December 18, 1999.

While Hill gained a large measure of celebrity from her actions, another protestor was not so lucky. On September 17, 1998, Earth First! activist David "Gypsy" Chain died on land owned by Maxxam/Pacific Lumber Company when logger A. E. Ammons felled a tree that crushed the activist's skull. A debate over culpability ensued. Activists produced a video taken shortly before Chain's death on which Ammons could clearly be heard shouting obscenities at the environmentalists and threatening to bring his handgun to work. Earth First! activists said that "the loggers were aware that activists were in the woods and deliberately felled trees in their direction . . . in an apparent attempt to target activists."[85] Pacific Lumber maintained that the death of Chain was accidental and that the logging crew thought the activists had left the area before Ammons resumed cutting. The exact amount of time between the videotaped confrontation and Chain's death remained an unresolved issue, as environmentalists called for an investigation into Pacific Lumber and Ammons. Instead, law enforcement officials told Chain's mother that they were considering bringing manslaughter charges against the other activists present at the time of her son's death.

The debate over the use of monkeywrenching and civil disobedience raged within Earth First! throughout the 1990s. Following Foreman's arrest, some who remained convinced that sabotage was the best way to further environmental causes went underground and began operating under the name Earth Liberation Front (ELF). In February 1994, Judi Bari published an article in the *Earth First! Journal* recommending that Earth First! mainstream itself in the United States, leaving criminal acts other than peaceful, unlawful protests to the new movement.

THE SAGEBRUSH REBELLION AND WISE USE

While Earth First! activists used sabotage and civil disobedience in response to what they viewed as the tepid efforts of mainstream environmentalists, another movement used similar tactics as a reaction against environmentalism in all its forms. The Sagebrush Rebellion of the 1970s and the more recent wise use movement were populist movements primarily based in the West that sought to claim state sovereignty over federally owned public lands and to replace the conservationist and preservationist ethics with a system that would allow private mining, logging, and ranching interests to utilize public land for personal profit.

Corporations such as Chevron and DuPont offered financial support to wise use groups in the 1990s but later shifted their attention to think tanks and public relations efforts. As a result, some of the leading wise use groups ceased operation, citing declines in funding and membership. However, the movement received a boost in early 2001, when President George W. Bush added wise use advocates to his cabinet. Interior Secretary Gale Norton's previous employer, Mountain States Legal Foundation, gave free legal advice to such groups, while Agriculture Secretary Ann Veneman represented the Nevada Access and Multiple Use Stewardship Coalition in her law practice. Of the 58 Bush appointees to the Interior Department, 12 were active in the wise use movement.

The Sagebrush Rebellion grew out of a clash in values between the Old and New West that has fueled the use of extreme tactics by both environmentalists and anti-environmentalists. Beginning in the late 1800s, ranchers, miners, and loggers in the American West became so accustomed to virtually free and untrammeled use of public lands that they began to see them as their own domain. The threat of restrictions or increased fees inaugurated by the conservation movement, supported by environmentalists, and imposed by the federal government has been seen as an infringement of basic rights by many in the West who cling to the 19th-century cowboy ideal.

The "rebellion" proper began in 1979, when the Nevada legislature passed the Sagebrush Rebellion Act, allowing the state to claim sovereignty over federally owned public lands with the eventual goal of turning the lands over to private resource extraction and ranching interests. The act was regarded as little more than a "sentiment" bill by the federal government and was not challenged in court. The legislation did, however, open a floodgate of hostility toward employees of the U.S. Forest Service, Bureau of Land Management, and National Park Service throughout the West and Alaska as large landowners sought to wrest control of the land and its resources from the federal government. Initiatives similar to the one passed in Nevada appeared in legislatures in Utah, Colorado, Wyoming, and Alaska. Utah senator Orrin Hatch called the movement "the second American revolution," and President Ronald Reagan, shortly after his election, sent a telegram to Nevada politicians declaring that he, too, was a Sagebrush Rebel. Reagan also appointed Sagebrush Rebellion advocate James Watt to the post of secretary of the interior. Before he was forced to resign in 1983 for uttering a sequence of ethnic slurs, Watt had transferred or sold more than 20 million acres of federal land to states.

Ecoterrorism

The Sagebrush Rebellion was not all politics. Extreme elements of the movement threatened and sometimes attacked government officials and vandalized federal property. According to author David Helvarg, the problem became so bad in Utah that County Commissioner Calvin Black "warned BLM employees to travel in pairs or groups along back roads to avoid being shot at by local people."[86] In several cases, vigilantes who opposed the federal government's closing of roads on public land for environmental reasons bulldozed them open again. On July 4, 1980, the local county commission in Moab, Utah, bulldozed a road into public land that the BLM had identified as a study area for possible wilderness designation. The incident, Dave Foreman once acknowledged, hardened his resolve to make Earth First! a force to reckoned with in the West.

The Sagebrush Rebellion lost impetus throughout the 1980s, but in 1988, Ron Arnold organized the first Multiple Use Strategy Conference (later renamed the Wise Use Leadership Conference) in Reno, Nevada, which inspired the drafting of the 25-point "Wise Use Agenda." Among its points were the "immediate wise development of the petroleum resources of the Arctic National Wildlife Refuge"; the creation of a national mining system under which "all public lands including wilderness and national parks shall be open to mineral and energy production under wise use technologies"; and support for the National Parks Reform Act, which stated that "private firms with expertise in people moving such as Walt Disney should be selected as new transportation concessioners to accommodate and enhance the national park experience without degrading the environment." The wise use ideology, essentially a counterrevolutionary response to the 30-year-old mainstream environmental movement, was broad enough to include land rights activists, resource extraction industries, ranchers, off-road vehicle enthusiasts, free enterprise capitalists, and anyone else who felt they were being strangled by environmental regulation, big government, and a perceived bias in the media.

As with environmentalists, the majority of wise use proponents were law-abiding citizens engaged in grassroots fund-raising and lobbying efforts to further their agenda. The volatile rhetoric of Arnold, however, immediately put environmentalists on the defensive. He once stated that the aim of wise use was "to destroy the environmental movement once and for all" and declared "holy war against the new pagans who worship trees and sacrifice people."[87] He also asserted that environmentalism had created many of the nation's more pressing social problems:

When you come into a town and decide a factory has to close because it violates environmental regulations, you see behavior patterns change. Domestic violence, child abuse, the use of drugs and alcohol will go up to a new plateau as the community disintegrates. Is it the environmentalists' fault? You're damn right it is.[88]

Such accusations prompted the left-wing *Seattle Weekly* to brand Arnold "the most dangerous man in America" for his ability to present himself as mainstream when his politics, especially on environmental issues, were as radical as those of Earth First![89] In response to Arnold's frequent appearances in mainstream media discussions of radical environmentalism, David Helvarg, an environmentalist who wrote *War Against the Greens*, once said that relying on the wise use founder for analysis of radical environmental activism is "like asking [Ku Klux Klan leader] David Duke to assess the rise of black militants."[90]

Some wise users sought to take Arnold's ideas a step further. Retired timber baron William Holmes once suggested that attendees at a California logging conference should begin a "Hate Them" campaign against environmentalists to destroy them as a political force. He said it should be a "fun program" in which participants "should be prepared to kick someone in the crotch." He also suggested that funding should be disguised so it could not be traced back to timber companies. In June 1990, former Reagan interior secretary James Watt told a gathering of cattlemen that "if the troubles from environmentalists cannot be solved in the jury box or at the ballot box, perhaps the cartridge box should be used."[91]

In 1990, *Dirt Bike* magazine editor Rick Sieman founded the Sahara Club in protest of the BLM's cancellation of the Barstow-to-Vegas off-road motorcycle race (the course passed through endangered desert tortoise habitat). The organization quickly expanded its interests to include the multiple-use concerns of loggers, miners, and ranchers. Sahara Club newsletters routinely published the names, addresses, phone numbers, and vehicle license plate numbers of environmental activists, with instructions to "track them down and perhaps 'reason' with them about the error of their ways"[92] or to "do the right thing; and let your conscience be you guide."[93] One newsletter offered $100 to anyone who supplied information leading to the arrest of an Earth First! activist. The article continued,

We were thinking of offering $150 reward if the Earth Firster [sic] was delivered to the cops with a bloody nose and a few broken bones, but our lawyer advised us against it, saying it was illegal. Then there's the fact that so many of them are homos, that you might get splashed with AIDS-tainted blood.[94]

In some cases, the rhetoric of radical wise use factions has been matched and even exceeded by actions that are often more dangerous than the activities of the ELF/ALF because they target people rather than property. At the February 2002 congressional hearings on ecoterrorism, Michael Roy Pendleton, a social scientist at the University of Washington, testified that the vast majority of property crime and violent acts committed in national forests are by people who subscribe to "a twisted view" of wise use. He cited a drive-by shooting of a ranger station using automatic weapons in which the perpetrators, before they were caught, actually stopped to reload and make a second pass. This, according to Pendleton, was only "one among many examples of blown gates, car bombings, and arsons where land management employees are the clear targets of violence" by wise use advocates.

Also speaking at the hearing was Gloria Flora, former forest supervisor of Lewis and Clark National Forest and Humboldt-Toiyabe National Forest. She spoke of her decision to resign from the USFS in 2000 to protest the threat of "harassment, intimidation, and lawlessness that haunts Forest Service employees" by extremist wise use advocates. Flora cited the growing violence of off-road enthusiasts who gather annually on Thanksgiving weekend in California's Imperial Valley: "In recent years, [BLM] rangers have been attacked by mobs, run down by vehicles and assaulted with weapons by off-roaders yelling anti-government epithets." During the 2001 holiday weekend, BLM agents "dealt with two deaths, 220 medical emergencies, 50 arrests, nearly 1,000 citations, several shootings, and one ranger run over by an angry 3-wheeler."[95]

Flora also produced statistics showing that "beatings, shootings, threats and other incidents of violence against federal resource managers, primarily in the West" rose sharply in 2000 and had done so every year but one since 1995. She went on to speak of hostile wise users who have threatened to break the law using "remember Waco" as a rallying cry and who have called her and other federal employees Nazis. "To evoke the image of fascism and compare it to contemporary public land management in America," she told the gathered congressional representatives, "is at best delusional and, at worst, a disgrace to the memories of those who suffered unimaginable terror at the hands of the Nazi regime."[96]

Flora detailed the case of Guy Pence, who had worked as the district ranger of the Carson District of Toiyabe National Forest, which includes Nye County, Nevada, "the heart of the anti-environmental 'wise-use' movement."[97] On March 30, 1995, a bomb was placed outside Pence's office at USFS headquarters in Carson City, Nevada, blowing out the windows. No one was injured. In August 1995, a bomb destroyed Pence's family van and blew out the front window of his house. Pence was later transferred to the USFS office in Boise, Idaho, which has since received several bomb threats.

Although no one took credit for the bombings, Flora believes wise users were to blame. Pence agrees. "I've always been proud of my relationship with conservation folks," he once said. "My contests do not come from that side."[98] Wise use advocates had reason to be angry with Pence. He had gained a reputation for suspending or canceling the permits of grazers, loggers, and miners who violated permit conditions and environmental laws. He once issued a citation to Nye County commissioner Dick Carver, a private rancher and wise use leader who "gained national attention (including the cover photo of *Time* magazine) in the mid-1990s, when he drove a bulldozer toward Forest Service rangers in an attempt to open a road that had been closed by the agency." Carver later described the incident at a wise use rally, boasting, "All it would have taken was for [one of the rangers] to draw a weapon, and fifty people with sidearms would have drilled him."[99]

THE EARTH LIBERATION FRONT AND THE ANIMAL LIBERATION FRONT

The Earth Liberation Front (ELF) was founded in 1992 in Brighton, England, by Earth First! activists who refused to abandon sabotage as a tactic when others wished to mainstream the movement. In September of the following year, the ELF and the Animal Liberation Front (ALF) issued a joint press release declaring their solidarity of action. This alliance marked a departure from a previous separation between the environmental and animal rights movements. The ALF itself was founded in England in 1979, having grown out of that nation's burgeoning radical animal liberation movement that included such groups as the Band of Mercy, which was dedicated to disrupting fox hunts. Since then, the ALF has conducted hundreds of arsons, fire bombings, and other acts of destruction against furriers, butchers, restaurants, veterinarians, zookeepers, mink farms, and medical research facilities. Another group based in England, Stop Huntingdon Animal Cruelty (SHAC), has focused its ire on Huntingdon Life Sciences, Europe's largest animal testing laboratory.

Since the 1980s, the ALF has been active in the United States, where its efforts are applauded by People for the Ethical Treatment of Animals (PETA), the largest and best known radical animal rights organization in the world. The PETA web site compares the ALF to the French Resistance of World War II and the Underground Railroad of 19th-century America. Founder Ingrid Newkirk says the group has a moral right to its illegal actions, but she insists that PETA does not participate in them. PETA has, however, been criticized for helping pay the legal fees of ALF members, a practice Newkirk defends by saying PETA merely wants to ensure that ALF members get fair trials.

Extremists who act in the name of the ELF/ALF operate in secrecy and in small independent cells with no identifiable leader or hierarchy. There are no membership lists, no annual fees, and no magazines or journals. According to

ELF/ALF web sites and printed material, one "joins" the movement simply by taking action that adheres to a set of widely available guidelines. Among these are "to cause as much economic damage as possible to a given entity that is profiting off the destruction of the natural environment and life for selfish greed and profit," "to educate the public on the atrocities committed against the environment and life," and "to take all necessary precautions against harming life."[100] The web sites have also published detailed primers on how to encrypt e-mail, stake out targets, deal with FBI investigations, and set fires.

The lack of structure has made it difficult for the FBI to infiltrate or stop the movement. The U.S. Justice Department, having abandoned the "soft-core" distinction it afforded Earth First! in the 1980s, now labels the ELF/ALF as the number one "domestic terrorist" threat to the United States, surpassing the antigovernment militia extremists who dominated the attention of the FBI during much of the 1990s. According to James Jarboe, the FBI's top domestic terrorism officer, the ELF/ALF are "the most active" and "cause the most damage" of any U.S. terrorist organization.[101]

Faced with the difficulty of identifying and arresting ELF/ALF perpetrators, law enforcement has focused its attention on the groups' highly visible spokespersons. According to writer Daniel Glick, arsonists acting in the name of the ELF/ALF developed a pattern of issuing claims of responsibility via untraceable, anonymous e-mails to spokespersons who, even while releasing the information to the media, "maintained plausible deniability of firsthand knowledge of the crime or its perpetrators."[102]

From 1997 to 2001, the spokespersons for the ELF were Craig Rosebraugh and Leslie James Pickering. In 1996, the two activists became involved with Portland, Oregon's, Liberation Collective, an organization dedicated to conducting protest and direct action campaigns against vivisection, war, globalization, and other issues. In 1997, Rosebraugh and Pickering began receiving and publishing anonymous communiqués taking credit for ELF/ALF actions. In 2000, they split from the Liberation Collective and founded the North American Earth Liberation Front Press Office (NAELFPO), which immediately became the target of repeated federal law enforcement raids. Between 1997 and 2001, Rosebraugh was served with seven subpoenas to testify before federal grand juries investigating the ELF, during which he maintained that he was not a member of the group and that his knowledge of the movement's activities was limited to communiqués he passed on to the media. He refused to answer further questions and was never directly implicated in any of the ELF's actions.

In September 2001, less than a week before the 9/11 terrorist attacks, Pickering and Rosebraugh both resigned from NAELFPO, although Pickering briefly reemerged as an ELF spokesperson in February 2002 to criticize the "war on terrorism," the USA PATRIOT Act of 2001, and congressional hearings on ecoterrorism for which Rosebraugh had been subpoenaed to testify. During these hearings, Rosebraugh invoked the Fifth Amendment against self-incrimination more than 50 times. He did, however, submit 11 pages of written testimony in which he argued that the ELF's "noble pursuit" of destroying the property of "those who are engaged in massive planetary destruction," rather than constituting terrorism, "seeks to abolish it." He went on to characterize the U.S. government as "by far . . . the most extreme terrorist organization in planetary history."[103]

The hearings, held on February 12, 2002, were hosted by Colorado representative Scott McInnis, chairman of the House Resources Subcommittee on Forests and Forest Health. Testimony was supplied by members of Congress, individuals representing companies targeted by the ELF/ALF, law enforcement officials, and industry representatives, many of whom gave detailed accounts of ELF/ALF attacks and called for additional legislation dealing with ecoterrorism. Aside from Rosebraugh (the sole representative of the environmentalist point of view, mainstream or radical), nearly everyone present agreed that the ELF/ALF were terrorist organizations on par with al-Qaeda and that no distinction should be made between the hijackers who flew airliners into the World Trade Center and those who use arson to burn empty buildings. Boise Cascade Corporation logging manager Michael S. Hicks summed up the prevailing view when he said, "Terrorism is terrorism, plain and simple."[104]

Pickering, meanwhile, did little to assuage widespread fears among those at the hearing that ELF/ALF tactics would grow increasingly bold. During his second stint as NAELFPO spokesperson, which lasted into summer 2002, he began issuing increasingly anti-authoritarian and violent rhetoric, claiming that the ELF was part of a larger struggle for revolutionary change. In early 2003, Rosebraugh published an open letter calling on activists protesting the war in Iraq to abandon peaceful tactics in favor of attacks against property at U.S. military installations, corporations, government buildings, and media outlets. The two activists subsequently cofounded the Arissa Media Group, an emerging revolutionary effort whose stated mission was to "rid the world of one of the greatest terrorist organizations in planetary history, the U.S. government."[105]

Despite the increasing frequency of ELF/ALF activity, as well as growing efforts by federal law enforcement officials to deal with the problem, few arrests have been made in connection with either group. In 1994, Rodney Coronado, one of the perpetrators of the Sea Shepherd Conservation Society's 1985 Raid on Reykjavik and ALF spokesperson during the early 1990s, was arrested for setting fire to animal experimentation labs at Michigan State University. He was sentenced to 57 months in prison and ordered to pay more than $2.5 million in restitution. In January 2001, Frank Ambrose became the first person to be arrested in connection with ELF activity. He was accused of a tree spiking incident in Indiana for which the ELF took credit. Ambrose, Midwest coordinator of the American Lands Alliance, was a longtime environmentalist who denied involvement with the ELF or the tree spiking incident. Activists have pointed to his arrest as an example of how authorities harass aboveground activists in order to intimidate radical environmentalists. In February 2001, three minors (Jared McIntyre, Matthew Rammelkamp, and George Mashkow) and one adult (Connor Cash) were arrested and charged with arson and arson conspiracy for burning homes under construction on Long Island. As part of a plea bargain, Mashkow and Rammelkamp pleaded guilty as adults and agreed to cooperate in investigations into the ELF/ALF. The ELF subsequently branded them traitors to the cause on its web site.

This latter incident, which involved burning luxury homes under construction in order to protest sprawl, is one incident in a growing trend among ELF activists to attack urban-based targets, such as SUV dealerships, fast-food restaurants, and housing developments. The group's concerns have also grown beyond environmentalism, illustrated by an attempted arson in April 2001 at a Nike outlet store in Albertville, Minnesota, in protest of the shoe manufacturer's use of sweatshop labor overseas and its role in globalization. On March 29, 2003, a truck at the Naval Recruiting office in Montgomery, Alabama, was set on fire. Graffiti calling for an end to the war in Iraq and signed "ELF" was spray painted onto five nearby military vehicles.

The ELF describes itself as being concerned with "positive social and political change" and with attacking the ideology of "capitalism and the mindset that allows it to exist," which is thought to be the root cause of injustice and the destruction of nature.[106] This idea is shared more by social ecologists and later members of Earth First! than by the deep ecologists who founded the militant organization in 1980. The activists involved in the ELF have not only moved away from a sole concern about "big wilderness" propounded by Earth First! founders but have also, with their alliance with the ALF, left behind the proud meat-eating, redneck behavior of Foreman and company in favor of vegan lifestyles.

This continued diversification of radical environmentalism into the realms of animal rights and social justice may be seen as a positive step by activists like Pickering and Rosebraugh, who consider the ELF/ALF to be a mere component of a more widespread revolutionary struggle. As this movement widens its scope, however, it will become increasingly difficult to predict what rhetoric and what tactics people will use under the unstructured banner of the ELF/ALF. As Foreman realized in the 1980s, lack of hierarchy and leadership often means lack of control. He and others faced fallout from Christopher Manes's 1987 AIDS essay, and on one occasion Foreman publicly reprimanded activists who sabotaged logging equipment belonging to a small, family-owned timber company and draped an Earth First! banner nearby. The destruction, he insisted, was more akin to petty vandalism than to well-considered monkeywrenching that targeted corporate logging operations.

The ELF/ALF may face similar problems. It has become a well-worn cliché among the most vocal critics of the movement to say that it is "only a matter of time" before someone is killed in an ecoterror attack. While condemning a group for an event that has not occurred signals a questionable willingness to allow emotions to trump logic, the ELF's contention that "an action similar to one performed by the ELF" that "resulted in an individual becoming physically injured or losing their life . . . would not be considered an ELF action"[107] is equally disingenuous. Accidents do happen, and any loss of life connected with an arson attack in the name of a revolutionary movement would, in the minds of many people, clarify the cloudy debate over whether the ELF/ALF deserve to be called terrorist organizations.

THE UNABOMBER

Even those radical environmentalists who exhibit no qualms about destroying property have taken great care to avoid injury to humans. The exception to this rule is Theodore Kaczynski, who in 1978 began a one-man, 18-year bombing campaign that resulted in 23 injuries and three deaths. Dubbed the Unabomber for targeting universities and airlines, Kaczynski wrote a manifesto charging that the Industrial Revolution had been a disaster for the planet and calling for the overthrow of the "industrial-technological" system. Although many deep ecologists share these sentiments, the vast majority of militant environmentalists have disavowed the Unabomber's methods.

Kaczynski's first act of terrorism occurred on May 25, 1978, when he left a package bomb in the parking lot near the Science and Engineering Building of the Chicago Circle campus of the University of Illinois. The package, which was stamped and addressed to a professor at Rensselaer Polytechnic Institute in Troy, New York, was found by Mary Gutierrez. Unable to fit it into a nearby mailbox, she took it home and contacted Northwestern University computer science professor Buckley Crist, Jr., whose name was on the return address. Crist sent a messenger to pick it up, but when he did not recognize the package, he turned it over to campus security. The bomb exploded when officer Terry Marker began to unwrap it. He sustained only slight injuries. Of the incident, Kaczynski wrote in his journal, "I hoped that a student—preferably one in a science and technology field—would pick it up and would either be a good citizen and take the package to post office to be sent to Rensselaer, or would open the package himself and blow his hands off, or get killed."[108]

The FBI's hunt for a single suspect in connection with the multiple bombings began with Kaczynski's third attack. On November 14, 1979, he mailed a package from Chicago to Washington, D.C., that contained explosives wired to ignite when they reached 2,000 feet in altitude. The bomb exploded inside a mail carrier container onboard American Airlines passenger flight 444, causing cabin pressure to drop and filling the body of the plane with smoke. Although no one was injured, the plane was forced to make an emergency landing at Washington's Dulles Airport. The disappointed terrorist wrote in his journal, "Plan was to blow up airliner flight . . . Unfortunately plane not destroyed, bomb too weak."[109] Meanwhile, FBI special agent Chris Ronay found similarities between this bomb and the one that had injured Marker, as well as a third that had injured Northwestern University graduate student John Harris on May 9, 1979. The search for the Unabomber was on.

The stakes increased on December 11, 1985, when Kaczynski, on his 11th attempt, finally succeeded in killing his target. On that day, Hugh Scrutton walked out the back door of the computer rental store he owned in Sacramento, California, and saw on the ground a block of wood with nails protruding from each end. When he picked it up, an explosion tore through his chest and blew off his right hand. He died 30 minutes later. Kaczynski was exultant. The victim "was killed, blown to bits," he wrote. "Excellent. Humane way to eliminate somebody. He probably never felt a thing."[110] Kaczynski was also flattered that the FBI was now offering a $25,000 reward for information leading to the arrest of the Unabomber, whose increasingly sophisticated and powerful bombs, law enforcement officials knew, were capable of taking more lives.

The FBI may have felt it got a break in February 1987, when a witness saw Kaczynski leave a bomb in the parking lot of a computer store in Salt Lake City, Utah. Store owner Gary Wright sustained severe injuries to his face, left arm, and hand when he picked it up. Although the witness supplied a description that resulted in the famous FBI sketch of the hooded Unabomber, the ensuing years brought the agency no closer to solving the crimes. This was partly because Kaczynski took a six-year break from terrorism following the Salt Lake City incident, during which he perfected a new type of bomb that used a more powerful explosive mixture.

The first victim of this new recipe was world-renowned geneticist Charles J. Epstein, who received a package at his Tiburon, California, home on June 22, 1993. The bomb inside, Kaczynski's 13th, blew Epstein across the room, knocked him to the floor, and injured his right arm. Two days later, Yale University computer science professor David Gelernter was the victim of a similar bomb, which blew the thumb and little finger from his right hand and badly mangled the remaining digits. Of these explosions Kaczynski wrote, "The effect of both of them was adequate but no more than adequate."[111]

Kaczynski mailed two more bombs before his arrest, both of which resulted in death. On December 10, 1994, Thomas Mosser, an executive at the public relations firm Burson-Marsteller, died at his home in North Caldwell, New Jersey, when he opened a package bomb sent by Kaczynski. The bomber wrote that the "device . . . gave a totally satisfactory result."[112] On April 24, 1995, Gilbert Murray, president of the California Forestry Association (CFA) in Sacramento, California, became the third and final person killed by the Unabomber when Murray opened a package addressed to William Dennison of the Timber Association of California (TAC). (The TAC had recently been renamed the CFA, and Dennison had served as the former organization's president.) The explosion packed such force that staff biologist Bob Taylor, who had left the room 30 seconds earlier, was unable to find Murray's body. He had literally been blown to pieces.

While Kaczynski had perfected his bombs using impressive homemade technology, his downfall was the correspondence he initiated with the media in 1993. On June 24, the *New York Times* received a letter signed by "an anarchist group calling ourselves FC." Half of the bombs linked to the Unabomber had been affixed with a metal tag inscribed with the letters *FC*, later explained by the terrorist to stand for "Freedom Club." Although the Unabomber used the plural *we* in his letters, the FBI long thought the bombing spree was the work of an individual rather than a group. This first note, mailed from the same location and on the same date as the bombs that injured Epstein and Gelernter, merely pointed out that the letter's postmark preceded "a newsworthy event."[113]

On April 27, 1995, Gelernter himself received a more substantial communication from FC that criticized the computer science professor's contention, in his book *Mirror Worlds*, that technological advancements have made a computer-dominated world inevitable. "If the developments you describe are inevitable," Kaczynski wrote, "they are not inevitable in the way old age and bad weather are inevitable. They are inevitable only because techno-nerds like you make them inevitable. . . . But we do not believe that progress and growth are inevitable."[114]

On April 24, 1995, the *New York Times* received its second letter from FC, this one explaining that Thomas Mosser had been killed because the company he worked for, Burson-Marsteller, was in the business of developing "techniques for manipulating people's attitudes," including cleaning up Exxon Corporation's public image following the *Exxon Valdez* oil spill in Alaska's Prince William Sound. The letter went on to explain, "Through our bombings we hope to promote social instability in industrial society, propagate anti-industrial ideas and give encouragement to those who hate the industrial system."[115]

In the last week of June 1995, the *New York Times*, the *Washington Post*, and *Penthouse* magazine all received copies of a 35,000-word essay by FC titled "Industrial Society and Its Future," soon to be commonly known as the "Unabomber Manifesto." Notes affixed to the *New York Times* and *Washington Post* copies promised that the bomber would "permanently desist from terrorism" if the essay was published. Although the newspapers were reluctant to allow themselves to be coerced into printing the manifesto of a serial killer, Attorney General Janet Reno convinced them to do so in the hope that someone would recognize its authorship. Before that, however, the FBI allowed approximately 50 college professors to read the document, hoping that one of them would remember a former student who used the same grammatical oddities (such as using "consist in" instead of "consist of") apparent in the manuscript. When this bore no fruit, "Industrial Society and Its Future" was jointly printed by the *Times* and the *Post* in its entirety on September 19, 1995.

In the end, Reno's intuition proved correct. When Ted's brother, David, read the manifesto in the newspaper, his suspicions were aroused by its similarity to an antitechnology essay Ted had written in 1971. Although reluctant to believe that his brother was capable of the crimes ascribed to the Unabomber, he finally contacted the FBI in February 1996. The investigation quickly focused on Ted, who was placed under surveillance and then arrested at his small cabin in Lincoln, Montana, on April 3.

The trial began in fall 1997. The backbone of the government's case, according to Assistant U.S. Attorney Robert Cleary, was the diary found in Kaczynski's cabin, which contained admissions that the former math professor had played a role in all 16 bombings. A typewriter found in the cabin was also linked to letters sent by FC. Kaczynski attorneys Quin Denvir and Judy Clarke based their defense strategy on proving that the Unabomber was too insane to deserve the death penalty. Part of this strategy included moving Kaczynski's Montana cabin to Sacramento, California, as evidence. "In some ways," Denvir said, "the cabin spoke a lot more to his mental state than the testimony of an expert."[116]

Kaczynski argued against his defense team's strategy. In December, he wrote a letter to the judge asking to be assigned new lawyers and explaining that he would "rather die, or suffer prolonged physical torture" than be portrayed as a madman at the trial. After the judge refused to allow Kaczynski to represent himself or change lawyers, Denvir and Clarke agreed to abandon the insanity defense. On January 4, however, Kaczynski was stunned to learn that his lawyers were still planning on presenting nonexpert mental-state testimony during the guilt phase of the trial. Four days later, Kaczynski, unhappy that his attorneys had worked behind his back to mount an insanity defense despite his wishes to the contrary, again asked the permission of the court to represent himself. The judge refused the request. In the meantime, court-appointed psychiatrist Sally Johnson had examined Kaczynski and issued a report finding that although the defendant suffered from "schizophrenia, paranoid type," he appeared to be in "remission" and therefore competent to stand trial and to represent himself.

In light of this psychiatric report, which had been ordered by the judge, many legal experts were surprised by the court's refusal to allow Kaczynski to represent himself. The judge's explanation ranged from the claim that Kaczynski had waited too long to make the request to the accusation that the request was merely a tactic to delay the trial. In any case, the January 22 decision to deny Kaczynski's request was followed within hours by a plea bargain. In exchange for the government's agreement to not seek the death penalty, Kaczynski pled guilty to 13 federal bombing offenses (three of which resulted in death) and took responsibility for the string of 16 bombings lasting from 1978 to 1995. On May 4, he was sentenced to four consecutive life terms plus 30 years.

Part of Kaczynski's plea bargain included assurances that he would not appeal his sentence, but on June 16, 1999, he did just that on the grounds that the court, by refusing to allow him to fire his attorneys, had violated his constitutional right to mount his own defense. The Justice Department maintained that Kaczynski was aware of the consequences of his plea bargain and that it should stand. The appeal brought up some tricky legal questions. Vermont Law School professor Michael Mello, author of *The United States of America Versus Theodore Kaczynski* (1999), believed the trial pointed to bigger issues concerning a lawyer's responsibility to respect a client's wishes. "For me," he said, "the bottom line is that it's the client's crime, it's the client's trial, and it's the client's life. And it ought to be the client's choice."[117] Colorado public defender Michael Katz disagreed, arguing that "the call for determining the strategy for a defense is ultimately the lawyer's," who has an obligation to protect his or her client.[118] The Ninth Circuit Court rejected the appeal in February 2001, and the Supreme Court declined to hear the case, effectively ending Kaczynski's options.

Although these questions of self-representation were batted around by legal experts, of greater interest to the public was the way the protracted trial denied everyone a closer look at the life, beliefs, and motivations of the Unabomber. Anyone interested in analyzing Kaczynski was forced to rely on a sparse collection of court documents and on his writings.

Chief among his writings is the "Unabomber Manifesto," a rambling document whose special brand of logic is overshadowed by the contradiction of attempting to create a society that respects individual freedom using a means that shows no respect for individual life. It has been suggested by author Alston Chase, however, that most people were made uncomfortable by the manifesto "not because its ideas were so foreign, but because they were so familiar. Except for the call to violence, its message was ordinary and unoriginal. The concerns it evinced, about the effects of technology on culture and nature, are widely shared."[119] Environmentalists in particular were appalled that the Unabomber's chosen "positive ideal" was, as he wrote, "WILD nature," and that nature advocacy could prompt someone to commit murder.

Not surprisingly, Kaczynski and his manifesto supplied anti-environmentalists with ammunition for assaults on environmentalism in general. Syndicated columnist Tony Snow went so far as to write an article linking then-vice president Al Gore to terrorism by pointing out similarities in language between the "Unabomber Manifesto" and Gore's 1992 book *Earth in the Balance*. Ralph Reiland attempted the same connection based on the observation that a "page-worn and well-underlined" copy of *Earth in the Balance* was found in Kaczynski's cabin.[120] Such accusations by conservatives exhibited the same kind of unrealistic guilt-by-distant-association used by some on the left side of the political fence in the 1990s in attempts to connect the wise use/property rights network to the terrorist militia movement.

Some critics of radical environmentalism have also attempted to link the Unabomber's campaign of terrorism to Earth First! This theory began to take shape immediately after Kaczynski's arrest, when ABC News correspondent Brian Ross reported that authorities believed that Kaczynski had been present at a November 1994 meeting at the University of Montana at which Earth First! activists had plotted strategy against multinational corporations. Ross further stated that "the bomb last year that killed Gil Murray, the head of the California Forestry Association, clearly can be traced back to a hit list published in one radical environmental journal." In one report, Ross added, "Much as Timothy McVeigh may have been inspired and inflamed by the militia, it's possible, perhaps, that Kaczynski was inspired and guided by the radical environmental groups."[121]

This information was supplied to Ross by Barry Clausen, who had once attempted to infiltrate Earth First! on behalf of timber companies but was unable to uncover any information of interest. Clausen purported to be in possession of a list of attendees at the Missoula conference that included the name "T. Casinski," although he refused to show reporters the document. Organizers of the conference said they found no names on the roster even remotely resembling Kaczynski or Casinski. The conference itself, despite its ominous description in news reports, was actually an open timber conference attended by 500 people, including Oklahoma congressman Mike Synar and representatives from the U.S. Forest Service, the Fish and Wildlife Service, and timber companies Weyerhaeuser and Louisiana-Pacific.

The "hit list" in question was originally published in the radical environmental publication *Live Wild or Die* and consisted of a roster of 75 companies that had sponsored the 1989 wise use National Wilderness Conference in Reno, Nevada. Number one on the list was the Timber Association of California, to which Kaczynski had addressed the bomb that killed Gilbert Murray, even though the organization had changed its name to the California Forestry Association. Number three on the list was Exxon Corporation. A June 21, 1993, article in the *Earth First! Journal* had blasted public relations firm "Burston-Marsteller" for cleaning up Exxon's image after the spill (an accusation that turned out to be false). The article incorrectly added the letter *t* to Burson-Marsteller so it read "Burston-Marsteller," a mistake duplicated in the April 24, 1995, letter Kaczynski sent to the *New York Times* to explain why he had targeted Thomas Mosser. Kaczynski confessed at his brief trial to having read the *Earth First! Journal* article. While it is possible that Kaczynski also saw the offending issue of *Live Wild or Die* and picked two of his targets from its pages, the "hit list," widely reported as if its purpose was to incite Unabomber-like violence, merely called on readers to boycott the listed corporations.

Earth First!, meanwhile, was quick to disavow the connection. *Earth First! Journal* editor Craig Beneville pointed out that "the Unabomber has been bombing people for a lot longer than Earth First! has even been in existence."[122] Another *Journal* editor, Leslie Hemstreet, said that linking the group to the Unabomber's deeds "is like blaming the pope for people who are killing abortion doctors."[123]

More troubling than these tenuous connections is the inspiration that Kaczynski seems to be affording the "green anarchist" movement. Theresa Kintz, writer for *Green Anarchist* magazine, was the first person Kaczynski granted an interview after his arrest, and the spring 2002 issue listed Kaczynski as "prisoner of war." Kaczynski also published an article in the magazine calling on anarchists to "eliminate the entire techno-industrial system" by attacking its "vital organs," among them the electric power grid, communications, computers, and the "propaganda industry." This latter, according to Kaczynski, includes "the entertainment industry, the educational system, journalism, advertising, public relations," and the "mental health industry." The best target, however, would be the leadership of the biotechnology industry: "You have to strike at its head."[124] John Zerzan, one of *Green Anarchy*'s editors, has corresponded regularly with Kaczynski and has visited him in prison. Zerzan is also thought by many to be the mastermind of the more violent aspects of 1999 anti-globalization "Battle in Seattle," having incited his followers to smash windows and destroy property belonging to offending corporations.

Kaczynski, meanwhile, has registered his support for the actions of the ELF/ALF. In a letter to Denver television reporter Rick Sallinger, he wrote, "I fully approve of [the 1998 Vail arson] and I congratulate the people who carried it out."[125] This laudatory comment certainly does not imply a reciprocation of appreciation on the part of the ELF, particularly since the ELF expressly forbids harming humans and animals in its actions. However, there does seem to be a potentially volatile cross-affinity of purpose among the green anarchists, the ELF/ALF, and Kaczynski, even if they do not agree on methods. Aside from the suggestion to target the leadership of the biotechnology industry, Kaczynski's advice to green anarchists is strikingly similar to Craig Rosebraugh's call for attacks against property at U.S. military installations, corporations, government buildings, and media outlets in protest of the U.S. invasion of Iraq in 2003. The ELF's concern with attacking the ideology of "capitalism and the mindset that allows it to exist,"[126] furthermore, is reflected by the ideals that fueled the Seattle protests, which are embodied in the writings and followers of John Zerzan.

The difference among these factions is that Kaczynski is the only one who has intentionally targeted and taken human lives and is therefore the only one who virtually everyone agrees is a terrorist. Earth First! and the ELF/ALF have also been identified as such by the FBI, but jurists in the Judi Bari and Darryl Cherney trial of 2002 chided federal investigators for violating the First and Fourth Amendments in their efforts to brand the Earth First! activists as terrorists. Civil libertarians maintain that extreme care must be taken in deciding who deserves such a label, warning that in the course of its "war on terror," the U.S. government runs the risk of repeating the mistakes of the cold war, when thousands of people were falsely accused of affiliations with the Communist Party. They further warn that legislation like the USA PATRIOT Act of 2001, if popularly perceived to intrude into the private lives of ordinary people, runs the risk of triggering an increase in the deep feelings of alienation that have, since the time of the Revolutionary War, prompted Americans to abandon mainstream political efforts in favor of questionable criminal tactics.

---

[1] Earth Liberation Front communiqué, quoted in Leslie James Pickering, *The Earth Liberation Front: 1997–2002.* South Wales, N.Y.: Arissa, 2003, p. 22.

[2] Peter C. List, *Radical Environmentalism: Philosophy and Tactics.* Belmont, Calif.: Wadsworth, 1993, p. 1.

[3] Ron Arnold, *Ecoterror: The Violent Agenda to Save Nature/The World of the Unabomber.* Bellevue, Wash.: Free Enterprise Press, 1995, pp. 121–122.

[4] List, *Radical Environmentalism*, p. 131.

[5] Paul Watson, quoted in List, *Radical Environmentalism*, p. 167.

[6] Dave Foreman, *Confessions of an Eco-Warrior.* New York: Crown, 1991, p. 113.

[7] Edward Abbey, quoted in List, *Radical Environmentalism*, p. 252.

[8] Pickering, *The Earth Liberation Front*, p. 77.

[9] William J. Bratton, quoted in Jill Leovy, "3 Held in Drive-By Killings." *Los Angeles Times*, September 12, 2003, pp. B1 ff.

[10] John Elvin, "Lumping the ELF and the ALF with Al-Qaeda." *Insight on the News*, vol. 18 (March 25, 2002), p. 34.

[11] Scott McInnis, quoted in Valerie Richardson, et al., "FBI Targets Domestic Terrorists." *Insight on the News*, vol. 18 (April 22, 2002), p. 30.

[12] James V. Hansen, quoted in Richardson, et al., "FBI Targets Domestic Terrorists," p. 30.

[13] Elvin, "Lumping the ELF and the ALF with Al-Qaeda," p. 34.

[14] Henry David Thoreau, quoted in James Bishop, Jr., *Epitaph for a Desert Anarchist: The Life and Legacy of Edward Abbey.* New York: Atheneum, 1994, p. 223.

[15] Thoreau, quoted in Bishop, *Epitaph for a Desert Anarchist*, p. 132.

[16] George Perkins Marsh, quoted in Benjamin Kline, *First Along the River: A Brief History of the U.S. Environmental Movement.* 2d ed. San Francisco: Acada, 2000, p. 47.

[17] Aldo Leopold, *A Sand County Almanac and Sketches Here and There.* New York: Oxford University Press, 1949, p. 130.

[18] Leopold, *A Sand County Almanac and Sketches Here and There*, pp. 224–225.

[19] Quoted in List, *Radical Environmentalism*, p. vii.

[20] Gaylord Nelson and Denis Hayes, quoted in Susan Zakin, *Coyotes and Town Dogs: Earth First! and the Environmental Movement.* Tucson: University of Arizona Press, 2002, pp. 33–35.

[21] Richard Nixon, quoted in Kline, *First Along the River*, p. 80.

[22] Richard Nixon, quoted in Christopher Manes, *Green Rage: Radical Environmentalism and the Unmaking of Civilization.* Boston: Little, Brown, 1990, p. 47.

[23] Barry Weisberg, quoted in List, *Radical Environmentalism*, pp. 3–4.

[24] List, *Radical Environmentalism*, p. 4.

[25] Sam Love and David Obst, eds. *Ecotage!* New York: Pocket Books, 1972, p. 14.

[26] Quoted in Love and Obst, *Ecotage!*, pp. 14–15.

[27] Quoted in Love and Obst, *Ecotage!*, p. 88.

[28] Mike Royko and the Fox, quoted in Love and Obst, *Ecotage!*, pp. 144–145.

[29] Quoted in Love and Obst, *Ecotage!*, p. 151.

[30] Quoted in Zakin, *Coyotes and Town Dogs*, pp. 59–60.

[31] List, *Radical Environmentalism*, p. 7.

[32] Arne Naess, quoted in List, *Radical Environmentalism*, p. 19.

[33] Arne Naess, quoted in List, *Radical Environmentalism*, p. 7.

[34] Arne Naess, quoted in List, *Radical Environmentalism*, pp. 19–20.

[35] Arne Naess, quoted in List, *Radical Environmentalism*, pp. 20–22.

[36] Ron Arnold, *Ecoterror*, p. 7.

[37] Carolyn Merchant quoted in List, *Radical Environmentalism*, p. 49.

[38] List, *Radical Environmentalism*, pp. 9–10.

[39] Gary Snyder, quoted in List, *Radical Environmentalism*, p. 12.

[40] Jim Dodge, quoted in List, *Radical Environmentalism*, p. 115.

[41] List, *Radical Environmentalism*, p. 12.

[42] Judith Plant, quoted in List, *Radical Environmentalism*, p. 92.

[43] List, *Radical Environmentalism*, p. 3.

[44] Quoted in List, *Radical Environmentalism*, pp. 134–135.

[45] James F. Jarboe, "Statement of James F. Jarboe, Domestic Terrorism Section Chief, Counterterrorism Division, Federal Bureau of Investigation, on The Threat of Eco-Terrorism Before the House Resources Committee, Subcommittee on Forests and Forest Health." Federal Bureau of Investigation. Available online. URL: http://www.fbi.gov/congress/congress02/jarboe021202.htm.

[46] Paul Watson, quoted in List, *Radical Environmentalism*, p. 172.

[47] List, *Radical Environmentalism*, p. 174.

[48] Quoted in List, *Radical Environmentalism*, p. 173.

[49] Edward Abbey, *Desert Solitaire: A Season in the Wilderness*. New York: Ballantine Books, 1968, p. 188.

[50] List, *Radical Environmentalism*, p. 149.

[51] Edward Abbey, quoted in Bishop, *Epitaph for a Desert Anarchist*, p. 29.

[52] Edward Abbey, *One Life at a Time, Please*. New York: Henry Holt, 1988, p. 30

[53] Edward Abbey, quoted in List, *Radical Environmentalism*, p. 149.

[54] Abbey, *One Life at a Time, Please*, p. 44.

[55] Abbey, *Desert Solitaire*, p. 20.

[56] Bishop, *Epitaph for a Desert Anarchist*, p. 46.

[57] Edward Abbey, quoted in List, *Radical Environmentalism*, p. 252.

[58] Dave Foreman, quoted in List, *Radical Environmentalism*, p. 254.

[59] Quoted in Bishop, *Epitaph for a Desert Anarchist*, p. 4.

[60] Edward Abbey, *The Monkey Wrench Gang*. New York: Avon Books, 1975, p. 65.

[61] Foreman, *Confessions of an Eco-Warrior*, p. 20.

[62] Dave Foreman, quoted in List, *Radical Environmentalism*, p. 188.

[63] Quoted in Manes, *Green Rage*, p. 73.

[64] Edward Abbey, quoted in List, *Radical Environmentalism*, pp. 190–91.

[65] Dave Foreman, quoted in List, *Radical Environmentalism*, p. 190.

[66] Dave Foreman, quoted in List, *Radical Environmentalism*, p. 189.

[67] Dave Foreman, quoted in List, *Radical Environmentalism*, p. 188.

[68] Leslie Lyon, quoted in Mark Dowie, *Losing Ground: American Environmentalism at the Close of the Twentieth Century*. Cambridge, Mass.: MIT Press, 1995, p. 210.

[69] Christopher Manes, quoted in Dowie, *Losing Ground*, p. 210.

[70] Dave Foreman, quoted in Dowie, *Losing Ground*, p. 210.

[71] Foreman, *Confessions of an Eco-Warrior*, p. 121.

[72] Foreman, *Confessions of an Eco-Warrior*, p. 23.

[73] Foreman, *Confessions of an Eco-Warrior*, p. 114.

[74] Foreman, *Confessions of an Eco-Warrior*, p. 214.

[75] Robert Smith, quoted in Manes, *Green Rage*, p. 12.

[76] Dave Pease and Harry Merlo, quoted in Manes, *Green Rage*, p. 177.

[77] Mike Roselle, quoted in Manes, *Green Rage*, pp. 177–178.

[78] Gerry Spence, quoted in Mark Shaffer, "'Eco-terrorism' Trial Underway," *Arizona Republic*, June 20, 1991, p. B1.

[79] Mike Fain, quoted in Martha F. Lee, *Earth First! Environmental Apocalypse*. Syracuse, N.Y.: Syracuse University Press, 1995, p. 132.

[80] Dave Foreman, quoted in Sam Negri, "Earth First! Setup Alleged," *Arizona Republic*, April 25, 1990, p. B2.

[81] Foreman, *Confessions of an Eco-Warrior*, pp. 217–220.

[82] John Davis, *The Earth First! Reader: Ten Years of Radical Environmentalism*. Salt Lake City, Utah: Peregrine Smith, 1991, p. 14.

[83] Judi Bari, "The Feminization of Earth First!" *Ms*, vol. 2 (May 1992), p. 84.

[84] Quoted in Dean Kuipers, "Busting the FBI: The Judi Bari Verdict Bares Government Lies and Deceit." *LA Weekly*, June 21–27, 2002, p. 27.

[85] Quoted in Russell Mokhiber, "Manslaughter in the Woods." *Multinational Monitor*, vol. 19 (September 1998), p. 31.

[86] David Helvarg, *War Against the Greens: The "Wise Use" Movement, the New Right, and Anti-Environmental Violence*. San Francisco: Sierra Club Book, p. 65.

[87] Ron Arnold, quoted in Dowie, *Losing Ground*, pp. 93–94.

[88] Ron Arnold, quoted in Dowie, *Losing Ground*, p. 96.

[89] Quoted in Daniel Glick, *Powder Burn: Arson, Money, and Mystery on Vail Mountain*. New York: PublicAffairs, 2001, p. 216.

[90] David Helvarg, quoted in Andrew Hsiao, "The Green Menace." *The Village Voice*, vol. 43 (November 10, 1998), p. 26.

[91] James Watt, quoted in Dowie, *Losing Ground*, p. 97.

[92] Quoted in David Darlington, *The Mojave: A Portrait of the Definitive American Desert*. New York: Henry Holt, 1996, p. 301.

[93] Quoted in Dowie, *Losing Ground*, p. 97.

[94] Quoted in Darlington, *The Mojave*, p. 302.

[95] Gloria Flora, quoted in Pickering, *The Earth Liberation Front*, p. 262.

[96] Gloria Flora, quoted in Pickering, *The Earth Liberation Front*, p. 267.

[97] Gloria Flora, quoted in Pickering, *The Earth Liberation Front*, p. 264.

[98] Guy Pence, quoted in Helvarg, *War Against the Greens*, p. 428.

[99] Dick Carver, quoted in Helvarg, *War Against the Greens*, p. 421.

[100] Quoted in Pickering, *The Earth Liberation Front*, p. 73.

[101] Jarboe, "Statement of James F. Jarboe, Domestic Terrorism Section Chief, Counterterrorism Division, Federal Bureau of Investigation, on The Threat of Eco-Terrorism Before the House Resources Committee, Subcommittee on Forests and Forests Health." Federal Bureau of Investigation. Available online. URL: http://www.fbi.gov/congress/congress02/jarboe021202.htm.

[102] Glick, *Powder Burn*, p. 97.

[103] Craig Rosebraugh, quoted in Pickering, *The Earth Liberation Front*, pp. 193–194.

[104] Michael S. Hicks, quoted in Pickering, *The Earth Liberation Front*, p. 242.

[105] Arissa Media Group, "Arissa Media Group Mission." Available online. URL: http://www.arissa.org/mediamission.html.

[106] Quoted in Pickering, *The Earth Liberation Front*, pp. 62–64.

[107] Quoted in Pickering, *The Earth Liberation Front*, p. 85.

[108] Theodore Kaczynski, quoted in Alston Chase, *Harvard and the Unabomber: The Education of an American Terrorist*. New York: W. W. Norton, 2003, p. 52.

[109] Theodore Kaczynski, quoted in Chase, *Harvard and the Unabomber*, p. 52.

[110] Theodore Kaczynski, quoted in Chase, *Harvard and the Unabomber*, p. 66.

[111] Theodore Kaczynski, quoted in Chase, *Harvard and the Unabomber*, p. 72.

[112] Theodore Kaczynski, quoted in Chase, *Harvard and the Unabomber*, p. 75.

[113] Quoted in Chase, *Harvard and the Unabomber*, p. 72.

[114] Theodore Kaczynski, quoted in Chase, *Harvard and the Unabomber*, pp. 72–73.

[115] Theodore Kaczynski, quoted in Chase, *Harvard and the Unabomber*, pp. 75–76.

[116] Quin Denvir, quoted in Michael Higgins, "A Difficult Client." *ABA Journal*, vol. 84 (March 1998), p. 18.

[117] Michael Mello, quoted in Jillian Lloyd, "Should the Accused Direct Own Trial Strategy? Unabomber Ted Kaczynski's Appeal Raises Issue of Whether a Lawyer's Obligation to Save a Client's Life Is Paramount." *Christian Science Monitor*, June 6, 2000, p. 2.

[118] Michael Katz, quoted in Lloyd, "Should the Accused Direct Own Trial Strategy?," p. 2.

[119] Chase, *Harvard and the Unabomber*, p. 89.

[120] Ralph Reiland, "Inspiring the Unabomber." *The American Enterprise*, vol. 9 (May/Jun 1998), pp. 10–11.

[121] Brian Ross, quoted in Alexander Cockburn, "Earth First!, the Press and the Unabomber." *The Nation*, vol. 262 (May 6, 1996), p. 9.

[122] Craig Beneville, quoted in Stephen Budiansky, "Academic Roots of Paranoia." *U.S. News & World Report*, vol. 120 (May 13, 1996), p. 33.

[123] Leslie Hemstreet, quoted in Richard Leiby, "Madman or Eco-Maniac? Conspiracy Theorists See Environmental 'Hit List' as Unabomber Fodder." *The Washington Post*, April 17, 1996, p. C1.

[124] Theodore Kaczynski, quoted in Chase, *Harvard and the Unabomber*, p. 371.

[125] Theodore Kaczynski, quoted in Chase, *Harvard and the Unabomber*, p. 360.

[126] Quoted in Pickering, *The Earth Liberation Front*, p. 64.

CHAPTER 2

THE LAW AND ECOTERRORISM

Domestic terrorism, as a problem that crosses state lines, is generally a matter of federal law. Several western states, however, have sought to pass legislation to increase penalties for activists involved in ecoterrorist activities. The federal government also presides over laws concerning the creation and stewardship of federally owned public lands, as well as the protection of endangered species.

FEDERAL ANTITERRORISM LEGISLATION

Current federal legislation is found in the U.S. Code, a compendium of all federal laws. Several provisions are relevant to the study of ecoterrorism.

ANIMAL ENTERPRISE PROTECTION ACT OF 1992

Enacted in response to an increasing number of attacks by animal rights activists, this legislation makes it a federal offense to cause more than $10,000 in damage while engaged in "physical disruption to the functioning of an animal enterprise by intentionally stealing, damaging, or causing the loss of, any property (including animals or records) used by the animal enterprise." Such crimes are punishable by fine and/or imprisonment for up to one year, plus payment of restitution for costs associated with loss of property, data, animals, food production, and farm income, or with repetition of interrupted or invalidated animal experiments. Attacks causing serious bodily harm or death are subject to increased imprisonment penalties (up to 10 years and life, respectively). "Animal enterprise" is defined as "a commercial or academic enterprise that uses animals for food or fiber production, agriculture, research, or testing; a zoo, aquarium, circus, rodeo, or lawful competitive animal event; or any fair or similar event intended to advance agricultural arts and sciences." The legislation also stipulated a joint study by the attorney general and the secretary of agriculture, resulting in the 1993 *Report to Congress on the Extent and Effect of Domestic and International Terrorists on Animal Enterprises.*

ANTITERRORISM AND EFFECTIVE DEATH PENALTY ACT OF 1996

The Antiterrorism and Effective Death Penalty Act of 1996 revised segments of the U.S. Code in response to the Oklahoma City bombing of 1995 and, to a lesser extent, the World Trade Center bombing of 1993. Several aspects of the act faced charges of unconstitutionality. In 2001, for example, a U.S. district judge in Los Angeles struck down portions of the law that barred individuals from providing "training" or "personnel" to organizations identified as terrorist. The judge declared that those terms were too vague to be constitutionally acceptable (see *Humanitarian Law Project v. Ashcroft* below). Many provisions of this body of legislation were updated by the USA PATRIOT Act of 2001.

USA PATRIOT ACT OF 2001

The awkwardly titled Uniting and Strengthening America by Providing Appropriate Tools Required to Intercept and Obstruct Terrorism (USA PATRIOT) Act of 2001 was passed with little debate in response to the September 11, 2001, terrorist attacks on New York City and Washington, D.C. It is described in the text as a set of laws designed "to deter and punish terrorist acts in the United States and around the world, to enhance law enforcement investigatory tools, and for other purposes."

Many organizations and individuals concerned with civil liberties have questioned the constitutionality of the USA PATRIOT Act and worry about its potential to seriously undermine the principles of free speech, due process, and equal protection under the law. Of particular concern are the over-broad definition of domestic terrorism, the FBI's enhanced powers of search and surveillance, and the indefinite detention of both citizens and noncitizens without formal charges. Among the more controversial aspects of the legislation are sections of Title II (Enhanced Surveillance Procedures) that expand the ability of federal authorities to monitor the activities and communications of suspected terrorists. To safeguard against long-term civil liberties abuses, Title II includes a "sunset clause" that renders many of these laws ineffective after December 31, 2005.

Constitutionality concerns prompted several lawmakers—independents, Republicans, and Democrats alike—to take action against the USA

PATRIOT Act. Among these, Vermont representative Bernie Sanders introduced the Freedom to Read Protection Act in March 2003, a bill whose purpose was to repeal Section 215. On July 21, 2003, Idaho representative C. L. "Butch" Otter drafted an amendment to the Commerce, Justice, State, and Judiciary Appropriations Bill of 2004 to withhold funding for "sneak and peek" searches of private property enacted under Section 213 of the act. The motion passed in the U.S. House of Representatives by a count of 309 to 118 in favor. In August 2003, Alaska senator Lisa Murkowski introduced the Protecting the Rights of Individuals Act, intended to put some checks and balances into the PATRIOT Act. This includes requiring a court order for law enforcement agencies to conduct electronic surveillance and increased judicial reviews before law enforcement agencies monitor some telephone and Internet usage. It would also limit the FBI's ability to look at personal information, including medical, library, and Internet records, without demonstrating specific suspicion to a judge.

U.S. Attorney General John Ashcroft has sought to defend the act against accusations by civil libertarians, who he says "scare peace-loving people with phantoms of lost liberty" and "only aid terrorists" by "erod[ing] our national unity and diminish[ing] our resolve." In September 2003, the Justice Department released data showing that the provisions of Section 215 had not yet been used. Ashcroft, meanwhile, chided the American Library Association, which has criticized the law, for engendering "baseless hysteria" about how the provision was being implemented. Civil libertarians were not impressed by the declassified data, saying that the Justice Department could begin using the Section 215 provisions at any time and that the case will not become moot until the law is repealed.

The PATRIOT Act is divided into 10 titles, several of which are further divided into subtitles. Each title encompasses a number of subsections that specify and detail legislation. Although most of the act concerns international terrorism, Title II increases the FBI's powers of domestic surveillance, while Title VIII expands the definition of "domestic terrorism." Below is an outline of the titles and subtitles, followed by a summary of many provisions contained within Title II. The complete text (Public Law No. 107–56) can be found on the Internet at http://www.cdt.org/security/010911response.shtml. A section-by-section analysis of the act can be found on the Internet at http://www.fps.crs_reps/tssal210.pdf.

TITLE I: Enhancing Domestic Security Against Terrorism
TITLE II: Enhanced Surveillance Procedures
TITLE III: International Money Laundering Abatement and Anti-Terrorist Financing Act of 2001

Ecoterrorism

Subtitle A: International Counter Money Laundering and Related Measures
Subtitle B: Bank Secrecy Act Amendments and Related Improvements
Subtitle C: Currency Crimes and Protection
TITLE IV: Protecting the Border
Subtitle A: Protecting the Northern Border
Subtitle B: Enhanced Immigration Provisions
Subtitle C: Preservation of Immigration Benefits for Victims of Terrorism
TITLE V: Removing Obstacles to Investigating Terrorism
TITLE VI: Providing for Victims of Terrorism, Public Safety Officers, and Their Families
Subtitle A: Aid to Families of Public Safety Officers
Subtitle B: Amendments to the Victims of Crime Act of 1984
TITLE VII: Increased Information Sharing for Critical Infrastructure Protection
TITLE VIII: Strengthening the Criminal Laws Against Terrorism
TITLE IX: Improved Intelligence
TITLE X: Miscellaneous

Title II: Enhanced Surveillance Procedures

Section 201 stipulates that suspicion of either terrorist activities or production of chemical weapons enables the government to obtain a wiretap of the suspected party's telephone, oral, and electronic communications. Because the government already had substantial authority under the Foreign Intelligence Surveillance Act of 1978 (FISA) to obtain a wiretap of suspected terrorists, the primary effect of this section is to allow wiretapping of U.S. citizens suspected of domestic terrorism.

Section 204 authorizes federal investigators to obtain permission to search a suspect's voice-mail communications and e-mail through a search warrant rather than through more stringent wiretap orders. Messages stored on an answering machine tape remain outside the scope of the statute.

Section 206 grants federal investigators "roving surveillance" authority, which allows the FBI to monitor all communications transmitted to and from public facilities—such as libraries, university computer labs, and cybercafés—if they suspect an intelligence target might be using that facility. This raises the possibility that the communications of any innocent, law-abiding citizen using the facility in question might be intercepted and monitored. Critics complain that the statute violates the Fourth Amendment's requirement that any search warrant particularly describe the place to be searched.

64

Section 210 expands the type of information that an Internet service provider must disclose to investigators. Under prior law, investigators could use a subpoena to obtain "the name, address, local and long distance telephone toll billing records, telephone number or other subscriber number or identity, and length of service or a subscriber to or customer of such service and the type of services the subscriber or customer utilized." The new statute expands this list to include, among other things, records of session times and duration, any temporarily assigned network address, and any means or source of payment. This heightened authority to use subpoenas (rather than court orders) for a broader list of information is not limited to investigations of suspected terrorist activity.

Section 213 authorizes federal district courts to delay required notices of the execution of a warrant if immediate notice may have an adverse result and under other specified circumstances. This statute eliminates the prior requirement that law enforcement provide a person subject to a search warrant with a notice at the time of the search. It also permits seizure of any tangible property or communications where the court finds "reasonable necessity" for this seizure. The law requires that notice be given within an undefined "reasonable period," which can be extended by the court for "good cause." The statute is not limited to investigations of terrorist activity, which people concerned with civil liberties say constitutes a radical departure from Fourth Amendment standards and could result in routine, no-knock, surreptitious (dubbed "sneak and peak") searches of private residences by law enforcement agents.

Section 215 authorizes the FBI to apply for a court order requiring production of certain business records for foreign intelligence and international terrorism investigations. This includes the ability to search bookstore, library, medical, and other personal records without probable cause or a warrant. It also imposes a "gag order" on booksellers, librarians, doctors, and others forced to turn over information, which prohibits them from telling anyone about the searches.

Section 216, along with section 220, allows a federal court to authorize the installation of surveillance devices and the issuance of search warrants anywhere in the United States in investigations of domestic or international terrorism. Previously, the law permitted the issue of such orders only within the geographic jurisdiction of the issuing court.

Section 218 expands allowable electronic surveillance or search warrants to include situations in which foreign intelligence gathering is merely "a significant" purpose of the investigation rather than, as prior law stipulated, the sole or primary purpose. Because the term *significant* is not defined many civil libertarians argue that this vagueness could lead to inconsistent application and potential overuse of the new law, including investigations concerning domestic crimes.

Section 224 is the "sunset clause" that terminates several Title II provisions enhancing electronic surveillance authority on December 31, 2005. The sunset clause does not apply to any foreign intelligence investigation beginning before that date, or any offense or potential offense that began or occurred before it. Also excluded are the expansion of electronic surveillance to the Internet, authority to share grand jury information, expansion of law enforcement authority over cable providers, expanded scope of subpoenas for electronic evidence, authority for delaying notice of the execution of a warrant, and expansion of jurisdictional authority of search warrants for terrorism investigations.

Title VIII: Strengthening the Criminal Laws Against Terrorism

Definition of Domestic Terrorism
Section 802 defines "domestic terrorism" as follows:
   (5)   *the term "domestic terrorism" means activities that*
   (A)   *involve acts dangerous to human life that are a violation of the criminal laws of the United States or of any State;*
   (B)   *appear to be intended —*
    (i)   *to intimidate or coerce a civilian population;*
   (ii)   *to influence the policy of a government by intimidation or coercion; or*
   (iii)   *to affect the conduct of a government by mass destruction, assassination, or kidnapping; and*
   (C)   *occur primarily within the territorial jurisdiction of the United States*

FEDERAL ENVIRONMENTAL LEGISLATION

Federal laws regarding the creation of protected areas and the stewardship of public lands are of concern to both environmentalists and wise use advocates: The former wish to see federal protection become more widespread and more stringent, while the latter fight to shift control of public land to the states and eventually to private interests. Disagreements over how to apply such laws as the Endangered Species Act and provisions of the National Environmental Policy Act have resulted in lawsuits from both sides of the debate. Some radical environmentalists and anti-environmentalists, when they think that the courts or the federal government have misapplied the laws, have rejected lobbying efforts in favor of civil disobedience, sabotage, or even physical violence.

FOREST RESERVE ACT OF 1891

This legislation gave the president authority to set aside federal forest reserves (now called national forests) from the public domain (unsettled federal lands). Section 24 reads,

> *That the President of the United States may, from time to time, set apart and reserve, in any State or Territory having public land bearing forests, in any part of the public lands wholly or in part covered with timber or undergrowth, whether of commercial value or not, as public reservations; and the President shall, by public proclamation, declare the establishment of such reservations and the limits thereof.*

However, the act did not define the purposes of the reserves, which were initially viewed as preserves or parks in which all mining, logging, and grazing was prohibited. By the end of the first decade of the 20th century, this view was replaced by Gifford Pinchot's multiple-use conservation ethic. The Forest Reserve Act also repealed several earlier acts, including the Timber Culture Act of 1873, which had granted homesteaders 160 acres of land in the Great Plains if they agreed to plant trees on 40 of the acres. Before expiration of his term, President Benjamin Harrison designated almost 13.5 million acres of western land as forest reserves.

YELLOWSTONE PROTECTIVE ACT OF 1894

This landmark legislation provided for the administration of Yellowstone National Park, which had been established in 1872. It also established Yellowstone as the first inviolate wildlife refuge in the country. It was the first legislation to establish definitive national park management rules.

LACEY ANTIQUITIES ACT OF 1906

This act allowed "the President to declare by public proclamation historic landmarks . . . and other objects of historic or scientific interest that are situated on (federal) land to be national monuments." The law was primarily intended to preserve prehistoric Native American ruins and artifacts in the desert Southwest, but more than 200 national monuments, including many large, scenic parklands, have been established. President Jimmy Carter, for example, invoked the Antiquities Act to set aside 56 million acres in Alaska as national monuments in order to preserve many pristine areas. A majority of national parks created by Congress since 1906 were first designated as national monuments by various presidents. President Theodore Roosevelt used his new power to declare Devils Tower in Wyoming as the first national monument on September 24, 1906. The Antiquities Act is the first of three legislative acts that have been referred to as the "Magna Carta of American Conservation." The other two are the National Park Service Organic Act of 1916 and the Wilderness Act of 1964.

NATIONAL PARK SERVICE ORGANIC ACT OF 1916

This act created the National Park Service (NPS) as a division of the Department of the Interior. The stated goal of the new agency was to "promote and regulate the use of the Federal areas known as national parks, monuments, and reservations . . . which purpose is to conserve the scenery and the natural and historic objects and the wildlife therein and to provide for the enjoyment of the same in such manner and by such means as will leave them unimpaired for the enjoyment of future generations." The protections granted by the NPS are generally stricter than the multiple-use plans under which the U.S. Forest Service manages national forests and grasslands.

MULTIPLE-USE SUSTAINED-YIELD ACT OF 1960

This act stipulates that national forests are to be administered for outdoor recreation, grazing rangeland, timber, watershed, and fish and wildlife purposes. It also directs the secretary of agriculture to administer national forest renewable surface resources for multiple use and sustained yield. *Multiple use* is defined as "management of all the renewable surface resources of the national forests to meet the needs of the American people," while *sustained yield* is identified as the "achievement and maintenance of a high-level regular output of the renewable resources of the national forest without impairment of the land's productivity."

WILDERNESS ACT OF 1964

This act, the third of the three laws sometimes called the "Magna Carta of American Conservation," established a new 9.1-million-acre land management system based on the concept of "wilderness," defined as "an area where the earth and its community of life are untrammeled by man, where man himself is a visitor who does not remain." Mechanisms were also put in place to facilitate the designation of additional wilderness areas on lands managed by the U.S. Forest Service, National Park Service, Bureau of Land Management, and Fish and Wildlife Service. As of 2003, an additional 97 million acres of lands had been designated as wilderness, approximately 48 million acres of which were in the lower 48 states, with the balance in Alaska.

Wilderness areas allow such activities as hiking, camping, horseback riding, hunting, fishing, and limited grazing. Activities that are generally banned from wilderness include the use of all mechanized vehicles, such as motorcycles, all-terrain vehicles, and snowmobiles, as well as mountain bikes. The act states, "there shall be no commercial enterprise and no permanent road . . . and, except as necessary . . . no temporary road, no use of motor vehicles, motorized equipment or motorboats, no landing of aircraft, no other form of mechanical transport, and no structure or installation within any such area." The rules include a provision to allow certain otherwise banned activities to ensure the health and safety of people, such as allowing the use of helicopters in emergencies and facilitating the control of fires, insects, and diseases within wilderness areas. Because wilderness designation is the strictest form of protection, environmentalists generally seek to maximize the amount of land managed under the provisions of the Wilderness Act.

NATIONAL ENVIRONMENTAL POLICY ACT OF 1969

The National Environmental Policy Act (NEPA) was signed on January 1, 1970, by President Richard Nixon as his first official act of what he called the new "environmental decade." The stated purpose of the legislation was to

> *declare a national policy which will encourage productive and enjoyable harmony between man and his environment; to promote efforts which will prevent or eliminate damage to the environment and biosphere and stimulate the health and welfare of man; to enrich the understanding of the ecological systems and natural resources important to the Nation; and to establish a Council on Environmental Quality.*

One important aspect of this plan was the establishment of the protocol for environmental impact statements (EIS), which require the managers of any major government project to assess the environmental impact of the project, propose alternative plans, and submit a report that is open to public scrutiny and comment. If the government's plans are deemed unsatisfactory, citizens can then initiate lawsuits to force revision.

ENDANGERED SPECIES PRESERVATION ACT OF 1973

In 1966, Congress passed the Endangered Species Preservation Act, which created a list of endangered native animal species and provided limited means for the protection of species so listed (including the acquisition of land). The Endangered Species Conservation Act of 1969 expanded protection to include species in danger of "worldwide extinction." Importing listed species was prohibited, as was their subsequent sale within the United States. A 1973 conference in Washington, D.C., resulted in the Convention on International Trade in Endangered Species of Wild Fauna and Flora (CITES), which restricted international commerce in plant and animal species believed to be actually or potentially harmed by trade. Later that year, the Endangered Species Preservation Act of 1973 was passed, which combined and considerably strengthened the provisions of its predecessors, and broke some new ground: U.S. and foreign species lists were combined, with uniform provisions applied to both; categories of "endangered" and "threatened" were defined; and plants and all classes of invertebrates were made eligible for protection. Perhaps most important was the requirement that all federal agencies undertake programs for the conservation of endangered and threatened species. This included a prohibition from authorizing, funding, or carrying out any action that would jeopardize a listed species or destroy or modify its "critical habitat." Amendments were enacted in 1978, 1982, and 1988, but the overall framework of the 1973 Act remained essentially unchanged.

NATIONAL FOREST MANAGEMENT ACT OF 1976

In 1974, Congress passed the Forest and Rangeland Renewable Resources Planning Act, which called for the management of renewable resources on national forest lands. The National Forest Management Act of 1976 reorganized, expanded, and otherwise amended the 1974 act. It became the primary statute governing the administration of national forests, requiring the secretary of agriculture to assess forest lands, develop a management program based on multiple-use and sustained-yield principles, and implement a resource management plan for each unit of the national forest system. The act required these steps be taken in accordance with the principles contained in the Multiple-Use Sustained-Yield Act of 1960 and the National Environmental Policy Act of 1969. Perhaps most important for the development of a radical segment of the U.S. environmental movement, the act legalized clear cutting of timber following a 1973 lawsuit over logging in West Virginia's Monongahela National Forest that had outlawed the practice. However, the National Forest Management Act required replanting of clear cuts and established the Reforestation Trust Fund to finance reforestation and timber stand improvements on national forest lands.

LAW AGAINST TREE SPIKING, 1988

In response to the tactics of Earth First! activists in the Pacific Northwest in the 1980s, a rider making tree spiking a felony was attached to the Drug Act of 1988. U.S. Code 18 Section 1864 reads as follows:

The Law and Ecoterrorism

Hazardous or injurious devices on Federal lands
(a) *Whoever —*
    (1) *with the intent to violate the Controlled Substances Act,*
    (2) *with the intent to obstruct or harass the harvesting of timber, or*
    (3) *with reckless disregard to the risk that another person will be placed in danger of death or bodily injury and under circumstances manifesting extreme indifference to such risk,*
uses a hazardous or injurious device on Federal land, on an Indian reservation, or on an Indian allotment while the title to such allotment is held in trust by the United States or while such allotment remains inalienable by the allottee without the consent of the United States shall be punished under subsection (b).
(b) *An individual who violates subsection (a) shall —*
    (1) *if death of an individual results, be fined under this title or imprisoned for any term of years or for life, or both;*
    (2) *if serious bodily injury to any individual results, be fined under this title or imprisoned for not more than 40 years, or both;*
    (3) *if bodily injury to any individual results, be fined under this title or imprisoned for not more than 20 years, or both;*
    (4) *if damage to the property of any individual results or if avoidance costs have been incurred exceeding $10,000, in the aggregate, be fined under this title or imprisoned for not more than 20 years, or both; and*
    (5) *in any other case, be fined under this title or imprisoned for not more than one year.*
(c) *Any individual who is punished under subsection (b)(5) after one or more prior convictions under any such subsection shall be fined under this title or imprisoned for not more than 20 years, or both.*
(d) *As used in this section —*
    (1) *the term "serious bodily injury" means bodily injury which involves —*
        (A) *a substantial risk of death;*
        (B) *extreme physical pain;*
        (C) *protracted and obvious disfigurement; and*
        (D) *protracted loss or impairment of the function of bodily member, organ, or mental faculty;*
    (2) *the term "bodily injury" means —*
        (A) *a cut, abrasion, bruise, burn, or disfigurement;*
        (B) *physical pain;*
        (C) *illness;*
        (D) *impairment of the function of a bodily member, organ, or mental faculty; or*
        (E) *any other injury to the body, no matter how temporary;*
    (3) *the term "hazardous or injurious device" means a device, which when assembled or placed, is capable of causing bodily injury, or damage to*

property, by the action of any person making contact with such device subsequent to the assembly or placement. Such term includes guns attached to trip wires or other triggering mechanisms, ammunition attached to trip wires or other triggering mechanisms, or explosive devices attached to trip wires or other triggering mechanisms, sharpened stakes, lines or wires, lines or wires with hooks attached, nails placed so that the sharpened ends are positioned in an upright manner, or tree spiking devices including spikes, nails, or other objects hammered, driven, fastened, or otherwise placed into or on any timber, whether or not severed from the stump; and

(4) *the term "avoidance costs" means costs incurred by any individual for the purpose of —*

　(A) *detecting a hazardous or injurious device; or*

　(B) *preventing death, serious bodily injury, bodily injury, or property damage likely to result from the use of a hazardous or injurious device in violation of subsection (a).*

(e) *Any person injured as the result of a violation of subsection (a) may commence a civil action on his own behalf against any person who is alleged to be in violation of subsection (a). The district courts shall have jurisdiction, without regard to the amount in controversy or the citizenship of the parties, in such civil actions. The court may award, in addition to monetary damages for any injury resulting from an alleged violation of subsection (a), costs of litigation, including reasonable attorney and expert witness fees, to any prevailing or substantially prevailing party, whenever the court determines such award is appropriate.*

COURT CASES

The following court cases deal with legal issues involving environmentalism and antiterrorism legislation. Note that the criminal cases most closely related to radical environmentalism and ecoterrorism are not represented. These include trials involving Ted Kaczynski, Dave Foreman, Judi Bari, the Animal Liberation Front, and the Earth Liberation Front. While such cases may be of great human interest, they are of little legal interest.

The sheer volume of challenges to environmental law by activist groups precludes any attempt to provide a comprehensive list of such cases. Between May 1990 and October 1991, for example, the Seattle office of the Sierra Club Legal Defense Fund was involved in at least 30 separate legal actions or decisions involving six major court cases, while during the 10-year struggle (1986–96) over the Headwaters Forest area of northern California, the Environmental Protection Information Center (EPIC) was involved in 15 lawsuits against logging company Maxxam/Pacific Lumber. Rather than a complete list of court cases, the following sample has been chosen to provide a look at how federal environmental laws, particularly the National Environmental Policy Act of 1969 and the Endangered Species Preservation Act of 1973, have been applied by lawmakers and challenged by activists in district court.

Also included is a challenge to the Antiterrorism and Effective Death Penalty Act of 1996, which may provide a model for how pending challenges to the USA PATRIOT Act of 2001 are decided. As of this writing, these challenges include a July 2003 lawsuit brought against Section 215 of the act by the American Civil Liberties Union (ACLU) on behalf of several Muslim-American community and activist groups. Members and clients of the groups contend that they were targets of investigation solely on the basis of their ethnicity, religion, and political association. Other lawsuits, including at least one based on the 2000 Antiterrorism and Effective Death Penalty Act decision, followed.

SIERRA CLUB V. MORTON, 405 U.S. 727 (1972)

Background

In the late 1940s, the U.S. Forest Service (USFS) began to consider development options for Mineral King Valley, an area of California's Sequoia National Forest adjacent to Sequoia National Park. In 1965, the USFS called for bids from private developers for the construction and operation of a ski resort in the valley that would also serve as a summer recreation area. The proposal of Walt Disney Enterprises was chosen from among six bidders. Its final plan, approved by the USFS in 1969, included an 80-acre, $35 million complex of motels, restaurants, swimming pools, and parking lots, as well as ski lifts, ski trails, a cog-assisted railway, and utility installations. To provide access to the resort, the state of California proposed to build a 20-mile-long highway, a section of which would go through Sequoia National Park. In 1969, representatives of the Sierra Club filed a lawsuit in the U.S. District Court for the Northern District of California, seeking a declaratory judgment that various aspects of the proposed development were illegal according to federal laws and regulations governing the preservation of national parks, forests, and game refuges, and also seeking preliminary and permanent injunctions revoking USFS permits in connection with the Mineral King project. The Sierra Club sued as a membership corporation with "a special interest in the conservation and the sound maintenance of the national parks, game refuges, and forests of the country."

Legal Issues

The primary legal question involved whether the Sierra Club even had legal standing to file its lawsuit. To seek judicial review under the Administration Procedure Act (APA), one must "show that he himself has suffered or will suffer injury, whether economic or otherwise." This required the Sierra Club to provide facts supporting alleged injuries resulting from the challenged action to gain the privilege of seeking its review. Instead, the Sierra Club sued as a membership corporation with "a special interest in the conservation and the sound maintenance of the national parks, game refuges, and forests of the country." The District Court accepted these terms, ruling that the Sierra Club's special interest in conservation and maintenance was sufficient to prove evidence of injury. The Court of Appeals for the Ninth Circuit reversed the decision, stating that the complaint failed to prove that members of the Sierra Club would be affected by completion of the Disney project "other than the fact that the actions are personally displeasing or distasteful to them." The Sierra Club appealed to the Supreme Court.

Decision

In the majority opinion delivered for the Supreme Court, Justice Potter Stewart questioned whether the Sierra Club had extended its interest in the controversy to show any personal injury or "personal stake in the outcome of the controversy." The Sierra Club claimed that it represented the public that used Mineral King and Sequoia National Forest, "for whom the aesthetic and recreational values of the area will be lessened by the highway and resort." In reality, however, Disney's plan divided public opinion. Many local residents welcomed the idea of a ski resort for economic and recreational benefits, while others were appalled at the negative environmental impacts to the national park. The Court contended that the Sierra Club failed to assert that its members were a part of this represented public who used Mineral King, concluding that none of the organization's members, which was who the club actually represented, "would be significantly affected by the proposed actions."

Impact

Although the Sierra Club lost its Supreme Court appeal, of much greater interest to environmentalists was the apparent strategic victory given by the dissenting opinion of Justice William O. Douglas. The justice offered environmental organizations a way to creatively use environmental law to establish the privilege of review by looking beyond the human race and proclaiming that nature itself had rights. Because "environmental objects can sue for their own preservation," and since "inanimate objects are sometimes parties in litigation . . . those who have that intimate relationship with an inanimate object about to be injured, polluted, or otherwise despoiled are its legitimate representative." The Sierra Club, whose purpose had been to protect the environment, therefore had established an intimate relationship with trees, land, and air. The Sierra Club, said Douglas, had failed to mention that Disney's plan would affect its relationship with an inanimate object. Instead, its standing rested on shaky grounds of public and organizational interest. Legally, Douglas suggested that direct relationships between inanimate objects and the Sierra Club would have been more substantial to win judicial review. Justices Harry A. Blackmun and William J. Brennan also offered dissenting opinions that endorsed the idea of legal standing for natural objects. In drafting his dissent, Douglas referred to University of Southern California law professor Christopher D. Stone's article, "Should Trees Have Standing? Toward Legal Rights for Natural Objects." In it, Stone argued that natural objects should be able to be plaintiffs for their own injuries in a court of law. The essay was prepared specifically for publication in the *Southern California Law Review* to influence the Supreme Court case. Douglas's opinion, in the long run, turned out to be more of a philosophical victory than a legal one. Following the 1972 Supreme Court decision, the U.S. District Court for the Northern District of California allowed the Sierra Club to amend its complaint to make further allegations concerning its standing to sue, to add additional parties to its complaint, and to add a third claim for relief under the National Environmental Policy Act (NEPA). The Sierra Club's subsequent success in blocking the Disney Corporation's efforts to build a ski resort at Mineral King (now part of Sequoia National Park) was based on the fact that its members hiked in the region and would therefore suffer injury from the development. Despite Douglas's opinion, the valley itself—its trees, streams, and wildlife—was denied legal standing.

WEST VIRGINIA DIVISION OF THE IZAAK WALTON LEAGUE OF AMERICA V. BUTZ, 367 F. SUPP. 422 (1973)

Background

On April 18 and 20, 1973, the U.S. Forest Service advertised three timber sales in the Monongahela National Forest in West Virginia. A lawsuit intended to prevent the logging of these tracts was brought by the West Virginia division of the Izaak Walton League of America; the Sierra Club; the Natural Resources Defense Council; the West Virginia Highlands Conservancy; and Forrest Armentrout, a resident of West Virginia who used the

Monongahela National Forest for recreation. The defendants were Secretary of Agriculture Earl L. Butz, chief of the Forest Service of the Department of Agriculture John R. McGuire, regional forester for Monongahela National Forest Jay H. Cravens, and forest supervisor of the Monongahela National Forest Alfred H. Troutt. On May 14, 1973, the court granted a temporary restraining order to stop the harvest and scheduled a hearing to consider the plaintiffs' motion for an injunction.

Legal Issues

The Organic Act, passed in 1897 to ensure a continuous supply of timber while preventing exploitative logging practices, required that only dead, mature, or large trees were to be cut; that all trees to be cut must be marked individually; and that contractors must remove all felled timber. The plaintiffs alleged that the defendants granted contracts for the sale of timber in the Monongahela National Forest that allowed the practice of clear cutting, which violated the three listed requirements of the Organic Act. The defendants claimed that the timber management and harvesting policies used on federal land were fully authorized under the Organic Act, which directed that the national forests be managed scientifically and left the choice of specific management practices to the discretion of the secretary of agriculture. The defendants claimed, among other things, that the term *maturity*, as used in the Organic Act, referred to economic desirability to harvest the tree rather than physiological development. Plaintiffs sought an injunction to ensure that all future timber harvesting contracts and sales within the Monongahela National Forest would adhere to the regulations of the Organic Act.

Decision

After reviewing the language of the Organic Act, the court concluded that the purpose of Congress at the time was to "firmly restrict the invasion of public lands and its timber resources for harvesting purposes" and to direct those charged with the administration of the national forests, that trees can be sold and cut only if they are "dead, matured, or large growth" and then may be sold only when the sale serves the purpose of preserving and promoting the younger growth of timber on the national forests. The court further disagreed with the defendants' interpretation of the word *mature* as meaning a condition that makes it economically desirable to cut the tree, arguing that "if any or every tree of the national forests can be cut whenever the persons in charge of administering the national forests consider it desirable, then the requirements, indeed the very terms, of the Organic Act are eliminated." The court therefore agreed with the plaintiffs' contention that the practice of clear cutting violated the Organic Act of 1897. It ordered the defendants to stop allowing the practice in the Monongahela National Forest and also ordered them to revise their regulations, manuals, and contracts in accordance with the injunction. Although the decision banned the practice of clear cutting from Monongahela National Forest, it did not affect the cutting of trees for the purposes of building highways, roads, and trails; protecting the forest from fire, insects, and disease; managing the forests for the uses (such as recreation and wildlife), other than timber harvest, permitted by the Multiple Use–Sustained Yield Act; thinning and improving the forests; and investigating, experimenting, and testing methods of reforestation and of growing and managing forest products.

Impact

This court case proved to be a short-lived victory for environmentalists. Faced with the fact that clear cutting was illegal under U.S. law, timber companies lobbied Congress to have the law changed in their favor. Their efforts succeeded with the passage of the National Forest Management Act of 1976, which legalized clear cutting of timber but established the Reforestation Trust Fund to finance reforestation and timber stand improvements on national forest lands. The legalization of clear cutting helped set the stage for the conflicts between radical environmentalists and logging interests that began to flare in the 1980s.

CALIFORNIA V. BLOCK, 690 F. 2ND 753 (1982)

Background

Under the Wilderness Act of 1964, the U.S. Forest Service (USFS) was directed to recommend to Congress "primitive" areas that should be added to the Wilderness System. Following an abortive first attempt to devise a national planning document for the management of "roadless areas" within the national forest system in 1972, the USFS made a second attempt, named the Roadless Area Review and Evaluation (RARE II), in 1977. This project inventoried all roadless areas within the national forest system and called for granting 15 million acres of land protection under the Wilderness Act, submitting 10.8 million acres to further studies to determine whether they should be afforded protection, and designating 36 million acres as "nonwilderness." On July 25, 1979, the state of California, along with the National Resources Defense Council, Trinity County, and the Clear Creek Legal Defense Fund, brought action in federal district court against the secretary of agriculture and the USFS, alleging that the USFS had conducted RARE II in a manner that violated the National Environmental Policy Act

(NEPA), the Multiple-Use Sustained-Yield Act (MUSY), and the National Forest Management Act (NFMA). The district court ruled in favor of the state of California. The USFS appealed the judgment, as well as an injunction against taking any action that might change the wilderness character of the disputed areas in California.

Legal Issues

California challenged the decision of the USFS to designate 47 RARE II areas in California as "nonwilderness." On January 8, 1980, the district court ruled that RARE II violated NEPA because the final environmental impact statement (EIS) did not contain sufficient site-specific data to support the "nonwilderness designations"; the EIS did not consider an adequate range of alternatives; and the USFS did not give the public an adequate opportunity to comment on the RARE II program. The district court enjoined the USFS from taking any action that might change the wilderness character of the disputed areas in California until it filed an EIS that satisfied NEPA's requirements and considered the impact of the decision upon the wilderness characteristics of these areas. The court did not reach a decision on the MUSY and NFMA claims.

Decision

The Ninth Circuit Court of Appeals affirmed most of the district court's decision, ruling that the USFS's final EIS for RARE II was inadequate to support the "nonwilderness" designations of 47 areas in California and therefore violated NEPA. The court agreed with the district court's ruling that the final EIS failed to satisfy NEPA guidelines because it did not describe adequately the wilderness characteristics of each area, assess the wilderness value of each area or the impact of nonwilderness designations on wilderness characteristics, consider the effect of nonwilderness classification on future opportunities for wilderness classification, or weigh the economic benefit of development against the wilderness loss it causes. The court further ruled that the final EIS did not consider a range of alternatives adequate to permit the requisite "reasoned choice" by the agency. In addition, the USFS violated NEPA by not circulating for public comment a supplemental draft EIS describing the action actually proposed even though it relied on a different standard than the draft seen by the public.

Impact

California v. Block was just one of a number of legal challenges to the findings of RARE II, the first of which (*California v. Bergland*) was filed in 1978 by California commissioner of natural resources Huey Johnson despite warnings from the Sierra Club and the Wilderness Society that such lawsuits would provoke a violent anti-environmental backlash. The impact of this state of affairs was twofold: The initial unwillingness of major environmental groups to challenge RARE II helped convince Dave Foreman and other activists to reject mainstream lobbying efforts in favor of more radical tactics, while the success of Johnson's lawsuit eventually convinced many of these same mainstream organizations to take part in similar legal action (thus the participation of the Natural Resources Defense Council in *California v. Block*). The collective result of these cases was that, at least in states where such legal challenges succeeded, site-specific environmental impact statements were required before any roadless area could be developed and that many national forest management decisions suddenly hinged on the outcome of statewide wilderness bills.

EPIC V. MAXXAM (1987)

Background

The Forest Practices Act of 1973 required timber companies, before beginning any logging operations, to submit timber harvest plans (THPs) for state approval. In 1986, Maxxam/Pacific Lumber Company devised three THPs to clear cut more than 400 acres of old-growth redwood and Douglas fir forestland in the Little South Fork Elk River, Salmon Creek, and Mattole River watersheds of Northern California. Two of the plans were located in the Headwaters Forest area. The Environmental Protection Information Center (EPIC), in its first lawsuit against Pacific Lumber, challenged the legality of these plans.

Legal Issues

The plaintiffs charged that the California Department of Forestry (CDF) was "rubber-stamping" THPs and had deliberately prevented other government agencies from providing legally required consultations on old-growth-dependent wildlife species.

Decision

The court ruled in favor of the plaintiffs, ruling that the CDF had not only "rubber-stamped" the THPs but also intimidated the Department of Fish and Game (DFG) and the Regional Water Quality Control Board staff from making any comments critical of THPs. Subsequently, the CDF had approved, on orders from the Board of Forestry, a number of old-growth THPs opposed by the DFG.

Impact

EPIC v. Maxxam was the first of 15 lawsuits, seven of them successful, filed by EPIC involving the old-growth groves of Headwaters Forest, an area that would only become more contentious in the years to come. In the short term, the ruling stopped two Maxxam/Pacific Lumber Company clear cuts totaling 274 acres in Headwaters Forest Grove. Court orders also led to a policy shift on the part of the DFG that forced the agency to conduct wildlife surveys and review some old-growth plans more carefully.

NORTHERN SPOTTED OWL V. MANUEL LUJAN, 758 F. SUPP. 621 (1991)

Background

In May 1988, 22 environmental organizations filed suit against the secretary of the interior, the U.S. Fish and Wildlife Service (FWS), and other federal defendants, alleging that the FWS's decision not to list the northern spotted owl under the Endangered Species Act (ESA) of 1973 was arbitrary and contrary to law. In that case *(Northern Spotted Owl v. Hodel)*, the U.S. District Court for the Western District of Washington agreed with the plaintiffs and remanded the matter to the FWS for further proceedings. In June 1989, the FWS proposed to list the northern spotted owl as a "threatened" species under the Endangered Species Act but refused to designate a critical habitat for the spotted owl on grounds that it was not "determinable." (A species is "threatened," and therefore eligible for protection under federal law, if it is "likely to become an endangered species within the foreseeable future throughout all or a significant portion of its range.") The plaintiffs petitioned the court to order the federal defendants to designate "critical habitat" for the northern spotted owl. (As defined under the ESA, "critical habitat" refers to geographic areas that are essential to the conservation of the species in question and that may require special management considerations or protection.)

Legal Issues

The plaintiffs' complaint was based on the ESA's requirement that the secretary of the interior, "to the maximum extent prudent and determinable," designate critical habitat at the same time that a species is listed as endangered or threatened. When critical habitat is not determinable at the time of the listing, the secretary must state the reasons for not making such a designation and is granted up to 12 additional months to do so. The plaintiffs charged that the secretary of the interior violated the ESA by failing to designate critical habitat concurrently with the listing of the northern spotted owl. The secretary countered that the inability to determine critical habitat at the time that the spotted owl was officially listed as threatened entitled him to a 12-month extension of time to make the determination.

Decision

The court reviewed the development of language in the ESA by pointing out that, as originally enacted in 1973, the law clearly stated that designation of critical habitat should coincide with the species listing determination, with no exceptions allowed. A 1978 amendment clarified that the secretary of the interior was required, "to the maximum extent prudent," to specify critical habitat "at the time [the species] is proposed [for listing]." A single exception was allowed when the habitat designation was not "prudent," defined as a rare situation in which designation of habitat would harm rather than help the threatened species. Frustrated at the slow pace of implementing the ESA, Congress in 1982 began allowing the secretary of the interior to defer the habitat designation for a maximum of 12 months upon finding that critical habitat is not "determinable" at the time a species is listed. In addition, the secretary was required to "justify listing a species without designating critical habitat" to support it. Based on this language, the court rejected the federal defendants' argument that the ESA authorized an automatic extension of time merely upon a finding that critical habitat is not presently determinable, even where no effort had been made to secure the information necessary to make the designation. The court also rejected the defendants' claim that critical habitat for the northern spotted owl was not determinable in June 1989 when the FWS proposed to list the species, or when the FWS issued its final rule one year later. The court pointed out that the issue of critical habitat received only brief discussion in the initial proposal and that almost identical language was used in the final ruling one year later, proving that no effort had been made in the intervening time to determine critical habitat. The defendants were further chastised for stating in their final ruling that the northern spotted owl was "overwhelmingly associated" with mature and old-growth forests and that, at present rates of timber harvesting, much of the remaining spotted owl habitat would be gone within 20 to 30 years. "Despite such dire assessments," the court wrote, "the [FWS] declined to designate critical habitat in its final rule, citing the same reasons it gave one year earlier." The court therefore ruled that the FWS "abused its discretion when it determined not to designate critical habitat concurrently with the listing of the northern spotted owl, or to explain any basis for concluding that the critical habitat was not determinable." The FWS was ordered to submit to the court by March 15, 1991, a written plan for completing its review of critical habitat for the northern spotted owl and to publish its proposed critical habitat plan no later than 45 days thereafter.

Impact

Northern Spotted Owl v. Manuel Lujan was just one of more than 20 major lawsuits brought by environmentalists against various federal agencies or timber companies to curb logging in the Pacific Northwest in the early 1990s. This particular case, along with *Northern Spotted Owl v. Hodel* (1991), forced the FWS to designate critical habitat for the owl. In July 1991, the service released a report concluding that 52 of its timber sales would jeopardize the owl but asked that 44 of these sales be exempt from critical habitat designation. In October 1991, Interior Secretary Manuel Lujan convened a cabinet-level Endangered Species Committee to consider the appeal. As a result, 13 of the timber sales were excluded from critical habitat designation, but the FWS was required to draft a recovery plan for these areas. Activists promptly challenged the committee's decision in court.

ROBERTSON V. SEATTLE AUDUBON SOCIETY,
503 U.S. 429 (1992)

Background

In June 1990, the northern spotted owl was listed as threatened under the Endangered Species Act of 1973. Environmentalists claimed that continued harvesting of timber in the Pacific Northwest would kill the owls. Local timber industries responded that restrictions on harvesting would devastate the region's economy. Lawsuits by the Seattle Audubon Society and the Portland Audubon Society, as well as other environmental groups, complained that amendments made to the USFS's regional timber harvesting plan afforded the owl too little protection according to a number of federal statutes, including the Migratory Bird Treaty Act (MBTA), the National Environmental Policy Act of 1969 (NEPA), and the National Forest Management Act of 1976 (NFMA). Other lawsuits brought by the Washington Contract Loggers Association, joined by various other industry groups, argued that the amendment afforded the owl too much protection. The district court twice dismissed the action brought by the Portland Audubon Society, decisions that were both reversed by the Court of Appeals for the Ninth Circuit, which also prohibited the USFS from continuing with some of the challenged harvesting pending appeal. In response to ongoing litigation from both environmental groups and logging companies concerning timber harvesting in the Pacific Northwest, Congress enacted the Northwest Timber Compromise of 1990, which established a comprehensive set of rules to govern harvesting within "the thirteen national forests in Oregon and Washington and [BLM] districts in western Oregon known to contain northern spotted owls." It expired on September 30, 1990, the last day of fiscal year 1990, except that timber sales offered under the act were to remain subject to its terms for the duration of the applicable sales contracts. The compromise simultaneously required harvesting to occur and expanded harvesting restrictions: The USFS and BLM were required to offer for sale specified quantities of timber from the affected lands before the end of fiscal year 1990, but harvesting was prohibited on various designated areas within those lands, while general environmental criteria were enacted to govern the selection of harvesting sites by the USFS.

Legal Issues

The first sentence of subsection (b)(6)(A) of the Northwest Timber Compromise stated in part that "Congress hereby determines and directs that management of areas . . . on the thirteen national forests in Oregon and Washington and Bureau of Land Management lands in western Oregon known to contain northern spotted owls is adequate consideration for the purpose of meeting the statutory requirements that are the basis" for many of the pending court cases, including those brought by the Seattle and Portland Audubon Societies, and that of the Washington Contract Loggers Association. After the compromise was enacted, both the Seattle and Portland Audubon defendants sought dismissal, arguing that the provision had temporarily superseded all statutes on which the plaintiffs' challenges had been based. In the Seattle Audubon case, the district court ruled that subsection (b)(6)(A) "can and must be read as a temporary modification of the environmental laws" and thereby reversed the Ninth Circuit Court of Appeal's preliminary injunction against timber harvesting. The Ninth Circuit subsequently reversed the district court's decision, holding that the first sentence of (b)(6)(A) did not "repeal or amend the environmental laws underlying this litigation," but rather directed the court "to reach a specific result and make certain factual findings under existing law in connection with" pending cases. Given that interpretation, the court held the provision unconstitutional under an 1872 court decision *(United States v. Klein)* that prohibited Congress from directing "a particular decision in a case, without repealing or amending the law underlying the litigation." Dale Robertson, chief of the USFS, then petitioned the Supreme Court to review the Ninth Circuit's judgment that the first sentence of subsection (b)(6)(A) was unconstitutional.

Decision

The Supreme Court reversed the decision of the Ninth Circuit, agreeing with the plaintiff's contention that the sentence in question replaced the legal standards underlying the two Audubon Society court challenges with subsections of the compromise stating that harvesting was prohibited on various designated areas within those lands and that general environmental criteria were enacted to govern the selection of harvesting sites by the USFS. The Court interpreted the language of the Northwest Timber Compromise as meaning that the federal agencies could satisfy their obligations in either, but not necessarily both, of two ways: by subscribing to the mandates of the Migratory Bird Treaty Act (MBTA), the National Environmental Policy Act of 1969 (NEPA), and the National Forest Management Act of 1976 (NFMA); *or* by managing their lands so as not to violate the harvesting prohibitions included in the compromise. Thus, the USFS and BLM could bypass the legal requirements of the earlier acts as long as they allocated timber harvests according to the rules stipulated in the Northwest Timber Compromise.

Impact

Robertson v. Seattle Audubon Society is one of the few legal cases involving the Endangered Species Act that have reached the U.S. Supreme Court. The first, and perhaps most famous, was *Tennessee Valley Authority v. Hill* (1978). This case resulted when the secretary of the interior brought to a halt construction of the Tellico Dam (which had begun before the ESA was enacted in 1973) after a small fish called the snail darter was declared to be endangered. Its habitat was thought to be limited to the part of the Little Tennessee River that was to be inundated by the reservoir behind the dam. The Supreme Court concluded that the ESA required an end to construction of the dam, even though $53 million had already been spent on the project. Eventually Congress directed that the Tellico Dam be completed, and President Jimmy Carter declined to veto the bill. This decision set the stage for the events surrounding *Robertson v. Seattle Audubon Society:* When the timber industry, labor unions, and homebuilding and real estate interests became sufficiently alarmed at the increased protection of the owl habitat, they lobbied Congress to change the law. Congress responded favorably by passing the Northwest Timber Compromise of 1990, which was upheld by the Supreme Court. Taken together, these two cases illustrate the willingness of the federal government to ignore or temporarily overturn environmental statutes when economic interests are compromised.

The Law and Ecoterrorism

HUMANITARIAN LAW PROJECT V. ASHCROFT, CV 03-6107 (2004)

Background

In 1996, Congress passed the Antiterrorism and Effective Death Penalty Act (AEDPA). Provisions within the act made it a crime, punishable by fines and up to 10 years in prison, to provide "material support" (including humanitarian aid, literature distribution, and political advocacy) to any foreign agency that the secretary of state has designated as *terrorist*. The Center for Constitutional Rights (CCR), contending that the federal government often used the label *terrorism* to brand groups and organizations that merely disagreed with U.S. foreign policy, challenged the "criminalization" of constitutionally protected activities. The CCR filed suit in federal court in Los Angeles on behalf of six organizations and two individuals who had supported and wanted to continue to support the political and humanitarian activities of two groups that the secretary of state had determined were terrorist: the Kurdistan Workers' Party (PKK), which advocated Kurdish independence from Turkey, and the Liberation Tigers of Tamil Eelam (LTTE), which advocated Tamil independence from Sri Lanka. Lead plaintiff Humanitarian Law Project (HLP), a Los Angeles–based nonprofit organization with consultative status to the United Nations, claimed to advocate the peaceful resolution of armed conflicts and worldwide compliance with humanitarian law and human rights law.

Legal Issues

The CCR maintained that the provisions of the AEDPA in question violated the First Amendment because they criminalized the acts of distributing literature, engaging in political advocacy, participating in peace conferences, training in human rights advocacy, and donating cash and humanitarian assistance, the sole purpose of which was to promote the lawful and nonviolent activities of the designated organizations. The HLP complained that the AEDPA imposed guilt by association by punishing moral innocents, not for their own culpable acts, but for the culpable acts of the groups they supported. The AEDPA, the plaintiffs pointed out, does not require any showing of intent to further terrorist or other illegal activity. Simultaneously with the filing of the complaint, the plaintiffs moved for a preliminary injunction that would declare the challenged provisions to be in violation of the First Amendment and that would enjoin the government from enforcing them.

Decision

Judge Audrey Collins of the Federal District Court for the Central District of California rejected the plaintiffs' argument that the provisions in question

85

violated the First Amendment insofar as they criminalized material support solely intended to further the lawful purposes and activities of an organization designated as terrorist. However, she did rule in favor of the plaintiffs by holding that the parts of the law criminalizing the provision of material support in the form of "personnel" and "training" were unconstitutionally vague. She found that these provisions did not "appear to allow persons of ordinary intelligence to determine what type of training or provision of personnel is prohibited" and, furthermore, "appeared to prohibit activity protected by the First Amendment: distributing literature and information and training others to engage in advocacy." Judge Collins also issued a preliminary injunction barring the government from prosecuting any of the eight plaintiffs in the suit or any members of the organizational plaintiffs for providing "personnel" or "training" to the PKK or the LTTE. On March 3, 2000, a three-judge panel of the Ninth Circuit affirmed Judge Collins's opinion in full and maintained her preliminary injunction. The Ninth Circuit agreed with CCR that AEDPA is unconstitutional to the extent that it bars the provision of "training" and "personnel." These terms are so vague that they could be understood to prohibit a wide range of speech protected by the First Amendment, from writing an opinion-based editorial to lobbying or teaching human rights advocacy. However, the Ninth Circuit did not agree with CCR that the provisions violated the First Amendment by imposing guilt through one's association rather than through one's own culpable acts. In March 2001, the U.S. Supreme Court declined to accept the case for review.

Impact

Following the appeal, the federal government asked the district court to dismiss the challenge to provisions regarding "training" and "personnel" on grounds of "mootness," arguing that the underlying policy had been amended by the USA PATRIOT Act of 2001. The court found that the government failed to show that its change in policy mooted the groups' claims. The court also found, as in the ruling on the preliminary injunction, that the language of statutes was impermissibly vague. In October 2001, the district court made permanent the injunction barring the government from prosecuting any of the eight plaintiffs in the suit or any members of the organizational plaintiffs for providing "personnel" or "training" to the PKK or the LTTE. Meanwhile, the federal government had filed an appeal with the Ninth Circuit court. On August 5, 2003, the CRR filed papers in the *Humanitarian Law Project v. Ashcroft* case challenging the provision of the USA PATRIOT Act that amended the AEDPA provision in question. The PATRIOT Act amended the definition of material support to include "expert advice and assistance" and made it a crime to provide such advice or assistance no matter what its intent and purpose, even when it has nothing whatsoever to do with furthering terrorism. On January 23, U.S. District Judge Audrey Collins ruled that the ban on providing "expert advice or assistance" was impermissibly vague and therefore in violation of the First and Fifth Amendments. She explained that the law, as written, does not differentiate between impermissible advice on violence and encouraging the use of peaceful, nonviolent means to achieve goals. The ruling marked the first court decision to declare unconstitutional a portion of the USA PATRIOT Act of 2001.

CHAPTER 3

CHRONOLOGY

This chapter presents a chronology of significant dates in the history of environmentalism and ecoterrorism in the United States. It is weighted heavily toward events that occurred in the 1970s and after, when environmentalists began using direct action tactics.

1811 to 1816

- Ned Ludd, a fabric weaver in Nottingham, England, incites a rebellion aimed at sabotaging new labor-saving looms over fears that he and his coworkers will lose their jobs due to automation of the weaving process. A government crackdown leads to the arrest of many Luddites, 14 of whom are hanged in January 1813 in York. Sporadic violence continues until 1816, when the movement ends.

1845

- Henry David Thoreau moves to Walden Pond, near Concord, Massachusetts, to write, live a simple life, and carefully observe his surroundings.

1849

- Thoreau publishes *A Week on the Concord and Merrimack Rivers*, in which he foreshadows contemporary direct action environmental tactics when he writes, "Who hears the fishes when they cry? I for one am with thee, and who knows what may avail a crowbar against Billerica dam."

1862

- The Homestead Act grants settlers in the American West 160 acres if they live on and develop the land for at least five years.

Chronology

1864

- George Perkins Marsh publishes *Man and Nature; or, Physical Geography as Modified by Human Action*. The book explains the vital interconnections among soil, water, and vegetation, a philosophy that later becomes central to the conservation movement. Marsh's writings help persuade the federal government to create parks such as Yellowstone in 1872 to curb the dwindling of wilderness.

1867

- *March:* John Muir, while working in a carriage factory in Indianapolis, Indiana, sustains a serious eye injury that temporarily blinds him in his right eye. During his long, painful recovery, he decides to dedicate his life to studying "the inventions of God." Later that year, he sets out on a 1,000-mile walk to the Gulf of Mexico, during which he documents his observations about the processes of nature in a journal.

1868

- *March 28:* Muir arrives in San Francisco, California. When he asks someone the fastest way to anywhere "that is wild," he is directed eastward to the Sierra Nevada. Fascinated by the landscape, Muir would dedicate most of the rest of his life to preserving the California mountain range from despoliation and development.

1870s

- During his tenure as U.S. secretary of the interior, Carl Schurz focuses on lobbying for preservation of federally owned forests and enforcing laws protecting government timber. His efforts help widen public support for saving the nation's dwindling woodlands.

1872

- Yellowstone National Park is created in Wyoming, Idaho, and Montana. It is the first publicly owned park in the world.

1873

- The Timber Culture Act gives homesteaders in the American West an additional 160 acres of land if they grow trees on 40 of the acres.

Ecoterrorism

1877

- The Desert Land Act offers 640 acres at $1.25 an acre in western states with little rainfall on the condition that the settler irrigates part of the parcel within three years.

1878

- The Timber and Stone Act offers 160 acres of western forestland to settlers for $2.50 an acre.

1889

- In his book *The Winning of the West*, Theodore Roosevelt argues for preserving wilderness to prevent modern Americans from becoming overcivilized.

1891

- Congress authorizes the U.S. president to designate public lands as forest reserves. During the 1890s, presidents Benjamin Harrison and Grover Cleveland use this power to protect more than 35 million acres of woodland.

1892

- *May 28:* John Muir founds the Sierra Club "to enlist the support and cooperation of the people and the government in preserving the forests and other natural features of the Sierra Nevada."

1903

- John Muir takes President Theodore Roosevelt on a camping trip in the Yosemite area and persuades him to pass additional legislation that will preserve public land in the United States. By the time he leaves office in 1909, Roosevelt has added more than 100,000 acres to the forest reserve (later national forest) system, and has created six new national parks, 53 wildlife reserves (later called wildlife refuges), and 18 national monuments.

1905

- President Theodore Roosevelt appoints Gifford Pinchot head of the U.S. Forest Service (USFS). Pinchot's approach to forestry is based, as he once wrote, on making "the forest produce the largest possible amount of whatever crop or service will be most useful." This utilitarian emphasis on natural resources (known as conservation), still preferred by the USFS, has been strongly criticized by radical environmentalists, who instead advocate preservation, or protecting nature for its own sake.

1906

■ President Theodore Roosevelt convinces Congress to pass the Lacey Antiquities Act, which gives presidents the authority to create national monuments to protect archaeological treasures. In his last years in office, he uses this new power to create 18 national monuments.

1908

■ *May:* The first Conservation Conference, organized by President Theodore Roosevelt, is held at the White House. Attending state governors and officials are urged to recognize that the main goal of conservation is protecting human health. This remains a main tenet of conservation and is considered by many to be a strong argument for regulating resource use. Gifford Pinchot excludes preservationist John Muir from the conference, preferring to promote conservationist views.

1913

■ Hearings on whether to allow the city of San Francisco to build the controversial Hetch Hetchy Dam are held before the Public Lands Committee of the U.S. House of Representatives. City officials, supported by Gifford Pinchot and President Theodore Roosevelt, argue that the dam is the only way to solve their water shortage and that it will provide a hydroelectric power source. Preservationists, led by John Muir and the Sierra Club, point out that the dam will flood a pristine valley within the protected Yosemite National Park. Despite widespread public condemnation, Congress passes the Hetch Hetchy bill by a large margin.

1916

■ Congress creates the National Park Service (NPS) to oversee the nation's national park system, which has grown to 16 parks since Yellowstone was created in 1872.

1924

■ *June 3:* At Aldo Leopold's recommendation, the Gila Wilderness Area is established in New Mexico, the first wilderness area in the national forest system. The designation lays the groundwork for passage of the Wilderness Act of 1964.

1934

- The Taylor Grazing Act is passed with the purpose of preventing additional erosion in the Great Plains states by limiting domestic animal grazing to designated districts.
- *February 6:* The three members of the President's Committee on Wild-Life Restoration—Jay Norwood Darling, Aldo Leopold, and Thomas Beck—release a report stating that the best way for the federal government to halt drastic declines in waterfowl populations is to purchase millions of acres of marginal farmland and turn it into new wildlife refuges. Darling is later appointed chief of the Bureau of Biological Survey, where he is instrumental in adding more than 900,000 acres to the National Wildlife Refuge System.

1936

- The Franklin D. Roosevelt administration outlaws the killing of predatory animals in national parks. Jay Norwood Darling founds the General Wildlife Federation with the goal of coordinating the work of the growing number of state and local conservation organizations across the United States. The organization evolves into the National Wildlife Federation.

1940

- The Roosevelt administration creates the U.S. Fish and Wildlife Service, which establishes 160 new wildlife refuges by the end of 1941.

1947

- *October:* Heavy smog settles for several days over Donora, a steel-mill town in Pennsylvania's Monongahela River Valley, resulting in 20 deaths and 6,000 cases of illness.

1949

- Aldo Leopold's *A Sand County Almanac* is published a year after the author's death. The compendium of notes and journal entries includes the essay "The Land Ethic," in which Leopold suggests extending ethics beyond human-to-human and human-to-society relations to include "man's relation to the land and to the animals and plants which grow upon it."

Chronology

1952

■ David Brower is appointed the first full-time paid executive director of the Sierra Club. He immediately expands the group's focus beyond the Sierra Nevada, becomes more aggressive in confronting environmental issues, and seeks to increase membership.

1953

■ During the summer, David Brower arranges float trips for journalists and politicians down the Green River through Dinosaur National Monument. His purpose is to publicize the beauty of the natural areas that would be inundated with water were a series of proposed dams to be built. His campaign is successful, and in 1955 Congress votes against construction of the dams.

1958

■ Edward Abbey and several coworkers at a Taos newspaper use saws to topple more than 10 billboards in the Las Vegas, New Mexico, area.

1962

■ *September:* Rachel Carson's *Silent Spring* is published. In it, she presents scientific evidence that widespread use of pesticides and herbicides is harmful to humans and wildlife. The book prompts President John F. Kennedy to establish the President's Science Advisory Committee to investigate the effects of pesticide use. By the end of 1962, 40 bills regulating the use of pesticides have been introduced in state legislatures across the country.

1963

■ The Clean Air Act sets aside federal funding to fight air pollution. The Sierra Club, under the direction of David Brower, begins a campaign to oppose the construction of two dams in the Grand Canyon. Toward that end, the organization takes out ads in major newspapers reading "Should we also flood the Sistine Chapel so tourists can get nearer the ceiling?" and "This time it's the Grand Canyon they want to flood. The Grand Canyon." This prompts a public outcry that ultimately leads the federal government to abandon the project but also prompts the Internal Revenue Service to revoke the Sierra Club's tax-exempt status for its "substantial" political lobbying.

- *March 25:* Senator Gaylord Nelson of Wisconsin, in his first speech in the Senate, tells the 99 other senators that they "cannot be blind to the growing crisis" of the environment; that the soil, water, and air "are becoming more polluted every day"; and that the nation's "most priceless natural resources—trees, lakes, rivers, wildlife habitats, scenic landscapes—are being destroyed." Since general environmental issues are not yet popular among politicians, he is largely ignored.
- *May:* The President's Science Advisory Committee, formed in reaction to Rachel Carson's *Silent Spring*, issues a report concluding that "elimination of the use of persistent toxic pesticides should be the goal."

1964

- *September 3:* The Wilderness Act is signed into law by President Lyndon Johnson after eight years of lobbying by the bill's original drafter, Howard Zahniser, who died only three months before the signing. The act, seen as a turning point for the U.S. environmental movement, gives legislative protection to 9 million acres of wilderness and includes mechanisms for designating more wilderness in the future. The National Park Service, U.S. Forest Service, and U.S. Fish and Wildlife Service are given task of reviewing their holdings for potential wilderness designation.

1968

- *February 1:* After months of intense lobbying by the Sierra Club, Secretary of the Interior Stewart Udall announces the cancellation of two dam projects that had been slated for the Grand Canyon. As an alternative, the federal government plans to help fund the construction of the Navajo Generating Station, one of six coal-fired power plants slated for the Four Corners region of Arizona, Colorado, New Mexico, and Utah. The Navajo plant will be fueled by coal from Black Mesa.

1969

- David Brower is forced to resign as executive director of the Sierra Club over disputes with the board of directors concerning the cost of publishing coffee-table books, the loss of tax-exempt status, and whether to oppose the construction of a nuclear power plant in California's Diablo Canyon. Under Brower's guidance, the club had grown in influence and from 7,000 members in 1952 to 77,000 in 1969. He immediately founds a new organization called Friends of the Earth. In the same year, a group of environmentalists in Vancouver, Canada, becomes concerned with nuclear tests being conducted in Alaska's Aleutian Islands by the U.S.

Atomic Energy Commission. In response, they form the Don't Make a Wave Committee, later to be renamed Greenpeace.

- *January:* An oil platform off the coast of Santa Barbara begins leaking, sending oil-slicked waves onto the heavily populated shoreline and killing wildlife.
- *June:* Theodore Kaczynski resigns from his mathematics professorship at the University of California at Berkeley. Two years later, he purchases 1.4 acres of land near Lincoln, Montana, and begins building the cabin that will become the base of operations for his bombing campaign.
- *June 22:* The heavily polluted Cuyahoga River catches fire in Cleveland, burning two railroad bridges. Heavy media coverage of this and the Santa Barbara oil spill helps the environmental movement gain momentum.
- *July:* California television and radio stations announce, "The children of Los Angeles are not allowed to run, skip, or jump inside or outside on smog alert days by order of the Los Angeles Board of Education and the County Medical Association."

1970

- Environmental activist Jack Loeffler begins a campaign to prevent Peabody Coal Company from strip mining 26,000 acres of Black Mesa, located on Navajo and Hopi land in Arizona. His organization, Black Mesa Defense Fund, appeals to the public through television appearances, radio interviews, and articles in national magazines. It also files six lawsuits, produces a film about the mine, and lobbies government agencies. Over a two-year period, an anonymous saboteur known as the Arizona Phantom, suspected of being a member of Black Mesa Defense Fund, vandalizes heavy equipment owned by Peabody Coal and makes a failed attempt to blow up the coal slurry line at the mining site. Also in 1970, the revised Clean Air Act identifies 189 smog-causing pollutants and establishes standards to regulate their emission. It also requires the installation of new anti-pollution technology in factories.
- *January:* Barry Weisberg, codirector of the Bay Area Institute in San Francisco and a critic of capitalism, argues that an authentic environmental movement has yet to develop but that it will when "something very basic and very revolutionary is done about the continued destruction of our life support system." He suggests that militant actions (including sabotage) against "corporate despoilers" will have to be part of this movement and predicts that "radical ecological actions" will take place by the end of the year.
- *January 1:* President Richard Nixon signs the National Environment Policy Act (NEPA) into law. It requires government agencies to consider

the environmental impacts of their actions, including the submission of environmental impact statements (EIS) for major projects.

■ *February:* In his State of the Union address, Nixon says that the 1970s "absolutely must be the years when America pays its debt to the past by reclaiming the purity of its air, its water. ... It is literally now or never."

■ *April 21:* A Miami-area group called Eco-Commando Force '70, claiming to be a five-person "clandestine guerilla organization," dumps yellow dye into tanks at six sewage treatment plants and flushes it down the toilets of two large hotels equipped with their own small sewage treatment facilities. The next day, the dye is apparent in many of the city's canals, illustrating the extent to which sewage pollutants affect the city's water system. A communiqué released by the group states, "Although we have committed a couple of misdemeanors—mostly trespass—we consider the risks worthwhile. Our crimes are minuscule compared to the hundreds of crimes that are being committed daily on our environment. We honestly believe we are fighting for our lives."

■ *April 22:* The first Earth Day is observed by 20 million people at 1,500 campuses and 10,000 schools across the nation. New York City bans cars from Fifth Avenue for two hours while 100,000 people march down it, and 250,000 people gather in Washington, D.C. Both houses of Congress recess to allow members to take part in events. In Alaska, however, Interior Secretary Walter Hickel announces plans for an 800-mile oil pipeline across the Arctic tundra, while the U.S. Department of Commerce grants a permit for a major oil refinery near Honolulu, Hawaii.

■ *July 3:* Eco-Commando Force '70 posts 800 official-looking signs on four major beaches warning holiday beachgoers that "potentially dangerous concentrations of pathogenic bacteria have been found at or near this location. Swimmers and fishermen risk infection and disease." A communiqué tells Miami residents that they should not be angered at the group for the holiday inconvenience, stating, "We have only done a job which the public officials charged with protecting your welfare have refused to do. Direct your anger at these malfeasants who endanger your health."

■ *September:* About 6,000 protestors blockade the U.S.-Canada border at Blaine, Washington, to protest nuclear tests being conducted in the Aleutian Islands by the U.S. Atomic Energy Commission.

■ *October 22:* Eco-Commando Force '70 sets out in a motor boat to an area where a 12,000-foot-long sewage treatment pipe pumps 40 million gallons of raw sewage into the Atlantic Ocean daily. They release 700 sealed bottles, each with a note explaining the release and pointing out that "this bottle has been moved by the same wind and water currents that move raw sewage. Wherever you find this bottle, you can assume that some of Miami's sewage was there also." People who find the notes are instructed to send them to the *Miami News*. Within two weeks, 70 have been sent to the newspaper, one from as far away as Melbourne, Florida, 140 miles distant from Miami.

1971

- Environmental Action, founded to focus public concerns on solutions to environmental problems, publishes *Earth Tool Kit* (1971). The book argues that it is necessary for serious environmentalists to use civil disobedience and "direct action tactics which break laws."
- *summer:* The anonymous Tucson Eco-Raiders begin an Arizona campaign involving cutting billboards, pulling up survey stakes from housing sites, pouring lead into locks of developers houses, ripping electrical and plumbing fixtures out of unsold houses, breaking windows, and sabotaging bulldozers. After tearing down hundreds of billboards, the perpetrators, five college-age boys fed up with rampant development, are finally caught in 1973.
- *September 15:* Activists set sail from Vancouver, Canada, on the 80-foot halibut boat *Greenpeace* and head for Amchitka Island (part of the Aleutian Islands) to protest nuclear testing by the United States. The voyage is endorsed by a large segment of British Columbia's population, as well as Canadian prime minister Pierre Elliot Trudeau. The 42-day trip is plagued by problems, including delays in the nuclear test program, worsening autumn weather, and an arrest by the U.S. Coast Guard.
- *November 4:* U.S. nuclear tests take place in the Aleutian Islands. Although the boat *Greenpeace Too* is 700 miles away from the site at the time, the negative publicity generated by activists in the United States and Canada had forced the Supreme Court to convene a special session to determine whether the test should be cancelled on environmental grounds. The test was allowed to go ahead by a margin of one vote, but the U.S. Atomic Energy Commission closes the test site the following spring and turns it into a bird sanctuary.

1972

- Inspired by the exploits of the Fox, Environmental Action holds a national contest calling on people to send in ideas for environmentally oriented direct action. Many of the suggestions are published later in the year in the book *Ecotage!* Also in 1972, the Environmental Protection Agency (EPA) bans the use of the pesticide dichloro-diphenyl-trichloroethane (DDT), while the Clean Water Act regulates the release of pollutants into waterways and reservoirs, and mandates the cleanup of waters that have already been polluted.

- *spring:* The leadership of the Greenpeace Foundation, consisting of people who had taken part in the 1971 voyages of *Greenpeace* and *Greenpeace Too,* turn their attention to French nuclear tests over Mururoa Atoll in the South Pacific. Retired Vancouver businessman and athlete David McTaggart and three volunteers sail *Greenpeace III* to the atoll, where they are confronted and eventually rammed by a French military vessel. The boat is towed to Mururoa, given minimal repairs, and towed back out to sea. The damaged vessel eventually makes its way to New Zealand.

1973

- The Endangered Species Act creates a system in which animal species may be listed as threatened or endangered without consideration of the economic consequences of the designations. Also, the Organization of Petroleum Exporting Countries (OPEC) initiates an oil embargo against the United States, dealing a blow to public enthusiasm for environmental protections as improving the economy becomes the priority of the Gerald Ford administration. Also in 1973, Norwegian philosopher Arne Naess introduces the basic tenets of deep ecology in an article published in the philosophical journal *Inquiry.*
- *summer:* David McTaggart sails the repaired *Greenpeace III* back into the Mururoa Atoll test area. French commandoes board the ship and beat McTaggart and navigator Nigel Ingram with rubber truncheons. As a result, McTaggart suffers partial loss of vision in his left eye.
- *July 17:* Senate passes an amendment, sponsored by Senator Mike Gravel of Alaska, to exempt the Trans-Alaska Pipeline from the provisions of the National Environment Policy Act (NEPA).
- *November:* A U.S. district court rules that excessive clear cutting in West Virginia's Monongahela National Forest is illegal under the Organic Act of 1897.

1974

- Murray Bookchin cofounds the Institute for Social Ecology in Plainfield, Vermont, which offers courses in ecophilosophy, social theory, and alternative technologies.
- *spring:* Faced with growing international and domestic pressure to stop nuclear testing in the South Pacific, French leaders announce that the upcoming tests will be the last atmospheric nuclear tests. Thereafter, they will be conducted underground.
- *March:* The Emergency Highway Energy Conservation Act is passed by the U.S. Congress, mandating a national maximum speed limit of 55 miles per hour.

1975

- In an effort to increase energy conservation in the midst of the energy crisis, the Energy Policy Conservation Act sets fuel efficiency standards for cars. Meanwhile, Edward Abbey publishes his novel *The Monkey Wrench Gang*, which chronicles the exploits of four characters who sabotage highway construction equipment in the southwestern United States. The book ultimately plays an important role in inspiring Dave Foreman and others to form Earth First!
- *January:* The Greenpeace Foundation announces it will turn its attention to whaling through Project Ahab, consisting of activists seeking out Soviet and Japanese whaling fleets and placing themselves between harpoons and whales.
- *April 27:* *Greenpeace V* and *Greenpeace VI* sail from Vancouver, accompanied by the cheers of 23,000 supporters. After 60 days, *Greenpeace V* confronts a Soviet whaling fleet 60 miles off the California coast. The environmental activists use high-speed inflatable rubber dinghies to place themselves between the ships and the whales they hunt, prompting the Soviets to back off. Film footage and photographs of confrontation shot by Greenpeace activists generate a tremendous amount of public sentiment against whaling.
- *June:* A French court rules that the ramming of David McTaggart's ship *Greenpeace III* by the French navy in 1972 violated international rules of the sea. Damages are assessed against French military authorities. However, the same court declares itself to be "without jurisdiction" in the matter of his beating by French commandoes later that year.

1976

- Legislation passed by Congress expands the Wilderness Act of 1964 to include lands under jurisdiction of the Bureau of Land Management (BLM).
- *August:* A U.S. district court orders a halt to further clear cutting in the national forests of eastern Texas, citing violations of the Multiple Use–Sustained Yield Act of 1960 and the National Environmental Policy Act of 1969.

1977

- President Carter creates the Department of Energy to regulate energy use. Paul Watson, ousted from Greenpeace for being too violent, forms the Sea Shepherd Conservation Society (SSCS) to pursue his more radical brand of direct action, making a project out of harassing ships engaged in whaling, sealing, and drift-net fishing. According to the FBI, this is the genesis of the ecoterrorism movement in the United States.

Ecoterrorism

1978

■ **May 25:** Theodore Kaczynski leaves a bomb in the parking lot near the Science and Engineering Building of the Chicago Circle campus of the University of Illinois. The package is found by Mary Gutierrez, who turns it over to the Northwestern University computer science professor listed on the return address. The bomb explodes and slightly injures campus security officer Terry Marker. This is the first known attack by the Unabomber.

1979

■ Howie Wolke and Mike Roselle begin campaigning to prevent Getty Oil from drilling in the Gros Ventre section of Wyoming's Bridger-Teton National Forest. Also in 1979, Statute 633 is introduced in the Nevada legislature, inaugurating the anti-environmental Sagebrush Rebellion. The statute seeks to transfer all BLM land in Nevada from federal to state control. Although it passes, it is regarded as little more than a "sentiment" bill by the federal government and is not challenged in court. As similar statutes pass in Utah, Colorado, Wyoming, and Alaska, Utah senator Orrin Hatch calls the Sagebrush Rebellion "the second American revolution." Ronald Reagan, shortly after his election as president of the United States in 1980, sends a telegram to Nevada politicians declaring that he, too, is a Sagebrush Rebel.

■ **January 4:** Rupert Cutler of the U.S. Department of Agriculture announces the results of the second Roadless Area Review and Evaluation (RARE II). Ten million acres of land in the lower 48 states and 5 million acres in Alaska are recommended for wilderness protection, while 36 million acres are opened for development and 11 million are set aside for further study. Frustrated environmentalists such as Dave Foreman and Howie Wolke, convinced that millions of acres were left out of the review because of poor map work and lobbying efforts by logging and mining interests, eventually use their anger over the findings as justification for radicalizing their views and founding Earth First!

■ **May 9:** Theodore Kaczynski leaves a bomb at Northwestern University's Technological Institute in Evanston, Illinois. Graduate student John Harris is slightly injured in the explosion.

■ **May 21:** Environmental activist Mark Dubois chains himself to a boulder on the bank of California's Stanislaus River just as the floodgates of a newly constructed dam close. He had left word of his protest with the Army Corps of Engineers, which is forced to postpone inauguration of the dam in order to locate and remove the protestor so he is not drowned by the rising waters. Dubois later justifies his actions by saying that he felt he "had to make a personal statement" and had hoped his action would delay completion of the dam long enough for a lawsuit to provide long-term protection for the area.

- *November 14:* Theodore Kaczynski mails a package from Chicago to Washington, D.C., containing a bomb wired to explode when it reaches 2,000 feet in altitude. It goes off inside a mail carrier container on board American Airlines flight 444, causing cabin pressure to drop and filling the body of the plane with smoke. Although no one is injured, the plane is forced to make an emergency landing at Washington's Dulles Airport.

1980

- *April 4:* In Arizona, on the way home from a trip to the Pinacate Desert in Mexico, Howie Wolke, Mike Roselle, Bart Koehler, Ron Kezar, and Dave Foreman decide to form a direct action environmental group. Foreman is credited with coming up with the name Earth First!, while Roselle designs the logo: a green fist in a circle. They agree that the motto will be "No compromise in defense of Mother Earth."
- *June 10:* United Airlines president Percy Wood suffers serious facial and leg wounds at his Lake Forest, Illinois, home when he opens a package containing a bomb sent by Theodore Kaczynski.
- *July 4:* The local county commission in Moab, Utah, bulldozes a road into public land that the Bureau of Land Management had identified as a study area for possible wilderness designation. The building of the illegal road is an action by the anti-environmental Sagebrush Rebellion, whose goal is the transfer of federal land to states and eventually to private owners.
- *November 1:* Earth First! publishes the first issue of its journal, at this point a photocopied newsletter titled *Earth First.* (The exclamation point was added later.) In winter 1981–82, the journal evolves into a newspaper-style newsletter that includes black-and-white photographs of Earth First! actions and activists.

1981

- *March 21:* Earth First! holds its first gathering at Glen Canyon Dam, where 75 activists brandish signs with such slogans as "Damn Watt, Not Rivers," "Free the Colorado," and "Let It Flow." The protest climaxes when five activists unfurl 300 feet of black plastic down the front of the dam, creating the impression of a growing crack. Edward Abbey speaks, telling those gathered to "oppose the destruction of our homeland" by politicians and industrialists. He adds that "if opposition is not enough, we must resist. And if resistance is not enough, then subvert."

Ecoterrorism

- **June 3:** A helicopter used to spray national forestland with pesticides is destroyed near Toledo, Oregon. A group of masked women calling themselves the People's Brigade for a Healthy Genetic Future claims responsibility.
- **October 8:** Theodore Kaczynski leaves his fifth known bomb in the University of Utah's Bennion Hall Business Building. A passing student begins to pick it up, then notices a wooden stick drop partway out of the bottom. Suspicions aroused, he notifies campus security, which calls the police bomb squad. The police disarm the bomb in a nearby women's bathroom.

1982

- David Brower founds his second environmental organization, Earth Island Institute.
- **May 5:** Theodore Kaczynski's sixth bomb, intended for computer science professor Patrick Fischer, arrives in the mail at Vanderbilt University in Nashville, Tennessee, with a return address from Brigham Young University professor Leroy Wood Bearnson. Using an outdated reference book, Kaczynski had mistakenly addressed the package to Penn State University (Fischer's previous employer), which forwarded it to Vanderbilt. Fischer's secretary Janet Smith opens the package and sustains severe facial burns and eye injuries.
- **May 31:** Five members of a group called Direct Action use explosives to destroy the $4.5 million British Columbia Hydro Substation on Vancouver Island, Canada. A letter claiming responsibility says that the group is "opposed to any further industrial development" and that their aim is to make Vancouver Island "an insecure and uninhabitable place for capitalists and their projects."
- **July 2:** Diogenes Angelakos, director of the University of California at Berkeley's Electronic Research Laboratory, picks up a package left in room 411 of Cory Hall Mathematics Building. The bomb inside, constructed by Theodore Kaczynski, inflicts severe injuries to Angelakos's right hand and arm.
- **July 4:** Five hundred activists begin rallying against Getty Oil Company's plans to build a seven-mile-long road into the Gros Ventre roadless area in Wyoming, which would exempt the region from future wilderness designation. Activists pull up survey stakes, destroy seismographic equipment, and physically block access to the area, bringing construction to a halt. Meanwhile, Bart Koehler files an administrative appeal that results in the Interior Board of Land Appeals rescinding Getty's drilling permit and ordering a new environmental impact statement that considers a no-drilling alternative. Gros Ventre is eventually designated a wilderness by Congress, protecting it from mining and oil drilling.

Chronology

- *October:* In *California v. Block*, the U.S. Ninth Circuit Court prohibits development in roadless areas in California due to inadequate environmental impact statements.

1983

- James Watt, the anti-environmental secretary of the interior appointed by President Reagan, is forced to resign after he utters a series of ethnic slurs that embarrasses the administration. Also in 1983, Paul Watson is arrested for interfering with Canada's seal hunt. His $10,000 bail is posted by television actor Mike Farrell of *M*A*S*H* fame.
- *April 25:* Earth First! activists Mike Roselle, Steve Marsden, Pedro Tama, and Kevin Everhart block construction on Bald Mountain Road in Oregon. Environmentalists worry that the road, slated to come within six inches of the Kalmiopsis Wilderness Area boundary in Siskiyou National Forest and destroy portions of the Illinois River Trail, will endanger local wildlife. After three hours, the activists are arrested by Josephine County sheriff's deputies and charged with disorderly conduct. They spend the night in jail.
- *May 4:* Seven Earth First! activists chain themselves to a bulldozer working on the Bald Mountain Road project. Operations are shut down for four hours. The activists are arrested, then released from jail that same day on their own recognizance.
- *May 10:* Dave Foreman and Dave Willis, along with a support crew of Earth First! activists, use a downed tree to create a roadblock 10 miles from the Bald Mountain Road construction project to prevent road builders from going to work. At 6 A.M., sheriff's deputies winch the log out of the way. Shortly afterward, a pickup truck containing five workers tries to go around Foreman and Willis, the latter confined to a wheelchair after losing his hands and feet to frostbite. The truck hits Foreman, then accelerates. Foreman runs backward to prevent himself from being run over, but finally loses his balance and falls under the vehicle. Deputies handcuff Foreman and arrest him for disorderly conduct. Police later tell the media that Foreman stepped in front of the truck in such a way that made it impossible for the driver to stop in time, but video footage captured by local television stations reveals that Foreman was intentionally run down and pushed more than 100 yards before he lost his footing. Faced with negative publicity, Plumley, the company hired by the USFS to build the road, orders its employees to refrain from further violence.
- *July 1:* In response to a lawsuit filed June 30 by Earth First!, the Oregon Natural Resources Council, and nine Oregon residents, U.S. District Judge James Redden orders the USFS to halt construction of the Bald

Mountain Road. After two weeks of hearings, the judge issues an injunction against construction, declaring road-building activities in the Siskiyou National Forest illegal. The decision is based on an earlier ruling by the Ninth Circuit Court of Appeals in San Francisco that the 1979 RARE II did not adequately consider the environmental impact of development on roadless areas not selected by the USFS for wilderness designation. In all, 44 activists are arrested during the road blockade.

- **October:** A U.S. district court issues an injunction against timber sales in the Kettle Planning Unit of Washington's Colville National Forest due to inadequate environmental impact statements.

1984

- **October:** Earth First! activists begin their first tree spiking campaign in Oregon's Hardesty Mountain roadless area, where 63 pounds of spikes (about 1,000 20-penny nails) are driven into trees that are part of a proposed timber sale. The USFS spends thousands of dollars removing the spikes.
- **November 17:** The Animal Liberation Front (ALF) claims to have poisoned Mars brand chocolate bars. The ensuing panic leads to millions of bars being removed from store shelves and destroyed.

1985

- Maxxam Corporation buys Pacific Lumber, a northern California logging company that had been family-owned and had cut timber according to sustainable practices since 1905. After the takeover, Pacific Lumber triples old growth redwood logging, purchases a fourth mill, and hires an extra shift of workers. Also in 1985, Dave Foreman publishes *Ecodefense: A Field Guide to Monkeywrenching.*
- **May 15:** John Hauser, an Air Force captain, picks up a booby-trapped spiral binder in room 264 of University of California at Berkeley's Cory Hall. He loses several fingers in the explosion, becoming the victim of Theodore Kaczynski's eighth bomb. Diogenes Angelakos, who had been injured three years earlier in the same building by one of Kaczynski's bombs, is on hand to stop Hauser's bleeding and call the hospital.
- **May 20:** Earth First! activist and rock climber Mike Jakubel originates the use of long-term tree sitting in the United States to stop a timber cut in Oregon. Although he is arrested and cited for criminal trespass after only one day, tree sitting is later refined by other activists and becomes an important tactic for radical environmentalists.
- **June:** A package postmarked May 8 arrives at Boeing Aircraft Fabrication Division in Auburn, Washington. Addressed to no specific person, it

sits in the mail room for several days before an employee starts to open it and finds an explosive device inside. Security personnel successfully disarm the bomb, which had been built and mailed by Kaczynski.

- *June 16:* Earth First! cofounder Howie Wolke is arrested after pulling up survey stakes along a five-mile stretch of road to be used by Chevron to explore for oil in Wyoming's Bridger-Teton National Forest. He is sentenced to six months in jail and a $750 fine and is ordered to pay $2,554 in restitution to Chevron.
- *July 10:* French commandoes place demolition charges on the hull of Greenpeace's ship *Rainbow Warrior* as it sits in New Zealand's Auckland harbor. The blast sinks the ship and kills Fernando Pereira, a Greenpeace photographer.
- *November 15:* Theodore Kaczynski's 10th bomb explodes in the University of Michigan office of professor James V. McConnell. The package, mailed from Salt Lake City, is accompanied by a note explaining that inside is a doctoral dissertation from a student named Ralph C. Kloppenburg. McConnell and his teaching assistant Nick Suino, who had opened the package, are both injured.
- *December 11:* Kaczynski leaves a package bomb in the parking lot behind a Sacramento, California, computer rental store called Rentech. Store owner Hugh Scrutton picks it up and is killed by the explosion. It is Kaczynski's 11th bomb, and the first time he has succeeded in killing someone.

1986

- The International Whaling Commission (IWC) begins a moratorium on commercial whaling. Icelandic and Norwegian whalers request scientific permits to kill whales to determine reasons for a decline in Fin and Sei whale populations in the North Atlantic. In rejecting the proposal, one member of the IWC's scientific committee states, "Iceland is seeking to prostitute science in an attempt to mask a commercial venture." Despite the moratorium, the Soviet Union, Japan, Iceland, Norway, and South Korea continue to hunt whales.
- *May:* Earth First! activists cut electrical power lines leading to the Palo Verde nuclear power plant in Arizona.
- *November 8:* Two Sea Shepherd activists break into a whale processing plant near Reykjavík, Iceland, and spend eight hours destroying refrigeration machinery, diesel engines, pumps, engine parts, laboratory equipment, and computers. Damage is later estimated at about $1.8 million. The activists then remove bolts from the saltwater sea valve flanges in two docked whaling ships, causing them to sink within 40 minutes. Damage for the two ships is estimated at $2.8 million.

Ecoterrorism

1987

- **February 20:** Theodore Kaczynski leaves a bomb in the parking lot of a computer store called CAAMS in Salt Lake City, Utah. When store owner Gary Wright picks it up, the explosion lifts him off his feet and drives shards of wood and metal shrapnel into his body. He sustains severe injuries to his face, left arm, and hand, which are left permanently numb. An employee at a nearby store sees Kaczynski in the parking lot shortly before the explosion, supplying the description that results in the famous FBI sketch of the hooded Unabomber.

- **May:** *EPIC v. Maxxam,* the first of seven successful environmental lawsuits brought by the Environmental Protection Information Center (EPIC), stops two Pacific Lumber clear cuts totaling 274 acres in Headwaters Forest Grove. Also, the first Earth First! tree sit and mass protest in the Headwaters area begins. At one point, 150 people block the main logging gate to Headwaters. Six women jump over the gate and are arrested.

- **May 1:** The *Earth First! Journal* runs an article in which a writer using the pseudonym Miss Ann Thropy suggests that AIDS is nature's way of dealing with overpopulation. The author writes, "I take it as axiomatic that the only real hope for the continuation of diverse ecosystems on this planet is an enormous decline in population," and continues, "If the AIDS epidemic didn't exist, radical environmentalists would have to invent one."

- **May 13:** A tree spike shatters a band saw in a Louisiana-Pacific lumber mill in Cloverdale, California, seriously injuring mill worker George Alexander. The next day, a Louisiana-Pacific spokesman publicly blames Earth First!, which denies the accusation by pointing out that environmentalists inform timber companies about its spiking activities, the point being to prevent logging, not harm workers. Although the media initially places the blame on radical environmentalists, several Northern California newspapers later issue apologies after they learn that the Mendocino County Sheriff Department's primary suspect is William Joseph Ervin, a radical libertarian upset by the logging occurring near his property line. However, they lack the evidence to bring charges against Ervin.

- **October 5:** Earth First! activists Mark Davis and Peg Millett use a propane cutting torch to damage the main cable chair lift at Fairfield ski resort in Arizona. Davis sends a letter, signed the Evan Mecham Eco Terrorist International Conspiracy (EMETIC), demanding that the ski resort stop a planned expansion onto sacred Indian land.

- **October 23:** During a protest against acid rain, Mike Roselle is arrested for attempting to unfurl a Greenpeace banner over George Washington's face at Mount Rushmore National Memorial in South Dakota. He is sentenced to four months in jail.

Chronology

1988

- Ron Arnold organizes the first Multiple Use Strategy Conference (later renamed the Wise Use Leadership Conference) in Reno, Nevada, which inspires the drafting of the 25-point "Wise Use Agenda." Also in 1988, congressional delegates from several Pacific Northwest states, led by Idaho senator James McClure and Oregon senator Mark Hatfield, successfully attach a rider to the Drug Act of 1988 making tree spiking a felony.
- *summer:* Earth First! activists begin a campaign to end logging in national forests in the Pacific Northwest. Over the next five years, protestors damage logging equipment, spike trees, blockade roads, and use the court system in an attempt to expand the definition of critical habitat for the northern spotted owl.
- *September 25:* Mark Davis, Peg Millett, and Ilse Asplund, operating under the name EMETIC, use a saw to topple poles supporting power lines leading to a uranium mine near the Grand Canyon in Arizona.

1989

- *March:* The oil tanker *Exxon Valdez* runs aground off the coast of Prince William Sound in Alaska. The 11-million-gallon oil spill damages 600 acres of coastal and marine habitat, kills thousands of sea otters and birds, and jeopardizes the herring and salmon industries.
- *April 3:* Animal Liberation Front (ALF) members break into a research facility at the University of Arizona and release more than 1,200 animals. They then set fire to the laboratory and a nearby administration building.
- *May 30:* FBI agents arrest Marc Baker and Mark Davis near Wenden, Arizona, while they are in the process of cutting down an electrical transmission tower. A third activist, Peg Millett, evades police but is arrested the next day. Dave Foreman, who was not on the scene, is also arrested on charges that he supplied $580 to the saboteurs. The FBI claims the incident is a dry run for a larger conspiracy to damage power lines leading to nuclear facilities in Arizona, California, and Colorado. The arrests are the result of a $2 million surveillance operation involving wiretaps, body wires, and infiltrators, marking the first time such tactics are used against an environmental group.
- *December:* Earth First! activist Ilse Washington Asplund is arrested and becomes one of the Arizona Five, along with Dave Foreman, Peg Millett, Marc Baker, and Mark Davis. She is charged with damaging a chairlift at the Fairfield ski resort near Flagstaff, Arizona, and planning sabotage at nuclear facilities in Arizona, California, and Colorado. Asplund later pleads guilty and is sentenced to one year in federal prison, five years probation, a $2,000 fine, and 100 hours of community service.

1990

- **March 1:** Trespassing Earth First! activists discover that Maxxam/Pacific Lumber Company is cutting an illegal road, 30 feet wide and one mile long, into the Headwaters Grove. Pacific Lumber claims the road is actually a trail for their biologist to perform wildlife studies ordered by the California Department of Forestry. EPIC and Sierra Club file suit, forcing Pacific Lumber to halt construction of the road.
- **May 24:** Earth First! activists and Redwood Summer organizers Judi Bari and Darryl Cherney are injured when a bomb explodes under the front seat of their car. Police claim Bari and Cherney were planning to use the bomb to disrupt logging operations, but the activists maintain that it was planted by the FBI or by supporters of the lumber industry. No charges are filed.
- **summer:** Redwood Summer, organized by Earth First!, brings thousands of activists from across the country to Northern California to confront Maxxam/Pacific Lumber Company's logging practices. Protests include marches, occupations of threatened groves, tree sits, blockades, rallies, and confrontations with loggers, some of which result in violence. The campaign gains national media attention.
- **June:** Under the Endangered Species Act, the northern spotted owl is listed as a threatened species in the Pacific Northwest. Timber companies complain that the designation will lead to widespread unemployment among loggers and others dependent on the timber industry in the region. Also in June, former interior secretary James Watt tells a gathering of cattlemen that "if the troubles from environmentalists cannot be solved in the jury box or at the ballot box, perhaps the cartridge box should be used."
- **August 13:** Paul Watson's boat *Sea Shepherd II* rams two Japanese drift net fishing boats after activists observe and document the fishermen violating the 1972 Convention for the Protection of Migratory Birds by catching birds in nets.

1991

- Dave Foreman, after quitting Earth First!, founds the Wildlands Project, whose purpose is to "re-wild" America by making 50 percent of its land off-limits to human occupation and development.
- **April:** Twenty-six Earth First! activists are arrested for blocking a Maxxam/Pacific Lumber Company clear cut on the edge of Headwaters Grove.
- **August 13:** Animal Liberation Front (ALF) activists break into Washington State University's Bustad Hall and free one mink, 10 mice, and seven coyotes. They also damage documents and interior facility fixtures.

Chronology

■ *December 22:* ALF arsonists destroy a single-story building at the Malecky Mink Ranch in Yamhill, Oregon. The ranch works with Oregon State University's research on mink breeding and nutrition.

1992

■ The Earth Liberation Front (ELF) is founded in Brighton, England, by Earth First! activists who refuse to abandon criminal acts as a tactic when others wish to "mainstream" Earth First!

■ *February 28:* Members of the Animal Liberation Front (ALF), Rodney Coronado among them, set fire to the Michigan State University office of Richard Aulerich, who uses mink in his experiments in the fields of toxicology and nutrition. An ALF-sponsored press release states that Aulerich "has killed thousands of mink in painful and scientifically worthless experiments." Aulerich defends himself by explaining the animals "are not allowed to suffer" and are often euthanized to avoid subjecting them to pain.

■ *October 24:* ALF sets fire to a Utah State University farm facility where coyotes are housed for research.

1993

■ *June 22:* After six years of inactivity, Theodore Kaczynski strikes again when his 13th bomb is delivered to the home of world-renowned geneticist Charles J. Epstein in Tiburon, California. The explosion sends Epstein across the room, knocks him to the floor, and injures his right arm.

■ *June 24:* Computer science professor David Gelernter receives a package containing one of Kaczynski's bombs at his Yale University office. The explosion blows the thumb and little finger from his right hand and badly mangles the remaining digits. Gelernter also sustains serious damage to his left hand, right leg, chest, and a lung.

■ *September:* The USFS approves 6,328 acres in the 76,000-acre Cove Mallard area in Idaho's Nez Perce National Forest for logging. Proponents say the logging and accompanying road building will lead to an influx of money and much-needed jobs in the community, but activists argue that the project will destroy the largest roadless area in the lower 48 states, threaten endangered species, and interfere with proposals to return wolves and grizzly bears to native habitat.

■ *September 22:* The ELF and the ALF publish a communiqué declaring their solidarity of action.

1994

■ *February:* Earth First! leader Judi Bari publishes an article in the *Earth First! Journal* recommending that Earth First! mainstream itself in the

United States, leaving criminal acts other than peaceful, unlawful protests to the ELF.

■ *summer:* Earth First! activists begin a campaign of peaceful disobedience based on tree sitting and human blockades to stop road building in the Cove Mallard area of Idaho's Nez Perce National Forest, approved for logging the previous year. In June, however, a Caterpillar tractor is disabled with sand in its fuel tank, smashed gauges, and cut fuel and hydraulic lines. The hostile reaction among local residents includes a poster in a nearby town sporting a drawing of an Earth First! activist with a bullet hole in his forehead. In another incident, a group of locals ambushes a lone activist on a remote road and beats him bloody. During the campaign, law enforcement officials make more than 50 arrests, issue more than 100 citations, and raid the Earth First! camp in an unsuccessful attempt to uncover evidence that the group was involved in the vandalism of logging and road-building equipment.

■ *December 10:* Thomas Mosser, an executive at the public relations firm Burson-Marsteller, dies at his home in North Caldwell, New Jersey, when he opens a package bomb sent by Kaczynski. Mosser's is the second death attributed to the Unabomber.

1995

■ Dave Foreman is elected to a three-year term as a Sierra Club director.

■ *April 24:* Gilbert Murray, president of the California Forestry Association in Sacramento, California, becomes the third person killed by the Unabomber when he opens a package bomb addressed to former association president William Dennison.

■ *June 24:* Theodore Kaczynski mails copies of "Industrial Society and Its Future," soon to be known as the "Unabomber Manifesto," to the *New York Times*, the *Washington Post*, and *Penthouse* magazine. The accompanying note claims that the bomber "will permanently desist from terrorism" if the manifesto is published.

■ *July 3:* Animal rights activist Rodney Coronado pleads guilty to firebombing research facilities at Michigan State University in 1992. He is sentenced to 57 months in federal prison, three years probation, and restitution of more than $2 million.

■ *September 19:* The *Washington Post*, in collaboration with the *New York Times*, publishes the "Unabomber Manifesto." Initially reluctant to run the manifesto, the two newspapers finally do so at the urging of Attorney General Janet Reno, who hopes that someone might recognize the authorship.

Chronology

1996

- *February 14:* Believing that the Unabomber's manifesto bears a striking resemblance to an earlier essay written by his brother, Theodore, David Kaczynski contacts the FBI through his attorney. Based on evidence provided by David, the FBI begins surveillance of Theodore's cabin in Montana.
- *April 3:* FBI agents arrest Theodore Kaczynski at his cabin.
- *September–November:* Earth First! organizes a direct action campaign to save Headwaters Forest. An estimated 5,000 activists attend a September 15 rally, during which hundreds of protesters (including Bonnie Raitt, Don Henley, Jello Biafra, and Dan Hamburg) are arrested for trespassing onto Pacific Lumber property. Actions over the next several weeks, which result in some 270 arrests, include more than 12 gate lockdowns, eight lockdowns to logging equipment inside the groves, a protest village where six sitters occupy a series of trees for 14 days, and demonstrations at the California Department of Forestry, the Department of Fish and Wildlife, the Democratic Headquarters in Eureka, Senator Diane Feinstein's office in San Francisco, and the Eureka Court House. On September 28, California and federal officials announce they have made a deal to purchase and permanently protect forestland from Pacific Lumber for $380 million dollars. Most local environmentalists oppose the deal, which they say offers less protection for the remaining redwood groves than they currently have and which creates a "tree museum" rather than saving an endangered ecosystem.
- *October 28:* A USFS pickup truck is set on fire in the parking lot of the Detroit Ranger District headquarters in Detroit, Oregon. The saboteurs spray-paint "Earth Liberation Front" and other graffiti on the building. An incendiary bomb that had failed to explode is later found on the roof of the building. Damage is estimated at $15,000. The ELF/ALF claim joint responsibility.
- *October 30:* Arsonists destroy the USFS Oakridge Ranger Station south of Eugene, Oregon. Law enforcement officials assert that the ELF/ALF have claimed joint responsibility for the destruction but fail to produce evidence to support this claim. Damage is estimated at $5.3 million.
- *November 7:* Jurors in Idaho award $150,000 in compensatory damages and $999,999 in punitive damages to Don Blewett, the owner of road building equipment that was destroyed by activists in central Idaho's Nez Perce National Forest. Blewett wins the damages from 12 Earth First! activists whom he accused of vandalizing the equipment during a 1993 protest of a timber sale in the Cove Mallard area.

Ecoterrorism

1997

- **March 14:** The ELF/ALF claim joint responsibility for spiking trees at a Robinson-Scott timber harvest site in the Mackenzie River watershed area of Oregon's Willamette National Forest.
- **April 20:** Douglas Joshua Ellerman turns himself in to law enforcement officers and admits to purchasing, constructing, and transporting five pipe bombs to the scene of the March 11, 1997, arson at the Fur Breeders Agricultural co-op in Sandy, Utah. Ellerman also admits setting fire to the facility. He is indicted on June 19, 1997, on 16 counts, and eventually pleads guilty to three. He is sentenced to seven years in prison and restitution of approximately $750,000. Though this incident was not officially claimed by the ALF, Ellerman indicates during an interview subsequent to his arrest that he is a member of the organization.
- **April 26:** More than 50 animal activists are arrested when they try to force their way into Emory University's Yerkes Regional Primate Center during a protest. They are charged with criminal interference with government property, trespassing, and obstruction of police.
- **July 21:** The ELF/ALF jointly set fire to Cavel West, a horse-rendering plant in Redmond, Oregon, that supplies horse tissue to the Pacific Coast Tissue Bank in Los Angeles to treat skull bone birth defects in children. Damages total $1 million.
- **November:** The highly anticipated trial of Theodore Kaczynski begins with jury selection.
- **November 29:** The ELF/ALF claim joint responsibility for burning a horse barn, chutes, pens, and equipment belonging to the U.S. Bureau of Land Management in Hines, Oregon. About 400 horses are released, but they are later recaptured. Damage is estimated at $474,000.
- **December 10:** Environmental activist Julia Butterfly Hill occupies a 180-foot-tall California Coast redwood tree with the aim of preventing it from being cut down. She lives in the tree until December 18, 1999.

1998

- **January 8:** Kaczynski, unhappy that his attorneys have worked behind his back to mount an insanity defense despite his wishes to the contrary, requests permission of the court to represent himself.
- **January 22:** Kaczynski's request for self-representation is denied. Within hours, in exchange for the government's agreement not to seek the death penalty, he pleads guilty to 13 federal bombing offenses (three of which resulted in death) and takes responsibility for a string of 16 bombings lasting from 1978 to 1995.

- *May 4:* Kaczynski is sentenced to four consecutive life terms plus 30 years for his bombing spree.
- *June 2:* The ELF/ALF claim joint responsibility for burning two U.S. Department of Agriculture wildlife stations near Olympia, Washington. Total damage is estimated at $1.9 million.
- *June 28:* ELF activists spray red paint on the Mexican consulate in Boston, Massachusetts, to protest the treatment of peasants in Chiapas, Mexico.
- *July 3:* ELF/ALF activists break into United Vaccines laboratory in Middleton, Wisconsin, and release 171 minks and ferrets.
- *July 5:* ALF activists break into the laboratory of a Cornell University professor and release dozens of woodchucks used to study liver cancer and hepatitis. The activists also remove data cards from cages, destroy log books, and allow vials of serum to spoil at room temperature.
- *September 17:* Earth First! activist David "Gypsy" Chain is killed on Pacific Lumber land in Humboldt County, California, when logger A. E. Ammons fells a tree that crushes the activist's skull. Although Pacific Lumber claims it "had no knowledge" that protestors were in the area, a video taken by an Earth First! activist before Chain's death captures the angry voice of Ammons shouting obscenities at the environmentalists and threatening to bring his pistol to work. The exact amount of time between the confrontation and the death becomes an issue, as Ammons says he assumed the protestors had left the area before he started cutting again. The lead investigator into the death later tells Chain's mother that activists present when he was killed could face criminal charges of manslaughter, while Ammons would go unpunished.
- *October:* The confrontation between Washington state's Makah Indians, who are attempting to revive a long-dormant whale hunting ritual, and the Sea Shepherd Conservation Society (SSCS) grows violent when angry tribal members throw rocks at the Sea Shepherd vessel *Sirenian*. Two SSCS crew members are injured, and the group's Zodiac raft is damaged. Three society members, including Gray Whale Campaign Expedition leader Lisa Distefano, are briefly detained by tribal police. As a result, the SSCS agrees not to land on Makah territory but vows to disrupt the hunt by other means. The first hunt ends in failure for the Makah, partly because frequent boat patrols and underwater broadcasts of predatory orca sounds by the SSCS keep the gray whales far offshore and away from the hunters.
- *October 10:* ELF/ALF activists in Rock Springs, Wyoming, cut the locks off horse pens at a Bureau of Land Management (BLM) corral and free about 40 wild horses. Incendiary devices are placed near a pickup truck and a building but fail to explode.

Ecoterrorism

- *October 19:* ELF activists set fire to a ski resort in Vail, Colorado, causing $12 million in damage. Four ski lifts, a restaurant, a picnic facility, and a utility building are destroyed. An ELF communiqué explains that the fire was set to stop proposed expansion of the resort into declining lynx habitat.
- *October 26:* ELF activists release 5,000 minks from Tom Pipkorn's Mink Farm in Powers, Michigan. An estimated 500 disappear or are killed by cars, starvation, or drowning in swimming pools. Damage is estimated at $100,000.
- *December 26:* ELF arsonists destroy U.S. Forest Industries' corporate headquarters in Medford, Oregon, causing $700,000 in damage. An ELF communiqué issued several weeks later by the Liberation Collective in Portland, Oregon, explains that the fire was intended as payback for company practices that include razing forests and killing wildlife for profit.

1999

- *April 5:* Vandals break into research facilities at the University of Minnesota, where animals are used in research for Parkinson's disease, cerebral palsy, Huntington's disease, and various forms of cancer. More than 100 research animals are stolen, research laboratories are ransacked, and computers, microscopes, and medical equipment are destroyed.
- *June 16:* Kaczynski appeals his sentence to the Ninth Circuit Court based on the complaint that the court, by refusing to allow him to fire his attorneys, had violated his constitutional right to mount his own defense.
- *August 7:* In Escanaba, Michigan, a fishing boat parked in the driveway of a veterinarian who once worked as a mink rancher is set on fire. The garage door is spray-painted with graffiti reading "Fur Is Murder. ELF." Damage is estimated at $15,000.
- *December 25:* Arsonists set fire to a Boise Cascade timber management office, causing $1 million in damage. A claim of responsibility sent to *The Oregonian* newspaper reads, "Let this be a lesson to all greedy multinational corporations who don't respect their ecosystems. The elves are watching."
- *December 31:* The ELF sets fire to the offices of Catherine Ives at Michigan State University in Lansing. The research facility had used funding from the Monsanto Corporation to develop genetically modified crops for use in Asia, Africa, and South America. Local newspapers report that the fire caused $400,000 in damage.

2000

- *January 23:* Arsonists destroy a luxury home under construction at the Sterling Woods Development in Bloomington, Indiana, and leave a sign that says, "No Sprawl—ELF." The perpetrators later send a statement to the Environmental News Service claiming that "the house was targeted because the sprawling development it is located in is in the Lake Monroe Watershed. This is the drinking water supply for the town of Bloomington, Indiana, and the surrounding area. It is already being jeopardized by existing development and roads."

- **February 25:** Greenpeace activists board and occupy a ship off the coast of Britain carrying 60,000 tons of genetically modified soya owned by the U.S. agricultural producer Cargill. The group seeks to highlight its campaign to end the importation of genetically modified foods into Europe. According to Cargill, the cargo is fully regulated and has been approved for use in food and feed products by the European Union since 1996, an approval questioned by Greenpeace. The six activists, who prevent the ship from moving for 17 hours, are arrested on board by police the next day.
- **April 30:** At a road construction site near Bloomington, Indiana, vandals sabotage logging and heavy construction equipment and set a trailer full of wood chips on fire. The ELF claims responsibility, stating that its aim is to punish those who have turned forestland into parking lots and "luxury houses for rich scum." Damage is estimated at $75,000.
- **May 21:** The ELF claims responsibility for fires at the University of Washington Center for Urban Horticulture in Seattle and at Jefferson Poplar Farms in Clatskaknie, Oregon.
- **July 20:** ELF activists cause $1 million in damage when they cut down thousands of experimental trees and spray-paint vehicles at a USFS research station in Rhinelander, Wisconsin. The ELF claims that the trees resulted from bioengineering experiments, but researchers maintain that the plants were bred naturally to grow faster and resist disease.
- **September 9:** In protest against plans to extend a nearby interstate highway, ELF activists set fire to the headquarters of the Monroe County Republican Party Committee in Bloomington, Indiana, resulting in $1,500 in damage.
- **October 18:** ELF activists in Shoals, Indiana, vandalize four pieces of heavy logging equipment in Martin State Forest by cutting hoses, slashing seats, destroying gauges, and pouring sand into engines, fuel tanks, and radiators. Among the slogans spray-painted on the equipment are "Earth Raper" and "Go Cut in Hell." Damage is estimated at $55,000.
- **November 27:** The ELF burns a luxury home in a new subdivision in Niwot, Colorado, to protest the defeat of a statewide ballot measure to control growth. A message sent to the *Boulder Weekly* newspaper reads, "Viva la revolution! The Boulder ELF burned the Legend Ridge mansion on November 27."

- *December 1:* Members of the ELF attack a new housing development in Middle Island, New York, smashing more than 200 windows, pulling up survey stakes to delay clear cutting, spraying antisprawl graffiti, and monkeywrenching 12 construction vehicles.
- *December 7:* The ELF/ALF claim joint responsibility for smashing windows and spray-painting slogans at the McDonald's corporate offices in Hauppauge, Long Island.
- *December 9:* An ELF communiqué claiming responsibility for a fire in a condominium under construction in Middle Island, New York, refers to the homes as "future dens of the wealthy elite" and declares "an unbounded war on urban sprawl." Damages add up to $200,000.
- *December 19:* The ELF sets fire to a house under construction in Miller Place, New York, causing $50,000 in damage. The claim of responsibility states, "Building homes for the wealthy should not even be a priority. Forests, farms and wetlands are being replaced with a sea of houses, green chemical lawns, blacktop and roadkill."
- *December 30:* The ELF sets fire to three luxury homes under construction in Mount Sinai, New York. A fourth home is painted with the slogan, "If you build it we will burn it."

2001

- *January 1:* Arsonists cause $400,000 in damage at the offices of Superior Lumber Company, the leading employer in the small town of Glendale, Oregon. An ELF communiqué calls the lumber company "a typical earth raper contributing to the ecological destruction of the Northwest."
- *January 14:* ELF activists burn an articulated loader and a pickup truck at Melo's Construction Corporation in Miller Place, Long Island.
- *January 23:* Activists break windows in two buildings under construction in Louisville, Kentucky, including a bank. The ELF claims that this minor action is the first strike in a long battle to stop urban sprawl in the area.
- *January 25:* Frank Ambrose is arrested and charged with spiking approximately 150 trees in Indiana state forests, an incident for which the ELF had claimed responsibility. It is the first arrest in the United States related to an ELF action. Activists maintain that Ambrose had nothing to do with the spiking and that his arrest is an incident of harassing an aboveground activist in order to intimidate radical environmentalists. Tree spiking, a felony, carries a sentence of up to three years in prison and up to a $10,000 fine.
- *February 12:* Kaczynski's appeal of his sentence is rejected by the Ninth Circuit Court. Judge Stephen Reinhardt dissents. Kaczynski appeals to the Supreme Court.

Chronology

- **February 15:** Officials in Suffolk County, New York, arrest four teenagers believed to be affiliated with the ELF. Jared McIntyre, 17; Matthew Rammelkamp, 16; George Mashkow, 17; and Connor Cash, 19; are charged in the December 9, 2000, arson of homes in Middle Island, New York; the December 19 arson in Miller Place, New York; and the December 30 arson in Mount Sinai, New York. Prosecutors charge Cash with arson conspiracy, claiming he procured gasoline for the other three and instructed them to carry out the arsons because he feared he would face greater charges as an adult if caught. Cash pleads not guilty, while McIntyre pleads guilty to arson conspiracy. As part of a plea bargain with federal prosecutors, Mashkow and Rammelkamp plead guilty as adults and agree to cooperate with investigations into the ELF/ALF.
- **February 20:** The ELF sets fire to the Delta and Pine Land Company Research cotton gin in Visalia, California. The company, according to the ELF, is responsible for the Monsanto Corporation's "terminator" seed technology, which renders seeds sterile and forces farmers to purchase a new supply from Monsanto each year.
- **March 5:** The ELF smashes windows and a neon sign at the Old Navy Outlet Center in Huntington, Long Island (New York). A communiqué attacks the Fisher family—which owns The Gap, Banana Republic, and Old Navy—for its plan to clear cut large sections of redwood forest on land they recently purchased in northern California.
- **April 4:** The ELF claims responsibility for an attempted arson at a Nike outlet store in Albertville, Minnesota, in response to the shoe manufacturer's use of sweatshop labor overseas and its role in globalization.
- **April 5:** Agents from the FBI, BATF, and Oregon State Police raid the Portland home and business of ELF press officers Craig Rosebraugh and Leslie James Pickering. Authorities seize computer equipment, phone books, videos, literature, and other items. Rosebraugh, who states that the raid "is nothing more than another attempt by the thugs of the state and federal government to stop the legal work of the North American Earth Liberation Front Press Office," is served a subpoena to testify before a federal grand jury. It is the seventh grand jury subpoena issued to him in relation to radical environmentalism since 1997.
- **May 21:** The ELF burns an office and 13 trucks at Jefferson Poplar Farms in Clatskanie, Oregon. On the same night, ELF activists burn down the office of Toby Bradshaw at the University of Washington. Both targets are involved in developing genetically engineered trees. The combined damage estimate is more than $3 million.
- **June 10:** The ELF removes survey stakes and paints graffiti reading "No GE" and "Go Organic" at a University of Idaho biotechnology building in opposition to genetic engineering.

117

Ecoterrorism

- **June 13:** The ELF/ALF claim joint responsibility for attacking five Bank of New York buildings on Long Island by gluing locks and ATM machines, spray-painting slogans, and smashing windows. The actions are part of a campaign to encourage the bank to end its association with Huntingdon Life Sciences (HLS), a Europe-based firm that conducts animal tests.
- **June 14:** Mark Sands is arrested on charges stemming from a series of arsons that targeted eight new homes under construction near the North Phoenix Mountain Preserve outside Phoenix, Arizona. A group calling itself the Coalition to Save the Preserves (CSP), whose stated goal is to stop development of previously undeveloped lands, had taken credit for the arsons, which caused damage estimated to be in excess of $5 million. On November 7, 2001, Sands pleads guilty to 10 counts of extortion and using fire in the commission of a federal felony. On February 12, 2002, he is sentenced to 18 years in prison.
- **July 14:** Fifteen Greenpeace activists and two journalists from eight different countries are arrested in California for delaying the test of a U.S. antiballistic missile system by swimming, diving, and boating beneath the flight path. They are charged with conspiring to violate a safety zone and violating an order, felony charges that carry possible prison terms of more than 10 years. On August 13, demonstrators gather at U.S. embassies around the world to show support for the arrestees. The charges are dropped several weeks later.
- **July 27:** An anonymous group of activists claims responsibility for spiking hundreds of trees in the Upper Greenhorn Timber Sale in Washington state's Gifford Pinchot National Forest.
- **September 5:** Craig Rosebraugh and Leslie James Pickering step down from their duties as press officers for the ELF, stating that if the ELF is to remain a viable movement, public concentrations of support must not be centered on one or two people.
- **October 5:** ELF activists burn the BLM's Litchfield Wild Horse and Burro Facility near Susanville, California. The fire causes approximately $85,000 in damages when a barn burns to the ground. In addition, the group cuts through four 60-foot sections of wooden fence on corrals holding more than 200 wild horses in an attempt to free them.
- **November 5:** Anonymous activists send a communiqué to the ELF press office claiming responsibility for spiking trees throughout the Otter Wing Timber Sale in Idaho's Nez Perce National Forest.

2002

- **January 29:** The ELF takes credit for setting fire to the Microbial and Plant Genomics Research Center under construction at the University of

Minnesota's St. Paul campus. The fire causes extensive damage to the main construction trailer and two pieces of heavy machinery before spreading into an adjacent crop research facility. An ELF communiqué states, "The construction of this research building is being funded by biotech giant Cargill Corporation who develop, patent, and market genetically modified crops, making people dependent on [genetically engineered] foods."

- **February 12:** The House Resources Subcommittee on Forests and Forest Health, chaired by Colorado representative Scott McInnis, holds hearings on ecoterrorism in Washington, D.C. Testimony is supplied by members of Congress, individuals representing companies targeted by the ELF/ALF, law enforcement officials, and industry representatives, many of whom give detailed accounts of ELF/ALF attacks and calls for additional legislation dealing with ecoterrorism. Elaine Close of the Mobilization for the Protection of Civil Liberties (MPCL) criticizes the hearing as being anti-environment and pro–big business because former ELF spokesperson Craig Rosebraugh is the sole representative of the environmentalist point of view.
- **March 18:** The Supreme Court declines to hear Kaczynski's last attempt to appeal his sentence.
- **June 11:** A jury in Oakland, California, rules that the FBI, while investigating a 1990 pipe bomb explosion that injured Earth First! members Judi Bari and Darryl Cherney, violated the two activists' First and Fourth Amendment rights. The court awards $4.4 million in damages, of which $2.9 million go to the estate of Bari, who died of breast cancer in 1997.
- **July 8:** Members of the ELF paint the words "Stop Sprawl" and "Respect" on the wall of a new Wal-Mart building in Louisville, Kentucky. A construction trailer in the parking lot is also painted, and its tires are slashed. Also, the locks on the main construction trailer are glued, and its four windows are smashed out. An anonymous communiqué claims that "the ELF is only beginning in the Kentucky region" and that it "will not stop until the developers and oligarchs do."
- **July 30:** Canadian authorities raid the British Columbia home of ALF spokesperson David Barbarash. All charges stemming from the raid are dropped in March 2003, after a judge learns that the search warrant obtained by police was based solely on evidence gathered from a single photocopied newspaper article about ALF activities.
- **July 31:** ALF activists strike the Meadowbrook Golf Club on the eve of the PGA Lightpath classic, digging three-foot trenches on the greens and remove metal casings and flags from the holes. A communiqué explains that the attack is part of a direct action campaign against sponsor

Ecoterrorism

Huntingdon Life Sciences (HLS), a biomedical research company that tests on animals.

- **August 11:** ELF activists set fire to a USFS research station in Irvine, Pennsylvania, causing approximately $700,000 in damages. The facility had gained international recognition for its studies on ecosystems in the Allegheny Plateau region, on forest sustainability, and on the effects of acid deposition from air pollution. An ELF communiqué dated September 3, 2002, explains that the research station was "strategically targeted" and that if rebuilt, it "will be targeted again for complete destruction." The communiqué also warns that "other U.S. Forest Service administration and research facilities" will likely be targeted in the future.

- **August 15:** The ELF press office receives an anonymous message claiming that hundreds of metallic and nonmetallic spikes have been placed in units 28 and 29 of the Kirk Timber Sale in Washington state's Gifford Pinchot National Forest.

- **August 18:** ALF activists release approximately 1,200 domesticated minks from a small farm near Waverly, Iowa. A communiqué warns that the ALF will continue to target local farms and research facilities "until every animal confinement operation is empty and every slaughterhouse is burned to the ground," adding that "in the fight for the freedom of these animals, all is justified."

- **September–October:** Over a period of several weeks, more than 25 sport utility vehicles (SUVs), two local restaurants, and heavy equipment at several construction sites in the Richmond, Virginia, area are targeted by graffiti. Local attacks on SUVs, including slashed tires and the use of glass-etching cream, date back to July 2002. Evidence suggests that the perpetrators may be ELF sympathizers. Damages are estimated at approximately $45,000.

- **October 8:** During a protest near Mount Madonna County Park in Santa Cruz, California, Earth First! activist Robert Bryan dies after removing his safety harness and falling 100 feet from a redwood tree where he had been living.

- **November 26:** The ELF/ALF claim joint responsibility for firebombing the feed barn at a 60-year-old mink farm in Erie County, Pennsylvania, causing an estimated $50,000 in damage. The attack is the third against the farm in less than one year. In September and May, ALF activists had released a total of more than 200 minks. An ELF communiqué warns that if the farm does not close, the perpetrators will return and demolish it.

- **December 23:** ELF activists strike a house and several construction vehicles at a new housing development in a suburb of Philadelphia, Pennsylvania. Damage to the vehicles includes broken windows, glued locks, disconnected hoses, contaminated gas tanks, and graffiti.

Chronology

- **December 23:** More than a dozen sport utility vehicles (SUVs) parked in two separate neighborhoods in Newton, Massachusetts, are vandalized with aerosol spray paint and markers. Among the graffiti are the slogans "gas guzzler," "I'm changing the environment," and "no blood for oil," as well as the "circle-A" anarchy symbol.

2003

- **January 1:** One SUV, one car, and two pickup trucks are destroyed by arsonists at the Bob Ferrando Ford Lincoln Mercury car dealership outside of Erie, Pennsylvania. The ELF claims responsibility.
- **January 6:** David Barbarash resigns from his post as the ALF's North American spokesperson.
- **February 2:** The ALF takes credit for cutting refrigeration and brake lines on 48 vehicles at a Chicago-based seafood distribution company. Damage estimates exceed $50,000.
- **February 10:** A log loader belonging to an Oregon-based timber company is sabotaged at a Northern California logging site. Perpetrators stuff wood bark in the oil fill tube, place sticks inside the engine, tamper with the fuel pump, remove the air filter, and remove one of the retaining straps. Investigators note that the engine's coverings had been carefully removed and replaced in order to conceal the damage, estimated at more than $20,000. At the time of the sabotage, Earth First! is active in the area, with members conducting tree sits and road blockades, although no one takes responsibility.
- **February 13–14:** California State University at Fresno hosts an academic conference on "revolutionary environmentalism." Among the speakers is convicted arsonist Rodney Coronado. Critics complain that inviting radical environmentalists amounts to condoning their views, but Steve Best, chairman of the philosophy department at University of Texas, El Paso, says that "property destruction and civil protest" are part of American heritage, citing the Boston Tea Party as a historical example.
- **February 27:** Activists steal more than 100 chicks from housing units at an animal research facility in Berlin, Maryland. An ALF communiqué posted to the Stop Huntingdon Animal Cruelty (SHAC) web site explains that the laboratory was specifically targeted because of its connections to drug testing company Huntingdon Life Sciences (HLS) and warns, "Any friend of HLS is an enemy of the ALF. We know who their clients are. We are out there, and you're next."
- **March:** Former ELF spokesperson Craig Rosebraugh publishes a manifesto via the Internet calling on antiwar activists to use direct action to disrupt U.S. military establishments, corporations, government buildings,

and media outlets. "An action is only good," he writes, "if it will serve to severely disrupt the political system of the country, its economy and the corporate interests that drive this society."

- **March 3:** Two firebombs left outside a McDonald's restaurant in Chico, California, fail to ignite. The attackers spray-paint "Animal Liberation Front" and "Meat Is Murder" across the exterior wall of the restaurant. A typewritten note left at a pay phone near the building taking responsibility for the bombs is signed by the ALF, as is another sent to a local newspaper. It states that "McDonald's has been targeted because of their prevalent connection to the farming industry. McDonald's is the world's largest user of beef."
- **March 10:** Employees at another McDonald's in Chico, California, find evidence of a small fire made with combustible material outside the restaurant. Red graffiti reading "liberation" and "ALF" is found on the building's exterior.
- **March 11:** Two McDonald's and one Arby's restaurants in Albuquerque, New Mexico, are attacked by Molotov cocktails and crude incendiary grenades. The Arby's sustains an estimated $80,000 in damages, not including revenue loss while repairs are made.
- **March 21:** Arsonists set fire to a home under construction at an Ann Arbor, Michigan, housing development. The fire spreads to a second vacant home, then embers from the burning houses force a family in a third house to evacuate. Damages to the two vacant homes are estimated at about $150,000 each. Although no official claim of responsibility is made, "ELF" and "No Sprawl" are spray-painted on the garage door of a nearby home also under construction.
- **March 22:** Arsonists pour a flammable liquid across the galvanized metal roofing and set fire to a slaughterhouse building in Santa Rosa, California. The perpetrators also shatter the skylights and spray-paint "Stop the killing" on the back of the building. Three years earlier, arsonists had set off incendiary devices in three separate buildings at the slaughter facility, causing $250,000 in damages.
- **March 27:** ALF activists scrawl "HLS SCUM" in red paint across the garage door of an employee of drug and chemical testing company Huntingdon Life Sciences (HLS) in San Diego, California. The perpetrators also slash three tires and dump a gallon of red paint on the car parked in the driveway.
- **March 29:** A large truck at the Naval Recruiting office in Montgomery, Alabama, is set ablaze. Graffiti calling for an end to the war in Iraq and signed "ELF" is spray-painted onto five nearby Navy vehicles. Investigators believe the arson falls in line with former ELF spokesperson Craig

Rosebraugh's manifesto calling for antiwar activism based on direct action with the aim of manufacturing "an atmosphere of severe unrest."

- *April 4:* A butcher shop in a suburb of Chicago, Illinois, is set on fire one day after the shop's owner and 15 other individuals are convicted of trading and selling endangered tiger meat. An official ALF communiqué claims the arson was conducted to "further extend the sentence handed down by federal courts." It warns those involved in the exotic meat scandal to "be careful, because we know who you are and where you live. Pray for extended jail time." Damages are estimated at $100,000.

- *April 8:* Bright yellow and blue paint is used to scrawl "No Blood for Oil," "SUVs Suck," "Killer," "ELF," and other slogans on at least 60 trucks and sport utility vehicles in the Santa Cruz, California, area. A local Ford and Lincoln Mercury car dealership sustains most of the damage, although several vehicles belonging to nearby residents are also targeted.

- *May 3:* Two plastic jugs filled with a flammable liquid are left under two SUVs at a Chico, California, car dealership. FBI investigators determine that the incendiary devices are similar to those used in the failed firebombing of a local McDonald's on March 3, 2003. An anonymous communiqué sent to the *Chico Enterprise Record* claims the attack is in protest of SUVs as "death machines," "gas hogs" and an "elite status symbol for the upper class."

- *May 18:* The FBI suspects Stop Huntingdon Animal Cruelty (SHAC) in an attack on Legacy Trading in Oklahoma City, Oklahoma, during which vandals break a window and the glass on the front door of the company's main office. Red paint is also poured inside the building and on the sidewalk outside. The damage is estimated at $4,000. At the time of the attack, Legacy Trading was one of the few investment firms still trading the stock of drug and chemical tester Huntingdon Life Sciences.

- *June 2:* Arsonists set fire to a vacant house at the Sterling Oaks development in Chico, California, and leave graffiti reading "Save Our Bio Region. ELF." The fire causes little damage because water released from a melted PVC tube douses the flames.

- *June 4:* Two houses in late stages of construction in a suburban development in Washington Township, Michigan, are burned to the ground. Graffiti reading "ELF" and "Stop Sprawl" is spray-painted on nearby construction equipment. The houses had a combined value of $700,000.

- *June 23–25:* An international agricultural conference in Sacramento, California, draws hundreds of activists protesting the development and use of bioengineered food. The nonviolent civil disobedience results in 75 arrests, most of them for failure to disperse.

- *August 1:* Arsonists destroy a five-story apartment under construction in San Diego's upscale University Towne Centre district, causing $50 million in damage. A banner found nearby says, "If you build it, we will burn it. ELF."

- **August 22:** The ELF claims responsibility for attacks on four auto dealerships and several privately owned cars in Southern California's San Gabriel Valley. Two fires at the Clippinger Chevrolet dealership in West Covina damage a warehouse where service parts are stored, destroy 20 H2 Hummers, and seriously damage 20 more, causing an estimated $1 million in damage. Cars at the other dealerships are sprayed with graffiti reading "earth raper," "I'm a greedy little pig," "I love pollution," "Fat lazy Americans," and "ELF." On September 12, 2003, federal authorities arrest 25-year-old Josh Connole, a peace activist living in a Pomona commune, in connection with the arsons. He is released 48 hours later because authorities lacked evidence to charge him with a crime.
- **August 25:** Animal activists release 10,000 Blue Iris minks from the Roesler Brothers Fur Farm in Sultan, Washington. The ALF claims responsibility.
- **August 28:** Two homemade bombs explode outside the headquarters of Chiron Corporation in Emeryville, California. Chiron, a biotech firm, had contracted in the past with Huntingdon Life Sciences (HLS) to perform animal experiments with medical compounds it had developed. A group called Revolutionary Cells, which the FBI believes is part of the ALF, takes credit. Chiron officials say that the bombings follow a long string of "harassment incidents" that started in May and included etching the words "Puppy Killer" in acid on a company executive's car, dumping rotten fruit at the home of another company executive, and leaving "stink bombs" in employee mailboxes.
- **September 10:** In the midst of increasing criticism of the USA PATRIOT Act by civil libertarians and many politicians, President George W. Bush calls on Congress to "untie the hands of our law enforcement officials so they can fight and win the war against terror." Among his proposals are allowing the attorney general to obtain phone records and other information about suspected terrorists without getting a search warrant, adding terrorism to the list of crimes for which defendants would be denied bail without needing to prove they pose a danger to the community or a flight risk, and increasing the number of terrorism-related crimes subject to the death penalty, including attacking a national defense installation and sabotaging a nuclear facility.
- **September 19:** Arsonists set fire to upscale homes under construction at two different sites in San Diego, California. Four homes are destroyed and two are damaged. Banners are left at both sites, one of which reads, "Development equals destruction. Stop raping nature. The ELFs are mad."

- **September 24:** Animal rights activists destroy roughly $300,000 worth of computers and equipment at the Inhalation Toxicology Research facility at Louisiana State University in Baton Rouge. The Animal Liberation Front (ALF) mails a letter to the university's student newspaper, *The Reveille*, taking credit for the act and calling on environmental medicine professor Dr. Arthur Perm to end his "cruel" research into the effects of pollutants on animals.
- **September 26:** A small predawn bomb breaks windows and cracks stucco at Shaklee Corporation's headquarters in Pleasanton, California. Shaklee had earned a place on People for the Ethical Treatment of Animal's list of companies that do not test on animals, but its parent company, Huntingdon Life Sciences, has been targeted by animal rights extremists. Although no one takes credit, a member of Stop Huntingdon Animal Cruelty says, "It is appropriate that Shaklee would receive pressure to put pressure on their bosses to drop Huntingdon."
- **October 16:** Representative Chris Chocola of Indiana introduces the Stop Terrorism of Property Act of 2003 to the House of Representatives. The legislation would create a new category of federal crime specifically aimed at ecoterrorism and anyone who "intentionally damages the property of another with the intent to influence the public with regard to conduct the offender considers harmful to the environment." Chocola's proposal was prompted by the Earth Liberation Front's repeated attacks on Humvees, which are assembled at a factory in his district.
- **October 24:** A Wal-Mart retail store under construction in Martinsville, Indiana, is vandalized, resulting in more than $10,000 in damages. Windows are smashed, tires are slashed, fuel tanks are filled with sand, and hydraulic hoses are severed on more than a dozen pieces of heavy equipment left overnight on the site. "Stop the Wal-Mart Empire," "Take that, Wal-Mart Giant," and other slogans are painted on some of the vehicles, as well as on a block wall on the site. The Earth Liberation Front takes credit for the incident but retracts its claim on November 3, saying that the earlier announcement was made in error.

2004

- **January 15:** The Sport Utility Vehicle Owners of America (SUVOA) calls on Attorney General John Ashcroft and Secretary of Homeland Security Tom Ridge to increase efforts to arrest and prosecute activists involved in the Earth Liberation Front.
- **January 23:** U.S. District Judge Audrey Collins rules that the USA PATRIOT Act's ban on providing "expert advice or assistance" is impermissibly vague and therefore in violation of the First and Fifth Amendments. She explains that "the USA Patriot Act places no limitation on the

type of expert advice and assistance which is prohibited and instead bans the provision of all expert advice and assistance regardless of its nature." The ruling marks the first court decision to declare a portion of the USA PATRIOT Act of 2001 unconstitutional.

- *March 9:* Federal Bureau of Investigation (FBI) agents arrest physics graduate student William Cottrell in Los Angeles in connection with fire-bomb and graffiti attacks on SUVs in Southern California on August 22. Authorities accuse him of using an alias to send e-mails to the *Los Angeles Times* boasting of the crimes and taunting the FBI. As proof of his involvement in the attacks, the author of the e-mails had mentioned a math equation that was written on one of the SUVs but not publicized. Cottrell, 23, faces arson and vandalism charges.
- *March 15:* Michael James Scarpitti (Tre Arrow), an environmental activist who had been added to the FBI's Most Wanted List in December 2002 on charges that he vandalized logging equipment in Oregon, is arrested in Victoria, British Columbia, Canada. He is charged with shoplifting and lying about his status in Canada, and his bail is set at $2,500. However, authorities continue to hold him in jail to face proceedings for deportation to the United States.
- *May 8:* Greenpeace activists tie themselves to mechanical loaders to prevent a freighter docked in Brazil's port of Paranaguá from mixing conventional soybeans with genetically modified beans. A spokeswoman for the group says that the freighter, called the *Global Wind*, was carrying 30,000 tons of genetically modified soybeans and had docked to pick up another 10,000 tons of natural beans before sailing to Turkey. As a result of Greenpeace's action, the freighter leaves Paranaguá on May 9 without the natural soybeans.

CHAPTER 4

BIOGRAPHICAL LISTING

This chapter provides brief biographies of important American environmentalists and anti-environmentalists. The number of known people accused of direct involvement in ecoterrorism activities is quite small. Therefore, it is important to note that many of these biographical listings have been included for historical perspective, and their subjects should not be considered terrorists. Many of these individuals are or have been affiliated with organizations detailed in Chapter 8. Additional information on these and other activists can be found in books listed in the bibliography in Chapter 7.

Edward Abbey, anarchist philosopher whose writings helped inspire the formation of Earth First! Born in rural Pennsylvania in 1927, Abbey traveled west for the first time during summer 1944 before serving in the military in Italy from 1945 to 1947. During this time, his growing distrust of military regulations steered him toward the study of anarchism, and his anti-draft stance led the FBI to begin a file on him in 1947. Abbey earned his graduate degree in philosophy at University of New Mexico in 1956, arguing in his master's thesis that anarchism was a positive philosophy because it meant maximum democracy, as well as the dispersal of political, economic, and military power. Abbey also rejected the idea that there was a necessary relationship between anarchism and violence, using Russian author Leo Tolstoy and Indian activist Mohandas K. Gandhi to illustrate the melding of anarchism and pacifism. The year after graduation, Abbey studied creative writing under Wallace Stegner at Stanford University, by which time he had already published the novels *Jonathan Troy* (1954) and *The Brave Cowboy* (1956; later made into the movie *Lonely Are the Brave,* starring Kirk Douglas). He went on to write more than 20 books, both fiction and nonfiction, including *Desert Solitaire* (1968), *One Life at a Time, Please* (1987), *The Fool's Progress* (1988), and *Hayduke Lives* (1989). Anger over the construction of Glen Canyon Dam in northern Arizona moved Abbey to write the novel *The Monkey Wrench Gang* (1975), which chronicled the exploits of four characters who sabotage highway construction equipment in southwestern United States. The book ultimately inspired Dave Foreman and others to form Earth First!, and Abbey took part in the group's inaugural media event: a symbolic cracking of the dam he so despised. He died in Tucson, Arizona, on March 14, 1989, of an incurable pancreatic disease. Following written instructions Abbey had left behind, his friends wrapped his body in a sleeping bag, transported it in the bed of a pickup truck to a secret location in the Arizona desert, and buried it illegally under a pile of rocks.

Frank Ambrose, community activist involved with Earth First!, Industrial Workers of the World (IWW), Speak Out for Animals, and the American Lands Alliance. Ambrose was arrested in 2001 and charged with spiking approximately 150 trees in Indiana state forests, an incident for which the Earth Liberation Front (ELF) claimed responsibility. It was the first arrest in the United States related to an ELF action. Activists maintained that Ambrose had nothing to do with the spiking and that his arrest, based on circumstantial evidence, was an incident of harassing an aboveground activist in order to intimidate radical environmentalists.

Ron Arnold, founder of the wise use movement. A longtime journalist who has written many articles from an anti-environmental point of view, Arnold was appointed executive vice president of the Center for the Defense of Free Enterprise (CDFE) in 1984, an organization whose primary purpose has been to counter the efforts of the environmental movement. In 1987, he founded the Free Enterprise Press as an outlet for authors who share his point of view. His own published books include *At the Eye of the Storm: James Watt and the Environmentalists* (1982), *Ecology Wars: Environmentalism As If People Mattered* (1987), *Ecoterror: The Violent Agenda to Save Nature/The World of the Unabomber* (1997), and *Trashing the Economy: How Runaway Environmentalism Is Wrecking America* (1998). In 1988, through the CDFE, Arnold organized the first Multiple Use Strategy Conference (later renamed the Wise Use Leadership Conference) in Reno, Nevada, which inspired the drafting of the 25-point "Wise Use Agenda." Among the points were the "immediate wise development of the petroleum resources of the Arctic National Wildlife Refuge"; the creation of a national mining system under which "all public lands including wilderness and national parks shall be open to mineral and energy production under wise use technologies"; and the National Parks Reform Act, which states that "private firms with expertise in people moving such as Walt Disney should be selected as new transportation concessioners to accommodate and enhance the national park experience without degrading the environment." Arnold has also held positions as an advisory board

member for the National Federal Lands Conference, as a consultant for
Dow Chemical, and, from 1989 to 1991, as the head of the Washington
state chapter of the American Freedom Coalition, the political arm of the
Reverend Sun Myung Moon's Unification Church.

Ilse Washington Asplund, Earth First! activist. One of the Arizona Five,
she was arrested in December 1989 and charged with damaging a chairlift at the Fairfield ski resort near Flagstaff, Arizona, and planning sabotage at the Central Arizona Project and Palo Verde nuclear generating
stations in Arizona; the Diablo Canyon Nuclear Facility in California;
and the Rocky Flats Nuclear Facility in Colorado. Asplund pleaded guilty
and was sentenced to one year in federal prison, five years probation, a
$2,000 fine, and 100 hours of community service.

Marc Baker, biologist and Earth First! activist. One of the Arizona Five, he
was arrested by the FBI in 1989 on charges related to damaging a chairlift at the Fairfield ski resort near Flagstaff, Arizona, and planning sabotage at the Central Arizona Project and Palo Verde nuclear generating
stations in Arizona; the Diablo Canyon Nuclear Facility in California;
and the Rocky Flats Nuclear Facility in Colorado. Also arrested were
Mark Davis, Peg Millet, Dave Foreman, and later Ilse Asplund. Baker
pleaded guilty and was sentenced in September 1991 to one year in federal prison, five months probation, a $5,000 fine, and 100 hours of com-
munity service.

David Barbarash, a former ALF member who served as the group's North
American spokesperson from his home in British Columbia, Canada. A
former associate of Rod Coronado, Barbarash is one of the few ALF activists who has been caught by authorities: He served four months in jail
for releasing 29 cats used in medical research at the University of Alberta
in 1992. He has also faced charges in Canada for mailing letters booby-
trapped with razor blades to fur farmers in 1996. Barbarash denied involvement, pointing out that his adherence to principles of nonviolence
prohibits him from such violent activities as sending razor blades to people. The charges were dropped in 2000 after the Canadian government
was unwilling to disclose evidence from an investigation into Barbarash's
activities. Later charges stemming from a July 2002 raid on Barbarash's
home were also dropped after a judge discovered that the search warrant
used by police was based solely on evidence gathered from a single photocopied newspaper article. In January 2003, Barbarash resigned from his
position as the ALF's North American spokesperson.

Judi Bari, Earth First! activist and organizer. Bari first became interested in
political organizing as a university student in Maryland during the Vietnam War. During the Reagan administration, she moved to Santa Rosa,
California, where she began organizing a civil disobedience crusade

against the U.S.-backed wars in Nicaragua and El Salvador. In 1986, she moved to Mendocino County and worked as a carpenter. Building redwood decks out of 2,000-year-old trees for rich people, she claimed, later convinced her to join Earth First! Bari immediately clashed with members of the movement who felt that using sabotage and tree spiking was justified to protect nature. Bari disagreed, arguing that large, nonviolent demonstrations would do more to alert the nation to the travesty of clear cutting redwood forests in California. She put her theory into practice by organizing the 1990 Redwood Summer campaign, a nationwide call for activists to converge in Northern California for nonviolent demonstrations. In her efforts to form alliances with radical unions representing loggers, she publicly renounced the use of tree spiking. Bari was subsequently criticized by some Earth First! activists of "selling out" and attempting to mainstream the movement. During the run-up to Redwood Summer, Bari received a series of anonymous death threats, which she reported to police. As the campaign was getting under way, on May 24, 1990, Bari and her partner, Darryl Cherney, were injured after a bomb exploded in their car as they drove through Oakland. Bari's pelvis and lower backbone were shattered, leaving her permanently disabled. When she awoke 12 hours later, representatives of the Oakland Police Department and the FBI were on hand to arrest her for possessing explosives. The charges were dropped six weeks later after prosecutors decided there was not enough evidence to secure a conviction. Bari and Cherney later sued the government, claiming their rights had been violated. Meanwhile, she continued her affiliation with Earth First!, suggesting in 1994 that the group mainstream itself and leave sabotage to the ELF. Several weeks before she died of cancer in 1997, Bari videotaped her testimony for the trial, which finally occurred in 2002. The jury found that six of the seven defendants violated Bari and Cherney's First and Fourth Amendment rights by arresting the activists, conducting searches of their homes, and carrying out a smear campaign in the press, calling Earth First! a terrorist organization and calling the activists bombers. Cherney and the estate of Bari were awarded a total of $4.4 million.

Murray Bookchin, anarchist philosopher who developed the theory of social ecology. Born in New York City in 1921 to immigrant parents who had been active in the Russian revolutionary movement, Bookchin became involved in the Communist youth movement and in organizing support for anarchists fighting in the Spanish Civil War. After serving in the U.S. Army during World War II, he worked in an auto factory and became deeply involved in labor organizing. During the 1950s, he became a libertarian socialist and began publishing articles about ecological issues in the United States and West Germany. This, as well as his involvement in countercultural and New Left movements, led Bookchin to develop the concept of social ecology during the 1960s. He wrote several books during this period, including *Our Synthetic Environment* (1962) and *Crisis in Our Cities* (1965). In the late 1960s, he taught at the Alternative University in New York, then at City University of New York in Staten Island. In 1974, he cofounded and directed the Institute for Social Ecology in Plainfield, Vermont, which featured courses in ecophilosophy, social theory, and alternative technologies. From 1974 to 1983, he also taught at Ramapo College in New Jersey. He has continued to develop his theory of social ecology, publishing his ideas in numerous articles and books, including *Toward an Ecological Society* (1981), *The Ecology of Freedom* (1982), *Remaking Society* (1989), *The Philosophy of Social Ecology* (1990), and *Reenchanting Humanity* (1996).

David Brower, former executive director of the Sierra Club, thought by many to be the person most responsible for the creation of the modern environmental movement. Brower attended the University of California at Berkeley but was forced to drop out in 1931 due to financial hardships created by the Great Depression. While working in a candy factory in San Francisco, he spent his spare time hiking and developing his skills as a mountain climber. In 1933, he met members of the Sierra Club for the first time while on a seven-week backpacking trip in the Sierra Nevada. That same year he also met and began a lifelong friendship with outdoor photographer Ansel Adams. In 1935, he began a job as an office worker in Yosemite National Park, climbing and hiking on his days off, but he soon gave up this position to work as an editor at the University of California Press. Brower joined the U.S. Army in 1942, where he taught climbing techniques to soldiers in the elite U.S. Mountain Troops. He was awarded the Bronze Star while serving as an intelligence officer in combat in Italy. After the war, he returned to his editorial position and increased his involvement with the Sierra Club. In 1952, he was appointed the organization's first full-time paid executive director and immediately expanded the group's focus beyond the Sierra Nevada, became more aggressive in confronting environmental issues, and sought to increase membership. During the 1950s, he fought federal plans to build dams in Colorado's Dinosaur National Monument by taking journalists and politicians on float trips through the area to show them the beauty of the landscape that would be submerged by the resulting reservoirs. He also traveled the country giving public speeches about the effect dams would have on public lands that he said belonged to all of them. Finally, he published a photo book called *This Is Dinosaur* and handed a copy to every member of Congress when he testified about his opposition to the dam. This unprecedented lobbying blitz paid off when, in 1955, Congress voted not to build the dam. As part of a compromise, however, Brower agreed not to oppose the construction of the Glen Canyon Dam, a decision that haunted him for the rest of his life, particularly when radical environmentalists later chose the dam as a symbol of everything wrong with the federal government's environmental policies. In 1963, Brower led the Sierra Club in defeating a proposal to build two dams in the Grand Canyon. The campaign involved taking out full-page ads in major newspapers that prompted many people to register their opposition to the project with their congressional representatives. As a result, the Sierra Club's membership grew by 10,000 people, but the organization lost its tax-exempt status when the Internal Revenue Service determined that it had engaged in "substantial" political lobbying. During his tenure as executive director, Brower oversaw a program in which the Sierra Club began publishing coffee-table books featuring photographs of the American wilderness to gain public support for protecting the environment. He also played a major role in the creation of Kings Canyon, Redwood, North Cascades, and Great Basin national parks; in the expansion of the Arctic National Wildlife Refuge; in the creation of national seashores at Point Reyes, Cape Cod, and Fire Island; and in passage of the Wilderness Act of 1964. By the late 1960s, under Brower's guidance, the Sierra Club had come to be considered the most powerful environmental organization in the United States, and membership had grown from 7,000 members in 1952 to 77,000 in 1969. Despite this success, Brower was forced to resign as executive director in 1969 over disputes with the board of directors over the cost of the coffee-table books, the loss of tax-exempt status, and whether to oppose the construction of a nuclear power plant in California's Diablo Canyon. (At the time, many environmentalists saw nuclear power as a nonpolluting alternative to coal; Brower was one of the few who opposed it.) He never completely severed his ties, and in 1977 the Sierra Club awarded Brower its highest honor, the John Muir Award. Immediately after his ouster, he became executive director of the John Muir Institute, which he had founded in 1968, and formed and became president of the new organization Friends of the Earth (FoE). Brower retired as president in 1978 and resigned from the board in 1984, two years after founding Earth Island Institute. Brower continued lending his energy to environmental issues until his death in 2000 at age 88.

Rachel Carson, biologist and author whose writings helped inspire the modern environmental movement. Carson graduated from Johns Hopkins University in Baltimore in 1932 with a degree in zoology. In 1936, she was hired as a biologist with the U.S. Bureau of Fisheries, only the second woman to work at the agency in a nonclerical position. She remained in the agency when it merged with the Bureau of Biological

Survey to become the U.S. Fish and Wildlife Service in 1940. In 1946, Carson was promoted to information specialist, and in 1949 she became biologist and chief editor, a title she retained until she retired in 1951 to focus on writing full time. Her early books included *Under the Sea-Wind* (1941), *The Sea Around Us* (1951), and *The Edge of the Sea* (1955), but she is most famous for *Silent Spring* (1962), in which she presented scientific evidence that widespread use of pesticides and herbicides was harmful to humans and to wildlife, especially birds. The book led President John F. Kennedy to establish the President's Science Advisory Committee to investigate the effects of pesticide use. By the end of 1962, 40 bills regulating the use of pesticides had been introduced in state legislatures across the country. In 1972, as a result of the efforts of Carson and others, the United States banned the use of the pesticide dichloro-diphenyl-trichloro-ethane (DDT).

Connor Cash, environmental activist and arsonist. Cash, 19 years old, was arrested in February 2001 with teenagers Jared McIntyre, Matthew Rammelkamp, and George Mashkow for a series of arsons and attempted arsons of new home construction sites in Long Island, New York. Prosecutors charged Cash with arson conspiracy, claiming he bought gasoline for the other three and instructed them to carry out the arsons because he feared he would face greater charges as an adult if caught. McIntyre stated that these acts were committed in sympathy with the ELF movement.

Darryl Cherney, Earth First! activist and organizer. He moved from New York to Northern California in 1985 and became involved with the Environmental Protection Information Center (EPIC), which used lawsuits to stop logging of old-growth redwoods. He soon found a place in the Earth First! movement as an organizer and a folk singer, writing and performing such songs as "This Monkeywrench of Mine," "Ballad of the Lone Tree Spiker," and "Spike a Tree for Jesus." Cherney met Judi Bari in 1987 and convinced her to join Earth First! despite her misgivings about its macho image and her disagreement with tree spiking as a tactic. Cherney and Bari immediately began organizing resistance to the destruction of ancient redwood forests around Mendocino County, culminating in the 1990 Redwood Summer campaign. Also in 1990, Cherney appeared on *60 Minutes.* When asked by the interviewer what kind of protest action he would consider undertaking if he had a terminal illness and only weeks to live, he replied, "I would definitely do something like strap dynamite on myself and take out the Glen Canyon Dam. Or maybe the Maxxam/Pacific Lumber Company building in Los Angeles after it's closed up for the night," a response he immediately realized was a mistake and that the logging industry used to criticize Earth First! On May 24, 1990, Cherney and Bari were injured after a bomb exploded in their car as they drove through Oakland. The explosion punctured both of Cherney's eardrums and filled one eye with shattered glass. He was taken by ambulance to a hospital, where he was questioned by FBI agents before being moved to another location for six more hours of interrogation. He was arrested for possessing explosives, charges that were dropped six weeks later due to lack of evidence. Bari and Cherney sued the government, claiming their rights had been violated. The trial, held in 2002, ended with the jury ruling that six of the seven defendants violated Bari and Cherney's First and Fourth Amendment rights by arresting the activists, conducting searches of their homes, and carrying out a smear campaign in the press, calling Earth First! a terrorist organization and calling the activists bombers. Cherney and the estate of Bari were awarded a total of $4.4 million. "The message to the FBI from this," Cherney said, "is that American citizens are going to take you to court if you violate their civil rights."

Rodney Coronado, environmental and animal rights activist. In 1985, at age 19, Coronado joined the crew of the Sea Shepherd Conservation Society (SSCS) and later took part in the "Raid on Reykjavík," during which he and another activist caused $1.8 million in damage to a whale processing plant and sank two illegal Icelandic whaling ships. During the early 1990s, he acted as the media spokesperson for the ALF, then lived underground for three years while authorities sought to arrest him for setting fire to the Michigan State University office of Richard Aulerich, who used minks in his experiments in the fields of toxicology and nutrition. Coronado was finally caught on September 27, 1994. In 1995, he was sentenced to 57 months in prison and three years probation and was ordered to pay more than $2.5 million in restitution for his role in firebombing the research facilities at Michigan State University. Following his release from jail, he continued his activism by joining the staff of the *Earth First! Journal* and traveling the country speaking about the environment.

Mark Davis, Earth First! activist. One of the Arizona Five, he was arrested by the FBI along with Peg Millett, Marc Baker, Dave Foreman, and later Ilse Asplund for damaging a chairlift at the Fairfield ski resort near Flagstaff, Arizona, and planning to sabotage the Central Arizona Project and Palo Verde nuclear generating stations in Arizona; the Diablo Canyon Nuclear Facility in California; and the Rocky Flats Nuclear Facility in Colorado. He pleaded guilty and received the harshest sentence of all five defendants: six years in federal prison. He was also ordered to pay restitution to Fairfield in the amount of $19,821.

Bill Devall, deep ecology theorist. A sociologist at Humboldt State University in California, Devall, along with George Sessions, is credited with helping articulate the concept of deep ecology for environmentalists in the United States. During the 1970s, Devall and Sessions published an ecophilosophy newsletter, and their book *Deep Ecology* (1986) became a standard introduction to the concept.

Douglas Joshua Ellerman, animal rights activist. In April 1997, Ellerman turned himself in and confessed to purchasing, constructing, and transporting five pipe bombs to the scene of the March 11, 1997, arson at the Fur Breeders Agricultural co-op in Sandy, Utah. He also admitted setting fire to the facility. He was indicted on June 19, 1997, on 16 counts, and eventually pleaded guilty to three. Ellerman was sentenced to seven years in prison and restitution of $750,000. Though this incident was not officially claimed by the ALF, Ellerman indicated during an interview subsequent to his arrest that he was a member of the group.

Mike Fain, special agent of the Phoenix office of the FBI. During the 1980s, Fain infiltrated Earth First! under the name Mike Tait as part of the federal agency's THERMCON (THERMite CONspiracy) investigation. The operation resulted in the arrests of radical environmentalists Dave Foreman, Mark Davis, Marc Baker, Peg Millett, and Ilse W. Asplund.

Dave Foreman, environmental activist and cofounder of Earth First! In 1964, as a high school student, Foreman campaigned for Republican Barry Goldwater's presidential campaign. He attended the University of New Mexico, where in 1966 he became state chair of Young Americans for Freedom, a conservative libertarian youth organization. The following year, at the height of the Vietnam War, he joined the U.S. Marines Corps but soon realized he had made a mistake. Declaring himself a communist, he deserted and was later discharged after spending one month in jail. In 1971, he became involved in environmental activism with the Black Mesa Defense Fund and later with the New Mexico Wilderness Study Committee. In 1973, Foreman was hired as the Wilderness Society's southwest representative, working as a watchdog during the U.S. Forest Service's first Roadless Area Review and Evaluation (RARE). In 1978, he moved to Washington, D.C., to work as the Wilderness Society's coordinator of Wilderness Affairs, a liaison between the field operation and the lobbying staff. After the results of RARE II were announced the following year, the frustrated Foreman returned to New Mexico and resumed work as the organization's southwest representative. His resentment over making too many compromises during his lobbying efforts led Foreman to resign in June 1980. Shortly afterward, he cofounded the radical group Earth First! as a means to take direct action on environmental issues. The group's first public protest occurred the following year, when members used black plastic to create the illusion of a crack in the Glen Canyon Dam, a symbol of the environmental destruction of the

Ecoterrorism

American Southwest. In 1985, Foreman published *Ecodefense: A Field Guide to Monkeywrenching*, which provided instructions on how to spike trees, disable heavy equipment, and destroy billboards. A few years later, Foreman divorced himself from the movement, declaring himself uncomfortable with the countercultural, leftist bent of many new Earth First! activists. In 1991, he was tried on charges of conspiring with four others to sabotage nuclear power plants in California, Colorado, and Arizona. Through a plea bargain, Foreman escaped jail time. The same year, he founded the Wildlands Project, whose purpose was to "re-wild" America by making 50 percent of its land off-limits to human occupation and development. He also cofounded the conservation journal *Wild Earth*. In 1995, he was elected to a three-year term as a Sierra Club director. After stepping down, Foreman refocused his attention on his work with the Wildlands Project.

The Fox, an anonymous activist who committed a number of widely publicized acts of sabotage against polluting corporations in Illinois in the early 1970s. Among the Fox's acts were plugging a drain at a soap manufacturing plant with bales of straw, rocks, and logs; installing a cap on the chimney of an aluminum processing company; hanging signs attacking U.S. Steel all over Chicago, including a 60-foot banner on a railroad bridge over the Indiana Toll Road that, mocking a current ad campaign by the company, read "We're Involved—in Killing Lake Michigan. U.S. Steel"; and walking into the Chicago office of a vice president of U.S. Steel and dumping a container of sewage the Fox had collected from the U.S. Steel drains. The Fox also sent thousands of self-adhesive stickers to sympathizers around the country to stick on bars of Dial soap, warning consumers that the company pollutes the air. These exploits, which the Fox equated to stopping someone who was beating a dog or strangling another human to death, were widely reported by *Time*, *Newsweek*, and the *National Observer*, and the Fox even granted an interview with *Chicago Daily News* columnist Mike Royko. Despite efforts to catch the Fox, including a rumored reward offered by at least one manufacturing firm, the activist was never caught or identified.

Elizabeth Dodson Gray, ecofeminist author and theologian. She is most well known for her book *Green Paradise Lost* (1981), which ties feminist critiques of Western philosophy, religion, and psychology with ecological ideas. Dodson Gray has also served as codirector of the Bolton Institute for a Sustainable Future and coordinator of the Theological Opportunities Program at Harvard Divinity School.

Julia Hill (Butterfly Hill), environmental activist. Hill attracted worldwide attention for living in a 180-foot-tall California Coast redwood tree from December 10, 1997, to December 18, 1999, with the aim of preventing it from being cut down. In 2001, she published an account of her effort titled *The Legacy of Luna.*

Mike Jakubel, Earth First! activist and rock climber. Jakubel is credited with originating the use of tree sitting in the United States in 1985 to stop a timber cut in Oregon. Although he was arrested after only one day, the tactic was refined by other activists and became an important tactic for radical environmentalists.

Theodore Kaczynski (the Unabomber), a former mathematics professor who became known as the Unabomber for sending letter bombs to people involved in technology-based industries. In 1967, having attended Harvard University as an undergraduate, Kaczynski earned his Ph.D. from the University of Michigan and moved to California to teach math at the University of California at Berkeley. In 1969, he resigned from his teaching position and two years later moved into a cabin he had built on land he and his brother, David, had purchased near Lincoln, Montana. This became Kaczynski's base of operations for a homemade bombing campaign that, between 1975 and 1995, killed three people and injured 23. In 1995, assured that the bombings would stop if it complied, the *Washington Post* and the *New York Times* published the Unabomber's anti-industrial manifesto. Kaczynski's brother, recognizing Theodore's writing style, tipped off the FBI. Kaczynski, convicted for the killings, pled guilty and received four life sentences plus 30 years. A later appeal was unsuccessful.

Ron Kezar, a member of the Sierra Club and a seasonal worker for the Park Service credited with cofounding Earth First! along with Dave Foreman, Bart Koehler, Mike Roselle, and Howie Wolke during a trip to the Sonora Desert in 1980.

Bart Koehler, cofounder of Earth First! Koehler graduated from the University of Wyoming's outdoor recreation, resource management, and planning program. His thesis, *An Evaluation of Roadless Areas in the Medicine Bow National Forest,* was used for years by environmentalists in disputes with the U.S. Forest Service. He began working part-time as Wilderness Society field representative in Wyoming in 1973, and also worked as executive director of the Wyoming Outdoor Council. In 1975, he became a full-time representative for the Wilderness Society. In 1980, angry over the findings of the USFS's RARE II, Koehler disavowed his work with mainstream environmental organizations and cofounded Earth First! along with Dave Foreman, Ron Kezar, Mike Roselle, and Howie Wolke. Koehler later became director of the Southeast Alaska Conservation Council.

Aldo Leopold, preservationist and nature writer. A graduate of the Yale School of Forestry, Leopold joined the U.S. Forest Service in 1909 and began work inventorying potential timber resources in the White

Mountains of eastern Arizona. While there, he and his crew shot a wolf. Of the incident, Leopold famously wrote that seeing the "fierce green fire dying" in the wolf's eyes changed his view of the wilderness, and he realized that animals deserved to exist for their own sake. In 1911, Leopold transferred to Carson National Forest in New Mexico and was promoted to supervisor in 1912. His experience led him to publish a guidebook for foresters titled *Game and Fish Handbook* (1915) and also establish the New Mexico Game Protective Association (NMGPA) to reform wildlife law enforcement and establish new game refuges. Leopold and forester Arthur Carhart successfully lobbied for the preservation of an undeveloped area in Colorado's White River National Forest in 1921. Three years later, at Leopold's urging, the USFS designated a 574,000-acre area in New Mexico's Gila National Forest as the first official wilderness area in a national forest; this later became the template for passage of the Wilderness Act of 1964. Also in 1924, he was appointed associate director of the Forest products laboratory in Madison, Wisconsin, but resigned from the USFS in 1928 when a promised promotion to director never occurred. The University of Wisconsin created a chair of game management for him in 1934 so he could teach *Game Management*, a book he had written based on a large-scale survey of game populations while working as a consultant for the Sporting Arms and Ammunitions Manufacturers Association. In teaching the class, he became the first professor of game management in the United States. Also in 1934 he, along with Jay Norwood Darling and Thomas Beck, was appointed by President Franklin D. Roosevelt to serve on the President's Committee on Wild-Life Restoration, formed to devise a plan to reverse the rapid decline in waterfowl populations across the nation. The resulting report urged the federal government to restore nesting areas by creating several million acres of new wildlife refuges. Later that year, Leopold helped establish the arboretum at the University of Wisconsin, a 245-acre parcel of land that students and faculty members tried to restore to its natural state. Leopold began a similar project the following year on his own land in Sauk County, Wisconsin, and also became one of the eight cofounders of the Wilderness Society. During the 1940s, he wrote *A Sand County Almanac*, a compendium of notes and journal entries focusing on his nature restoration work at the family farm. In 1948, after a long search, he found a publisher but died seven days later of a heart attack sustained while fighting a grass fire on a neighbor's farm. The book was published in 1949 and included "The Land Ethic," in which he suggested extending ethics beyond human-to-human and human-to-society relations to include "man's relation to the land and to the animals and plants which grow upon it." It was here that he wrote his often-quoted belief: "A thing is right when it tends to preserve the integrity, stability, and beauty of the biotic community. It is wrong when it tends otherwise." Leopold was posthumously honored in 1978 with the John Burroughs Medal for his lifework and for his authorship of *A Sand County Almanac.*

Jack Loeffler, environmental activist. In 1970, Loeffler began a campaign to prevent Peabody Coal Company from strip mining 26,000 acres of Black Mesa, located on Navajo and Hopi land in Arizona. His organization, Black Mesa Defense Fund, appealed to the public through television appearances, radio interviews, and articles in national magazines. It also filed six lawsuits, produced a film about the mine, and lobbied government agencies. Members of the organization were also suspects in a failed attempt to blow up the coal slurry line at the mining site.

Ned Ludd, a fabric weaver in Nottingham, England, during the 19th century. Fearing that he and his coworkers would lose their jobs due to automation of the weaving process, Ludd incited a rebellion (lasting from 1811 to 1816) aimed at sabotaging the new looms. The term *Luddite* has come to denote anyone who is critical of new technology. Ludd was considered a hero to many original Earth First! activists, who sometimes referred to themselves as neo-Luddites.

Thomas Malthus, 18th-century British writer who theorized that the world's population would increase more rapidly than the capacity to grow food, leading to mass starvation. The term *Malthusian* is now often used to describe any person who predicts imminent disaster for the human race as a result of environmental degradation.

George Perkins Marsh, author who defined the basic principles of conservation. In his book *Man and Nature* (1864), Marsh used examples from nature to illustrate the relations among soil, water, and plants. He wrote that humanity's "power to transform the natural world should entail a commensurate sense of responsibility" and theorized that many past civilizations had failed because they wasted natural resources, an idea that contradicted the widespread view that nature existed to be tamed and conquered. The philosophy of the book became central to the conservation movement and helped persuade the federal government to create parks such as Yellowstone in 1872 to curb the dwindling wilderness.

George Mashkow, environmental activist. Mashkow, along with Jared McIntyre, Matthew Rammelkamp, and Connor Cash, was arrested in February 2001 for a series of arsons and attempted arsons of new home construction sites in Long Island, New York. At age 17, he pled guilty as an adult to charges of arson and arson conspiracy and agreed to cooperate with investigations into the ELF/ALF.

Jared McIntyre, environmental activist. McIntyre and three others were arrested in February 2001 and charged with arson and arson conspiracy in relation to a series of arsons and attempted arsons of new home construction sites in Long Island, New York. He pled guilty to the charges and stated that these acts were committed in sympathy with the ELF.

David McTaggart, Canadian Greenpeace activist. In spring 1972, McTaggart and three volunteers sailed the boat *Greenpeace III* to the Mururoa Atoll in the Pacific Ocean to protest nuclear tests by the French government. A video recording showing a French military vessel ramming and damaging McTaggart's boat generated worldwide publicity and placed the nuclear tests under scrutiny. In New Zealand and Australia, the negative publicity helped elect officials who promised to oppose the tests. In summer 1973, McTaggart sailed the repaired *Greenpeace III* back to the Mururoa Atoll, where French soldiers boarded the ship and beat McTaggart and navigator Nigel Ingram with rubber truncheons. McTaggart suffered permanent partial loss of vision in his left eye. In June 1975, a French court ruled that the ramming of *Greenpeace III* by the French navy violated international rules of the sea but claimed the court was "without jurisdiction" in the matter of the beating. Meanwhile, public pressure in France forced the ruling Gaullist party to end atmospheric nuclear tests in spring 1974.

Carolyn Merchant, professor of environmental history, philosophy, and ethics at the University of California at Berkeley. Merchant's book *The Death of Nature* (1980), considered a classic of ecofeminist philosophy, explores the idea that the view of the cosmos as an organism was replaced by the scientific revolution of 16th- and 17th-century Europe with the idea that the universe works more like a machine. This mechanical model, she claimed, has allowed those in power to justify the domination of both nature and women.

Peg Millett, Earth First! activist. She received a bachelor's degree in natural history and liberal arts at Prescott College in Arizona in 1983. In 1985, she attended the Round River Rendezvous sponsored by Earth First! and became an active member. One of the Arizona Five, she was arrested by the FBI in 1989 on charges related to damaging a chairlift at the Fairfield ski resort near Flagstaff, Arizona, and planning sabotage at the Central Arizona Project and Palo Verde nuclear generating stations in Arizona; the Diablo Canyon Nuclear Facility in California; and the Rocky Flats Nuclear Facility in Colorado. Also arrested were Marc Baker, Mark Davis, Dave Foreman, and later Ilse Asplund. As the result of a plea bargain, she pled guilty and was convicted of "aiding and abetting in the malicious destruction" of the chairlift at Fairfield. Millet served three years in federal prison without parole, and was ordered to pay restitution to Fairfield in the amount of $19,821.

John Muir, founder of the Sierra Club. Born in Scotland in 1838, he moved to the United States with his family in 1849 and settled in Wisconsin. In

1867, after studying botany and chemistry at the University of Wisconsin, Muir incurred a severe eye injury while fixing a machine belt (from which he ultimately recovered) that prompted him to dedicate his life to studying "the inventions of God." He set out that same year on a 1,000-mile walk through the southern United States to the Gulf of Mexico, keeping a meticulous journal of observations of nature (published in 1916 as *A Thousand-Mile Walk to the Gulf*) along the way. Muir reached San Francisco in 1868, from where he traveled to the Sierra Nevada for the first time and worked herding sheep and sawing lumber. While there, his observations led him to develop the now-accepted theory that Yosemite Valley was carved by glaciers rather than shaped by a cataclysmic earthquake as most geologists of the time believed. During the 1870s, Muir began publishing articles on the natural wonders of the Sierra Nevada, a venture he put on hold during much of the 1880s to concentrate on running a farm near San Francisco with his wife. In 1889, he returned to writing articles, published in Robert Underwood Johnson's *Century* magazine, in an effort to gain public support for the idea of turning Yosemite Valley into a national park, a goal that was achieved by an act of Congress in 1890. Two years later, Muir founded the Sierra Club with the goal of enlisting "the support and cooperation of the people and the government in preserving the forests and other natural features of the Sierra Nevada." Success in the Yosemite Valley campaign inspired Muir to spend the 1890s successfully pressuring the federal government to establish a system of forest reserves (later national forests) in the surrounding region. In 1903, Muir spent four days in Yosemite with Theodore Roosevelt, prompting the president to take legislative action to halt the widespread degradation of American wilderness. Muir's most famous defeat came in 1913, when officials from the city of San Francisco, citing the need for more water and power, built a dam in Yosemite National Park that flooded picturesque Hetch Hetchy Valley. Muir fought to stop construction of the dam because he thought it would undermine the integrity of the park system and because he did not want to see the valley flooded. He died of pneumonia on Christmas Eve the year after Congress approved construction of the dam.

Arne Naess, Norwegian philosopher who developed the concept of deep ecology. Naess earned his doctorate in 1936 and worked as a professor of philosophy at the University of Oslo from 1939 to 1969, then as a freelance philosopher and naturalist. A veteran of the international peace movement, he became active in environmental issues and developed the philosophy of deep ecology during the early 1970s. He has written numerous books and articles on deep ecology and other philosophical subjects, and he founded *Inquiry*, an interdisciplinary journal of philosophy.

Ecoterrorism

Ingrid Newkirk, cofounder of People for the Ethical Treatment of Animals (PETA). In 1972, while living in Maryland and studying to become a stockbroker, she witnessed nearly a dozen cats being "put down" at an animal shelter. The incident prompted her to quit the brokerage business and start working at the shelter, where she sought to protect the animals from the abuse of coworkers. After a brief time at the shelter, Newkirk worked as a deputy sheriff for Montgomery County, Maryland, focusing on animal cruelty cases. In 1976, she was put in charge of the Washington, D.C., Commission on Public Health's animal disease control division. By 1980, she had become a vegetarian and decided that it was morally unacceptable to use animals for food, clothing, or entertainment. Along with Alex Pacheco, Newkirk founded PETA as a radical alternative to existing animal welfare organizations. The group first made headlines in 1981 when Pacheco investigated the treatment of experimental monkeys in a Silver Spring, Maryland, laboratory, resulting in the first police raid of a U.S. research laboratory on suspicion of animal cruelty. PETA has since grown into the world's largest and best-known animal rights organization. In 1999, Pacheco left PETA to pursue other goals, leaving Newkirk as the sole leader of the group.

Leslie James Pickering, former ELF press officer and cofounder of Arissa. In 1996, after dropping out of high school, Pickering became involved with the Liberation Collective, a Portland, Oregon, based organization dedicated to conducting protest and direct action campaigns against vivisection, war, globalization, and other issues. The following year, Pickering and Craig Rosebraugh began to receive and publish anonymous communiqués declaring certain actions to be caused by the ELF. Pickering served as the ELF's press officer through the Liberation Collective until 2000, when he and Rosebraugh split from the collective and founded the North American Earth Liberation Front Press Office (NAELFPO). The new office immediately became the target of repeated federal law enforcement raids and grand jury subpoenas. In 2001, less than a week before the 9/11 terrorist attacks, Pickering and Rosebraugh both resigned from NAELFPO. Pickering briefly reemerged as an ELF spokesperson in February 2002 to criticize the "war on terrorism," the USA PATRIOT Act of 2001, and congressional hearings on ecoterrorism for which Rosebraugh had been subpoenaed to testify. During this time, Pickering began using increasingly violent rhetoric, claiming that the ELF was part of a larger struggle for revolutionary change. Following his second resignation, he cofounded Arissa, which he described as "an emerging revolutionary effort."

Gifford Pinchot, first head of the U.S. Forest Service (USFS). Pinchot graduated from Yale University in 1889. The first American to choose

142

forestry as a career, he enrolled in the French Forest School in Nancy, France, since no schools in the United States taught such a curriculum. After returning to the United States in 1892, Pinchot worked as a forester at Biltmore (George W. Vanderbilt's North Carolina estate), then as chief forester of the U.S. Department of Agriculture. In 1905, President Theodore Roosevelt appointed him head of the newly created USFS. Pinchot's approach to forestry was based, as he once wrote, on making "the forest produce the largest possible amount of whatever crop or service will be most useful." This utilitarian emphasis on natural resources (known as conservation), still preferred by the USFS, has been strongly criticized by radical environmentalists, who instead advocate preservation, or protecting nature for its own sake.

Matthew Rammelkamp, environmental activist. In February 2001, Rammelkamp, Jared McIntyre, George Mashkow, and Connor Cash were arrested for setting fire to a series of new homes in Long Island, New York. Rammelkamp, along with Mashkow, pled guilty as an adult (he was 17 at the time of his arrest) and agreed to cooperate with investigations into the ELF/ALF.

Theodore Roosevelt, conservation-minded 26th president of the United States. Born in New York City, Roosevelt developed an appreciation for nature while growing up on the western plains of the United States. When he became president in 1901, he declared that conservation would be one of his administration's top priorities. He took a utilitarian approach, emphasizing the practical use of resources rather than preservation of nature for its own sake. In 1903, he spent several days in Yosemite Valley under the guidance of John Muir, who persuaded the president to cede the area to federal control so it could be declared a national park. During his tenure in office, Roosevelt expanded the national forest system from 42 million acres to 172 million acres, and urged Congress to create six new national parks and 51 national wildlife refuges. He also promoted passage of the Lacey Antiquities Act, which gave the president the power to create national monuments by executive order. Roosevelt promptly created 18 national monuments in the western United States. Many consider his greatest accomplishment to be the organization of the first Conservation Conference in 1908, during which he convinced state officials that the main goal of conservation was to protect human health. For conservationists, this remains one of the strongest arguments in favor of regulating the use of natural resources.

Craig Rosebraugh, former ELF spokesperson and cofounder of Arissa. The owner of a vegan bakery in Portland, Oregon, Rosebraugh began receiving anonymous ELF statements and communiqués in 1997, which he then prepared as press releases and sent to the media. Though he claimed not to be a member of the ELF and was never directly implicated in any of the group's actions, his office and apartment were repeatedly raided by federal authorities, who confiscated his computer equipment and other belongings. Between 1997 and 2001, Rosebraugh was served with seven subpoenas to testify before federal grand juries investigating the ELF. Following the September 11 terrorist attacks, Rosebraugh was quoted in *Details* magazine as saying, "Anyone in their right mind would realize the United States had it coming." He was subpoenaed to appear before a congressional hearing on ecoterrorism on February 12, 2002, during which he refused to discuss any of the ELF's activities and invoked the Fifth Amendment against self-incrimination more than 50 times. He did, however, submit 11 pages of written testimony in which he claimed that "the slaughter of Iraqi civilians by the U.S. military" during the 1991 Persian Gulf War had prompted him to become involved with the antiwar movement, after which he became active in the animal rights movement. Rosebraugh resigned as the ELF's spokesman shortly after being subpoenaed by Congress and later earned his master's degree from Murray Bookchin's Institute for Social Ecology, where he wrote a thesis titled "Rethinking Nonviolence: Arguing for the Legitimacy of Armed Struggle." In early 2003, he published an open letter calling on activists protesting the war in Iraq to abandon civil disobedience in favor of attacks against property at U.S. military installations, urban centers, corporations, government buildings, and media outlets. Also in 2003, Rosebraugh founded the Arissa Media Group, whose stated mission was to assist in building a "revolutionary consciousness" to "rid the world of one of the greatest terrorist organizations in planetary history, the U.S. government."

Mike Roselle, cofounder of Earth First! During the 1960s, Roselle was active in the anti–Vietnam War movement, taking part in the violent 1968 Democratic convention in Chicago. In 1975, while working in Wyoming, he met Howie Wolke, who introduced him to environmental issues. After reading Edward Abbey's *The Monkey Wrench Gang*, Roselle bought a saw and began cutting down billboards around the city of Jackson. In 1979, he and Wolke began a public relations and monkeywrenching campaign to stop Getty Oil from carrying out its plan to drill in the Gros Ventre section of Wyoming's Bridger-Teton National Forest. That same year, Roselle's environmental views were further radicalized when the U.S. Forest Service, as part of its RARE II findings, recommended fewer than 700,000 acres for wilderness protection in Wyoming. RARE II helped prompt Roselle, Wolke, Dave Foreman, Ron Kezar, and Bart Koehler to renounce mainstream environmentalism and found Earth First! in 1980. In 1986, Roselle, who had always preferred civil disobedience over monkeywrenching as a means to sway public opinion, quit Earth First! and became national campaign coordinator for Greenpeace USA. In the 1990s, he founded the Ruckus Society to train activists in the use of nonviolent direct action, the planning of strategy, the establishment of coalitions, and the use of effective media outreach.

Justin Samuel, animal rights activist. On September 16, 1998, a federal grand jury in Wisconsin indicted Samuel on charges of animal enterprise terrorism stemming from his involvement in mink releases in Wisconsin in 1997 claimed by the ALF. Samuel was apprehended in Belgium and extradited to the United States. On August 30, 2000, Samuel pled guilty to two counts of animal enterprise terrorism and was sentenced on November 3, 2000, to two years in prison and two years' probation. He was also ordered to pay $364,106 in restitution.

Daniel Andreas San Diego, an animal rights activist wanted by the Federal Bureau of Investigation. San Diego is sought for his alleged involvement in the bombings of two corporate offices in California. On August 28, 2003, the Chiron Corporation, located in Emeryville, was bombed twice. On September 26, 2003, the Shaklee Corporation, located in Pleasanton, was bombed once. A federal arrest warrant was issued in the Northern District of California on October 5, 2003, charging San Diego with maliciously damaging and destroying, and attempting to destroy and damage, by means of explosives, buildings and other property. The FBI offered a reward of up to $50,000 for information leading to his arrest.

Mark Sands, environmental activist and arsonist. Sands was arrested on June 14, 2001, on charges stemming from a series of arsons that targeted eight new homes under construction at the edge of the North Phoenix Mountain Preserve near Phoenix, Arizona. Sands had invented a group calling itself the Coalition to Save the Preserves (CSP), whose stated goal was to stop development of previously undeveloped lands, to take credit for the arsons, which caused damage estimated to be in excess of $5 million. On November 7, 2001, Sands pled guilty to 10 counts of extortion and using fire in the commission of a federal felony. He was sentenced to 18 years in prison.

Michael James Scarpitti (Tre Arrow), a radical environmentalist thought to be affiliated with the Earth Liberation Front and sought by the Federal Bureau of Investigation. Scarpitti, also known as Tre Arrow, is wanted for his alleged involvement in the arson of a sand and gravel company in Portland, Oregon, on April 15, 2001. Incendiary devices caused more than $200,000 in damage to three concrete mixing trucks. Scarpitti was indicted by a federal grand jury in Oregon for the incident and charged with four felonies on October 18, 2002. He is also wanted for his alleged involvement in the June 1, 2001, arson at a logging company in Eagle Creek, Oregon. The remains of four incendiary devices were found at the scene along with four unexploded devices. Two logging trucks and a front loader were damaged. Three other activists were arrested for the crime in August 2002, but Scarpitti eluded capture. In December 2002 he was added to the FBI's Most Wanted List with a reward of up to $25,000 for information leading directly to his arrest. On March 15, 2004, Scarpitti was arrested in Victoria, British Columbia, Canada, for shoplifting. Although his bail was set at $2,500, authorities continued to hold him for proceedings to deport him to the United States to face the FBI's charges.

Gerry Spence, trial lawyer from Wyoming who gained a national reputation for representing ordinary people against large corporations. Perhaps most well known for winning a $1.8 million lawsuit brought against Kerr-McGee Corporation by whistleblower Karen Silkwood's family, Spence agreed to defend Dave Foreman pro bono (for the public good, or free of charge) after the Earth First! cofounder's 1989 arrest by the FBI.

Henry David Thoreau, American essayist and poet. In 1845, Thoreau moved to a cabin at Walden Pond near Concord, Massachusetts, to write, live a simple life, and carefully observe his surroundings. In his writings, he rejected the view of nature as a vast wasteland to be conquered and used as raw material for human progress. Instead, he believed that the American wilderness should be preserved for spiritual benefit of everyone, and that preservation of nature was more rewarding than material gain. This deep reverence for nature laid the foundation for contemporary environmental ethics and continues to influence environmental thought to this day.

Karen J. Warren, ecofeminist and professor of philosophy at Macalester College in St. Paul, Minnesota. In the early 1970s, she wrote her doctoral dissertation on the moral and legal status of nonhuman natural objects, such as trees, rivers, and ecosystems. She went on to edit and co-edit several books on ecofeminist philosophy and environmental ethics, and wrote *Ecofeminist Philosophy* (2000) and numerous articles.

Paul Watson, founder of the Sea Shepherd Conservation Society (SSCS) and captain of the vessel *Sea Shepherd II.* One of the founders of Greenpeace, Watson was later ousted because his views were considered too violent. He formed the SSCS in 1977 to pursue his more radical brand of direct action, which included harassing ships engaged in whaling, sealing, and drift-net fishing. Despite his militancy, Watson gained widespread support among environmental activists and celebrities. Watson's group has been referred to as the navy of Earth First!

James Watt, secretary of the interior under President Ronald Reagan. Watt's support for the ethics and actions of the Sagebrush Rebellion prompted environmentalists to demand his removal from office. After Republican congressional defeats in the 1982 election, a "Dump Watt" petition drive gathered momentum and collected nearly 1 million signatures. He was forced to resign in 1983.

Barry Weisberg, codirector of the Bay Area Institute in San Francisco during the 1960s. In 1970, he argued that an authentic environmental movement had yet to develop but that it would progress when "something very basic and very revolutionary is done about the continued destruction of our life support system." Weisberg suggested that militant actions against "corporate despoilers," including sabotage, would be a necessary component of this movement.

Howie Wolke, cofounder of Earth First! Wolke enrolled in the University of New Hampshire's forestry department but became disillusioned when he learned that the program was based on managing tree yields for logging. He switched to a new conservation studies program and graduated in 1974. He then moved to Wyoming and volunteered for the Sierra Club for a short while before meeting Bart Koehler, who helped him get a job with David Brower's Friends of the Earth. Wolke also met Mike Roselle in winter 1975, and in 1979 the two activists began campaigning to prevent Getty Oil from drilling in the Gros Ventre section of Wyoming's Bridger-Teton National Forest. That same year, the U.S. Forest Service, as part of its RARE II findings, recommended fewer than 700,000 acres for wilderness protection in Wyoming. In 1980, an angry Wolke joined Koehler, Roselle, Dave Foreman, and Ron Kezar for a trip to the Sonora Desert, during which Earth First! was founded. In the 1990s, Wolke dedicated himself to protecting the roadless Greater Salmon–Selway ecosystem in Idaho and went on to found Big Wild Adventures, a wilderness guiding service based in the Bitterroot Valley of Montana.

Howard Zahniser, executive director of the Wilderness Society in the 1950s. In 1951, Zahniser drafted a bill that called for congressional designation of wilderness areas. The first version of this Wilderness Act was introduced to Congress by Senator Hubert Humphrey and Representative John Saylor in 1955. After eight years of hearings and 66 revisions, the Wilderness Act was finally signed into law on September 3, 1964, by President Lyndon Johnson. Zahniser, however, had died three months before. The legislation, which protected 9 million acres of wilderness and included mechanisms for designating more wilderness in the future, gave increased impetus to preservation efforts in the United States.

CHAPTER 5

GLOSSARY

This chapter provides definitions for relevant terms that often arise in discussions and literature concerning ecoterrorism.

anarchism   From the Greek term meaning "without a chief or head," this political philosophy asserts that government is inherently corrupt and that justice can only be brought about through the abolition of the state and all other authoritarian institutions. These formal power arrangements should be replaced by organizations based on cooperative agreement among autonomous individuals. Many early members of Earth First! subscribed to Edward Abbey's definition of anarchism as "the maximum possible dispersal of power: political power, economic power, and force—military power," as well as his view that an anarchistic society "would consist of a voluntary association of self-reliant, self-supporting, autonomous community." To many radical environmentalists, such an arrangement would consist of small communities that utilized appropriate technology and operated under the principles of deep ecology rather than anthropocentrism. Others subscribe to the principle of social ecology, which criticizes the role of hierarchies of power in the destruction of wilderness.

animal liberationist   A militant animal rights activist who believes that humans have a moral obligation to free animals from testing laboratories and farms to end their suffering. Many animal liberationists also believe that the by-products of animal exploitation, such as fur coats, should be destroyed.

anthropocentrism   The belief that humans have a special, privileged status in the biosphere. The philosophy of deep ecology opposes this idea, claiming that all living things have equal status.

appropriate technology   For environmentalists, small-scale, renewable, and sustainable energy sources (such as solar or wind power) that would allow small communities to exist without reliance on a centralized public power grid. The desire for such energy is based on the idea that modern

Glossary

technology has spun out of control and is responsible for much of the damage to the environment. While critics see the desire for appropriate technology as proof that radicals are hostile to the notion of progress, environmentalists argue that widespread use of renewable energy would require technological advances that would move society beyond reliance on combustible, Industrial Revolution–era energy sources.

Arizona Five   Originally the Arizona Four, the group of Earth First! activists arrested on May 31 and June 1, 1989, as the result of an FBI investigation called THERMCON (THERMite CONspiracy) for trying to topple an electrical tower in Arizona with a cutting torch. The "four" consisted of Earth First! cofounder Dave Foreman, and activists Mark Davis, Marc Baker, and Peg Millett. In December 1989, activist Ilse W. Asplund became the fifth defendant when she was charged with helping the others destroy an energy facility.

biocentrism   *See* **deep ecology.**

biological diversity (biodiversity)   A measure of the health of a particular ecosystem or of the biosphere as a whole based on the number of different plant and animal species that thrive within it. The most extreme form of biodiversity loss is extinction. Although these losses may be triggered by natural causes, such as natural disasters or competition between species, environmentalists focus on reducing the impact of human causes. These include overexploitation of species (such as overfishing), introduction of exotic species, destruction of habitat (often blamed on the explosive growth of human population), and pollution.

bioregionalism   The belief that the ideal human community should be organized in close accordance with the natural patterns of the specific ecological region in which it exists. These small-scale, self-reliant settlements would allow humans to live in harmony with nature, thereby reducing the overall impact of humans on the planet.

biosphere   Coined by Russian scientist Vladimir Vernadsky in 1929, the term refers collectively to the regions of Earth that are capable of supporting living organisms. This includes areas on land, in the oceans, and in the atmosphere.

biospheric egalitarianism   *See* **deep ecology.**

civil disobedience   A form of public protest that generally involves breaking the law to register discontent about laws or policies that activists deem unjust or unethical. Such actions, usually nonviolent and nondestructive, are generally not intended to subvert the government but rather to persuade authorities to change the law to rectify the perceived injustice. Unlike saboteurs or monkeywrenchers, who operate in secret to avoid arrest and punishment, participants in civil disobedience are usually willing to accept the consequences of their actions by not resisting arrest and by accepting legal penalties imposed on them.

clear cutting The controversial practice among timber companies of logging all the trees in a designated area in one operation. Critics of the practice complain that clear cutting reduces habitat for wildlife by eliminating native forest ecosystems, increases erosion, reduces the recreational value of forestland, and increases the susceptibility of forests to insect damage and diseases. Alternatives to clear cutting advocated by some environmentalists include "selection management," in which individual trees are marked and cut, creating small clearings that allow the forest to regenerate through natural reseeding from remaining trees.

conservation The view that undeveloped forests and grasslands should be managed with the aim of ensuring that future generations will have an adequate supply of the natural resources harvested from these areas. This philosophy resulted in the formation of the U.S. Forest Service (USFS) to manage large areas of the nation's public lands for multiple uses, including logging, hunting, and recreation. Most radical environmentalists reject conservation management in favor of preservation.

deep ecology (biocentrism) Conceived by Norwegian philosopher Arne Naess in the early 1970s and accepted by many radical environmentalists, deep ecology calls for a fundamental shift in human consciousness away from anthropocentrism toward a philosophy that emphasizes the intrinsic value of all natural things and sees all species as having equal worth. Proponents believe that humans, rather than being at the center of life on Earth, are only part of it and that the fate of all life on Earth is intertwined. In response to criticism that this view leads people to value animals above humans, deep ecologists claim that rather than condemning humans in favor of animals, they condemn forms of human behavior that are destructive to life, both human and nonhuman, on the planet. Naess used the term *deep ecology* to distinguish it from *shallow ecology*, a term he says focuses on fighting pollution and resource depletion with the sole aim of preserving the health and affluence of people in industrial countries.

ecofeminism A philosophy developed in the 1970s that synthesizes feminist and environmental concerns. Although ecofeminism encompasses a broad and diverse array of ideas and influences, all variations are based on the notion that the oppression of nature and the oppression of women both stem from the patriarchal structure of Western civilization. Many proponents of the philosophy, for example, perceive a direct connection between the impulses that lead to the rape of women and those impulses that result in the destruction of wilderness.

ecology The scientific study of the relationships between organisms and their environments. The coining of the term is usually attributed to Ernst Haeckel, a 19th-century German natural scientist and philosopher.

Glossary

ecosystem A distinct system of interdependent plants and animals, along with their physical environment.

environmental impact statement (EIS) Mandated by the 1970 National Environmental Policy Act, a required assessment of the environmental impacts of any major government project. Submission of the EIS is followed by a period during which the public can comment on the project's impact and initiate lawsuits against the government if the plans are deemed unsatisfactory.

land ethic A holistic morality originated by naturalist Aldo Leopold in the 1940s that extended the concept of ethics to include entities that are not sentient. Leopold wrote that such a belief system would change "the role of *Homo sapiens* from conqueror of the land community to plain member and citizen of it," a view taken up by proponents of deep ecology in the 1970s. The land ethic was based on three key concepts: Land was not just soil, but a fountain of energy flowing through an interdependent circuit of soils, plants, and animals; the concept of community should be expanded to include soil, water, plants, and animals (collectively known as "the land"); and the health of the land, and therefore its capacity for self-renewal, must be preserved.

Luddite Originally, a follower of 19th-century British fabric weaver Ned Ludd, who convinced fellow workers to destroy labor-saving textile machinery out of fear that its use would diminish employment. During the 1980s some radical environmentalists who favored monkeywrenching as a tactic began referring to themselves as neo-Luddites. The term is sometimes used as a generic description for anyone who is critical of technology.

Malthusian One who predicts imminent disaster for the human race based on overpopulation and environmental degradation. The term stems from the name of Thomas Malthus, an 18th-century British writer who theorized that the world's population would increase more rapidly than the capacity to grow food, leading to mass starvation.

monkeywrenching (ecotage, ecosabotage) Sabotage for the purpose of protecting the environment from development or overuse. Such tactics include destroying heavy equipment, spiking trees, removing survey stakes, defacing or destroying billboards, and slashing the tires of off-road vehicles. The term was taken from Edward Abbey's 1975 novel *The Monkey Wrench Gang*, which helped inspire the formation of Earth First!

neo-paganism A broad term denoting a contemporary religion that has been reconstructed and revived from the beliefs and practices of pre-Christian faiths, including Celtic, Norse, Roman, and Egyptian traditions. Since many of these faiths envision nature as a sentient, all-encompassing presence, they have attracted a number of adherents among environmentalists, radical and otherwise.

---

old-growth forest (ancient forest)   Generally defined as woodland consisting of trees that are more than 250 years old. Radical environmentalists have focused their anti-logging activism on these areas, using tactics such as tree spiking and tree sitting in efforts to stop or slow logging operations.

preservation   The view that undeveloped natural areas have intrinsic value and deserve to exist for their own sake rather than as depositories of natural resources for human use. The Wilderness Act of 1964 originally preserved 9 million acres of wilderness in the United States, and put in place legislative mechanisms to extend protection to more land in the future. Radical environmentalists generally reject conservation in favor of preservation.

restoration ecology   A concept popular among environmentalists that involves repairing damaged ecosystems in an attempt to return them to their natural state. This work may involve removal of exotic species, reintroduction of extirpated species, and removal of human-made structures such as dams, roads, and power lines.

road blockade   A form of nonviolent civil disobedience in which activists use their own bodies to physically prevent the construction of logging roads or to stop access to logging, mining, or oil-drilling areas on already existing roads.

Roadless Area Review and Evaluation (RARE and RARE II)   The first review was initiated by the U.S. Forest Service (USFS) in fall 1971 to determine what areas in national forests were eligible for wilderness designation under the Wilderness Act of 1964. The agency studied nearly 1,500 roadless areas totaling 55.9 million acres, held 300 public meetings, and received 50,000 comments from the public. However, the USFS's refusal to include the impacts of logging and mining in their review led to a widespread threat of lawsuits by environmental groups. The USFS backed down and agreed to re-evaluate its holdings, leading to RARE II in the late 1970s. The second evaluation recommended 10 million acres of land in the lower 48 states and 5 million acres in Alaska for wilderness protection, while 36 million acres were opened for development and 11 million were set aside for further study. These findings prompted another round of intense criticism from environmentalists, who accused the USFS of failing to consider millions of acres that should have been eligible for wilderness designation. The perceived failure of RARE II prompted angry activists, including Earth First! cofounder Dave Foreman, to abandon mainstream lobbying efforts in favor of more radical tactics.

Sagebrush Rebellion   A conservative, anti-environmentalist movement that began in 1979 when the Nevada legislature passed the Sagebrush Rebellion Act, allowing the state to claim sovereignty over federally owned public lands. Proponents sought to replace the conservationist and preservationist ethics with a system that would allow private mining, logging, and ranching interests to utilize the land for personal profit. The grassroots Sagebrush Rebellion was replaced by the corporation-backed wise use movement during the 1980s and 1990s.

shallow ecology   *See* **deep ecology.**

social ecology   A philosophy developed by anarchist Murray Bookchin and inspired by Russian revolutionary Peter Kropotkin that sees the global ecological crisis as a direct outgrowth of the hierarchical and authoritarian social, economic, and political structures that dominate western society. As opposed to nature, where animal and plant communities cooperate to further evolutionary goals, contemporary society is organized to emphasize dominance over nature and other humans. The solution, according to social ecologists, is to reject free-market capitalism in favor of new forms of democratic community, economic production, and technology based on decentralization and minimizing human impact on nature. Bookchin and other proponents have criticized deep ecology as being antihumanist and hopelessly naïve about the need for social change.

strategic lawsuit against public participation (SLAPP)   A civil lawsuit brought by a corporation against citizens who protest its actions. More than 80 percent of SLAPPs are dismissed before trial for lack of merit, and the vast majority end without a cash settlement. However, citizens defending themselves are forced to spend thousands of dollars in legal fees. SLAPPs are often used by logging companies to intimidate environmentalists, as in 1987 when the Alaskan timber company Shee Atika brought a $40 million damage suit against the Sierra Club for the organization's attempt to prevent logging on the traditional hunting grounds of Alaskan natives.

terrorism   As defined by the U.S. government, "premeditated, politically motivated violence perpetrated against noncombatant targets by subnational groups or clandestine agents, usually intended to influence an audience." The USA PATRIOT Act of 2001 broadened the definition of "domestic terrorism" to encompass acts occurring primarily within the territorial jurisdiction of the United States that are "dangerous to human life" and "are a violation of the criminal laws of the United States or of any State" or acts that "appear to be intended to intimidate or coerce a civilian population; to influence the policy of a government by intimidation or coercion; or to affect the conduct of a government by mass destruction, assassination, or kidnapping." Many radical environmentalists argue that monkeywrenching should not be considered an act of terrorism since it is intended to prevent destruction of wilderness rather than to hurt people. Others, however, consider the destruction of objects to be an act of violence. During the 1980s the FBI classified Earth First! as a "soft-core" terrorist group to distinguish its focus on the destruction of property from the killing of people perpetrated by "hard-core" terrorists. This distinction later disappeared in federal discussions of the ELF/ALF.

tree sitting   A form of nonviolent civil disobedience in which activists reside in the upper branches of trees for long periods of time to prevent loggers from cutting them down. Tree sitters rely on support from ground-based sympathizers, who bring them food and other supplies.

tree spiking   A form of monkeywrenching first used by Earth First! in 1984 that involves hammering long nails into the trunks of old-growth trees slated to be logged on public land. Critics argue that the spikes are capable of shattering chain saw blades, putting loggers in danger of injury or even death. Proponents say that proper tree spiking protocol involves warning logging companies and the U.S. Forest Service (USFS) that an area has been spiked, forcing corporations to decide whether the cost of removing spikes is worth the profit to be made. The hope among radical environmentalists is that if the cost of spike removal is too high, the cut will not be made, or that a decreased profit margin will discourage logging in areas where environmental radicals are known to be active. In 1988, Congress, led by Idaho senator James McClure and Oregon senator Mark Hatfield, attached a rider to the Drug Act making tree spiking a felony. In 1990, in an effort to build alliances with unionized timber workers in California, an increasing number of Earth First! activists began denouncing the tactic of tree spiking.

tribalism   The belief among some radical environmentalists that studying the lifestyles of indigenous people around the world can provide valuable lessons for how humans can live in the natural world with minimal impact on the environment.

veganism   A form of vegetarianism that advocates an entirely plant-based diet and rejects the consumption of all animal-based materials, including meat, eggs, honey, milk, butter, and cheese. Defined by proponents not as a mere diet but rather as a philosophy and lifestyle that emphasizes reverence for all life, veganism also encourages the manufacture and use of clothing, shoes, and other commodities made from nonanimal materials.

vivisection   The act of cutting into or dissecting the body of a living animal for the purpose of scientific research or education.

wilderness   As defined by the Wilderness Act of 1964, an area of undeveloped federal land at least 5,000 acres in size that is protected with the purpose of retaining its "primeval character" and natural condition without permanent improvements or human habitation. No temporary roads, no motor vehicles or other forms of mechanical transport, and no structures or installations are allowed in such areas. Although numerous loopholes exist, wilderness designation also curtails such activities as mining, cattle grazing, and oil drilling. Wilderness designation is the most rigorous form of protection a natural area can achieve; environmentalists have therefore sought to maximize the amount of land preserved by the Wilderness Act.

wise use movement   A conservative, anti-environmentalist movement of the 1980s and 1990s that grew out of the earlier Sagebrush Rebellion. While the two movements held similar philosophies, wise use was more successful in growing beyond the grassroots level and gaining the support of industry, right-wing political groups, and fundamentalist Christians. Among other activities, wise use organizations have provided legal aid to private land holders and local industry groups in disputes with the federal government and environmental groups.

PART II

GUIDE TO FURTHER RESEARCH

CHAPTER 6

HOW TO RESEARCH
ECOTERRORISM

Before beginning any research project, it is important to have a topic or theme, a list of key terms and searchable words, and a general idea of how to use the variety of research tools that are now available. This chapter suggests a number of web sites, indexes, and catalogs that will help organize and define the research process and will provide a wide range of information, from a variety of points of view, pertaining to ecoterrorism.

THE INTERNET

The Internet and the World Wide Web offer virtually unlimited amounts of information on ecoterrorism, the wise use movement, and environmentalism. Keep in mind, however, that web sites reflect the agenda and biases of their creators. This is particularly important to keep in mind when visiting sites created by environmentalist groups and wise use organizations, both of which are capable of manipulating or exaggerating statistics to support their point of view. Many public policy research organizations claim to present unbiased information when, in fact, they adhere to a particular political agenda. The authors of these web sites often declare that their information is based on rigorous, objective scientific research, then go on to accuse the opposition of "politicizing" the debate for their own ends. Realize, however, that there are political elements on all sides of the ecoterrorism debate; any information should therefore be weighed against opposing points of view supplied by other web sites and non-Internet resources. For this reason, it is also important, when using statistical information in a report, to cite the source in case questions of validity arise.

Like any research tool, the Internet is most useful if time is taken to learn the various tricks that will allow the researcher to efficiently tap into all the resources and information it has to offer. It is important to remember, however, that although the World Wide Web is an incredible resource, it is best used as a supplement to, rather than a replacement for, research materials that are available only by visiting a public or school library.

Unlike books, newspapers, periodicals, and video documentaries, the Internet is a nonlinear research medium, meaning that the information is not offered in a straight line. The user, rather than the author or producer, decides where to search for information and in what order the information will be received and reviewed. A single web site can provide links to a number of other sites, each of which may, in turn, lead to additional sites. One site that does not appear relevant to the topic at hand may provide access to one or more sites that deal precisely with the subject matter being researched. Therefore, diligence is important. Navigating in this manner can provide large amounts of information, but following a seemingly endless array of links can also cause the researcher to lose track of useful pages. Most Web-hosting services aid in research organization by offering the ability to store "favorite" or "bookmarked" sites that are likely to be revisited in the future. The exact method of bookmarking a web site may vary among Internet providers, but generally there is an icon in the upper right-hand corner that will save the web page being viewed to a "favorites" folder. Another useful feature is the "history" menu, which is a linear list of all sites visited during a research session or in the recent past. This acts as a sort of "bread-crumb trail" that allows surfers to retrace their steps or revisit any site or link that has been hit along the way.

"Surfing the Web" by following links can, as has already been mentioned, lead to large amounts of information, but this inherently haphazard method can also cause researchers to miss important web sites altogether. Using web indexes and search engines can fill in these information gaps.

INDEXES

A web index, or guide, is a site that offers a structured, hierarchical listing or grouping of key terms or subject areas relating to the topic requested. This allows researchers to focus on a particular aspect of a subject and find relevant links and web sites to explore.

Web indexes possess several advantages over random or blind Internet surfing. First, they offer a structured hierarchy of topics and terms that simplify the process of homing in on a specific topic, related subtopic, or link. Second, sites are screened and evaluated for their usefulness and quality by those who compile the index, giving the researcher a better chance of finding more substantial and accurate information. This feature also has its down side, however, which is that the index user is at the mercy of the indexer's judgment about which sites are worth exploring. As with all other research tools, web indexes should therefore be used in conjunction with other tools and methods.

The most popular and user-friendly web index is Yahoo! (http://www.yahoo.com). Researchers can use the homepage's top-level list of topics and follow them to more specific areas, or they can type one or more key words into the search box and receive a list of matching categories and sites. To explore subjects relevant to environmentalism via Yahoo!, the researcher can click on the "Society and Culture" link, then "Environment and Nature." From there, the user can choose from a variety of subtopics, such as "Conservation," "Environmental History," "Ethics," or "Wilderness," depending on the focus of the research. Terrorism in general can also be explored through the "Society and Culture" link, followed by "Crime," then "Types of Crime," and finally "Terrorism." These topics are just suggestions to get started, of course. Since ecoterrorism encompasses a number of social, scientific, political, philosophical, and even religious disciplines, it is useful to keep an open mind about where information can be found. The user should not limit research to the obvious, but should supplement browsing with a direct search to ensure the most comprehensive results.

About.com (http://www.about.com) is similar to Yahoo! but gives greater emphasis to guides prepared by experts in various topics. Information on environmentalism may be found by browsing "News and Issues," then "Environmental Issues" (offering a variety of more specific links), "Globalization Issues" (then "Environment"), "Conservative Politics: U.S." (then "Environment"), or "Liberal Politics: U.S." (then "Environment"). To access information about terrorism, click on "News and Issues," then "Crime/ Punishment," and finally "Terrorism."

Another example of a useful web index is AskJeeves (http://www.ask.com). This site attempts to answer plain-English questions, such as "What year was Earth First! formed?" Sometimes it directly answers the question, and other times it provides a number of possibly useful links it obtains by scanning a series of search engines.

SEARCH ENGINES

When beginning an online research project, several organizations' web sites may come to mind, but there are many more out there that may not be so well known but are highly valuable. This is where search engines come into the picture. A search engine scans web documents for key words or terms provided by the researcher and comes up with a list of relevant web sites to explore. Instead of organizing topically in a top-down fashion, search engines work their way from the bottom up, meaning that they search the Web for key terms and compile their findings into an index. Next, the search engine takes that index and matches the search words to those links that have been flagged as key term matches. Finally, the engine compiles a list based on the sites within the index that match the entered searchable words.

There are hundreds of search engines. Among the most user-friendly and popular are:

Alta Vista (http://www.altavista.com)
Excite (http://www.excite.com)
Google (http://www.google.com)
Hotbot (http://www.hotbot.com/Default.asp)
Lycos (http://www.lycos.com)
WebCrawler (http://www.webcrawler.com)

Search engines are easy to use by employing the same kinds of key words that work with web indexes and library catalogs. A variety of web search tutorials are available online, including one published by Bright Planet (http://www.brightplanet.com/deepcontent/tutorials/search/index.asp).

There are some basic rules for using search engines. When looking for something, use the most specific term or phrase. For example, when researching wildlife affected by logging in the Pacific Northwest, using the phrase *"northern spotted owl"* will result in more useful information than simply entering *"endangered species."* Note that phrases should be placed in quotation marks in the search field if you want them to be matched as phrases rather than as individual words.

When searching for a more general topic, use several descriptive words (nouns are more reliable than verbs), such as *"domestic terrorism statistics."* Most search engines will automatically put pages that match all three terms first on the results list.

Use "wildcards" when a search term may have more than one ending. For example, typing in *"ecoterroris*"* will match both *"ecoterrorism"* and *"ecoterrorist."*

Most search engines support Boolean (AND, OR, NOT) operators that can be used to broaden or limit a search topics. Use AND to narrow a search: *"logging AND protest"* will match only pages that have both terms. Use OR to broaden a search: *"monkeywrenching OR ecotage"* will match any page that has either term. Use NOT to exclude unwanted results: *"ecoterrorism NOT United States"* finds articles about ecoterrorism occurring in countries other than the United States.

Each search engine has its own method of finding and indexing results and will therefore come up with a unique list. It is therefore a good idea to use several different search engines, particularly for a general query. Several "metasearch" programs automate the process of submitting search terms to multiple search engines. These include Metacrawler (http://www.metacrawler. com) and Search.com (http://www.search.com).

FINDING ORGANIZATIONS AND PEOPLE

Web sites of organizations can often be found by entering the name into a search engine. Generally, the best approach is to put the name of the organization into quotation marks, such as *"Earth Liberation Front."* If this does not yield satisfactory results, another approach is to take a guess at the organization's likely web address. The Earth Liberation Front's site, for example, can be found by typing in http://www.earthliberationfront.com. The American Civil Liberties Union is commonly known by the acronym ACLU, so it is no surprise that this agency's web site is http://www.aclu.org. (Keep in mind that noncommercial organization sites normally use the *.org* suffix, government agencies use *.gov,* educational institutions use *.edu,* and businesses use *.com*).

There are several ways to find people on the Internet. One can enter the person's name (in quotes) in a search engine and may find that person's homepage on the Internet. Another way is to contact the person's employer, such as a university for an academic or a corporation for a technical professional. Most such organizations have web pages that include a searchable faculty or employee directory. Finally, one can try one of the people-finder services such as Yahoo! People Search (http://people.yahoo.com) or Big-Foot (http://www.bigfoot.com). This may yield an e-mail address, regular address, and/or phone number.

SPECIFIC RESOURCES

A variety of government, educational, and private web sites offer background material, news, analysis, and other material on topics, groups, and people associated with ecoterrorism research. The following are some of the more useful major sites, broken down by category.

Government Sites

The Federal Bureau of Investigation (http://www.fbi.gov) has information on domestic terrorism, including ecoterrorism. Particularly useful are the annual report *Terrorism in the United States* (http://www.fbi.gov/publications/ terror/terroris.htm) and Domestic Terrorism Section Chief James F. Jarboe's 2002 report *The Threat of Eco-Terrorism* (http://www.fbi.gov/congress/ congress02/jarboe021202.htm).

Ecoterrorism

The Bureau of Alcohol, Tobacco, Firearms and Explosives (http://www.atf.gov), a law enforcement agency within the U.S. Department of Justice, is in charge of investigating arson and suppressing traffic in the illegal use of explosives. The web site contains information that students may find relevant to the study of ecoterrorism.

Radical environmentalists are concerned with the fate of public lands, which are overseen by several government agencies. The U.S. Forest Service (http://www.fs.fed.us) is an agency of the U.S. Department of Agriculture that manages national forests and grasslands. The National Park Service (http://www.nps.gov) oversees the preservation of national parks and monuments. The Bureau of Land Management (http://www.blm.gov/nhp/index.html) is an agency within the U.S. Department of the Interior that administers 261 million acres of public lands, located primarily in the western United States. The U.S. Fish and Wildlife Service (http://www.fws.gov/) is a bureau within the Department of the Interior that manages the National Wildlife Refuge System, as well as thousands of small wetlands and other special management areas. These web sites provide information on projects, policies, research, and recreational opportunities, with links to publications and specific regions under the stewardship of each agency throughout the Unites States.

Academic and Environmental News Sites

Academic sites are primarily concerned with research and building databases of archival information. General information on terrorism can be found at the web site of the Terrorism Research Center (http://www.terrorism.com), which includes links to many other organizations and agencies. The University of Pittsburgh School of Law's Terrorism Law and Policy web site (http://jurist.law.pitt.edu/terrorism.htm) is a good source for relevant news, policy papers, antiterrorism law, and academic commentary.

Many environmental news sites frequently report on events related to radical environmentalism and ecoterrorism. Econet (http://www.igc.org/econet/) provides access to stories and editorials written from an environmentalist and activist perspective. The EnviroLink Network (http://www.envirolink.org) is a nonprofit organization that provides access to thousands of online environmental resources. The Environment News Service (http://www.ens-newswire.com) is a daily international wire service that presents late-breaking environmental news. Issues and events covered include legislation, politics, conferences, lawsuits, international agreements, demonstrations, science and technology, and renewable energy. The Environmental News Network (http://www.enn.com) offers timely environmental news, live chats, interactive quizzes, feature stories, and debate forums aimed at educating users about major environmental issues.

Civil Liberties Sites

Many extremist organizations maintain that laws intended to curb their activities violate their own civil liberties. The American Civil Liberties Union (http://www.aclu.org) is a good source for news and advocacy materials. The web site has several issue pages that are relevant to domestic terrorism:

Criminal Justice: http://www.aclu.org/CriminalJustice/
CriminalJusticeMain.cfm
Free Speech: http://www.aclu.org/FreeSpeech/FreeSpeechMain.cfm
National Security: http://www.aclu.org/NationalSecurity/
NationalSecurityMain.cfm

Civil liberties groups that focus on computer-related issues are also relevant, since much of the legislation concerning extremism and counterterrorism is aimed at increasing law enforcement capabilities in eavesdropping on and monitoring communication. The Electronic Privacy Information Center (http://www.epic.org), the Electronic Frontier Foundation (http://www.eff.org), and the Center for Democracy and Technology (http://www.cdt.org) are all useful for keeping up with these issues.

Radical Environmental and Anti-Environmental Sites

Many radical environmental and anti-environmental groups have their own web sites. Addresses to many of these sites can be found in Chapter 8 (Organizations). Discretion is advised when deciding whether to visit or use sites that may be involved in the promotion of extremist ideologies.

BIBLIOGRAPHIC RESOURCES

Although the Internet and World Wide Web provide virtually unlimited resources for the researcher, libraries and bibliographic resources are still vital assets to any research project. A bibliographic resource is any type of index, catalog, or guide that lists books, texts, periodicals, or printed materials containing articles or chapters related to a subject.

LIBRARY CATALOGS

Most public and academic libraries have placed their card catalogs online. This allows the user to access a library's catalog from any Internet connection, even from home. Viewing a library catalog in advance enables the researcher to develop a comprehensive bibliographic resource list and reserve these resources before signing offline, saving time and frustration.

The Library of Congress (http://catalog.loc.gov) is the largest library catalog available. This site provides advice on search techniques, lists of resources, and catalogs of books, periodicals, maps, photographs, and more.

Online catalogs can be searched by author, title, and subject headings, as well as by matching keywords in the title. Thus a title search for "ecoterrorism" will retrieve all books that have that word somewhere in their title. However, since all books about ecoterrorism may not have that word in the title, it is still necessary to use subject headings to get the best results.

General Library of Congress subject headings under which information on ecoterrorism and radical environmentalism can be found include, but are certainly not limited to, the following:

Animal Liberation Front
Deep Ecology
Earth First!
Earth Liberation Front
Ecoterrorism
Ecoterrorism—United States
Environmental Policy—United States—Citizen Participation
Environmentalism—Political Aspects
Forest Conservation
Green Movement—Citizen Participation
Green Movement—Political Aspects
Old Growth Forests
Sabotage—United States
Terrorism—United States

Once the record of a book or other item has been found, it is a good idea to check for additional subject headings and name headings that may have been previously overlooked. These can be used for additional research.

BOOKSTORE CATALOGS

Another valuable resource is online bookstore catalogs such as Amazon.com (http://www.amazon.com) and Barnes&Noble.com (http://www.barnesand-noble.com). These sites not only offer a convenient way to purchase books related to ecoterrorism but also provide publisher information, lists of related topics and books, and customer reviews. These features allow online bookstore catalogs to be used as another source for annotated bibliographies.

PERIODICAL DATABASES

Most public libraries subscribe to various database services, such as Info-Trac, which offer detailed indexes of hundreds of current and back-issue periodicals. These databases can perform searches based on titles, authors, subjects, or keywords within the text. Depending on the service, the database can provide a listing of bibliographical information (author, title, pages, periodical name, issue, and date), a synopsis and abstract (a brief description of the article), or the article in its entirety.

Many public and academic libraries now have dial-up or Internet access, allowing these periodical databases to be searched from home, school, or the local cybercafé. The periodical database search can often be found in the library's catalog menu or on its homepage. Sometimes a library membership card may be necessary to access the information available on a library's web site, so always check with the desired library for its specific policies.

Another extensive but somewhat time-consuming option for searching for periodicals is to visit the web site of a specific periodical related to environmental or domestic terrorism topics. Often the web address is the periodical's name with *.com* (if commercial), *.gov* (if it is a governmental publication), *.edu* (if it is a university published journal), or *.org* (if it is a publication produced by a public organization) added. Some of these publications may have several years of back issues online.

LEGAL RESEARCH

Gathering and understanding legal research can be more difficult than simply reading through bookstore catalogs and bibliographical indexes. Once again, the Internet proves to be extremely useful by offering a variety of user-friendly ways to research laws and court cases without paging through volumes of court cases in legal libraries (to which the public may not have access).

FINDING LAWS

When federal legislation passes, it becomes part of the U.S. Code, a massive compendium of federal law. The U.S. Code can be searched online at several locations. Perhaps the easiest and most comprehensive is the U.S. Code database compiled by the Office of the Law Revision Counsel (http://uscode. house.gov). Another option is the web site of Cornell University Law School (http://www4.law.cornell.edu/uscode/). The University of Pittsburgh School of Law's Terrorism Law and Policy web site (http://jurist.law.pitt.edu/ terrorism.htm) is a good source for relevant news, policy papers, antiterrorism law, and academic commentary. In general, the fastest way to retrieve a law is by its title and section citation, but phrases and keywords can also be used.

The codes of many states' laws are also available online. Links to the codes for specifics states can be found on the 'Lectric Law Library (http:// www.lectlaw.com/inll/1.htm).

KEEPING UP WITH LEGISLATIVE DEVELOPMENTS

When performing legal research, some pertinent legislation may be pending. Pending legislation can frequently be found by looking at advocacy group sites for both national and state issues.

The Library of Congress's Thomas web site (http://thomas.loc.gov) is a Web-based, user-friendly interface that has many valuable features for keeping up with legislative developments and legal research. The Thomas site allows the user to access proposed legislation to each Congress by entering key terms or a bill number. For example, if the researcher is looking for domestic-terrorism-related legislation, either the bill number can be entered or, if that is not known, key words ("domestic terrorism," for example) can be searched, and a listing of relevant legislation will be compiled.

Clicking on the bill number of one of the items found will display a summary of the legislation, the complete text, its current status, any floor actions, and any other information available. If the bill number is known from the beginning, the legislation can be accessed directly by entering it into the search field.

FINDING COURT DECISIONS

Similar to laws, legal decisions are recorded and organized using a uniform system of citations. The basic elements are *Party 1 v. Party 2*, followed by the volume number, the court, the report number, and the year in parentheses. Here are two examples to illustrate the naming method:

- *Sierra Club v. Morton,* 405 U.S. 727 (1972): In this example, the parties are the Sierra Club (plaintiff) and Morton (defendant). The case can be found in volume 405 of the *United States Supreme Court Reports,* report number 727, and the case was decided in 1972. (The name of the court is not indicated in Supreme Court decisions.)
- *Northern Spotted Owl v. Manuel Lujan,* 758 F. Supp. 621 (1991): In this U.S. Court of Appeals citation, the parties are the northern spotted owl (plaintiff, represented by a consortium of environmental organizations) and Manuel Lujan (defendant), the case can be found in volume 758 of the *Federal Reporter* (covering U.S. Circuit Court and U.S. Court of Appeals decisions) on page 621. The case was decided in 1991.

To locate a decision made by the federal court, the level of the court involved must first be determined: district (lowest level, first stage for most trials), circuit (the main court of appeals), or the Supreme Court. Once this question is answered, the case and the court's ruling can be located on a number of web sites by searching for either the citation or the names of the parties. There are two sites in particular that are useful for calling up cases. The first, the Legal Information Institute web site (http://supct.law. cornell.edu/supct/), contains every Supreme Court decision made since 1990, plus 610 of the most well known and referenced Supreme Court cases. The site also provides several links to other web sites that contain earlier Supreme Court decisions.

The other site, Washlaw Web (http://www.washlaw.edu), maintains a comprehensive database of decisions made at all court levels. In addition, the site has a large list of legal topics and links, making it an excellent resource for any type of legal research.

For more information and tips on researching legal issue, read the "Legal Research FAQ" at http://www.eff.org/legal/law_research.faq. The EFF site also explains advanced research techniques, including "Shepardizing," so called for *Shepard's Case Citations*, which explains how a decision is cited in subsequent cases and whether or not the case was later overturned.

CHAPTER 7

ANNOTATED
BIBLIOGRAPHY

This bibliography lists a representative sample of sources on environmentalism, animal rights, ecoterrorism, and the wise use movement, ranging from scholarly sociological studies to opinion pieces aimed at the general public. Sources have been selected for usefulness to the general reader, currency (though a significant number of "classic" books published before 1990 have been included), and variety of points of view.

Listings in this bibliography are grouped according to the subjects listed below and, within each of these subjects, by type (books, articles, Internet documents, and videos):

General Terrorism
General Environmentalism
General Animal Rights
Radical Environmentalism
Greenpeace and the Sea Shepherd Conservation Society
Earth First!
The Earth Liberation Front and the Animal Liberation Front
Unabomber
Wise Use and Anti-Environmentalism

Note that many of the articles listed here are accessible through periodical databases available on the Internet or at the local library, or on the web sites of the periodicals in which they were published. Also be aware that Web addresses change frequently, and sites can disappear altogether. In entries for Internet documents, a "downloaded" date refers to when the site was last verified as existing online. "Posted" refers to either the date the material was posted on the Web or, if the material originally appeared in another form, the date the material was originally published. In general, listings are current as of mid-2004.

GENERAL TERRORISM

BOOKS

Bovard, James. *Terrorism and Tyranny: Trampling Freedom, Justice and Peace to Rid the World of Evil.* New York: Palgrave Macmillan, 2003. Bovard, a journalist who has written for the *Wall Street Journal* and the *American Spectator,* argues that homeland security measures enacted by the Bush administration in response to September 11 have set dangerous legal precedents that allow the federal government to trample personal liberty. Among the topics covered are the USA PATRIOT Act (which he says "treats every citizen like a suspected terrorist"), attempts to tighten airline security, increased surveillance of individuals, and the detainment of terrorism suspects without legal representation.

Cole, David, and James X. Dempsey. *Terrorism and the Constitution: Sacrificing Civil Liberties in the Name of National Security.* New York: New Press, 2002. The authors, experts on civil rights law, examine the 1996 Anti-Terrorism Act and the 2001 USA PATRIOT Act and conclude that they were passed under the "influences of emotion and political posturing." They argue that the Bush administration's response to the attacks of September 11 repeat past mistakes made by federal policies enacted to combat communists in the 1950s, Central American activists in the 1980s, and Palestinians in the 1990s, all of which sacrificed civil liberties without making the world a safer place. Cole and Dempsey conclude by suggesting ways that the government can fight terrorism without restricting the rights of innocent individuals.

Cronin, Isaac, ed. *Confronting Fear: A History of Terrorism.* New York: Thunder's Mouth Press, 2002. This book is less a comprehensive history and more a collection of essays on various aspects of worldwide terrorism. The introduction doubles as a brief glossary of terms, while essays in the "Pre-History" section cover the 1894 bombing of the Greenwich Observatory and the assassination of U.S. president William McKinley. Subsequent sections include "Political Terrorism," "Religious Terrorism," "Fringe Terrorism" (which includes excerpts from the Unabomber Manifesto), and "Confronting Terrorism."

Laqueur, Walter. *The New Terrorism: Fanaticism and the Arms of Mass Destruction.* New York: Oxford University Press, 1999. Written before the terrorist attacks of September 11, 2001, this book traces the history of terrorism and analyzes the trend away from political radicalism toward acts of terror committed by small groups bent on vengeance and simple destruction. Laqueur covers everything from right-wing militias based in the United States to radical Muslim groups, and speculates on the implications of the use of chemical, biological, and nuclear weapons by terrorists.

The chapter on "exotic terrorism" includes informative sections on ecoterrorism and animal rights activists, although the unquestioning contention that Earth First! activists Judi Bari and Darryl Cherney were injured when a pipe bomb "in their possession" exploded reveals either bias or sloppy research on the part of the author. Strong evidence, including a jury decision against the FBI, supports the theory that that bomb was planted in the car rather than "possessed" by the activists.

Leone, Richard C., and Greg Anrig, Jr., eds. *The War on Our Freedoms: Civil Liberties in an Age of Terrorism.* New York: PublicAffairs, 2003. This collection of essays by top thinkers, scholars, journalists, and historians attempts to show how government officials in the United States have used the perception of an imminent threat from terrorists as an excuse to undermine the judiciary, intimidate the press, and invade the privacy of individuals. As a whole, the book focuses on how the suppression of information by the federal government is antithetical to American values and ideals, and how the war on freedom is just as real and dangerous as the war on terrorism.

Simon, Jeffrey D. *The Terrorist Trap: America's Experience with Terrorism.* 2d ed. Bloomington: Indiana University Press, 2001. Although only passing reference to ecoterrorism is made in the introduction, this book provides a comprehensive history of terrorism around the world, as well as attempts by the U.S. government to combat it. In-depth coverage effectively ends in 1994, the year the first edition was published. In the second edition, more recent events are covered briefly in a new introduction. The book includes black-and-white photographs, endnotes, and a list of interviews conducted by the author in the course of research.

ARTICLES

Tell, David. "The Patriot Act's Surprising Defenders." *The Weekly Standard,* November 3, 2003, p. 9. This article reports on support of the USA PATRIOT Act from Senators Joe Biden of Delaware and Dianne Feinstein of California, both Democrats. Tell writes that the support of more Democrats for the legislation is essential to prevent many Americans from viewing it as an attack on civil liberties.

Wallace, Bill. "The Patriot Act Reconsidered." *PC World,* vol. 22, December 2003, pp. 38+. Wallace looks at those portions of the USA PATRIOT Act that allow the federal government to collect personal data with fewer restrictions on law enforcement, less oversight, and less public accountability for surveillance of electronic communications. Also discussed are eight bills intended to alter the legislation, which is set to expire in 2005.

Annotated Bibliography

INTERNET DOCUMENTS

Jarboe, James F. "Statement of James F. Jarboe, Domestic Terrorism Section Chief, Counterterrorism Division, Federal Bureau of Investigation, on The Threat of Eco-Terrorism Before the House Resources Committee, Subcommittee on Forests and Forest Health." Federal Bureau of Investigation. Available online. URL: http://www.fbi.gov/congress/congress02/jarboe021202.htm. Posted on February 12, 2002. Jarboe provides an overview of ecoterrorism in the United States from the perspective of federal law enforcement, including a brief history of "monkeywrenching" and a run-down of recent arrests.

Lynch, Timothy. "Executive Branch Arrests and Trials (Military Tribunals)." Cato Institute. Available online. URL: http://www.cato.org/testimony/ct-tl120401.html. Posted on December 4, 2001. This article is the transcript of testimony given by Lynch, director of the Cato Institute's Project on Criminal Justice, before the Senate Judiciary Committee. Lynch argues against the use of military tribunals to prosecute U.S. citizens charged with terrorism, claiming that such a process violates the Fourth Amendment. Lynch accuses President George W. Bush of violating the separation of powers inherent in the Constitution by signing an executive order with respect to the indefinite detention, treatment, and trial of those accused of terrorist activities.

Morrison, Greg, and Joseph Airey. "Special Event Safety and Security: Protecting the World Alpine Ski Championships." *FBI Law Enforcement Bulletin.* Available online. URL: http://www.fbi.gov/publications/leb/2002/april2002/april02leb.htm. Posted in April 2002. This article provides interesting insight into how the FBI addresses security concerns at high-profile sporting events. The agency was on heightened alert for this particular event because it occurred on Vail Mountain in January and February 1999, only three months after the Earth Liberation Front's arson attacks on the resort and its subsequent warning for skiers to choose other destinations.

VIDEOS

"Counterterrorist Teams." New York: A&E Television Network, 2001. Video (VHS). 50 minutes. This video profiles elite military units, including the U.S. Marine Corps and Great Britain's Special Air Forces, that are trained to deal with every imaginable terrorist situation, from hostage situations to biochemical attacks.

"Mad Bombers." New York: A&E Television Network, 1996. Video (VHS). 50 minutes. This video chronicles the rising occurrence of bombings in the United States, from "mad bomber" George Metesky, who planted 33 bombs in New York City from 1940 to 1956, to Ted Kaczynski and Timothy McVeigh. Also covered are the Weather Underground and the 1993 bombing of the World Trade Center.

"Terrorism: Aims and Objectives." Directed by Tony Stark. Princeton, N.J.: Films for the Humanities and Sciences, 1995. Video (VHS). 3 vols. 52 minutes each. This series explores the motivations behind terrorist activities, the reasons why terrorists are so difficult to catch, and the temptation by governments to bend or break their own laws in order to bring the culprits to justice.

"Wartime Justice." New York: A&E Television Network, 2003. Video (VHS). 50 minutes. This documentary reports on controversies surrounding the way suspected terrorists have been investigated and detained since the September 11 attacks.

GENERAL ENVIRONMENTALISM

BOOKS

Byrnes, Patricia. *Environmental Pioneers*. Minneapolis, Minn.: Oliver Press, 1998. Byrnes presents information on environmentalists John Muir, Jay Darling, Rosalie Edge, Aldo Leopold, Olaus and Margaret Murie, Rachel Carson, David Brower, and Gaylord Nelson. Each chapter includes biographical details about its subject, as well as an overview of the issues on which he or she focused. A short section titled "America's Public Lands" describes the national park and forest systems, while lists of government agencies, environmental organizations, and books point the way to additional information.

Carson, Rachel. *Silent Spring*. Boston: Houghton Mifflin, 1962. Biologist Carson uses scientific evidence to uncover the devastating effects of pesticides on bird populations and human health. This important book opened the eyes of many to widespread environmental degradation at the hands of humans and is credited with helping start the mass environmental movement of the 1960s and beyond.

Chase, Alston. *Playing God in Yellowstone: The Destruction of America's First National Park*. San Diego, Calif.: Harcourt Brace Jovanovich, 1987. Like many radical environmentalists, Chase blames the degradation of Yellowstone National Park on the policies of the National Park Service, the federal agency whose job it is to take care of the park. He shows in great detail how political policies have continually trumped science in the struggle to maintain the integrity of the park, leading to the extinction of the Rocky Mountain gray wolf and the elimination of several other species from a park originally intended to protect them.

Annotated Bibliography

Doherty, Brian. *Ideas and Actions in the Green Movement.* New York: Routledge, 2002. Doherty explores the philosophical basis of the contemporary environmental movement and examines how activists have modified old ideas to deal with ever-changing political landscapes.

Dowie, Mark. *Losing Ground: American Environmentalism at the Close of the Twentieth Century.* Cambridge, Mass.: MIT Press, 1995. Award-winning journalist Dowie traces the development of the U.S. environmental movement from the days of Thoreau and Muir through the 1990s. He contends that the political accommodation of mainstream organizations, such as the Sierra Club, during the Ronald Reagan and George H. W. Bush administrations undermined much of what had been accomplished by earlier environmentalists. Dowie, however, sees the multicultural environmental justice movement that gained momentum during the 1990s as supplying the vision and grassroots anger necessary to rejuvenate environmentalism. Appendices include transcripts of the Principles of Environmental Justice (adopted at the 1991 First National People of Color Environmental Leadership Summit), the 1992 Sierra Club Centennial Address, and Alan M. Gottlieb's 25-point Wise Use Agenda.

Dunning, Joan. *From the Redwood Forest: Ancient Trees and the Bottom Line: A Headwaters Journey.* White River Junction, Vt.: Chelsea Green, 1998. This book reports on the struggle to save a stand of redwood trees in the Headwaters Forest area of coastal Northern California. Writing in a first-person, journalistic style, nature writer Dunning clearly harbors great reverence for the region and sympathizes with the activists. She provides a list of organizations involved in the struggle to end logging in the area, a selection of books pertaining to ancient forest, and contact information for politicians. Color photographs by Doug Thron show the majesty of the area.

Durbin, Kathie. *Tree Huggers: Victory, Defeat, and Renewal in the Northwest Ancient Forest Campaign.* Seattle, Wash.: The Mountaineers, 1996. Durbin provides an account of the struggles between environmentalists and logging interests in the Pacific Northwest from the early 1970s to the mid-1990s. Among the topics covered are the spotted owl controversy; the arrival of Earth First! in the early 1980s, which ushered in an era of direct action and civil disobedience in the region; and attempts by the Clinton administration to develop a compromise forest strategy, which drew mixed reviews from both sides of the debate. The book is interspersed with black-and-white photographs and ends with a chronology of events.

Ehrlich, Greta. *John Muir: Nature's Visionary.* Washington, D.C.: National Geographic, 2000. Nature writer Ehrlich's chronicle of the life of Sierra Club founder Muir is greatly enhanced by her access to the preservationist's unpublished journals. The book also features Lynn Johnson's landscape photography, as well as numerous archival images.

Hirt, Paul W. *A Conspiracy of Optimism: Management of the National Forests Since World War Two.* Our Sustainable Future series. Lincoln: University of Nebraska Press, 1994. Hirt traces the impact of the U.S. Forest Service's attempt to achieve the dual mandate of production and conservation by increasing the intensity of management in national forests. This policy, according to Hirt, led to high levels of resource extraction (such as massive clear cuts), which polluted waterways, reduced wildlife populations, and marred scenery. The eventual discovery of this widespread destruction of forest ecosystems by environmentalists initiated decades of conflict that continues to the present. Informative photos, diagrams, and graphs are interspersed throughout the text.

Huber, Peter. *Hard Green: Saving the Environment from the Environmentalists: A Conservative Manifesto.* New York: Basic Books, 1999. Huber argues that the environmentalism of the Left—a "Soft Green" faction run by scientists, regulators, and lawyers—is actually destroying nature rather than saving it. Huber proposes the privatization of major pollutants and argues, among other things, that fossil fuels are greener than renewable energy sources because they extract more power from less of the Earth's surface; modern agriculture practices (including the use of pesticides and genetic engineering) allow farmers to use less land more efficiently than they otherwise would; and wealth is necessary to provide the means to conserve wilderness. Huber also argues the importance of maintaining and extending wilderness protection, but he is careful in his manifesto to distance himself from deep ecology and similar philosophies: "We accept the traditional Judeo-Christian teaching, that man and nature are not equal," he writes, but he also believes that "aesthetic standards" such as those found in nature "can and must be maintained."

Kaufman, Wallace. *No Turning Back: Dismantling the Fantasies of Environmental Thinking.* New York: Basic Books, 1994. This book argues that the U.S. environmental movement, rooted as it is in romantic rejections of technology and science, is doing more harm to nature than good. Contrary to Henry Thoreau's often-quoted idea that "in Wildness is the preservation of the world," Kaufman believes that the preservation of wilderness hinges on maintaining civilization and relying on reason, planning, and inventiveness. Included is an annotated bibliography of important books for understanding environmental thinking.

Kline, Benjamin. *First Along the River: A Brief History of the U.S. Environmental Movement.* 2d ed. San Francisco: Acada, 2000. Kline provides an easy-to-read overview of all the important events and currents of thought that led to the creation of the modern environmental movement in the

United States. He begins with the philosophical foundations for the domination of nature found in the Bible and ends with the final year of the Clinton administration. Along the way, he explores the concept of Manifest Destiny and the settling of the American West, the development of the conservation movement as a reaction to the Industrial Revolution, the building of momentum for creation of a mass environmental movement throughout much of the 20th century, the conservative backlash against environmentalism during the Reagan administration, and much more. Radical groups like Earth First! and the Animal Liberation Front are discussed only briefly but are placed in the context of larger social and political trends. Each chapter concludes with endnotes, and the book concludes with an extensive glossary and a list of suggested readings.

Kuletz, Valerie L. *The Tainted Desert: Environmental and Social Ruin in the American West*. New York: Routledge, 1998. Kuletz, who grew up at a military test center in the Mojave Desert, where her father worked as a weapons scientist, explores the environmental and social repercussions of the "secret nuclear holocaust" caused by decades of nuclear testing in the American Southwest. The book is divided into two parts, the first of which shows how nuclear experimentation has been kept secret from the public and how this "invisible nuclear landscape" has been superimposed upon a landscape already occupied by Native Americans. These desert regions are considered "wastelands" by the U.S. government and therefore useless for anything other than large-scale weapons testing and nuclear waste disposal. As a result, many indigenous people have been driven from land they see as sacred, while several reservations located downwind from test sites have suffered increased incidences of cancer, birth defects, and disease. Part two discusses Yucca Mountain in southern Nevada, under consideration as a disposal site for high-level nuclear waste. Kuletz claims that the U.S. government has ignored independent scientists who maintain that earthquake faults under the mountain make it a poor choice for waste storage. For Kuletz, Yucca Mountain represents the tendency of scientists employed by the government to ignore alternatives that may be contrary to U.S. political objectives. It also illustrates the U.S. government's policy of "nuclear colonialism," in which indigenous people and their land are seen as expendable.

Langston, Nancy. *Forest Dreams, Forest Nightmares: The Paradox of Old Growth in the Inland West*. Seattle: University of Washington Press, 1995. Langston investigates why millions of acres of once-healthy forestland in northeastern Oregon and southeastern Washington are now threatened by fire, insect epidemics, and disease. She concludes that federal fire suppression policies, intended to save the forests, allowed firs to grow in areas once dominated by ponderosa pine. When drought hit, the firs

177

proved vulnerable to insects, diseases, and fires. The book features photographs, notes, and a selected bibliography.

Lansky, Mitch. *Beyond the Beauty Strip: Saving What's Left of Our Forests.* Gardiner, Maine: Tilbury House, 1992. Lansky provides an intensely critical look at federal forest management practices, stating, among other claims, that the "jobs versus the environment" argument used to support widespread logging is a false dichotomy. The book presents a number of issues—such as regional development, community welfare, use of herbicides—and then attempts to debunk the "myths" used by the U.S. Forest Service and resource extraction industries to justify their management policies. The title refers to the strip of unlogged trees that timber companies maintain along Forest Service roadways to hide clear cuts from passing motorists.

Leopold, Aldo. *A Sand County Almanac and Sketches Here and There.* New York: Oxford University Press, 1949. Leopold holds a place alongside John Muir and Henry Thoreau in the pantheon of environmental writers. This book, published shortly after Leopold's death, is considered one of the most important and influential nature books ever written. The almanac itself consists of observations of the cycles of nature in Wisconsin throughout the course of one year. Among the other essays is Leopold's widely read "The Land Ethic," in which he suggested extending ethics beyond human-to-human and human-to-society relations to include "man's relation to the land and to the animals and plants which grow upon it." It was here that he wrote his often-quoted belief, "A thing is right when it tends to preserve the integrity, stability, and beauty of the biotic community. It is wrong when it tends otherwise."

Lowenthal, David. *George Perkins Marsh: Prophet of Conservation.* Seattle: University of Washington Press, 2000. Lowenthal was inspired to update his 1958 biography of Marsh by the availability of new primary source material, as well as by new perspectives offered by radical developments in the U.S. environmental movement since the late 1950s. Biographical information is interspersed with great detail about historical events, providing historical perspective on the development of Marsh's influential theory on the negative impact that humans have had on nature.

Marsh, George Perkins. *Man and Nature; or, Physical Geography as Modified by Human Action.* Seattle: University of Washington Press, 2003. Originally published in 1864, this book challenged the widespread belief that human impact on the environment was negligible and blamed the collapse on ancient Mediterranean civilizations on the abuse of nature. Marsh explains the vital interconnections among soil, water, and vegetation, a philosophy that later becomes central to the conservation movement. These observations helped persuade the federal government to create Yellowstone National Park in 1872 to preserve the dwindling wilderness. An introduction by David Lowenthal evaluates the significant role the book played in the development of the U.S. environmental movement and provides biographical information on Marsh.

Miller, Char. *Gifford Pinchot and the Making of Modern Environmentalism.* Douglas, England: Shearwater, 2001. History professor Miller recounts the life story of Pinchot, first head of the U.S. Forest Service and one of the men most responsible for creating the multiple-use, conservationist vision by which much federal land in the United States is managed to this day.

Muir, John. *Our National Parks.* San Francisco: Sierra Club Books, 1991. First published in book form in 1901, this collection of 10 essays that originally appeared in *Atlantic Monthly* magazine details the natural attractions of Yosemite, Yellowstone, Sequoia, and General Grant national parks. The beauty of these writings helped increase public support for preservation of wilderness in the United States, eventually leading to the creation of the National Park Service.

———. *A Thousand-Mile Walk to the Gulf.* Boston: Houghton Mifflin, 1998. Through journal entries and notes compiled at the end of his life, Muir recounts his 1867 walk from Indiana across Kentucky, Tennessee, North Carolina, Georgia, and Florida to the Gulf of Mexico. It was the beginning of a life of adventure that led Muir to San Francisco and the Sierra Nevada, which in turn inspired him to found the Sierra Club. This book was originally published in 1916, three years after Muir's death.

———. *The Yosemite.* San Francisco: Sierra Club Books, 1988. Written when Muir was 73 years old, this book recounts the Sierra Club founder's observations and adventures during a lifetime of exploring Yosemite Valley. A foreword by longtime Sierra Club executive director David Brower puts the book into historical perspective and details Muir's passion for California's Sierra Nevada in general and Yosemite National Park in particular. Appendices, provided for historical interest, include discussions of legislation about Yosemite enacted from 1864 to 1905, a table of distances within the park, and transportation rates in and around Yosemite Valley at the time of the book's writing.

Nash, Roderick Frazier. *The Rights of Nature: A History of Environmental Ethics.* Madison: University of Wisconsin Press, 1989. This classic book traces the evolution of ethics and the expansion of the concept of rights, beginning with the Magna Carta of 1215 and broadening over centuries to include slaves, women, and minorities. According to Nash, the Endangered Species Act of 1973 marked the extension of rights to include nature, possibly the most dramatic expansion of morality in the history of human thought. Nash's study of environmental ethics reaches from the ancient Romans to radical contemporary groups, such as Greenpeace and Earth First!, and includes discussions of Aldo Leopold, Christianity, and deep ecology.

————. *Wilderness and the American Mind.* 4th ed. New Haven, Conn.: Yale University Press, 2001. Nash presents a comprehensive review of changing perceptions of ecological diversity and wilderness in the context of the European settlement of North America. The book includes chapters on the philosophy of wilderness, the irony of victory in official wilderness designation, and an international perspective on the environmental movement. Of particular interest are in-depth discussions of the importance of Muir, Thoreau, and Leopold in the development of deep ecology.

O'Leary, Richard. *The Environmental Mafia: The Enemy Is Us.* Flemington, N.J.: Agathon Press, 2003. O'Leary criticizes uncontrolled bureaucratic regulation of the environment, which he believes often causes more harm than good to both the environment and society. He presents evidence, for example, that reintroduced or protected species often outstrip habitat that has been reduced by human development, creating safety and sanitation problems for both animals and humans.

Pinchot, Gifford. *Breaking New Ground.* New York: Harcourt, Brace, 1947. In this autobiography, Pinchot recounts his role in the creation of the U.S. Forest Service and in shaping the philosophy of conservation that came to dominate federal forest policy. The book is illustrated with photographs and political cartoons from the first decades of the 20th century that support Pinchot's view of how natural resources should be managed.

Sale, Kirkpatrick. *Dwellers in the Land: The Bioregional Vision.* San Francisco: Sierra Club Books, 1985. Sale, a founding member of the North American Bioregional Congress, articulates the bioregional philosophy, which envisions allowing natural geographic regions (rather than arbitrary political borders) to dictate human settlement and cultural patterns. Sale uses examples from Greek city-states, Native American cultures, and regionalist movement in the United States to show how an ecocentric worldview will restore harmony between humans and nature, thereby averting environmental disaster.

Snyder, Gary. *The Old Ways.* San Francisco: City Lights Books, 1977. This brief book contains six essays by the well-known American poet, one of which presents his influential ideas on bioregional re-inhabitation.

————. *Turtle Island.* New York: New Directions, 1974. This collection of essays and poems by the Pulitzer Prize–winning poet includes the deep ecology manifesto "Four Changes" (1969), which suggests that ecology and Buddhism are complementary belief systems.

Switzer, Jacqueline Vaughn. *Environmental Activism.* Santa Barbara, Calif.: ABC-CLIO, 2003. This book covers the U.S. environmental movement

from 1900 to the present, presenting information on organizations ranging from the mainstream Sierra Club to radical groups, such as the Earth
Liberation Front. The "Reports, Documents, Cases, and Testimony" section provides researchers with lists of primary-source materials, and the
list of organizations includes addresses, phone and fax numbers, web sites,
and e-mail addresses.

Thoreau, Henry David. *Walden and Civil Disobedience*. New York: Penguin,
1986. Two of Thoreau's greatest and most well known works are presented in a single volume. *Walden* is Thoreau's autobiographical account
of the time he spent living alone in a cabin near Concord, Massachusetts,
a simple existence that allowed him to focus on contemplating nature and
humanity. "On the Duty of Civil Disobedience," one of the most famous
essays ever written, formulates Thoreau's idea that government actions
that infringe on fundamental personal liberties are best met with nonviolent resistance. This model would later be followed by Greenpeace and
other radical environmental organizations.

ARTICLES

Carlton, Jim. "Unions, Environmentalists Form Group to Exert Pressure
for Jobs, Resources." *Wall Street Journal*, October 4, 1999, p. A20. This
article reports on the announcement of the formation of the Alliance for
Sustainable Jobs and the Environment, an alliance between about 400
members of large unions such as the United Steelworkers and Teamsters
on one hand, and environmental groups including Earth First! and the
American Lands Alliance on the other. Organizers claim that another 120
environmental groups and about 100 unions endorsed the move. The
nonprofit organization, based in Eureka, California, is run by representatives from both groups and seeks to exert pressure on corporations whose
practices they believe jeopardize U.S. jobs and threaten natural resources.

Drexel, Karl W. "Will the Real Sierra Club Please Stand Up?" *Christian Science Monitor*, May 24, 1996, p. 19. This article reports on a recent vote by
the Sierra Club's national membership to adopt a policy of supporting a
ban on all logging on all public lands. Drexel believes this is an "ill-
conceived posture" that moves the normally mainstream environmental
group into the ranks of radical environmental organizations, such as
Earth First! and Greenpeace. Chad Hanson, the author of the new policy, responds that the environmental movement has become "too oriented toward compromise" and that it is necessary to fight for the defense
of ecosystems "as passionately and forcefully as we are able." Drexel questions whether this new policy is a turning point that will transform the
Sierra Club into a radicalized preservationist organization.

Ecoterrorism

Golden, Frederic. "Who's Afraid of Frankenfood?" *Time,* November 29, 1999, pp. 49–50. Golden reports on European anxieties over genetically modified (GM) crops, as well as efforts by environmentalists to publicize the potential dangers of bioengineering. Food producers have begun fighting back, however, supporting the testimony of scientists who claim GM foods could benefit health by delivering more nutrients, reducing spoilage, and curtailing chemical contamination. The public relations struggle will have repercussions in the political arena: Although regulators in the United States have approved dozens of genetically modified plants for human consumption, a bipartisan group of 20 members of Congress introduced legislation requiring labeling of all genetically engineered food.

Guterl, Fred. "The Fear of Food: One by One, Countries Are Coming Out Against Crops with Engineered Genes. America Is Isolated." *Newsweek,* January 27, 2003, p. 40ff. Guterl reports on the rejection of U.S.-produced genetically modified (GM) food by a large number of other nations. While Greenpeace sees the rejection of what it terms "Frankenfood" by African nations "a triumph of national sovereignty," some U.S. officials have called Europe's moratorium on new GM foods "immoral" and "Luddite." They say that GM foods have reduced the amount of pesticides farmers have had to spray on their cornfields, which is good for both the environment and human health. Many nations remain unconvinced, equating GM foods with U.S. agriculture and trusting neither. Such views, Guterl suggests, often have as much to do with politics and public opinion as with science.

Hunt, Ed. "Remember the Environment?" *Christian Science Monitor,* December 24, 2001, p. 9. Hunt explores the effect the September 11, 2001, terrorist attacks on the United States had on the amount of attention paid to environmental issues. A September 10 decision by a federal judge in Eugene, Oregon, for example, stripped Oregon's coho salmon of Endangered Species Act protections, opening the way for logging that jeopardized the endangered species status of more than 20 other stocks of salmon. Normally a story that would have been featured prominently in the national news media, few heard of the decision until three days later. Meanwhile, many mainstream environmental groups postponed mailers and advertisements critical of the Bush administration, and even the hotly contested issue of whether to open the Arctic National Wildlife Refuge (ANWR) to oil and gas drilling was quietly dropped for a while.

Kenny, Andrew. "The Green Gestapo." *The Spectator,* vol. 290, September 7, 2002, pp. 21–22. Kenny argues that the best way to save the planet is to rely on science, reason, and capitalism to ensure that everyone in the world becomes rich as quickly as possible. He writes that poor people chop down trees for firewood, foul the rivers, have more children than the rich, and are too busy surviving to care for the environment. Against the background of the 2002 World Summit on Sustainable Development (WSSD) in Johannesburg, South Africa, Kenny faults Greenpeace (an "eco-fascist organization whose flair for publicity is a match for Hitler in the 1930s") for rejecting technologies that could help raise Africans from poverty and thus help the environment. These include genetically engineered foods and nuclear power. ("Nuclear power at the WSSD," writes Kenny, "was like a Jew at a Nazi rally.") The article ends with the admonition that Africa is involved in a race against time: If the continent can industrialize and use modern technology to grow food, all will be well. Continued poverty, on the other hand, will lead to environmental disaster.

Klee, Kenneth. "The Big Food Fight: Europeans Are Railing Against 'Frankenstein Foods'—Genetically Modified Crops that Abound in America. And Exporters Have Been Forced to Listen." *Newsweek*, September 13, 1999, p. 22. In 1992, the U.S. Food and Drug Administration (FDA) issued a key ruling that brought foods containing genetically modified (GM) foods to market quickly, and without labels. By 1998, 40 percent of U.S. corn crops and 45 percent of its soybeans were genetically modified. French and British, however, have witnessed a rise in activism against the U.S. desire to export GM crops and foods. Several companies in the United States that conduct business overseas have responded to this pressure: Agribusiness giant Archer Daniels Midland (ADM) told its suppliers that they should start segregating their GM crops from conventional ones because that was what foreign buyers wanted, while Heinz and Gerber announced that they would go to the considerable trouble of making their baby foods free of GM organisms.

Miller, Karen Lowry. "Pin-Striped Protesters: Activists Are Learning to Work the Capitalist System." *Newsweek*, February 25, 2002, p. 26. Miller reports that although Greenpeace activists continue to use direct action tactics (just before this article was written, felony charges were dismissed against 15 members who attempted to disrupt a missile test launch on a California Air Force base), the events of September 11, 2001, have inspired a number of activists to rethink theatrical protest strategies. Many groups have begun to rely on more businesslike tactics by using the Internet to recruit members with business expertise, commissioning financial studies, collecting advice from sympathetic investment bankers, poaching talent from the corporate world, and eschewing direct protest in favor of financial protest. Among the latter are the use of social investment funds, which use the threat of embarrassing shareholder resolutions to pressure companies to adopt more responsible social or environmental policies.

Pezzella, Mike. "Despite NAS OK, Some Still Call It Frankenfood." *Biotechnology Newswatch*, September 16, 2002, pp. 1ff. A report by the National Academy of Sciences (NAS) sponsored by the Food and Drug Administration has concluded that food from genetically modified (GM) animals poses no significant danger to humans, aside from a low probability of triggering allergic reactions. The panel urged a revamping of federal oversight of animal biotechnology to address unique problems associated with animal biotechnologies. Despite the report's assessment that bioengineering poses minimal risk to humans and the environment, GM plant products continue to be rejected by many nations. Among them is Zambia, where food shortages caused by drought and poor management have exposed millions of people to the dangers of starvation. The African nation's leadership has cited safety and environmental concerns as its reasons for the rejection. Meanwhile, several environmental groups that have opposed GM foods maintain they would make an exception for Zambia. "When it comes to famine, telling anybody not to eat GM food in this situation is a position we absolutely can't take," Greenpeace's Annette Cotter said, while Friends of the Earth's Juan Lopez added, "We're not saying no to GM food in the middle of the famine."

Sanction, Thomas, and John Skow. "Trouble in Paradise." *Time*, vol. 146, September 18, 1995, p. 85. Worldwide protest greeted France's decision to resume nuclear tests in the South Pacific, including a 36-hour rampage in Papeete, Tahiti, during which several hundred rioters virtually destroyed Tahiti's international airport, smashed storefront windows, and torched several buildings before French Foreign Legionnaires and paramilitary troops arrived.

INTERNET DOCUMENTS

Ercelawn, Ayesha. "End of the Road: The Adverse Ecological Impacts of Roads and Logging: A Compilation of Independently Reviewed Research." Natural Resources Defense Council. Available online. URL: http://www.nrdc.org/land/forests/roads/eotrinx.asp. Posted December 1999. This lengthy report reviews independent research providing evidence that road building and logging in national forests harms wildlife, spreads tree diseases, promotes infestations of bark beetles and other insects, facilitates the spread of non-native plant and animal species, damages soil resources and tree growth, and negatively impacts aquatic ecosystems.

Snape, William, III, and John M. Carter III. "Weakening the National Environmental Policy Act: How the Bush Administration Uses the Judicial System to Weaken Environmental Protections." Defenders of Wildlife.

Annotated Bibliography

Available online. URL: http://www.defenders.org/publications/nepareport. pdf. Downloaded September 10, 2003. This report shows how the Bush administration has used judicial nominees and the federal court system to undermine laws that have long been used by environmentalists to curb abuses of public lands by developers and natural resource extraction industries.

Wilkinson, Todd. "Thinning the Ranks." *National Parks Conservation Association Magazine.* Available online. URL: http://www.npca.org/magazine/2003/september_october/privatization.asp. Posted in September/October 2003. This article reports on a proposal by the George W. Bush administration to privatize as many as 70 percent of the jobs in the National Parks Service. Wilkinson writes that the replacement of passionate, knowledgeable federal personnel with less experienced employees will lessen the value of work being done in the parks and provide a disservice to visitors.

VIDEOS

"The Boyhood of John Muir." Directed by Lawrence R. Hott. Oley, Pa.: Bullfrog Films, 1997. Video (VHS). 78 minutes. This dramatic feature film follows the early life of Muir, from his days working on a Wisconsin farm to the industrial accident that nearly blinded him and caused him to dedicate his life to observing nature.

"David Brower." Directed by John de Graaf. Oley, Pa.: Bullfrog Films, 1995. Video (VHS). 56 minutes. This film, shot when Brower was 84 years old, recounts the environmental activist's life, then moves on to an interview conducted by Scott Simon, host of National Public Radio's "Weekend Edition." The discussion ranges from nuclear power to the preservation of national parks.

"The Four Corners: A National Sacrifice Area?" Directed by Christopher McLeod. La Honda, Calif.: Earth Image Films, 1983. Video (VHS). 58 minutes. McLeod documents the environmental and cultural impacts of mining and oil shale development in the Four Corners region of the desert Southwest. This film is of interest to students of radical environmentalism because it examines the Peabody Coal Company's Black Mesa strip mine, target of Black Mesa Defense Fund (for which Dave Foreman volunteered in the early 1970s) and of fictional sabotage in Edward Abbey's 1975 novel, *The Monkey Wrench Gang.*

"Our Vanishing Forests." Directed by Arlen Slobodow. Oley, Pa.: Bullfrog Films, 1993. Video (VHS). 58 minutes. This history of the U.S. Forest Service is presented from an environmentalist's perspective, showing how the agency has abandoned its conservation ethic and now favors the interests of the timber industry.

185

GENERAL ANIMAL RIGHTS

BOOKS

Cavalieri, Paola. *The Animal Question: Why Nonhuman Animals Deserve Human Rights.* Translated by Catherine Woollard. New York: Oxford University Press, 2001. Cavalieri uses arguments based in ethics and science to advocate extending human rights to include animals. Her controversial use of the term *human rights* in this regard is intentional, as she believes that such rights "are not the prerogative of the species *Homo sapiens.*" She also argues that the history of "moral progress" consists of a history of "replacing hierarchical visions with presumptions in favor of equality." She therefore views the extension of rights to animals as part of the larger, ongoing process of cultural evolution.

Cohen, Carl, and Tom Regan. *The Animal Rights Debate.* Lanham, Md.: Rowman & Littlefield, 2001. This point/counterpoint book is split into three parts: In the first, philosophy professor Cohen presents his view that animals should not be endowed with the same rights as humans and argues in favor of using animals for scientific research. He concludes with a chapter presenting advancements made in various fields of research (such as heart failure, vaccines, Alzheimer's disease, cancer, and diabetes) using animals. The second part consists of philosophy professor Regan's arguments in favor of extending rights to include animals. In the third part, each author is given about 40 pages to respond to the opposing arguments presented earlier in the book.

Francione, Gary L. *Introduction to Animal Rights: Your Child or the Dog?* Philadelphia: Temple University Press, 2000. Francione presents his case that humans should reject the use and treatment of animals as resources and property. This includes not just regulating but abolishing the use of animals for food, scientific research, and entertainment. The appendix consists of the answers to 20 common questions concerning animal rights that Francione has been asked since he became interested in the issue. Graphic black-and-white photos reveal the treatment of animals in slaughterhouses, factory farms, rodeos, circuses, and research laboratories.

Kistler, John M., ed. *People Promoting and People Opposing Animal Rights in Their Own Words.* Westport, Conn.: Greenwood Press, 2002. Kistler asked the same 12 questions concerning animal rights to 42 people representing a variety of viewpoints on the subject. Each chapter consists of the answers supplied by each one of the contributors, a list that includes wise use advocate Ron Arnold, former Animal Liberation Front (ALF) member David Barbarash, and People for the Ethical Treatment of Animals (PETA) founder Ingrid Newkirk. Appendices included a list of the

Annotated Bibliography

12 interview questions, the participant letter Kistler sent to prospective contributors, and a list of organizations.

Regan, Tom. *The Case for Animal Rights.* Berkeley: University of California Press, 1983. Regan argues that animals, like humans, are individuals with value independent of their usefulness to others that possess a basic moral right to be treated in ways that show respect for that independent value. He then presents a disciplined moral theory on animal rights that, if accepted by society at large, would necessitate such cultural changes as the elimination of commercial animal agriculture, a ban on commercial and sport hunting and trapping, and the abolition of the use of animals in scientific research.

Rudacille, Deborah. *The Scalpel and the Butterfly: The Conflict Between Animal Research and Animal Protection.* Berkeley: University of California Press, 2000. Rudacille traces the parallel histories of animal research and the antivivisection movement, examining the central question of whether "enhancement of human life justifies the use of animals for research." Her discussion of animal rights activists includes both those who work within the system and those who work outside the law, including the Animal Liberation Front (ALF). A list of resources includes scientific and research organizations and animal protection organizations.

Singer, Peter. *Animal Liberation.* 2d ed. New York: Random House, 1990. Originally published in 1975, this book is considered by many to have inspired the worldwide animal rights movement. Singer argues that inflicting suffering on animals for scientific study and meat production is morally indefensible and wasteful. The second edition includes Singer's thoughts on the development of the radical animal rights movement between 1975 and 1990, as well as an updated list of books and organizations, and suggestions for where to buy "cruelty-free" products.

Stand, Rod, and Patti Strand. *The Hijacking of the Humane Movement.* Wilsonville, Oreg.: Doral, 1993. This scathing critique of animal rights activism contends that the movement has been taken over by hateful radicals whose violent tactics cause more harm than good to animals. Case studies involving such organizations as People for the Ethical Treatment of Animals (PETA) and Animal Liberation Front (ALF) are included. A list of organizations supplies complete addresses for those that advocate animal testing and experimentation, while animal rights groups are identified only by name and city. A list of 20th-century medical advances through animal research and testing is provided.

ARTICLES

Berman, Richard. "Animal Groups Callous, not Cute." *USA Today*, April 16, 2003, p. A1. Berman criticizes People for the Ethical Treatment of

Animals (PETA) for placing "animal life above human tragedy," citing campaigns lamenting the use of pigeons and chickens by U.S. troops in Iraq to detect chemical weapons and complaining that dolphins locating mines in the Persian Gulf "have not volunteered" for service. The article goes on to examine the activities of Stop Huntingdon Animal Cruelty (SHAC) and Animal Liberation Front (ALF), the latter classified by the FBI as "a serious terrorist threat" within the United States. Taylor ends by debunking the idea that animal rights radicals who use arson have anything in common with civil rights activists who used civil disobedience as a tactic.

Black, Jason Edward. "Extending the Rights of Personhood, Voice, and Life to Sensate Others: A Homology of Right to Life and Animal Rights Rhetoric." *Communication Quarterly*, vol. 51, Summer 2003, pp. 312+. This scholarly, footnoted article explores similarities in the language used by animal rights activists and antiabortionists in their attempts to extend rights to animals and human fetuses, respectively.

Fiala, Jennifer. "Animal Activism Runs Rampant through States." *DVM*, vol. 34, October 2003, p. 29. Fiala discusses efforts by animal rights activists to introduce legislation in Florida, New Jersey, and California with a variety of aims, including increasing the value of pets, protesting bans on feral cat programs, and making the declawing of cats illegal.

Morrison, Adrian R. "Ethical Principles: Guiding the Use of Animals in Research." *The American Biology Teacher*, vol. 65, February 2003, pp. 105+. Morrison presents his personal code of ethics on the use of animals in biological and medical research, which stresses the belief that although humans are more important than animals, scientists are obligated to treat research animals humanely.

Nordlinger, Jay. "PETA vs. KFC." *National Review*, December 22, 2003, p. 27. This look into People for the Ethical Treatment of Animals' campaign against the KFC fast-food franchise begins with the premise that PETA "does not, or should not, inspire trust in normal people" because it is an extremist group that supports terrorism. The author explores how the group has enjoyed success in previous protests against McDonald's, Burger King, and Wendy's, and how it is now using similar tactics in its efforts to force KFC to treat its chickens more humanely.

Orlean, Susan. "Animal Action Popular Chronicles." *The New Yorker*, November 17, 2003, pp. 92+. This long article profiles American Humane's Film and Television Unit, the official monitor of animals in most Hollywood film and television productions. Orlean also covers the history of animal abuse in movies and follows the events that led to reforms in 1980, when the Screen Actors Guild/Producer's Agreement was amended to include rules requiring the proper treatment of animals.

Annotated Bibliography

Karen Rosa, the director of the Film and Television Unit, indicates the seriousness with which she takes her job when she says, "A cockroach in a movie is an actor. Like any other actor, it deserves to go home at the end of the day."

Samuel, Dave. "Animal Rightists Reveal Real Agenda." *Bowhunter*, vol. 33, October/November 2003, p. 180. Samuel, a wildlife biologist, discusses efforts by animal rights activists to stop all forms of hunting and airs his concerns that such an agenda may do more harm than good to overall wildlife populations.

Specter, Michael. "The Extremist." *The New Yorker*, vol. 79, April 14, 2003, p. 52. This long article profiles Ingrid Newkirk and the organization she founded in the early 1980s, People for the Ethical Treatment of Animals (PETA). Specter also examines the group's tactics, which he says are "often repulsive" but have cemented its reputation as having a "Barnum-like genius for attracting attention." To protest the use of fur in the pages of *Vogue*, for example, a PETA activist once placed a dead raccoon on the plate of editor Anna Wintour while Wintour was eating lunch at the Four Seasons restaurant in Manhattan. Specter devotes the final portion of the essay to exploring the ways that the beef and poultry industries have improved treatment of animals in recent years, which may or may not have anything to do with agitation on the part of PETA and other animal rights organizations.

Sunstein, Cass R. "The Rights of Animals." *The University of Chicago Law Review*, vol. 70, Winter 2003, pp. 387–402. Sunstein approaches questions concerning animal rights from a scholarly legal perspective, suggesting that although some demands made by radical activists should be rejected, an argument can be made for stronger regulation of many current uses of animals. Among these are the use of animals in entertainment, scientific experiments, and agriculture.

INTERNET DOCUMENTS

People for the Ethical Treatment of Animals. "PETA Annual Review 2002." People for the Ethical Treatment of Animals. Available online. URL: http://www.peta.org/feat/ar2003/. Downloaded on September 10, 2003. This report provides a detailed review of PETA's activist and advertising campaigns, an overview of work done by the organization's education department, and numerical data concerning operating expenses and vital statistics about the web site and activism. This is an excellent resource for researchers of animal rights activism interested in studying the scope of activity in the movement.

VIDEOS

"Animal Rights and Their Human Consequences." Directed by Frances B. N. Ommanney. Princeton, N.J.: Films for the Humanities and Sciences, 1994. Video (VHS). 28 minutes. This video explores the ethics of animal rights and the dilemma of breaking the law to prevent the suffering of animals.

"Humans and Animals: Bridging the Gap." Directed by Steve Barney. Oshkosh, Wis.: Animal Liberation Action Group, 1996. Video (VHS). 53 minutes. This video consists of an unedited lecture given by Peter Singer on April 20, 1995, at the University of Wisconsin in Madison.

"In Defense of Animals." Directed by Julie Akeret. Oley, Pa.: Bullfrog Films, 1998. Video (VHS). 28 minutes. This video provides a portrait of Peter Singer, the Australian philosopher who inspired the worldwide animal rights movement with the publication of his 1975 book *Animal Liberation*. At the core of his argument is the idea that it is unethical for humans to discount the suffering of nonhuman animals.

RADICAL ENVIRONMENTALISM

BOOKS

Abbey, Edward. *Desert Solitaire: A Season in the Wilderness*. New York: Ballantine Books, 1968. Generally considered to be Abbey's best book, *Desert Solitaire* recounts the author's six-month stint as a volunteer park ranger in Utah's Arches National Monument during the 1950s. The narrative is characterized by careful observation of life and death in the arid regions of the southwestern United States—exemplified by Abbey's admonition in the introduction that the only way to truly see the desert is to "crawl, on hands and knees, over the sandstone and through the thornbush and cactus"—and several rants about the continued degradation of the wilderness. Indeed, the seeds of the novel *The Monkey Wrench Gang* are sown in this book: Abbey recounts his removal of five miles of survey stakes placed by a National Park Service crew planning on building a paved road through the monument, and during a rafting trip down Colorado River through Glen Canyon, which will soon be submerged due to construction of the Glen Canyon Dam, he daydreams about an "unknown hero" who will use a rucksack full of dynamite to blow up the dam. *Desert Solitaire* has long been famous among those opposed to radical environmentalism for Abbey's claim that as a humanist, he would "rather kill a *man* than a snake," a criticism that many fans say ignores the strong current of sarcasm and caustic wit that runs throughout the book and virtually all of Abbey's work.

———. *Hayduke Lives!* Boston: Little, Brown, 1990. Published a year after the author's death, Abbey's last book is a sequel to *The Monkey Wrench Gang.* Earth First! plays a prominent role in the narrative, and some of the fictional characters are based on real people involved in the radical environmental movement. Dave Foreman and Paul Watson even make cameo appearances. Although the book as a whole is considerably less entertaining than *The Monkey Wrench Gang,* the story articulates the ideals of radical environmentalism more successfully than the first novel.

———. *The Monkey Wrench Gang.* New York: Avon Books, 1975. Abbey's legendary novel, which follows the exploits of four disgruntled environmentalists who use sabotage in an attempt to halt the destruction of wilderness in Utah and Arizona, is credited with providing radical activists with a blueprint for action. Dave Foreman himself once wrote that one of the original purposes of Earth First! was "to inspire others to carry out activities straight from the pages of *The Monkey Wrench Gang.*" The fictional characters' ultimate aim of destroying the Glen Canyon Dam was even echoed by Earth First!'s inaugural public rally (attended by Abbey), during which activists used black plastic to create a fake crack down the face of the dam. Of particular interest is "The Raid at Comb Wash" chapter, which describes in detail the destruction of heavy equipment at a highway-building site. Interspersed throughout the extremely readable adventure story are radical musings about the more destructive aspects of industrial civilization, as well as Abbey's trademark descriptions of the beauty of the desert Southwest.

———. *One Life at a Time, Please.* New York: Henry Holt, 1988. This book is a collection of essays that originally appeared in such diverse publications as the *San Francisco Examiner, Harper's, New York Times Magazine, National Geographic, Architectural Digest,* and *Earth First! Journal.* Divided into four sections (Politics, Travel, Books and Art, and Nature Love), the book covers a wide range of topics, including cattle ranching, anarchism, river rafting, immigration, canyoneering, feminism, hunting, and transcendentalism. Included is the essay "Eco-Defense," which served as the introduction to Dave Foreman's book of the same name.

Bishop, James, Jr. *Epitaph for a Desert Anarchist: The Life and Legacy of Edward Abbey.* New York: Atheneum, 1994. This book provides biographical information on Abbey, as well as analysis of his writings and the influence his ideas has had on American culture in general and the environmental movement in particular. Bishop does a good job of pointing out the complexity of Abbey's work without attempting the impossible task of explaining the contradictions that have long confounded fans and critics alike.

Ecoterrorism

Bookchin, Murray. *The Ecology of Freedom: The Emergence and Dissolution of Hierarchy.* Palo Alto, Calif.: Cheshire Books, 1982. Bookchin presents an extensive study of communalism and hierarchy, contrasting organic society with mechanical society. He sees efforts to repair the split between humans and nature as the greatest hope for the future of the planet.

Butler, Tom, ed. *Wild Earth: Wild Ideas for a World Out of Balance.* Minneapolis, Minn.: Milkweed, 2002. This anthology collects essays from the first 10 years of the conservation journal *Wild Earth*, cofounded by Dave Foreman. The book is divided into three sections: Wild Science and Strategy, Wild Thinking, and Wild Places and Creatures. Among the well-known environmentalists represented here are Gary Snyder, Howie Wolke, Roderick Frazier Nash, Dave Foreman, Wendell Barry, Christopher Manes, and Barry Lopez.

Cockburn, Alexander, Jeffrey St. Clair, and Allan Sekula. *Five Days that Shook the World: Seattle and Beyond.* New York: Verso, 2000. The authors provide eyewitness accounts of leftist protests in Seattle; Washington, D.C.; Philadelphia; Los Angeles; Prague; and other cities, claiming that this new activism heralds the birth of a new radical movement in the United States and beyond.

Drengson, Alan, and Yuichi Inoue. *The Deep Ecology Movement: An Introductory Anthology.* Berkeley, Calif.: North Atlantic Books, 1995. This anthology covers a wide range of approaches to the philosophy of deep ecology, including ecofeminist, scientific, spiritual, and Gandhian viewpoints. Contributors include such deep ecology luminaries as Arne Naess, George Sessions, Gary Snyder, Bill Devall, Dolores LaChapelle, and Joanna Macy. Included is a list of books relevant to the deep ecology movement.

Gray, Elizabeth Dodson. *Green Paradise Lost.* New York: Roundtable Press, 1981. In this influential book, ecofeminist theorist Gray ties feminist critiques of Western philosophy, religion, and psychology with ecological ideas.

Keulartz, Josef. *The Struggle for Nature: A Critique of Radical Ecology.* Translated by Rob Kuitenbrouwer. New York: Routledge, 1998. This critique of deep ecology, ecofeminism, and eco-anarchism is based on discussions of contemporary European philosophy and may therefore be difficult for readers with little background in this area. However, the author's idea of "evolutionary ecology," in which the ever-changing dynamic between human society and nature is taken into consideration while drafting environmental policies, is worth exploring as an alternative to the philosophies upon which radical environmentalism is based.

Lewis, Martin W. *Green Delusions: An Environmentalist Critique of Radical Environmentalism.* Durham, N.C.: Duke University Press, 1992. Lewis, a moderate environmentalist, argues that radical environmentalism is based on ill-conceived notions that, if enacted, would exacerbate ecological problems rather than correct them. The book includes an appendix that compares extreme "Arcadian" environmentalism with its more moderate "Promethean" counterpart.

List, Peter C., ed. *Radical Environmentalism: Philosophy and Tactics.* Belmont, Calif.: Wadsworth, 1993. Essays in this collection explore radical environmentalism largely through the eyes of its proponents, including Arne Naess, Carolyn Merchant, Murray Bookchin, Dave Foreman, Edward Abbey, and Paul Watson. Among the topics explored are the philosophies of deep ecology, ecofeminism, social ecology, and bioregionalism, as well as the tactics of Greenpeace, Earth First!, the Sea Shepherd Conservation Society (SSCS), and others.

Love, Sam, and David Obst, eds. *Ecotage!* New York: Pocket Books, 1972. This book, in which the term *ecotage* was coined, was the result of a contest held by Earth Day organizers Environmental Action to gather direct-action techniques for fighting pollution and environmental degradation. Although most entries, sent in from across the United States, suggest relatively tame acts involving letter-writing campaigns and boycotts, a few touched on tactics that would later be espoused by Earth First!, including billboard destruction, putting sugar in gas tanks, and removing survey stakes. The final section of the book details the actions of the Fox, to whom the book is dedicated, and Miami-based Eco-Commando Force '70. In the epilogue, co-editor Sam Love writes that the task of ecosaboteurs "will be rewarding" and that they will win in the end because "man is not so far removed from nature that he has lost one of the basic natural drives, the survival instinct."

Merchant, Carolyn. *The Death of Nature: Women, Ecology, and the Scientific Revolution.* San Francisco: Harper & Row, 1980. Merchant, one of the most important theorists of the ecofeminist movement, takes a critical look at the "Scientific Revolution" of the 16th and 17th centuries, which marked the ascendance of technology and progress over nature. Merchant shows how this paradigm shift caused shortages in natural resources, disrupted long-established ways of life, and solidified the power of a patriarchal ruling class to the detriment of women and peasants. The book features 24 illustrations from the era under consideration, as well as a large number of endnotes.

———. *Reinventing Eden: The Fate of Nature in Western Culture.* New York: Routledge, 2003. Merchant examines the powerful hold that the biblical story of the Garden of Eden has on the Western imagination and explores how attempts to re-create or rediscover Eden have only led to further degradation of nature. These attempts, from Christopher Columbus's journey to the Americas to the development of gated communities, all spring from a utopian pastoral impulse that has resulted in the creation of national parks while the rest of the planet is exploited for human use. Merchant suggests a revolution of consciousness that would allow humans to view nature as an independent agent capable of autonomous action and would promote a balancing of human needs with those of nature.

Miller, Joseph A., and Rose M. Miller. *Eco-Terrorism and Eco-Extremism Against Agriculture.* Chicago: Joseph A. Miller, 2000. Approaching the subject of ecoterrorism from both a psychological and a legal perspective, the authors provide examples to support their charge that crimes committed for environmental or animal rights causes have harmed innocent people, endangered species, and the environment in general. Spiral bound and privately published, this book has the feel of a master's thesis, complete with well-documented footnotes.

Naess, Arne. *Ecology, Community, and Lifestyle: Outline of an Ecosophy.* Translated by David Rothenberg. Cambridge, U.K.: Cambridge University Press, 1990. Naess presents in detail the tenets of deep ecology, the philosophy he invented in the early 1970s that later inspired a large number of radical environmentalists to take action.

———. *Life's Philosophy: Reason and Feeling in a Deeper World.* Translated by Roland Huntford. Athens: University of Georgia Press, 2002. Norwegian philosopher Naess, the founder of the deep ecology movement, presents a meditation on the art of living based on preserving the environment and biodiversity. He believes that humans should strive to rely more on feelings and less on "pure reason," the latter of which has led humans to degrade the environment and their own culture. An integration of reason and emotion, he believes, will ultimately inspire humanity to make changes for the better.

Scarce, Rik. *Eco-Warriors: Understanding the Radical Environmental Movement.* Chicago: Noble Press, 1990. Approaching the subject from a sympathetic point of view, Scarce covers the beliefs, tactics, and personalities that form the foundation of such groups as Earth First!, the Sea Shepherd Conservation Society (SSCS), Greenpeace, and the Animal Liberation Front (ALF). The final section looks at the literature, music, art, and theater used by environmental activists to get their message across. The book ends with an essay on the future of radical environmentalism. Scarce was jailed in May 1993 for refusing to reveal the identity of his sources for this book to a grand jury.

Sessions, George, and Bill Devall. *Deep Ecology.* Layton, Utah: Gibbs Smith, 1986. Sessions and Devall articulate the concept of deep ecology for environmentalists in the United States. This book has become a standard introduction to the concept.

Annotated Bibliography

Taylor, Bron Raymond, ed. *Ecological Resistance Movements: The Global Emergence of Radical and Popular Environmentalism.* SUNY Series in International Environmental Policy and Theory. Albany: State University of New York Press, 1995. In this anthology of essays, environmental scholars examine the emergence of ecological resistance movements, some militant and some focusing on sustainable development, that have proliferated around the world. The book is divided into geographic sections (the Americas, Asia and the Pacific, Africa, and Europe), followed by a selection of articles that examine the philosophical roots, ethics, tactics, and impact of radical environmental organizations.

Thomas, Janet. *The Battle in Seattle: The Story Behind the WTO Demonstrations.* Golden, Colo.: Fulcrum, 2000. Thomas provides an eyewitness account of events in Seattle from the perspective of a protestor and passionate anti-globalization activist.

Warren, Karen J. *Ecofeminist Philosophy.* Lanham, Md.: Rowman & Littlefield, 2000. Philosophy professor Warren studies ecofeminism from a Western perspective, scrutinizing the variety of beliefs and positions within the movement, the distinctive nature of ecofeminist philosophy, and ecofeminism as an ecological position. She also looks at how the unjustified domination of women and other humans is connected to the unjustified domination of animals and nature, discusses the characteristics of oppressive systems, and explores how the ecofeminist perspective can help one understand issues of environmental and social justice. Answering such questions, Warren maintains, can help people understand and change patterns of domination, whether they are based in patriarchy or some other system.

Zerzan, John. *Elements of Refusal.* Seattle, Wash.: Left Bank Books, 1988. Anarchist Zerzan, thought by many to have been one of the driving forces behind the 1999 protests against the World Trade Organization in Seattle, ruminates in the origins of human alienation. Among the topics covered in his essays are time, agriculture, technology, unionism, Marxism, and war.

Zimmerman, Michael E. *Contesting Earth's Future: Radical Ecology and Postmodernity.* Berkeley: University of California Press, 1994. This is an in-depth look at the major philosophies that underpin much of radical environmentalist thought: deep ecology, social ecology, and ecofeminism. Most interesting are discussions concerning the often bitter differences among the three branches, particularly accusations by many social ecologists that deep ecology is, at root, an antimodernist, fascist ideology.

ARTICLES

Bandow, Doug. "American Terrorism, Environment-Style." *Human Events,* September 29, 2003, p. 27. Bandow, who is affiliated with the Cato Institute and the American Legislative Exchange Council (ALEC), presents a broad overview of individuals and environmental groups that have been accused of ecoterrorism, including the Fox and the Earth Liberation Front. He blames mainstream environmental groups of doing little to discourage "eco-saboteurs" and makes the case for supporting efforts by ALEC to draft legislation designed "to prohibit acts of or support for environmental terrorism, set penalties for violators, allow victims to sue for treble damages, target organizations that promote ecoterrorism, and allow forfeiture of property used in such offenses."

Bello, Walden. "Lilliputians Rising—2000: The Year of the Global Protest Against Corporate Globalization." *Multinational Monitor,* vol. 22, January/February 2001, pp. 33–36. Bello looks at the history of the World Trade Organization and the issues that led thousands of people to protest its policies and practices in Seattle and Washington, D.C., as well as several cities overseas.

Cockburn, Alexander. "'New' and 'Left' Are Not Oxymoronic." *Los Angeles Times,* April 20, 2000, p. B11. The author of this editorial commentary lauds the rise of the new leftist radicalism evidenced in well-attended antiglobalism protests in Seattle and Washington, D.C.

"Conservation's Ecocentrics." *Science News,* vol. 144, September 11, 1993, p. 168. This anonymous article examines the call by Dave Foreman, via the North American Wilderness Recovery (a.k.a. Wildlands) Project, to create a vast system of connected wilderness reserves across North America. Although the plan appears too radical for even mainstream environmentalists to accept, the article cites recent conservation science findings that justify some of project's underlying premises. Among these findings is the idea that protecting rare and endangered species is crucial, and that this protection must extend to "umbrella" species (plants and animals whose survival ensures that many other species will thrive) as well as to rare ones. A growing group of scientists and activists are finding that the current national park system is inadequate to achieve these goals and thus find merit in Foreman's large-scale preservation plan, even if most remain critical of the details.

DeLuca, Kevin Michael. "Unruly Arguments: The Body Rhetoric of Earth First!, ACT UP, and Queer Nation." *Argumentation and Advocacy,* vol. 36, Summer 1999, pp. 9–21. This article explores the tactics of three contemporary activist groups, including Earth First!, that are notable for rejecting formal public argument in favor of physical protests, such as tree sitting and blocking roads. Although DeLuca briefly explores the tendency of these groups to reject traditional organizational structures while forming radically democratic "disorganizations," he focuses on the idea that Earth First! activists have made their bodies, rather than language, central to their political arguments. Much of the long, scholarly essay explores the effectiveness of such tactics.

Greif, Mark. "Wreaking Ruckus." *The American Prospect*, vol. 11, August 28, 2000, pp. 18–22. The Ruckus Society was founded in 1995 by several alumni of Greenpeace actions to train people from other organizations in nonviolent direct action tactics. The group—which sets up temporary "action camps" on an as-needed basis rather than pursuing a steady campaign, a single issue, or a real doctrine—gained notoriety in 1999, when its training was credited with elevating the tactics of U.S. activists to a new level at the anti–World Trade Organization protests in Seattle. Greif reports on the Democracy in Action Camp set up in preparation for the 2000 Democratic National Convention in Los Angeles, during which activists focused on the Ruckus Society's efforts to expand beyond the white intellectual middle class and create a lasting, broad-based, populist movement. Toward this end, organizers invited black, Latino, Asian-American, and Native American trainers to join the camp as the partners of existing trainers; they also recruited "people of color" to make up the vast majority of participants.

Hawken, Paul. "On the Streets of Seattle." *The Amicus Journal*, vol. 22, Spring 2000, pp. 29–33ff. This eyewitness account of a protester at the 1999 anti–World Trade Organization (WTO) rally in Seattle is interspersed with background information on the WTO that will help readers understand exactly what thousands of people were demonstrating against.

Jensen, Derrick, and Chris Dodge. "You May Be an Anarchist—and Not Even Know It." *The Utne Reader*, May/June 2001, pp. 48ff. This is a lengthy interview with John Zerzan, an Oregon-based anarchist and author who is thought to be one of the masterminds behind the 1999 anti–World Trade Organization protests in Seattle, Washington. Sidebars to the interview provide biographical information on Zerzan and attempt to define anarchism. The article ends with a list of anarchist resources, such as books, magazines, and web sites.

Knickerbocker, Brad. "New Laws Target Increase in Acts of Ecoterrorism." *Christian Science Monitor*, November 26, 2003, p. 3. This article examines attempts by federal and state lawmakers to pass legislation aimed specifically at radical environmental and animal-rights activists. Many civil libertarians warn that such laws could be used by the government to punish peaceful political dissenters.

Kumar, Satish, and Jake Bowers. "Can the Use of Violence Ever Be Justified in the Environmental Struggle?" *The Ecologist*, vol. 30, November 2000, pp. 20–23. Peace activist Satish Kumar, editor of *Resurgence* magazine, and Jake Bowers, cofounder of Earth First! UK, engage in a lengthy debate over whether the use of violence is justified in the environmental struggle. Kumar argues against the use of violence on the grounds that police, the court system, and the mainstream media are powerful and are equipped to suppress such tactics. Believing there is no distinction between violence against people, property, or nature, she goes on to say that the means must be compatible with the ends: Violence only begets more violence, while nonviolent civil disobedience will ultimately lead to the peaceful and just society she envisions. Bowers, while not dismissing nonviolence as a viable path for protestors to take, is unwilling to make an unconditional commitment to peaceful disobedience on a personal level. He believes that destruction of inanimate objects does not constitute violence and that property should only be destroyed if no living thing is going to be hurt. Finally, he disagrees that nonviolent civil disobedience leads to a peaceful culture, pointing out the existence of nuclear weapons in Mohandas K. Gandhi's India and of the death penalty in Martin Luther King, Jr.'s, United States.

Levi, Margaret, and David Olson. "The Battle in Seattle." *Politics and Society*, vol. 28, September 2000, pp. 309–329. This is the introductory essay to a special issue of *Politics and Society* dedicated to the history of labor strife in Seattle, Washington. As such, it undermines perceptions of Seattle as a predominantly white, middle-class city and puts the 1999 anti–World Trade Organization protests in the context of a long tradition of militant Industrial Workers of the World (IWW) activity and radical labor practices, particularly among waterfront workers.

Malkin, Michelle. "Antiwar Greens Given Orders to Use 'Any Means Necessary.'" *Insight on the News*, vol. 19, April 15, 2003, p. 51. Malkin reports on the Internet publication of Craig Rosebraugh's manifesto calling on antiwar activists to take "direct actions" against U.S. military establishments, urban centers, corporations, government buildings, and media outlets. Excerpts from the manual are presented, followed by Malkin's recommendation that "green saboteurs" be treated as enemy combatants and that the government "use any means necessary to stop them in their terrorist tracks."

Morse, David. "Beyond the Myths of Seattle." *Dissent*, vol. 48, Summer 2001, pp. 39–43. Morse discusses how the media created a version of the 1999 anti–World Trade Organization protests in Seattle that made the protestors seem more violent than they actually were. In turn, police forces in cities where later protests were planned (such as Washington, D.C., Philadelphia, and Los Angeles) used this myth of violence to justify undermining civil liberties in the name of "keeping the peace."

Taylor, Paul. "Ecoterrorism: An Overlooked Threat to the U.S." *Insight on the News*, vol. 17, December 10, 2001, p. 46. Taylor writes that the September 11 terrorist attacks provided the excuse for a much-needed boost in national security measures after decades of political obsession with po-

Annotated Bibliography

litical correctness had "emasculated our military, intelligence, and criminal-justice systems." He then compares environmentalism with religion, and fundamentalism by implication, writing that "environmentalists can become radical, extreme, anarchist or nihilist entities." Taylor mentions Greenpeace and Earth First! in passing but focuses his attention on Earth Liberation Front (ELF) and Animal Liberation Front (ALF), comparing their hatred of "capitalism, political diversity, and corporate global trade" with the ideologies of terrorists based in the Middle East. He ends with the warning that ELF's attacks will eventually result in death and recommends that ecoterrorists be pursued with the same "awareness, focus, and prosecution priorities" as international terrorists.

Vanderpool, Tim. "Eco-Arson Sets Off Sparks in Desert: Phoenix Luxury Homes Are among U.S. Construction Sites Targeted by Eco-Terrorists." *Christian Science Monitor*, February 9, 2001, p. 2. Vanderpool discusses a string of arsons that burned nine luxury homes under construction near a Phoenix nature preserve. Mainstream environmentalists interviewed for the article are concerned that their efforts will be tainted by extremists, who draw attention away from issues that concern large numbers of Americans. Although Earth First! activist Nancy Zierenberg does not condemn Earth Liberation Front (ELF) tactics with the same passion as mainstream environmentalists, she also refuses to condone them, seeing them "an act of desperation and incredible frustration."

Wright, Evan Alan. "Hot Enemy of the State: Jeffrey Luers (A.K.A. Free)." *Rolling Stone*, August 30, 2001, p. 81. In June 2001, an Oregon court sentenced 22-year-old environmental activist Jeffrey Luers to nearly 23 years in prison for setting a fire at a car dealership and for his alleged role in a failed arson a few weeks earlier. Luers has paid the price for being one of the few activists whom authorities have successfully prosecuted. "The state came down so hard on him because they haven't been able to catch many activists," says Craig Rosebraugh, at that time spokesperson for Earth Liberation Front (ELF). "They wanted to make an example of him." He also added that the judge had "just handed the radical movement its first living martyr." The article traces Luers's journey from a mainstream environmentalist to one who began questioning nonviolent forms of protest. He also wrote a manifesto denouncing corporate-led destruction of the environment and calling on people to renounce their allegiance to the United States.

INTERNET DOCUMENTS

Zerzan, John. "New York, New York." *Green Anarchist*. Available online. URL: http://www.greenanarchist.org/pdf/ga70.pdf. Posted in Fall 2003.

Zerzan reports on the 24-hour blackout that hit New York City on July 13–14, 2003, seeing the widespread unrest as an indication of the fineness of the line between technology-mediated civilization and a free society. He refers to the looting that occurred as the "transformation of commodities into free merchandise."

VIDEOS

"30 Frames a Second: The WTO in Seattle." Directed by Rustin Thompson. Oley, Pa.: White Noise Productions/Bullfrog Films, 2001. Video (VHS). 72 minutes. Photojournalist Thompson documents the civil unrest that erupted during the 1999 World Trade Organization (WTO) meeting in Seattle. Engaging images of clashes between protestors and police are accompanied by a voice-over narrative in which Thompson acknowledges his inability to remain subjective despite his journalistic intentions.

GREENPEACE AND THE SEA SHEPHERD CONSERVATION SOCIETY

BOOKS

Bohlen, Jim. *Making Waves: The Origin and Future of Greenpeace*. Montreal, Quebec: Black Rose, 2000. This book traces the development of Greenpeace from early efforts of a handful of activists to publicize nuclear testing by the United States off the coast of Alaska to the establishment of offices in more than 30 countries with a total membership of more than 3 million people. Bohlen, who helped found Canada's Sierra Club chapter before breaking away to help form the group that would become Greenpeace, writes about the origin of the organization, the motivation and philosophy of the founders, and the development and execution of the direct action campaigns that helped Greenpeace gain notoriety in the environmental scene.

Morris, David B. *Earth Warrior: Overboard with Paul Watson and the Sea Shepherd Conservation Society*. Golden, Colo.: Fulcrum, 1995. Morris profiles Watson and provides an eyewitness account of a sea hunt during which the Sea Shepherds used their search-and-ram tactics to force the retreat of Japanese trawlers involved in drift-net fishing.

Watson, Paul. *Ocean Warrior: My Battle to End the Illegal Slaughter on the High Seas*. Toronto, Ontario: Key Porter Books, 1996. This book, the sequel to Watson's 1981 *Sea Shepherd*, chronicles actions by the Sea Shepherd Conservation Society (SSCS) during the 1980s and early 1990s.

———. *Sea Shepherd: My Fight for Whales and Seals.* New York: W. W. Norton, 1981. Watson details his break with Greenpeace, his founding of the Sea Shepherd Conservation Society (SSCS), and the early actions of his new organization.

ARTICLES

Bond, Michael. "A New Environment for Greenpeace." *Foreign Policy,* November/December 2001, pp. 66–67. Bond profiles Greenpeace on the 30th anniversary of its inaugural attempt to stop nuclear testing on Alaska's Amchitka Island. He traces the group's impact and its development into a global organization through three decades. Greenpeace International Executive Director Gerd Leipold then outlines the group's priorities for the 21st century, including a campaign against the biotechnology industry that has led to reductions in research funding.

Buckley, William F., Jr. "The Passions of the Greenpeacers." *National Review,* vol. 47, October 9, 1995, p. 71. Buckley takes a critical look at Greenpeace's hostility toward nuclear energy and nuclear testing.

Carmin, JoAnn, and Deborah B. Balser. "Selecting Repertoires of Action in Environmental Movement Organizations." *Organization and Environment,* vol. 15, December 2002, pp. 365–388. This long, scholarly article relies on organization and social movement theories to explore the criteria that environmental organizations use to determine what types of action will be most appropriate and effective to achieve their goals. The authors focus their attention on Greenpeace and Friends of the Earth, relying on interview and archival data from these organizations. Endnotes and a long list of cited works are provided.

Chisholm, Patricia. "Canada's 'Earth Warrior.'" *Maclean's,* vol. 107, July 25, 1994, p. 40. Chisholm profiles Paul Watson and reports on the Sea Shepherd Conservation Society's disruption of a whale hunt off the northern coast of Norway in which his ship and a Norwegian coast guard vessel collided.

"Cod Vanish; Grand Banks' Defender Faces Jail." *Earth Island Journal,* vol. 9, Spring 1994, p. 21. This anonymous article covers the trial of Paul Watson on charges stemming from a confrontation with Spanish and Cuban fishing boats in the international waters off the coast of Newfoundland, Canada. Watson says he was trying to protect the northern cod, an endangered species.

"Don't Invite Greenpeace." *Oil & Gas Journal,* vol. 100, September 16, 2002, p. 19. This anonymous editorial argues against the inclusion of Greenpeace representatives at the World Petroleum Congress, maintaining that although discourse is generally good (leading to compromise, enlightenment, and progress), the sort of "discord-conflict" provoked by extremist groups like Greenpeace precludes compromise. The article says that while it is "reasonable to dislike oil spills and air pollution and to worry about the possibility . . . that carbon dioxide generated by the combustion of hydrocarbons warms the planet," the extremist contention that "oil is not a clean and sustainable energy, and so it cannot be good for anybody" made by activist Benedict Southworth at the 1992 Earth Summit in Brazil undermines the credibility of Greenpeace and similar organizations. The author warns that Greenpeace has more political effect than most leaders of the oil and gas industry want to acknowledge, and therefore suggests that the industry, rather than ignoring environmentalists, should "respond more aggressively than it has done before to Greenpeace propaganda." This includes not inviting radicals to meetings "designed to foster constructive discussion about real problems."

Flynn, Julia, Heidi Dawley, and Naomi Freundlich. "Green Warrior in Gray Flannel: Why Business Listens to Activist Jeremy Leggett." *Business Week*, May 6, 1996, p. 96. The authors profile Jeremy Leggett, who at the time of this article was the director of Greenpeace International's solar campaign. He has found success in convincing insurance and bank executives that global warming could bankrupt their industries.

"Greenpeace Buys into Shell in Bid to Promote Solar Cells." *Professional Engineering*, vol. 13, March 22, 2000, p. 8. This anonymous article reports on Greenpeace's purchase of 140,000 shares in Shell oil company to help persuade it to invest in a large-scale solar panel factory. The organization is seeking to take advantage of a Dutch stock exchange rule that allows shareholders with an investment worth more than 70,000 to send proposals to fellow shareholders. Greenpeace has also united 100 BP Amoco shareholders with a total of more than 150,000 shares to oppose the company's controversial Northstar oil pipeline project in the Arctic Ocean.

"Greenpeace Protesters Face Felony Charges." *The Progressive*, vol. 65, October 2001, p. 17. This anonymous article provides evidence that Greenpeace, despite criticism by more radical environmental groups, has not entirely abandoned direct action tactics. On July 14, 2001, 17 people from eight different countries were arrested for delaying the test of a U.S. antiballistic missile system by swimming, diving, and boating beneath the flight path. They were charged with conspiring to violate a safety zone and violating an order, felony charges that carry possible prison terms of more than 10 years.

Gunther, Marc. "Green Is Good." *Fortune*, vol. 147, March 31, p. 58. Gunther interviews Greenpeace USA executive director John Passacantando, who majored in economics, once worked at a consulting firm, and has steered Greenpeace toward working with big companies, such as Coca-Cola and McDonald's, to make them more ecologically sound.

Holden, Constance. "Shell Pulls a U-Turn." *Science*, vol. 269, July 7, 1995, p. 33. Holden writes about Greenpeace's success in pressuring Shell oil company to abort plans to dump the *Brent Spar*, a decommissioned floating oil storage tank containing an estimated 100 tons of heavy-metal-laden sludge, in the North Atlantic. British government officials reacted angrily, claiming that disposing of the tank on land is more hazardous environmentally and would cost four times as much.

Judis, John B. "Activist Trouble." *The American Prospect*, January/February 1998, pp. 20–22. This article discusses the financial and organizational troubles faced by Greenpeace and Citizen Action during the late 1990s.

Kerlin, Katherine. "Giving Greenpeace a Chance." *E: The Environmental Magazine*, vol. 12, September/October 2001, pp. 12–16. Following internal unrest that culminated in the resignation of Greenpeace USA's entire board of directors, the organization was revitalized by new executive director John Passacantando. Since then, finances have become stable, and morale has risen in response to the change in leadership and by the sense of urgency the Bush administration has created in environmental groups worldwide. Kerlin discusses the effectiveness of Greenpeace's combination of behind-the-scenes lobbying efforts and its continued use of direct action tactics. According to Jerry Taylor of the conservative Cato Institute, Greenpeace remains ineffective in changing public policy but has been able to change the minds of corporations, which care about how they are perceived by consumers. Passacantando's tactics have included calling on leaders of *Fortune* 100 companies to clarify their position on the Kyoto Protocol.

Margulis, Charles. "Playing With Our Food." *Earth Island Journal*, vol. 17, Winter 2003, pp. S2–S3. Margulis, a genetic engineering (GE) specialist with Greenpeace, presents an argument against the production and consumption of GE foods, which he claims pose unknown risks to human health and the global environment. Greenpeace opposes any release of GE organisms, accusing the companies that produce them of a new form of "biological pollution" that is alive, that reproduces, and that moves through the environment. Margulis argues against biotech industry claims that there is no evidence that GE foods cause any harm; toward that end, he says lab evidence that insect-resistant GE corn could harm monarch and other endangered butterflies has been verified in the field. He also cites a 1996 article in *The New England Journal of Medicine* warning that the Food and Drug Administration's (FDA) policy on GE food left consumers at risk from potential new food allergies. Of particular note is the infamous StarLink incident, in which gene-altered corn that was never approved for human consumption contaminated more than 300 products sold in supermarkets and restaurants across the country. Greenpeace's tactics have included inciting consumer pressure that led McDonald's, Frito Lay, and McCain Foods to reject GE potatoes, and compiling a True Food Shopping List that connects consumers across the country in a grassroots effort to force food companies to stop using GE food. The article ends with a list of suggestions for getting active in the elimination of GE products, including links to organizations that have taken up the cause.

Motavalli, Jim. "A Violent Confrontation." *E: The Environmental Magazine*, vol. 10, January/February 1999, p. 27. The revival of a gray whale hunt by Washington state's Makah Indians drew protests from environmental groups, including the Sea Shepherd Conservation Society (SSCS). In October 1998, a confrontation between the Makah and SSCS grew violent when angry tribal members threw rocks at the Sea Shepherd vessel *Sirenian*, injuring two crew members and damaging the group's Zodiac raft. Three society members, including Gray Whale Campaign Expedition leader Lisa Distefano, were briefly detained by tribal police. As a result, SSCS agreed not to land on Makah territory but vowed to disrupt the hunt by other means.

Motavalli, Jim, and Maud Dillingham. "In Harm's Way." *E: The Environmental Magazine*, vol. 6, November 1995, p. 28. This article discusses Greenpeace's crusade to oppose French nuclear tests in the South Pacific, marking a return to its direct action roots in an effort to reestablish its commitment to the environment and its prowess as an efficient publicity machine. Paul Watson, founder of the Sea Shepherd Conservation Society, is also profiled.

Olson, Karen. "Be the Change You Want to See." *Utne Reader*, March/April 2003, pp. 65–66. Olson interviews Andre Carothers, a 20-year Greenpeace activist who founded the Rockwood Leadership Program. Based on Gandhi's idea that a person needs to be the change he or she wants to see in the world, Rockwood's Art of Leadership workshop teaches potential leaders of social movements that self-examination and improved communication skills are essential to creating a better world.

Parker, John. "Greenpeace Holds Ship in Protest." *Traffic World*, vol. 261, March 6, 2000, pp. 39–40. Parker discusses Greenpeace's boarding and occupation of a ship off the coast of Britain carrying 60,000 tons of genetically modified soya owned by the U.S. agricultural producer Cargill. The group sought to highlight its campaign to end the importation of genetically modified foods into Europe. According to Cargill, the cargo was fully regulated and had been approved for use in food and feed products by the European Union since 1996, an approval questioned by Greenpeace. The six activists, who prevented the ship from moving for 17 hours, were arrested onboard by police the next day.

Ridgeway, James. "Mururoa Mon Amour." *The Village Voice,* vol. 40, September 26, 1995, p. 23. Ridgeway analyzes the resumption of underground nuclear testing in the South Pacific by the French government, claiming it has jump-started the long-dormant, Greenpeace-led antinuclear movement.

———. "No Justice, No Greenpeace." *The Village Voice,* vol. 45, February 15, 2000, p. 44. This brief article reports on a threat by Greenpeace to commit nonviolent civil disobedience at Al Gore's headquarters in Manchester during the 2000 New Hampshire presidential primary. The group was angry over a 1992 campaign promise made by Gore to stop operations at a $167 million hazardous-waste incinerator in East Liverpool, Ohio, until a risk study was completed. After his election as vice president, Gore stalled on the pledge.

Rosenberg, Kirsten. "Whales Slip Past Makah." *The Animals' Agenda,* vol. 19, March/April 1999, pp. 9–10. In 1998, the Makah Indians of Neah Bay, Washington, were granted the right, based on a provision from an 1855 government treaty, to circumvent the existing global whaling ban and resume a whale-hunting ritual that their ancestors had abandoned in 1926. The first hunting expedition in 70 years ended in failure. Rosenberg speculates that stormy weather and the activities of the Sea Shepherd Conservation Society (which conducted frequent boat patrols and broadcast underwater orca sounds) may have kept the whales farther off the Pacific coast than usual, and therefore far away from the hunters, as they migrated south.

Selle, Robert R. "A Founder of Greenpeace." *The World & I,* vol. 18, March 2003, pp. 52–55. Selle profiles Patrick Moore, one of the 12 original Greenpeace activists who sailed to Alaska's Amchitka Island in 1971 in protest of a U.S. hydrogen bomb test. Moore later served as president of Greenpeace Canada for nine years and a director of Greenpeace International for seven years, but now believes that Greenpeace and other big environmentalist organizations have moved away from truly environmental concerns and into the realm of anticorporate socialist extremism. He left Greenpeace in 1986, and in 1991 he and his wife founded an eco-consulting company called Greenspirit, which favors a "big picture" approach to environmentalism rather than the piecemeal approach of Greenpeace, Sierra Club, and other organizations. As an advocate of sustainable development, in which human civilization grows without hurting the environment, he differs with many environmentalists on a number of issues. He favors, for example, the greatest possible use worldwide of genetically modified (GM) crops, which he says increase farm productivity and thereby reduce the pressure to cut down forests for expanding agricultural land. Moore is critical of the environmental movement's "logical inconsistency," citing as an example a sign carried by a protester at the 1999 antiglobalization rallies in Seattle that read, "Join the Worldwide Struggle Against Globalization."

Smith, Gar. "Whale War Heats Up." *Earth Island Journal*, vol. 9, Fall 1994, p. 18. Confrontations between Norwegian whalers and ships from Greenpeace and the Sea Shepherd Conservation Society (SSCS) are reported. SSCS's *Whales Forever* was damaged by depth explosives dropped by Norwegian commandoes, while Greenpeace's *MV Sirius* confronted a Norwegian whaler in the act of killing minke whales in international waters.

Watson, Paul. "For Cod and Country." *Whole Earth*, Fall 1998, pp. 28–29. Watson describes the efforts of the Sea Shepherd Conservation Society (SSCS) to draw the Canadian government into a confrontation with a foreign drag-trawler outside Canada's 200-mile nautical limit.

———. "Will We Be Prepared for the Next Spill?" *Newsweek*, vol. 137, March 12, 2001, p. 16. Watson, founder of the Sea Shepherd Conservation Society (SSCS), offers a firsthand account of the 2001 wreck of the Ecuadorian-registered oil tanker *Jessica* on a reef off San Cristobal Island in the Galapagos Islands. With help from the U.S. Coast Guard four days away, Watson says his crew was prevented from pumping 160,000 gallons of diesel fuel and 80,000 gallons of bunker fuel oil from the ship by local officials, who told him that the oil was the private property of Petroecuador. Any attempt to remove it would be considered theft by both the Ecuadorian Navy and Petroecuador. While Watson's crew stood by unable to act, *Jessica*'s hull cracked and began to ooze oil into the ocean. Although a greater disaster was prevented by evaporation and favorable currents, Watson says the incident offers a valuable lesson about the general lack of preparation among nations to deal with oil spills. He proposes the creation of an internationally recognized coalition of oil producers and conservationists, who could organize airborne teams equipped with wildlife-cleaning equipment and emergency pumps able to reach any spill or potential spill within 12 hours.

Zakin, Susan. "Oh, Stop Blubbering." *Field & Stream*, vol. 103, January 1999, p. 24. Zakin reports on the controversial exemption from International Whaling Commission restrictions granted to Washington state's Makah Nation and efforts by the Sea Shepherd Conservation Society (SSCS) to prevent the hunters from succeeding.

INTERNET DOCUMENTS

National Forest Protection Alliance and Greenpeace. "Endangered Forests, Endangered Freedoms." Greenpeace USA. Available online. URL: http://

www.greenpeaceusa.org/bin/view.fpl/8270/article/359.html. Downloaded on September 10, 2003. This Greenpeace publication reports on the dwindling acreage of forestland in the United States and what this means for American concepts of freedom and rugged individuality.

Watson, Paul. "How Many More Whales Will Iceland Need to Kill to Discover What We Already Know They Eat?" Sea Shepherd Conservation Society. Available online. URL: http://www.seashepherd.org/editorial07.shtml. Posted on August 25, 2003. In 2003, the Icelandic government released a question-and-answer fact sheet in an attempt to justify that nation's continued whaling operations in the North Atlantic despite an international ban on the practice. This article consists of the original questions and answers supplied by Iceland, followed by Watson's own commentary, which seeks to debunk Iceland's justifications. The title of the article refers to Iceland's claim that it needs to continue hunting whales for research purposes.

VIDEO

"Drumbeat for Mother Earth." Directed by Joseph Di Gangi and Amon Giebel. Oley, Pa.: Bullfrog Films, 1999. Video (VHS). 56 minutes. This video collaboration between Greenpeace and the Indigenous Environmental Network (IEN) brings together Native activists and U.S. environmentalists to explore the effects of persistent organic pollutants (POPs). These chlorine-based chemicals, which can be either pesticides (such as DDT) or byproducts of industrial processes, disproportionately affect (for a variety of reasons) indigenous people who follow a traditional lifestyle and consume traditional foods. The video addresses a number of key questions about POPs, including what they are, how they move through the environment, how they affect human and environmental health, how industry and government are responding, and what individuals and communities can do to mitigate the problem. "Drumbeat for Mother Earth" was recognized as the Best Environmental Documentary at the 1999 New York International Independent Film and Video Festival.

EARTH FIRST!

BOOKS

Bari, Judy. *Timber Wars.* Monroe, Maine: Common Courage, 1994. Through a series of essays and interviews, Bari recounts her work in organizing the 1990 Redwood Summer in Northern California, including efforts to form alliances between environmentalists and unionized timber workers. Her account of the car bombing that injured her and Darryl Cherney is highlighted by photographs of the mutilated car, taken by the Oakland Police Department.

Beach, Patrick. *A Good Forest for Dying: The Tragic Death of a Young Man on the Front Lines of the Environmental Wars.* New York: Doubleday, 2004. Beach tells the story of David "Gypsy" Chain, an environmental activist who died in September 1998 when he was crushed by a tree felled by Pacific Lumber logger A. E. Ammons. The author also looks at the history of the struggle between environmentalists and those with economic interests in the American West and traces the events that led to confrontations between loggers and activists in Northern California in the 1990s.

Chase, Alston. *In a Dark Wood: The Fight Over Forests and the Rising Tyranny of Ecology.* Boston: Houghton Mifflin, 1995. Chase tells the story of the battle over old-growth forests in the Pacific Northwest, offering the diverse points of view of loggers, foresters, environmental activists, scientists, and businesspersons. In examining the participation and impact of Earth First!, Chase considers the influence that the radical environmental philosophy of biocentrism has had on mainstream environmentalists and even on some government agencies. This well-researched book includes a long list of notes and resources.

Davis, John. *The Earth First! Reader: Ten Years of Radical Environmentalism.* Salt Lake City, Utah: Peregrine Smith, 1991. Davis, longtime managing editor of the *Earth First! Journal,* presents a collection of articles that appeared in the periodical between 1982 and 1990. The essays are arranged in chronological order within sections that include Earth First! Actions, Land Use Conflicts, Critiques of the Status Quo, Deep Ecology, Ecosystems and Their Members, Matters Spiritual, and Some Summary Thoughts on Earth First! This is a good source of material by those who were directly involved in the formative years of Earth First! when the founders were still involved. Included is a foreword by Dave Foreman and brief biographical sketches of contributors, several of whom wrote under pseudonyms.

Foreman, Dave. *Confessions of an Eco-Warrior.* New York: Crown, 1991. Although the title suggests an autobiographical work, Earth First! cofounder Foreman instead presents a series of essays that set forth his agenda and beliefs concerning the defense of the environment. The book includes several chapters on the virtues of monkeywrenching and tree spiking but ends with Foreman's announcement that although he will continue to applaud the efforts of Earth First!, the time has come for him to move on and work for environmental causes under an organization with a different name. In this final essay, he writes, "We do not engage in radical action because we are primarily motivated by opposition to authority . . . but because we are *for* something—the beauty, wisdom, and abundance of this living planet."

Foreman, Dave, and Bill Haywood, eds. *Ecodefense: A Field Guide to Monkeywrenching.* Tucson, Ariz.: Ned Ludd, 1985. Prefaced with the disclaimer that no person involved in the book's production "encourages anyone to do any of the stupid, illegal things contained herein," *Ecodefense* proceeds to supply the reader with detailed instructions on how to spike trees, disable heavy equipment, topple billboards, free wild animals from snares, and flatten the tires of off-road vehicles, among other things. It includes a foreword by Edward Abbey, whose novel *The Monkey Wrench Gang* helped inspire the Earth First! movement.

Hill, Julia Butterfly. *The Legacy of Luna: The Story of a Tree, a Woman, and the Struggle to Save the Redwoods.* San Francisco: HarperSanFrancisco, 2001. Hill recounts the two years she spent living in a California redwood that had been marked for the sawmill by Pacific Lumber. Highlights include enduring harassment from loggers, the media, food-stealing squirrels, and even from Earth First! activists who thought Hill was too independent. Hill also suffered frostbitten toes, and at one point she hosted an overnight visit by actor Woody Harrelson, who complained about the cramped conditions. Less compelling is the author's account, based largely on second- and third-hand sources, of radical environmental politics, the practices of Pacific Lumber, and the effects of logging and environmental activism on the residents of Humboldt County, California. Hill eventually helped win protection for the tree (which she named Luna) and others in the area.

Lee, Martha F. *Earth First! Environmental Apocalypse.* Syracuse, N.Y.: Syracuse University Press, 1995. Lee, a political theorist at the University of Windsor in Ontario, analyzes the ideology and infrastructure of Earth First! and links them with the mainstream ideology of millenarian reform movements in U.S. history. Basing her research on Earth First! publications, personal interviews, and a large number of secondary sources, Lee traces the movement from its origin in 1980 to the 1990 split between the old guard and younger activists. At the root of this schism was cofounder Dave Foreman's idea that Earth First! should be an environmentally activist "community outside the American mainstream" based on "tribal" or grass-roots egalitarianism. Although this lack of structured leadership hierarchy allowed radical environmentalists the freedom to focus on activism, it also prevented development of a sense of unity and common purpose, opening the way for division that led Foreman to quit the organization in 1990.

Manes, Christopher. *Green Rage: Radical Environmentalism and the Unmaking of Civilization.* Boston: Little, Brown, 1990. Manes, a former associate editor of the *Earth First! Journal*, provides an in-depth history of the early years of Earth First!, focusing on the frustrations and philosophies that drove the group to action. He explores deep ecology, civil disobedience, the history of the U.S. Forest Service, and critics of monkeywrenching, all from the perspective of a radical environmentalist. The book includes extensive endnotes and a selected bibliography.

Wall, Derek. *Earth First! and the Anti-Roads Movement: Radical Environmentalism and Comparative Social Movements*. London: Routledge, 1999. This book focuses on Earth First! activities in England, which coalesced in the early 1990s around opposition to road building.

Zakin, Susan. *Coyotes and Town Dogs: Earth First! and the Environmental Movement*. Tucson: University of Arizona Press, 2002. Written in a fast-paced journalistic style intended for a general audience, this book covers the early years of Earth First! Zakin begins with biographical information about the movement's cofounders and continues through the 1989 arrest and subsequent trials of Dave Foremen and others, providing along the way plenty of insight into the environmental battles of the 1970s and 1980s that increasingly radicalized many activists.

ARTICLES

Bari, Judi. "The Feminization of Earth First!" *Ms*, vol. 2, May 1992, pp. 84ff. Bari describes her activism in Earth First! from a feminist perspective. Initially wary of the "no compromise" direct action group founded by "macho beer-drinking men," Bari was eventually won over by the philosophy of deep ecology and by the realization that Earth First! activists "were the only people willing to put their bodies in front of the bulldozers and chain saws to save the trees." The loose structure of Earth First! allowed her to eschew the macho activism advocated by Earth First!'s male founders in favor of a more explicit nonviolence code based on the civil rights movement and on finding common ground with loggers. Bari also recounts the explosion that blew up her car and the death threats she received before the blast, many of which had a decidedly misogynistic tone. One, signed "The Avenging Angel," included a biblical quote from Timothy 2:11: "Let the woman learn in silence with all subjection. But I suffer not a woman to teach, nor to usurp authority over the man, but to be in silence."

Bergman, B. J. "Wild at Heart." *Sierra*, vol. 83, January/February 1998, pp. 24–29ff. The author profiles Dave Foreman, cofounder of Earth First! and later, at the time of the article's writing, a director of the Sierra Club. The article intersperses biographical information about Foreman with the author's account of a rafting trip on the Colorado River with Foreman and several others.

Annotated Bibliography

Bielski, Vince. "Environmental Legacy." *The Village Voice*, vol. 42, May 27, 1997, pp. 55–56. Two days before Earth First! activist Judi Bari died of cancer, her lawyer filed a brief that detailed the FBI's alleged attempt to "smear" her and fellow activist Darryl Cherney. This article profiles Bari and presents much of the evidence pointing to FBI misconduct, including the accusation that many of the claims about evidence in the Earth First! case made by FBI Crime Lab bomb expert David Williams were baseless. The Justice Department's inspector general had recently found that Crime Lab agents used flawed science and false testimony to help prosecutors in a number of cases, including the 1993 World Trade Center and 1995 Oklahoma City bombings. The inspector general went on to say that Williams "lacks the objectivity, judgment, and scientific knowledge that should be possessed by a Laboratory Examiner." Seven years after this article was written, this evidence convinced a 10-member jury that the FBI had indeed violated Bari and Cherney's civil rights.

Elvin, John. "Wild-Eyed in the Wilderness." *Insight on the News*, vol. 17, April 23, 2001, pp. 21–23. Elvin profiles Earth First! cofounder Dave Foreman, who discusses his long-term efforts to "re-wild" America through The Wildlands Project (TWP).

Fortgang, Erika. "The Girl in the Tree." *Rolling Stone*, July 8, 1999, pp. 66–67ff. This profile of Julia Butterfly Hill was written while the activist was 18 months into her two-year sit in a redwood tree to prevent its destruction. The article recounts many of her travails, including attempts by loggers to force her out by cutting safety lines, buzzing her with a helicopter, and intercepting her food supplies. Hill also endured repeated snowfalls and high winds induced by El Niño, as well as the cramped conditions of the tree platform. Hill believes a childhood spent traveling with her father (then a preacher), her mother, and her two brothers in a small trailer helped prepare her for this inconvenience. The article also touches on the federal government's unprecedented agreement to buy the land around Hill's tree to turn it into a forest preserve, a move that many environmentalists believed included too many concessions to Pacific Lumber.

Goodell, Jeff. "Death in the Redwoods." *Rolling Stone*, January 21, 1999, pp. 60–69ff. Goodell presents the story of David Chain, an Earth First! activist who was killed when a logger felled a redwood tree in Humboldt County, California. The article includes some background information on the struggle by radical environmentalists to save redwood trees from Pacific Lumber in Northern California, on repeated violations of the law by the logging company, and on the details of Chain's Texas upbringing and the circumstances that led him to California. The bulk of the article, however, consists of a well-written, detailed account of hours leading up to Chain's death, including the content of the video that catches A. E.

Ammons, the logger who cut the tree that killed Chain, shouting obscenities and threatening to get his pistol. The account of the aftermath included the author's interview with Ammons a week after Chain's funeral.

"High and Outside." *People Weekly*, vol. 50, December 28, 1998–January 4, 1999, pp. 145. This brief article profiles Julia Hill's efforts to save a grove of redwood trees in Northern California by living in one of them to prevent it from being cut down by Pacific Lumber.

Mokhiber, Russell. "Manslaughter in the Woods." *Multinational Monitor*, vol. 19, September 1998, p. 31. Mokhiber reports on the death of activist David Chain and calls by environmentalists for law enforcement agencies to investigate Pacific Lumber and one of its loggers. Earth First! has stated its belief that "the loggers were aware that activists were in the woods and deliberately felled trees in their direction . . . in an apparent attempt to target activists." Pacific Lumber says the death of Chain was accidental and that the logging crew did not see anybody in the area. A. E. Ammons, the logger who cut the deadly tree, had been caught on video threatening the activists shortly before Chain's death but claims he thought they had left the area before he resumed cutting.

Ridgeway, James. "Federal Bureau of Instigation." *The Village Voice*, vol. 47, July 2, 2002, p. 36. In the aftermath of a jury decision in favor of Earth First! activists Judi Bari and Darryl Cherney against the FBI, Ridgeway discusses the federal agency's questionable tactics concerning investigation into radical environmentalism. This includes THERMCON, an Arizona sting in which an FBI infiltrator pushed Earth First! activists into using thermite to topple a power line so the government could cast Dave Foreman as a terrorist who made use of explosives.

Shantz, Jeffrey A., and Barry D. Adam. "Ecology and Class: The Green Syndicalism of IWW/Earth First! Local 1." *The International Journal of Sociology and Social Policy*, vol. 19, pp. 43–72. This long, scholarly essay explores the international emergence of "syndical ecology" or "green syndicalism," manifested in the United States by the convergence of the radical labor group Industrial Workers of the World (IWW) and radical environmentalists Earth First! This alliance, which emerged in 1990 during the Redwood Summer campaign, was largely the work of Earth First! activist Judi Bari, who sought to build alliances with loggers in order to save old-growth forest in Northern California "and replace the corporate timber companies with environmentally responsible worker-owned cooperatives." The essay ends with a list of references.

Skow, John. "The Redwoods Weep." *Time*, vol. 152, September 28, 1998, pp. 70–72. This article on the death of Earth First! activist David Chain focuses on the shady history of Maxxam Corporation (owners of Pacific

Lumber) and the bad deal the federal government and the state of California made with the corporation to save a small tract of forest.

Smith, Gar. "Singing Under Oath." *Earth Island Journal,* vol. 17, Autumn 2002, pp. 35–37. Smith looks at the court case brought against the FBI by Earth First! activists Darryl Cherney and Judi Bari. The article provides background information on the Earth First! Redwood Summer campaign (during which the bombing occurred) and a detailed account of the trial, including the content of a videotape that Bari and her lawyers recorded several weeks before she died of cancer. The jury found that six of the seven defendants violated Bari and Cherney's First and Fourth Amendment rights by arresting the activists, searching their homes, and carrying out a smear campaign in the press by calling Earth First! a terrorist organization and calling the activists bombers.

Smith, Gar, and Judi Bari. "Uncovering the FBI Bomb School." *Earth Island Journal,* vol. 16, Winter 2001/2002, pp. 36–38. Smith recounts the pipe bomb explosion that injured Earth First! activists Judi Bari and Darryl Cherney and briefly discusses the (at the time of the article) upcoming trial based on the two activists' lawsuit against the FBI. The bulk of the article, however, consists of a 1994 essay written by Bari in which she presents extensive evidence that the FBI mishandled the investigation and may have even been responsible for the bombing. This includes the fact that, four weeks before the incident, four of the local FBI agents who investigated the explosion (including lead investigator Frank Doyle) attended a training course in which the federal agency blew up cars with pipe bombs to practice responding, thus creating virtually the same crime scene that was about to happen in Oakland. The article includes several sidebars, including a tribute to the recently deceased Bari written by David Brower.

INTERNET DOCUMENT

Earth First! "What Is Earth First!?: An Introductory Primer." Earth First! Journal. Available online. URL: http://www.earthfirstjournal.org/efj/primer/index.html. Updated on May 20, 1998. This overview is intended for environmental activists considering the use of direct action. Sections include "How Deep Is Your Ecology?," "Direct Action Gets the Goods," "Monkeywrenching: What's Up with That?," "Get It Together: Forming an Earth First! Group," and "EF! Campaigns and Projects."

VIDEOS

"Butterfly." Directed by Doug Wolens. San Francisco: Doug Wolens Film Library, 2000. Video (VHS). 80 minutes. This film recounts the story of

Julia Butterfly Hill, who spent two years living in a giant redwood to protest logging practices in Northern California. Interviews with lumber company spokespersons, loggers whose jobs were affected by the protest, Hill's father (a former evangelical minister), and people living in the nearby lumber town of Stafford provide multiple points of view. Rather than focusing on the philosophy of the radical environmental movement, the film examines aggressive logging methods based on maximizing short-term profits at the expense of long-term ecological damage.

"The Cracking of Glen Canyon Damn with Edward Abbey and Earth First!" Directed by Christopher McLeod. La Honda, Calif.: Earth Image Films, 1982. Video (VHS). 9 minutes. This video captures the legendary birth of Earth First! activism with the new group's unfurling of a 300-foot "crack" down the face of Glen Canyon Dam in 1981. It also features footage of Edward Abbey's famous speech from the back of a pick-up truck, during which he tells those gathered to "oppose the destruction of our homeland" by politicians and industrialists. He adds that "if opposition is not enough, we must resist. And if resistance is not enough, then subvert."

"Fire in the Eyes." Directed by James Ficklin. Redway, Calif.: Earth Films, 1999. Video (VHS). 32 minutes. This video, taped at various protests against logging in the Headwaters Forest region, shows police officers swabbing and spraying pepper spray on the eyelids of nonviolent protesters. The footage was used in an unsuccessful attempt to seek redress in court.

"Luna: The Stafford Giant Tree-Sit." Directed by James Ficklin. Redway, Calif.: Earth Films, 1998. Video (VHS). 22 minutes. Ficklin tells the story of Julia Butterfly Hill's two-year tree sit in an attempt to save a giant redwood she named Luna from being cut down by Maxxam/Pacific Lumber Company.

"Redwood Summer." Directed by Stuart Rickey. Oley, Pa.: Bullfrog Films, 1993. Video (VHS). 30 minutes. This video documents the 1990 Earth First! civil disobedience campaign against logging the Headwaters Forest region of Northern California. The perspectives of both radical environmentalists and local loggers are presented.

"Tree Sit: The Art of Resistance." Directed by James Ficklin. Redway, Calif.: Earth Films, 2000. Video (VHS). 120 minutes. Ficklin presents an overview of the struggle between Earth First! activists and logging interests in Northern California's Humboldt County. The action ranges from 1990 Redwood Summer and the car bomb that injured activist Judi Bari to the 1999 WTO protests in the streets of Seattle. In between, the video covers the establishment of "tree villages" in the branches of redwood trees hundreds of feet above the ground by Julia Hill and other activists.

THE EARTH LIBERATION FRONT AND THE ANIMAL LIBERATION FRONT

BOOKS

Glick, Daniel. *Powder Burn: Arson, Money, and Mystery on Vail Mountain.* New York: PublicAffairs, 2001. Glick, a *Newsweek* correspondent, examines the events surrounding the October 1998 arson that caused $12 million of damage at Vail, Colorado. Along the way, he uncovers deep-seated resentment among local residents aimed at the ski resort's questionable business practices, indicating that the list of arson suspects is long despite the Earth Liberation Front's unsubstantiated claim of credit. Glick even records the belief among some locals that Vail Associates set the fires themselves to gain sympathy so they could expand the resort without opposition.

Newkirk, Ingrid. *Free the Animals: The Story of the Animal Liberation Front.* New York: Lantern Books, 2000. This ostensibly true account of the life of "Valerie," the woman who started the Animal Liberation Front (ALF) in North America, is presented as a fictional story. Anecdotal chapters that detail ALF actions are accompanied by pictures of the animals that were rescued. Newkirk, the president of People for the Ethical Treatment of Animals, writes in a style that is suitable for young adult readers.

Pickering, Leslie James. *The Earth Liberation Front: 1997–2002.* South Wales, N.Y.: Arissa, 2003. Pickering, who along with Craig Rosebraugh served as press officer for the North American Earth Liberation Front Press Office (NAELFPO), has complied a collection of previously published documents relating to the ELF from its inception in 1997 through 2002. Chapters include a collection of all the ELF communiqués received at the press office during the time in question, the answers to a series of frequently asked questions concerning the group, reprints of three issues of the NAELFPO publication *Resist*, excerpts from statements made at the February 2002 congressional hearing on ecoterrorism, an interview of Pickering conducted by the Guerilla News Network, and Pickering's 2002 statement of resignation from NAELFPO. Publisher Arissa is an organization cofounded by Pickering and Rosebraugh with the purpose of inciting a violent revolution in the United States.

Rosebraugh, Craig. *Burning Rage of a Dying Planet: Speaking for the Earth Liberation Front.* Portland, Oreg.: Arissa Media Group, 2004. Rosebraugh presents an account of his own life, as well as a complete history of the Earth Liberation Front in North America.

———. *The Logic of Political Violence: Lessons in Reform and Revolution.* Portland, Oreg.: Arissa Media Group, 2003. Rosebraugh argues that violence has often been more effective than nonviolent civil disobedience in advancing the cause of political and social justice. He also advocates revolution in the United States using any means necessary.

ARTICLES

Belsie, Laurent. "Eco-Vandals Put a Match to 'Progress.'" *Christian Science Monitor,* July 5, 2001, p. 11. This article profiles the history and activity of ELF, focusing on its campaign against genetic engineering. Belsie points out that by targeting university scientists, the radical group may be doing itself more harm than good. Since the time of Galileo, he writes, history has been reluctant to turn scientists into villains. The few times that it does (the article cites Nazi anthropologists who tried to prove Aryan superiority), bad science is eventually trumped by more science rather than by ideology. ELF's opposition to biotech research, therefore, has allowed biotech supporters to seize the high ground.

Bosworth, Brandon. "America's Homegrown Terrorists." *The American Enterprise,* vol. 13, April/May 2002, pp. 48–49. This overview of ELF and ALF focuses on Craig Rosebraugh, spokesperson for ELF at the time this article was written. Rosebraugh claims the group contacted him anonymously in 1997 with assorted communiqués, which he then prepared as press releases and sent to the media. In response to charges that radical environmentalists are vandals, he replies, "If we are vandals, so were those who destroyed forever the gas chambers of Buchenwald and Auschwitz." Asked if ELF and ALF expect to win new converts through terrorism, Rosebraugh says, "That's not the immediate goal. The immediate goal is to cause economic damage."

Cloud, John. "Fire on the Mountain." *Time,* vol. 152, November 2, 1998, p. 77. Cloud reports on the fire, for which ELF claimed responsibility, that consumed seven structures at Colorado's Vail ski resort in October 1998. The radical group conducted what turned out to be history's costliest ecoterrorist strike (damage estimates reached $12 million) "on behalf of the lynx," into whose habitat the owners of Vail had planned to expand. The ELF communiqué continued, "This action is just a warning. . . . For your safety and convenience, we strongly advise skiers to choose other destinations." The "safety" part of the letter had law enforcement officials worried that future arsons could prove physically harmful to people. Aside from raising awareness of endangered lynx, however, Cloud believes that the arsons may have backfired on ELF. One result was a healing of the rift between the Vail Resorts company and locals, which may have raised previously wavering support for the planned expansion.

"Colorado Bill Eyes Eco-Terror." *Organized Crime Digest*, vol. 23, February 15, 2002, p. 5. In response to a growing number of attacks by radical groups like ELF and ALF, the Senate Agricultural Committee in Colorado approved a bill allowing judges to impose civil money penalties as well as criminal sentences for ecoterrorism.

Denson, Bryan. "Shadowy Saboteurs." *Investigative Reporters and Editors Journal*, vol. 23, May/June 2000, pp. 12–14. Denson reports on print media coverage of the rise in ecoterrorism in the American West since 1980, focusing on the investigative trail followed by reporters for *The Oregonian* (of which Denson was one) who produced the four-part series "Crimes in the Name of the Environment." The article also discusses public reaction to the series, ranging from support from industry groups, law enforcement, and conservationists who felt they had unfairly been linked with terrorists on one hand, to condemnation from critics angry that the newspaper had used the term *ecoterrorism* to describe the crimes when, in their view, the real terrorists were corporations that plunder nature for profit.

Elvin, John. "How Do You Spell 'Terrorist'? Try P-E-T-A (or E-L-F/A-L-F)." *Insight on the News*, vol. 18, April 15, 2002, p. 34. This article presents evidence collected by Richard Berman, executive director of the Center for Consumer Freedom, that People for the Ethical Treatment of Animals (PETA) has provided financial support for ELF and ALF. This evidence is based on PETA's tax filings, which show that in 2001 the organization contributed $1,500 to the North American ELF to "support their program activities" and gave $5,000 to the "Josh Harper Support Committee" to defend an ALF activist convicted of assaulting a police officer. PETA also reported a $45,200 contribution made in 1995 to the support committee for Rodney Coronado, convicted of firebombing a research facility at Michigan State University.

———. "Lumping the ELF and the ALF with Al-Qaeda." *Insight on the News*, vol. 18, March 25, 2002, p. 34. At the February 12, 2002, congressional subcommittee hearing on ecoterrorism, Richard Berman, executive director of the Center for Consumer Freedom, suggested that the FBI go after supporters of the ELF and the ALF with the "same vengeance" that they pursue supporters of al-Qaeda. Elvin questions the idea that destructive but nonlethal arsons committed by ecoterrorists are of the same caliber as the September 11 attacks by al-Qaeda that killed thousands of people. He concludes by suggesting that using the word *terrorist* to describe ELF and ALF activists may serve only to diminish the term, pointing out that while incidences of property destruction are not uncommon in American culture, "the wholesale slaughter of thousands of innocent civilians is a horror unique in its barbarity."

Ecoterrorism

"Enviro-Terror." *The American Enterprise*, vol. 12, October/November 2001, pp. 8–9. This anonymous article profiles ELF, characterized by the FBI as one of the most significant domestic American terrorist threats since the Weather Underground.

Glick, Daniel. "Fire on the Mountain." *Ski*, vol. 63, January 1999, pp. 23–24. Glick, author of the book *Powder Burn*, examines the impact that the 1998 ELF arson of the Vail resort had on the Colorado ski industry. He sees the fire as an escalation of the long-standing fight between pro-development and no-growth forces in resort towns. In recent years, the ski industry has made progress in meeting environmental concerns, from protecting wildlife habitat to mitigating water issues associated with snowmaking. However, some larger resorts, Vail among them, are still driven by development and real estate, continuing to expand to sell more condos rather than provide a better skiing experience. One result of the arson may be increased awareness of security. Glick writes, "It's a safe bet that anyone on the mountain at night who's not grooming or making snow will be viewed with more suspicion."

Hibbard, Courtney. "Targets of Opportunity." *E: The Environmental Magazine*, vol. 12, November/December 2001, p. 23. Hibbard reports on the fires that burned half-built homes in New York's Island Estates and the subsequent arrest of self-proclaimed members of ELF in relation to the crime.

Higgins, Sean. "The Terrorist Tactics of Radical Environmentalists." *Insight on the News*, vol. 18, April 22, 2002, pp. 44–45. This article presents the arsons and property destruction perpetrated by ELF and ALF as the "most virulent form" of domestic terrorism. Higgins examines the tactics of these two groups and reports on the support given to ALF by People for the Ethical Treatment of Animals (PETA), whose web site compares ALF to the French Resistance during World War II and the Underground Railroad.

Hsiao, Andrew. "The Green Menace." *The Village Voice*, vol. 43, November 10, 1998, p. 26. Hsiao examines media coverage of ELF in the weeks following the fires that engulfed the Vail ski resort in Colorado. The article accuses major media outlets of elevating "some of the anti-environmental movement's most virulent and dubious propagandists to the status of expert—without divulging their political ties." Among these are Barry Clausen, who has been employed by the timber industry and whose 1995 accusation that the Unabomber had connections to Earth First! is considered by many to be without merit. Another is Ron Arnold, founder of the wise use movement, who once said he was out to "destroy environmentalism once and for all." According to David Helvarg, author of *War on the Greens*, relying on Arnold and Clausen for analysis of radical Green activism is "like asking David Duke to assess the rise of black militants."

Hunt, Ed. "Ecoterror's Troubling Trend." *Christian Science Monitor,* October 7, 2002, pp. 9ff. In summer 2002, the Earth Liberation Front (ELF) announced an escalation in its attacks. Hunt explores the manner in which ELF actions are counterproductive because they make all environmentalists seem irrational and dangerous, while at the same time creating public acceptance for the harassment and persecution of nonviolent activists. This has allowed opponents of the environmental movement to lump bombing in with nonviolent tree sits, boycotts, lawsuits, and road blockades, branding them all as acts of ecoterrorism. The article also criticizes those who excuse ELF actions as a "legitimate form of protest" similar to the Underground Railroad and the Boston Tea Party, both of which, according to Hunt, were precursors to violent terrorism and bloody wars.

Jackson, David S. "When ELF Comes Calling." *Time,* vol. 157, January 15, 2001, p. 35. Jackson provides a brief overview of ELF's history and tactics, in addition to reporting the group's first actions in the eastern United States.

Knickerbocker, Brad. "Concerns Rise as Ecoterrorists Expand Aim: Biotech Research and Fur Farms Are the Latest Targets of Fringe Groups on the Far Left." *Christian Science Monitor,* April 3, 2000, p. 3. Knickerbocker reports on the expansion of ELF attacks beyond businesses thought to exploit wilderness and into the realm of organizations involved in genetic engineering. Lawmakers in Oregon and Wisconsin responded by proposing legislation that would make such crimes punishable under the federal Racketeer Influenced and Corrupt Organizations (RICO) Act, a law that would provide the stiffer penalties that have been used to prosecute militant antiabortion activists.

———. "Eco-terrorists, Too, May Soon Be on the Run: Congress Considers New Penalties against Pro-Environment Violence out West." *Christian Science Monitor,* February 15, 2002, p. 2. Knickerbocker explores the clash in values between the Old and New West that has fueled the use of extreme tactics by both environmentalists and anti-environmentalists. Congress is working on legislation that would stiffen penalties against ecoterrorists, while the FBI is deploying more agents to fight ELF and ALF. Meanwhile, theft of natural resources and attacks by anti-environmentalists (including fire-bombings aimed at employees of the U.S. Forest Service, the U.S. Bureau of Land Management, and other government agencies) have largely escaped the "terrorism" label.

———. "Firebrands of 'Ecoterrorism' Set Sights on Urban Sprawl: Burning of San Diego Mega-Condos Demonstrates Radical Environmentalists' Tactical Shift to Housing, Commercial Sites." *Christian Science Monitor,* August 6, 2003, p. 01. Knickerbocker examines the August 2003 arson attack that destroyed a housing development in San Diego. The Earth Liberation Front, he reports, seems to be focusing less on wilderness issues and more on urban sprawl, SUVs, and symbols of U.S. military strength.

————. "In U.S., a Rise of Violent Environmental Tactics: Arson and Death Threats Have Followed Ecoterrorists' Call for More Use of Force." *Christian Science Monitor,* September 26, 2002, pp. 1ff. Knickerbocker reports on the summer 2002 ELF communiqué in which the radical environmentalist group threatened an escalation of its attacks, vowing that they "will no longer hesitate to pick up the gun to implement justice." Although civil disobedience and property damage have long been the tools of radical environmentalists, he writes, ELF rhetoric increasingly warns of personal violence. Experts warn that ecoterrorists may become more violent as their efforts are frustrated by law enforcement crackdowns or by political administrations perceived as particularly unfriendly.

Markels, Alex, and Scott Willoughby. "Backfire: Environmentalists Had Forged an Unusual Coalition with Locals and Animal Rights Activists to Oppose Vail's Growth—Until Ecoterrorists Torched the Mountain." *Mother Jones,* vol. 24, March 1999, p. 60. Following ELF's 1998 arson of Vail Ski Resort, which caused $12 million in damage, mainstream environmentalists faced suspicion by locals who had supported opposition to Vail's expansion into the endangered lynx habitat.

Murphy, Kim. "Disruption Is Activists' Business." *The Los Angeles Times,* April 25, 2000, pp. A1ff. Murphy profiles the activities of ELF and its spokesperson Craig Rosebraugh, as well as unsuccessful efforts by law enforcement officials to arrest the perpetrators of the acts of ecosabotage for which the group claims responsibility.

Otis, Ginger Adams. "Terrorist Tactics." *The Village Voice,* November 12–18, 2003, p. 40. This article discusses efforts by New York assembly member Richard Smith to introduce state legislation that would define the Earth Liberation Front and Animal Liberation Front as terrorist organizations. The draft is based on model legislation written by the American Legislative Exchange Council, an influential conservative Washington, D.C., lobby group. Otis presents several provisions of the bill, as well as opponents' reactions.

Power, Matthew. "Guerrillas in Our Midst." *Builder,* vol. 24, March 2001, p. 46. Power reports on ELF tactics from the point of view of homebuilders, giving them credit for highlighting a deepening rift between conflicting worldviews about sprawl and the environment. Sandy Lonsdale, an Oregon-based conservation activist, is quoted as foreseeing a time when a large portion of the population will view ELF as an avenging Robin Hood rather than a sinister terrorist organization, a prediction that is still a long way from coming to fruition.

Richardson, Valerie, et al. "FBI Targets Domestic Terrorists." *Insight on the News*, vol. 18, April 22, 2002, pp. 30–33. This article examines how ecoterrorism has been taken more seriously as a domestic security threat since the September 11 terrorist attacks. "The general population is becoming a lot less tolerant toward these groups," says Representative Scott McInnis of Colorado. "The feeling is, if you're going to tolerate this, then why not tolerate al-Qaeda? We need to take away the Robin Hood mystique from these terrorists, which is what they are." Others also draw parallels between al-Qaeda and ecoterrorism, claiming that both believe "they are the sole proprietor of truth and righteousness," both believe they "have the right to impose their concepts of truth and righteousness on society," and both "attack people who they think have violated nature's or God's law." Activists complain that September 11 is being used to suppress the ideas of people who have nothing to do with terrorism, pointing out the fundamental difference between burning down an empty house and flying airliners into a building full of thousands of people.

Sanow, En. "Vandalism? Terrorism." *Law and Order*, vol. 50, May 2002, p. 4. This brief article provides an overview of ELF and ALF, warning that the late 1990s and early 2000s saw a sharp increase in the activity of animal rights and environmental extremists. Sanow points out that the Code of Federal Regulations defines terrorism as the "unlawful use of force and violence against persons or property to intimidate or coerce a government, the civilian population, or any segment thereof, in furtherance of political or social objectives." According to this definition, he writes, the activities of the ALF and the ELF are terrorism and should be treated as such by law enforcement officials.

Satchell, Michael. "An Eco-War Widens." *U.S. News & World Report*, vol. 125, November 2, 1998, p. 36. This article covers the 1998 ELF arson at Colorado's Vail ski resort that caused $12 million in damage. Satchell also provides a brief overview of the history of the radical environmental group.

Tauschek, Sam. "Domestic Terrorists." *Sports Afield*, vol. 224, May 2001, p. 27. This brief article reviews a *60 Minutes* television report detailing ELF's domestic terrorism activities. On the broadcast, FBI Special Agent Dave W. Szady characterized ELF as a "true domestic terrorism group that uses criminal activity to further their political agenda." Despite the radical group's claims that no one has been injured in one of its arsons, *60 Minutes* reported that several firefighters were nearly killed when ELF burned down the headquarters of the Boise Cascade Corporation in Monmouth, Oregon, in 2000.

"U.S. Links Radicals to Arsons in Northwest." *Organized Crime Digest*, vol. 22, July 20, 2001, p. 4. This anonymous article reports on simultaneous arsons that occurred more than 100 miles apart in Oregon and Washington on the night of May 21, 2001. The fires, which caused $3 million in damage, have been attributed to ELF.

Wilson, Robin. "Radical Group Takes Credit for Lab Fire." *The Chronicle of Higher Education*, vol. 46, February 11, 2000, p. A18. Wilson reports on a December 1999 ELF arson that destroyed the offices of a project at Michigan State University that brought biotechnology research to agricultural scientists in the Third World. ELF claimed it had set the fire in objection to research designed "to lobby developing countries to abandon their current agricultural practices and to rely on genetically engineered plants." The fire caused nearly $500,000 in damage.

Ziner, Karen Lee. "Burning Down the Houses: The Earth Liberation Front Targets Long Island Sprawl." *E: The Environmental Magazine*, vol. 12, May/June 2001, pp. 17–22. Ziner discusses ELF and its targeting of half-built luxury homes in Long Island's North Shore, located an hour east of New York City. An ELF communiqué quoted by Ziner attempts to justify such attacks: "Urban sprawl has undoubtedly served to alter nearly 90 percent of Long Island's habitats, either by physically removing them, paving them, or polluting them with toxic man-made materials, making them either undesirable or unsustainable for most species."

INTERNET DOCUMENTS

Animal Liberation Front. "ALF Primer." Animal Liberation Front web site. Available online. URL: http://www.animalliberationfront.com/ALFront/ALFPrime.htm. Downloaded on September 1, 2003. After providing a brief history of ALF, the bulk of this document consists of a how-to guide for illegal direct action, including guidelines for activity, how to find people to work with, how to plan, and how to prepare. The section on how to execute specific actions is followed by advice on how to deal with police, federal agents, and grand juries, and how to report actions.

Horner, Christopher C. "There Are No 'Acceptable' Terrorists." Competitive Enterprise Institute. Available online. URL: http://www.cei.org/gencon/019,02388.cfm. Posted on February 11, 2002. Horner writes that allowing "low-level" domestic terrorism (such as that conducted by ALF) to proliferate will only lead to escalation. Any war on terrorism must not distinguish between this type of activism and attacks like those that occurred on September 11.

UNABOMBER

BOOKS

Chase, Alston. *Harvard and the Making of the Unabomber: The Education of an American Terrorist.* New York: W. W. Norton, 2003. The author approaches his subject with an eye toward wedding the Unabomber's motivations to the culture of widespread American alienation that Chase claims grew out of the cold war. The author also questions the morality and long-term effects of a series of psychological experiments for which Kaczynski volunteered while attending Harvard University as a student during the 1950s. Whether the reader is convinced of the validity of these theories or not, *Harvard and the Unabomber* is packed with hard facts about Kaczynski's life and the 18-year effort to solve the Unabomber case. Included are a number of black-and-white photographs, a chronology of events, and endnotes.

Douglas, John E., and Mark Olshaker. *Unabomber: On the Trail of America's Most-Wanted Serial Killer.* New York: Pocket Books, 1996. Douglas, the FBI unit chief who created the first FBI profile of the Unabomber, and Olshaker provide an insider's view of the 18-year manhunt that ended with the arrest of Ted Kaczynski.

Gelernter, David. *Drawing Life: Surviving the Unabomber.* New York: Free Press, 1997. In 1993, Yale computer science professor Gelernter was nearly killed by a bomb sent by Ted Kaczynski. Using the publicity gained from the crime, as well as his sense of moral outrage, Gelernter criticizes contemporary American culture as lacking a moral compass. He blames this state of affairs on the 1960s, when, as he sees it, intellectuals took over elite institutions and began to teach tolerance of morally reprehensible behavior. Among the representations of the "cultural elite" derided by the author are feminists, opponents of the death penalty, the producers of Sesame Street, members of the media, and Ivy League professors. These are the people, he argues, who are responsible for the existence of the Kaczynskis of the world and who force the American public to see the Unabomber as a "mad genius" rather than a cold-blooded serial killer who deserves the death penalty.

Gibbs, Nancy, et al. *Mad Genius: The Odyssey, Pursuit, and Capture of the Unabomber Suspect.* New York: Warner Books, 1996. Written by a team of *Time* magazine journalists, this book traces the path that led Ted Kaczynski to isolate himself in a Montana cabin and begin his 18-year letter-bomb campaign. It includes 16 pages of photographs, a list of items seized in Kaczynski's cabin and used as evidence against him during the trial, and the complete manuscript of the Unabomber's antitechnology manifesto.

Ecoterrorism

Graysmith, Robert. *Unabomber: A Desire to Kill.* Washington, D.C.: Regnery, 1997. Graysmith not only traces the bombing career of Ted Kaczynski but also critiques the FBI's handling of the 18-year investigation and attempts to answer such conspiracy-oriented questions as whether the Unabomber had an accomplice who is still at large. The book includes eight pages of color photographs.

Kaczynski, Ted. *The Unabomber Manifesto: Industrial Society and Its Future.* Berkeley, Calif.: Jolly Roger Press, 1995. Originally published in the *Washington Post* under the pseudonym FC, thought at the time to be a terrorist group rather than an individual, this unedited version of Kaczynski's manuscript allows readers to judge for themselves the madness or merits of the philosophy that prompted him to commit murder.

Mello, Michael. *The United States of America Versus Theodore Kaczynski: Ethics, Power and the Invention of the Unabomber.* New York: Context Books, 1999. Author and law professor Mello closely examines the circumstances surrounding Kaczynski's trial. Although not sympathetic to the defendant's bombing campaign, Mello concludes that, contrary to what has been portrayed in the media, Kaczynski is not mentally ill and was therefore competent to stand trial. Furthermore, his defense lawyers denied him his right to a trial by attempting to use an insanity defense despite Kaczynski's wishes to the contrary.

Waits, Chris, and Dave Shors. *Unabomber: The Secret Life of Ted Kaczynski: His 25 Years in Montana.* Helena, Mont.: Montana Magazine, 1999. Waits, a neighbor to Kaczynski in Montana, and journalist Shors recount the events of the FBI investigation into the Unabomber following Kaczynski's arrest. The authors discuss the bomber's motives as revealed by the 22,000-page journal found in the cabin, but Waits regrets that Kaczynski's plea bargaining eliminated the need for a trial that surely would have revealed more about the killer's personality. The book contains color photographs and a foldout timeline.

ARTICLES

Budiansky, Stephen. "Academic Roots of Paranoia." *U.S. News & World Report,* vol. 120, May 13, 1996, p. 33. Budiansky discusses efforts by conservative columnists and talk show hosts to link the Unabomber's campaign of violence to radical environmental groups. Meanwhile, Earth First! has been quick to disavow the connection. "The Unabomber has been bombing people for a lot longer than Earth First! has even been in existence," points out Craig Beneville, editor of the *Earth First! Journal.* Although there is no evidence that the Unabomber had direct ties with environmental radicals, Budiansky explores similarities between the "Unabomber

Manifesto" and the writings of leading environmental and animal rights scholars, all of which contain strong indictments against science and technology-based society.

Chase, Alston. "Harvard and the Making of the Unabomber." *The Atlantic Monthly*, vol. 285, June 2000, pp. 41–65. This long article was the genesis of Chase's 2003 book of the same name. He argues that a series of purposely brutalizing psychological experiments for which Theodore Kaczynski volunteered in 1958 while attending Harvard may have influenced the future Unabomber's ideas about the evils of science.

Chepesiuk, Ron. "Surviving the Unabomber Media Circus: An Interview." *American Libraries*, vol. 29, March 1998, pp. 27–28. Chepesiuk interviews Sherri Wood, a librarian at the Lincoln, Montana, branch of the Lewis and Clark Public Library who had befriended Ted Kaczynski during the time he lived in the area. Wood discusses the FBI investigation and her difficult dealings with the media after the Unabomber story broke. She was mistakenly vilified as having broken Montana confidentiality laws concerning what reading material Kaczynski had supposedly taken out of the library; the information had actually been divulged by a library volunteer who used Wood's title.

Cockburn, Alexander. "Earth First!, the Press and the Unabomber." *The Nation*, vol. 262, May 6, 1996, p. 9. Cockburn accuses ABC News and reporter Brian Ross of sensationalizing reports that linked suspected Unabomber Theodore Kaczynski with Earth First! During interviews in the days immediately following Kaczynski's arrest, Ross attempted to trace the Unabomber's interest in several of his bombing victims to a 1994 meeting at the University of Montana at Missoula "attended by top Earth First! members," implying that the meeting was a secret gathering to discuss strategies aimed at weakening multinational corporations. Cockburn found, however, that the meeting was an open timber conference attended by 500 people, including the late Oklahoma representative Mike Synar and representatives from the Forest Service, the Fish and Wildlife Service, and timber companies Weyerhaeuser and Louisiana-Pacific. Meanwhile, a much-talked-about "hit list" published by Earth First! that supposedly incited the Unabomber to murder called for boycotts, not violence, against listed corporations. Cockburn does, however, criticize Earth First! cofounder Dave Foreman of being a "Barry Goldwater environmentalist" who, like the Unabomber, hated the left, eschewed politics, and "nourished the infantile romanticism of lone-wolf intervention, whether by bomb or tree spike," and whose Malthusian views existed "under the same big tent as the Nazi philosophy of nature."

———. "Land of the Free." *New Statesman*, vol. 8, September 1, 1995, p. 14. Cockburn analyzes the content of the Unabomber's manifesto, recently published jointly by the *Washington Post* and the *New York Times*. He finds a large contradiction between the Unabomber's professed desire to live in a society that respects individual freedom and his bombing campaign that left three people dead.

"Dear Diary, I Made Bombs." *Time*, vol. 148, September 30, 1996, p. 32. Investigators reveal the content of the diary taken from Theodore Kaczynski's Montana cabin, which they say is their best evidence that the suspect is the Unabomber and which is, according to Assistant U.S. Attorney Robert Cleary, "the backbone of the government's case." According to Cleary, the journal contains the admission that Kaczynski played a role in all 16 crimes, including inscriptions such as "I mailed that bomb" and "I sent that bomb," details of the outcome of bombings, and expressions of a "desire to kill." Kaczynski's typewriter was also linked to the Unabomber's correspondence. Federal defender Quin Denvir protested that publicizing the content of the diaries would make it harder to find impartial jurors. He said the defense would be challenging their admissibility as evidence.

Dubner, Stephen J. "I Don't Want to Live Long. I Would Rather Get the Death Penalty Than Spend the Rest of My Life in Prison." *Time*, vol. 154, October 18, 1999, pp. 44–49. Ted Kaczynski talks about his life in jail, his appeal plans, and his brother, David. He also discusses his book, *Truth Versus Lies*, an account of his life to date that does not address the Unabomber crimes. One aim of the book is to assert his sanity. When asked by Dubner if he considers himself insane, Kaczynski replies, "I'm confident that I'm sane, personally. I don't get delusions and so on and so forth. . . . I mean, I had very serious problems with social adjustment in adolescence, and a lot of people would call this a sickness. But it would have to be distinguished between an organic illness, like schizophrenia or something like that." Another purpose of the book is to attack his brother, David, who turned Ted in to the FBI. David's decision to turn him in, according to Ted, was less a moral or lawful one than "a way to settle a perversely complicated sibling rivalry." Much of this article consists of an in-depth exploration of the relationship between the two brothers over the years. Dubner also describes Kaczynski's life on "Celebrity Row," a group of eight cells protected from the prison's general population where he has contact with Ramzi Yousef, the mastermind of the 1993 World Trade Center bombing, and Timothy McVeigh.

Duffy, Brian. "The Mad Bomber?" *U.S. News & World Report*, vol. 120, April 15, 1996, p. 28. This article reports on the 18-year manhunt for the Unabomber, the arrest of Ted Kaczynski, and the evidence collected against him. A profile of Kaczynski is also presented.

Annotated Bibliography

———. "United States v. Kaczynski." *U.S. News & World Report*, vol. 120, April 22, 1996, p. 30. Duffy discusses the seemingly "airtight" case against Kaczynski based on evidence collected by the FBI.

Edwards, Tamala M. "Crazy Is as Crazy Does." *Time*, vol. 151, February 2, 1998, p. 66. Edwards discusses Ted Kaczynski's unwillingness to accept the insanity defense planned by his lawyers, leading to the guilty plea that traded his admission of guilt for a life sentence without the possibility of parole or the option to appeal.

Eftimiades, Maria. "Blood Bond." *People Weekly*, vol. 50, August 10, 1998, pp. 77–82. David Kaczynski speaks of growing up with his older brother, his realization that his brother may be the Unabomber, and his choice, after much agonizing, to turn Ted over to the FBI. David laments that the ruling that sent Ted to jail for life did little to answer the question of how a highly educated mathematics professor transformed into a cold-blooded murderer.

Elson, John. "Murderer's Manifesto." *Time*, vol. 146, July 10, 1995, p. 32. Elson reports on a flurry of correspondence initiated by the Unabomber that began with a letter to the *San Francisco Chronicle* claiming that he was "planning to blow up an airliner out of Los Angeles International Airport sometime during the next six days." A letter to the *New York Times* the following day apparently rescinded the threat, but the Federal Aviation Authority maintained strict security measures at California's major airports. Shortly afterward, the *New York Times*, *Washington Post*, and *Penthouse* magazine all received copies of the 35,000-word manuscript titled "Industrial Society and Its Future" with a letter offering to stop the bombings if the manifesto was published in its entirety.

Fitzgerald, Mark. "Decrying Public Journalism." *Editor and Publisher*, vol. 128, November 11, 1995, p. 20. At a speech given at the Society of Professional Journalists's annual convention, Iowa publisher Michael Gartner called public journalism a "menace" best exemplified by the decision of the *Washington Post* and *New York Times* to publish the Unabomber's manifesto. Gartner said, "The Unabomber decision—that was public journalism run amok."

Gibbs, Nancy. "Tracking Down the Unabomber." *Time*, vol. 147, April 15, 1996, p. 38. Gibbs discusses the arrest of Ted Kaczynski and efforts by federal agents to gather incriminating evidence against him.

Gleick, Elizabeth. "A Serial Bomber Strikes Again." *Time*, vol. 144, December 26, 1994, p. 128. The December 10, 1994, death of advertising executive Thomas Mosser as the result of a mail bomb sent by the Unabomber is discussed.

Gray, Paul. "Publish or Perish." *Time*, vol. 146, August 14, 1995, p. 43. Before its publication, the FBI allowed 50 or 60 college professors to read the 35,000-word manifesto the Unabomber sent to the *Washington Post* and *New York Times*. Investigators hoped that one of the professors would remember a former student who used the same grammatical oddities (such as using *consist in* instead of *consist of*) apparent in the manuscript.

Higgins, Michael. "Crazy Talk." *ABA Journal*, vol. 83, December 1997, p. 34. Higgins shows how diverse views of jurors in cases where mental illness evidence is produced, including that of Ted Kaczynski, often creates problems for the defense. A study of more than 8,900 insanity pleas in felony cases shows this defense is rarely used.

———. "A Difficult Client." *ABA Journal*, vol. 84, March 1998, pp. 18ff. Quin Denvir, attorney for Ted Kaczynski, discusses his defense strategy, which hinged on proving that the Unabomber was too insane to deserve the death penalty. Part of this strategy included moving Kaczynski's Montana cabin to Sacramento, California, as evidence. "In some ways," says Denvir, "the cabin spoke a lot more to his mental state than the testimony of an expert." Denvir and cocounsel Judy Clarke, however, were not able to pursue their defense strategy, as both sides accepted a plea bargain that precluded the need for a trial.

Howe, Rob, et al. "For the Greater Good." *People Weekly*, vol. 45, April 22, 1996, p. 50. This overview of Ted Kaczynski's life was published only three weeks after the accused Unabomber's arrest.

Jackson, David S. "Did a Student Crack the Unabomber's Code?" *Time*, vol. 151, May 11, 1998, p. 16. In 1995, Milton Jones, an American literature student at Brigham Young University, theorized that the Unabomber was using the literary device of "juxtaposition" in his construction of the bombs and his choice of victims. "By mailing a bomb to a person named Wood or someone living on Aspen Drive, the Unabomber was saying technology was destroying nature," writes Jackson, "But by making the bomb partly out of wood and selecting victims who represented the advance of technology, he was sending a second message: Technology was destroying both itself and nature." The FBI was interested enough to ask for more information from Jones, who predicted that the bomber "would be an intellectual, a conservationist, a loner, possibly a college teacher, familiar with the work of Joseph Conrad and see himself as if in a war to save the world."

———. "Man Behind the Mask." *Time*, vol. 150, November 17, 1997, p. 52. Jackson explores the problems faced by Kaczynski's defense team in their attempt to use the insanity defense against their client's wishes. Although defendants who claim insanity or mental disease in federal trials rarely succeed, the author sees disturbing parallels between some of the symptoms of paranoid schizophrenia and Kaczynski's behavior and life. These include resistance to diagnosis and a mystery illness that put Kaczynski in the hospital when he was only 10 months old. (Some researchers, says Jackson, "believe that schizophrenia could come from a virus that strikes pregnant mothers and infants, causing brain damage that usually doesn't become fully apparent until the teens or early 20s.")

King, Patricia. "He Will Never Kill Again." *Newsweek*, vol. 131, February 2, 1998, p. 4. King reports on Ted Kaczynski's guilty plea, which involved giving up the right to appeal and admitting that he was the criminal whose bombing campaign had killed three people and injured 29. In exchange, Kaczynski was spared the death penalty.

Klaidman, Daniel, and Patricia King. "Suicide Mission." *Newsweek*, vol. 131, January 19, 1998, pp. 22–25. Several weeks before accepting a plea bargain, Ted Kaczynski attempted to hang himself in his jail cell. The following day, he informed the court that he wished to represent himself. This article discusses the legal implications of these events and wonders whether the suicide attempt was the result of insanity or a trick to avoid the death penalty.

Lacayo, Richard. "A Tale of Two Brothers." *Time*, vol. 147, April 22, 1996, p. 44. Lacayo provides an early profile of brothers Theodore and David Kaczynski.

Lavelle, Marianne. "Defending the Unabomber." *U.S. News & World Report*, vol. 123, November 17, 1997, p. 18–22. This article, written one week before Ted Kaczynski's trial was set to begin, speculates that since the accused Unabomber would not allow psychiatrists to examine him, the best evidence for his defense team to prove him insane may revolve around his angry writings, his shack, and the testimony of his brother, David, who turned him in to authorities.

"Leaks Insufficient to Free Kaczynski." *Editor and Publisher*, vol. 129, November 9, 1996, p. 37. This anonymous article reports on Theodore Kaczynski's unsuccessful bid to convince the Supreme Court to free him because of news leaks. The justices refused to allow Kaczynski another chance to argue in a lower court his case that media leaks poisoned public opinion to such a great extent that the government should forfeit its right to prosecute him.

Lemonick, Michael D. "The Bomb Is in the Mail." *Time*, vol. 145, May 8, 1995, p. 70. Lemonick discusses the April 25, 1995, bomb that killed timber industry lobbyist Gilbert Murray, and recounts the 18-year history of the bombing spree linked to the Unabomber.

Lloyd, Jillian. "Should the Accused Direct Own Trial Strategy? Unabomber Ted Kaczynski's Appeal Raises Issue of Whether a Lawyer's Obligation to Save a Client's Life Is Paramount." *Christian Science Monitor*, June 6, 2000, p. 2. Lloyd reports on Kaczynski's attempt to appeal his plea bargain on the grounds that he was coerced into the guilty plea by court-appointed lawyers, who, contrary to Kaczynski's wishes, insisted on a defense strategy that would have portrayed him as a "grotesque lunatic." The Justice Department maintains that Kaczynski was aware of the consequences of his plea bargain and that it should stand. Michael Mello, a Vermont Law School professor who wrote *The United States of America Versus Theodore Kaczynski* (1999), believes that the case points to bigger issues concerning a lawyer's responsibility in respect a client's wishes. "For me," he says, "the bottom line is that it's the client's crime, it's the client's trial, and it's the client's life. And it ought to be the client's choice." Others disagree, including Michael Katz, Colorado's federal public defender, who believes that "the call for determining the strategy for a defense is ultimately the lawyer's," who has an obligation to protect his or her client.

Magner, Denise K. "Colleges Keep Security Measures Despite Arrest in Unabomber Case." *The Chronicle of Higher Education*, vol. 42, April 19, 1996, p. A25. After bombs seriously injured academics David Gelernter and Charles Epstein in separate incidents in June 1993, many colleges and universities became much more cautious about handling packages. Administrators on many campuses say that Ted Kaczynski's arrest will not cause them to ease their security procedures, which include having mailroom workers give special handling to suspicious packages.

"Media Gains Access to 'Unabomber' Psychiatric Report." *News Media and the Law*, vol. 22, Fall 1998, pp. 9–10. This anonymous article discusses a decision by a federal appeals panel in San Francisco (Ninth Circuit) that unanimously affirmed the media's right of access to Theodore Kaczynski's psychiatric report. The court held that "the public's legitimate interest in the disclosure of the report outweighed Kaczynski's right to privacy." The 47-page psychiatric report had been ordered by the court in 1998 to test Kaczynski's mental competence to stand trial after Kaczynski requested that he be allowed to represent himself, in part because his attorneys were planning to present a mental illness defense. The report concluded that Kaczynski was competent to stand trial but was probably a paranoid schizophrenic.

O'Donnell, Paul, and Carla Power. "Reaching Out." *Newsweek*, vol. 132, July 6, 1998, p. 6. Just two months into his life sentence, convicted Unabomber Theodore Kaczynski began efforts to prove his claim that the FBI and prosecutors "misrepresented" him during the trial.

O'Sullivan, John. "'Affable, Polite and Sincere.'" *National Review*, vol. 51, November 8, 1999, pp. 22–26. O'Sullivan argues against the idea of turning murderers into celebrities. He maintains that Kaczynski's interview with *Time* magazine's Stephen J. Dubner, the forthcoming (but later cancelled) publication of his book *Truth Versus Lies*, the publication of one of his short stories by a university-based literary magazine, and the donation of his personal papers to a university archive of anarchist literature all undermine "decent restraints in popular culture." O'Sullivan extends the discussion to include Timothy McVeigh and other convicted murderers.

Quinn, Judy. "Unabomber Book Blows Up." *Publishers Weekly*, vol. 246, November 15, 1999, p. 24. This article discusses the decision of Context Books to cancel publication of Ted Kaczynski's book *Truth Versus Lies*. While Kaczynski had stipulated that the manuscript could not be edited, Context lawyers asked for changes based on a legal review. In response, according to Context publisher Beau Friedlander, Kaczynski "was uncooperative and expressed himself in ways that made it impossible for the book to be published by Context or by anyone else." He acknowledged that Kaczynski had sought to dissolve the relationship first.

Quittner, Joshua. "The Web's Unlikely Hero." *Time*, vol. 147, April 22, 1996, p. 47. Despite his antitechnology message, the Unabomber became an antihero on the Internet. Three weeks after Kaczynski's arrest, copies of his manifesto were widely available on the Internet. One site offered a Unabomber theme song, another invited people to attend an online birthday party for Kaczynski, and a third gave away free "Official Unabomber" screensavers. The Unabomber Political Action Committee, meanwhile, ran a web site urging people to write in the name of suspect Theodore Kaczynski on the November 1996 ballot.

Reiland, Ralph. "Inspiring the Unabomber." *The American Enterprise*, vol. 9, May/June 1998, pp. 10–11. Reiland attempts to connect the murders committed by Theodore Kaczynski with Earth First! and, based on the fact that a "page-worn and well-underlined" copy of *Earth in the Balance* was found in Kaczynski's cabin, mainstream environmentalists like former vice president Al Gore.

Rubin, Mike. "An Explosive Bestseller." *The Village Voice*, vol. 41, June 4, 1996, p. 8. Rubin profiles Kristan Lawson of Jolly Roger Press, who downloaded the Unabomber's uncopyrighted manifesto and published it in book form as *Industrial Society and Its Future* by "FC." The book went on to become a best-seller in San Francisco.

Scarf, Maggie. "The Mind of the Unabomber." *The New Republic*, vol. 214, June 10, 1996, p. 20. Scarf profiles Houston psychiatrist Stuart Yudofsky, whose name appeared on a hit list found in Kaczynski's Montana cabin by federal agents. Although Yudofsky was puzzled about why he would be a potential target, Scarf speculates that it was the psychiatrist's interest in the neural substructure of human aggression that caught the Unabomber's attention. Scarf goes on to discuss the possibility that Kaczynski suffers from Narcissistic Personality Disorder, defined in the American Psychiatric Association's *Diagnostic and Statistical Manual of Mental Disorders* as a "pervasive pattern of grandiosity (in fantasy or behavior), need for admiration, and lack of empathy beginning by early adulthood and present in a variety of contexts." The characteristic features of narcissistic disturbances include an over-inflated sense of uniqueness, self-importance, and personal entitlement.

"35,000 Words—and Perhaps a Clue or Two." *U.S. News & World Report*, vol. 119, October 2, 1995, p. 16. This brief, anonymous article reports on the joint publication of the Unabomber's manifesto by the *Washington Post* and the *New York Times*. FBI officials, who had urged the newspapers to publish the 35,000-word manuscript, hoped that someone would read the manifesto and recognize the author through his writing style.

"The Usual Suspects?" *Environmental Action*, vol. 27, Fall 1995, p. 8. This anonymous essay reports that the FBI, in the course of investigating the Unabomber case, questioned a number of mainstream, nonviolent environmentalists.

Van Boven, Sarah, and Patricia King. "A Killer's Self Portrait." *Newsweek*, vol. 131, May 11, 1998, p. 38. Denied the trial that likely would have revealed much about Theodore Kaczynski's personality and motives, the media must rely on court documents to develop a profile of the Unabomber. These documents include the court psychiatrist's January report, which found that the defendant was competent to stand trial but suffered from paranoid schizophrenia, and a 30-page sentencing memorandum released by prosecutors that used quotes from Kaczynski's journal to show that he knew exactly what he was doing and therefore would probably not have escaped a death sentence. The defense called the memo "gratuitous and misrepresentative."

Vizard, Frank. "Matching Wits with the Unabomber." *Popular Science*, vol. 253, October 1998, pp. 68–73. When Ted Kaczynski was arrested, FBI agents discovered a live bomb, packaged and ready for mailing but unaddressed, in his cabin. Authorities needed the bomb defused intact for forensic evidence but realized that the task was beyond its capabilities. Vizard recounts in detail the work of an elite bomb squad consisting of Chris Cherry (a researcher at the federal weapons research facility Sandia National Laboratories), veteran Sandia assistant Rod Owenby, and Vic Poisson of the Riverside, California, police department. The team used a PAN disrupter to dismantle the bomb so it could be used as evidence.

Will, George F. "Intolerable Tolerance." *Newsweek*, vol. 131, May 11, 1998, p. 94. Will argues, based on the evidence of Theodore Kaczynski's journal, that the convicted Unabomber is quite sane and therefore should have been given the death penalty rather than a life sentence. He then expands his argument to criticize a widespread reluctance to impose the death penalty in murder cases.

Annotated Bibliography

Witkin, Gordon. "Did the FBI Ignore the 'Tafoya profile'?" *U.S. News & World Report*, vol. 123, November 17, 1997, p. 24. In June 1993, FBI agent Bill Tafoya joined the Unabomber case. Two months later, he, along with colleague Mary Ellen O'Toole, produced a profile of the suspect that differed greatly from a previous profile that had pictured the suspect as a man in his mid-30s to early 40s, with perhaps some college education, who worked as a blue collar aviation worker. By contrast, Tafoya's analysis concluded that the Unabomber was probably in his early 50s (Kaczynski was 53 at the time of his capture), had a graduate degree and maybe even a Ph.D., probably had a background in "hard" science (such as electrical engineering or math), and was likely an antitechnology Luddite. Tafoya contends that his eerily prescient profile was ignored by the FBI. Former San Francisco agent-in-charge Jim Freeman counters that profiles are only one component of any investigation and that investigators pursued several tracks, including the idea that the bomber might be an academic.

———. "What Does It Take to Be Crazy?" *U.S. News & World Report*, vol. 124, January 12, 1998, p. 7. Witkin reports on Theodore Kaczynski's refusal to use an insanity plea to avoid the death penalty, and examines the history and use of, as well as popular misconceptions about, the insanity defense in general.

Witkin, Gordon, and Ilan Greenberg. "End of the Line for the Unabomber." *U.S. News & World Report*, vol. 124, February 2, 1998, p. 34. The legal events leading up to Ted Kaczynski's plea bargain are discussed.

INTERNET DOCUMENTS

Johnson, Sally C. "Psychiatric Competency Report." Unabomber, The Sacramento Bee. Available online. URL: http://www.unabombertrial. com/documents/psych_report1.html. Posted on September 11, 1998. This is the full text of the psychiatric evaluation of Theodore Kaczynski ordered by the court during the trial. Johnson concluded that Kaczynski appeared to suffer from some form of paranoid schizophrenia but was competent to stand trial.

Kaczynski, Theodore. "Industrial Society and Its Future." Unabomber, The Sacramento Bee. Available online. URL: http://www.unabombertrial. com/manifesto/index.html. Posted in 1997. The complete online text of the so-called Unabomber Manifesto is accompanied by links to news items about the document, to a transcript of the Unabomber's letter to the *New York Times*, and to the statement by the *New York Times* and *Washington Post* upon initial publication of the manifesto.

The Sacramento Bee. "Court Transcripts." Unabomber, The Sacramento Bee. Available online. URL: http://www.unabombertrial.com/transcripts/index.html. Updated on January 22, 1998. This archive presents the full daily court reporting in Kaczynski's trial in Sacramento, California. It begins with the first day of jury selection on November 12, 1997, and ends with the January 1998 plea bargain.

VIDEOS

"The Bombing of America." South Burlington, Vt.: Nova Videos, 1996. Video (VHS). 60 minutes. This video focuses on the science of bomb explosions and the forensic evidence that helped solve bombings by the Unabomber and of the Oklahoma City federal building in 1995, the World Trade Center in 1993, and several abortion clinics in the Washington, D.C., area. It also looks into the technique of criminal profiling to pinpoint the identity of bombers.

"Hunt for the Unabomber." New York: A&E Television Networks, 1997. Video (VHS). 50 minutes. This video follows the 18-year search for the Unabomber, which ended when Ted Kaczynski's brother turned him in after recognizing Ted's writing style in the published "Unabomber Manifesto." It includes interviews with FBI profilers, arresting officers, prosecutors, and friends of Kaczynski.

"Ted Kaczynski the Unabomber." New York: A&E Television Networks, 1996. Video (VHS). 43 minutes. This video recounts the life of Kaczynski, whose use of logic allowed him to elude a massive FBI manhunt for nearly two decades.

WISE USE AND ANTI-ENVIRONMENTALISM

BOOKS

Arnold, Ron. *At the Eye of the Storm: James Watt and the Environmentalists.* Chicago: Regnery Gateway, 1982. This defense of James Watt, secretary of the interior during the early years of the Reagan administration, is part biography and part examination of U.S. environmental and public lands issues from the perspective of an author who went on to found the anti-environmental wise use movement. In the introduction, Arnold writes that "on several occasions Watt had told me flatly that if he ever became a political liability to President Reagan he would be honor-bound to offer his resignation." Despite the author's belief that there was "little chance of that happening," Watt did indeed resign the year following the publication of *At the Eye of the Storm.* The book is notable for its early use of the term *ecoterrorism* in the context of a brief discussion of environmental sabotage between 1980 and 1982. Appendices include a list of federal environmental laws passed between 1960 and 1982, and brief summaries of eight key court cases initiated by environmentalists from 1965 to 1977.

———. *Ecoterror: The Violent Agenda to Save Nature/The World of the Unabomber.* Bellevue, Wash.: Free Enterprise Press, 1995. This critical look at the use of violence by radical environmentalists was written by a founder of the wise use movement, which believes that public lands should be open to exploitation by private companies. Arnold goes to great lengths to catalog abuses of the law by environmentalists and to debunk accusations about the use of similar tactics by wise use advocates. Although poorly organized, the book is well researched and contains plenty of useful information. Of particular interest is a long, detailed chronology of sabotage and civil disobedience by environmentalists that begins in 1958 and ends in 1996. Each chapter concludes with a list of endnotes, and Arnold also provides a bibliography of books and articles.

Cawley, R. McGreggor. *Federal Land, Western Anger: The Sagebrush Rebellion and Environmental Politics.* Lawrence: University Press of Kansas, 1993. This is an in-depth analysis of the causes and connotations of the rebellion against tighter federal regulation of land in the western states. The author contends that "the Sagebrush Rebellion deserves to be listed with the conservation movement and the environmental movement as pivotal events in shaping the history of U.S. federal land policy."

Clausen, Barry, and DanaRae Pomeroy. *Walking on the Edge: How I Infiltrated Earth First!* Olympia, Wash.: Washington Contract Loggers Association, 1994. The first 80 pages of this autobiographical work, written in the third person, recount Clausen's work investigating drug dealers in Montana. The rest of the book follows his infiltration of Earth First! and his unsuccessful attempt to interest law enforcement officials in his findings, most of which came from reading readily available radical environmental newsletters. Among those who funded Clausen's investigation was the Washington Contract Loggers Association, which also published this book.

Echeverria, John, and Raymond Booth Eby, eds. *Let the People Judge: Wise Use and the Private Property Rights Movement.* Washington, D.C.: Island Press, 1995. This anthology of essays presents a wide range of views on the wise use movement and the controversies at the center of the debate between environmentalists and property rights advocates.

Helvarg, David. *The War Against the Greens: The "Wise Use" Movement, the New Right, and Anti-Environmental Violence.* San Francisco: Sierra Club Books, 1997. Journalist and private investigator Helvarg takes a critical look at the wise use movement, focusing on the more extreme elements that have used arson, bombings, and assault to intimidate environmentalists and federal employees.

Nelson, Robert H. *A Burning Issue: The Case for Abolishing the U.S. Forest Service.* Lanham, Md.: Rowman & Littlefield, 2000. Nelson argues that the U.S. Forest Service (USFS) has failed in its attempt to provide scientific management of the nation's forests, that it lacks a coherent vision, and that its policies are dictated by "fashionable environmental solutions," such as ecosystem management. The author suggests replacing the USFS with a decentralized management system. The book is published under the auspices of the Montana-based Political Economy Research Center, which advocates "free market environmentalism" and private property rights.

ARTICLES

"Counter Movement Backs Wise Use." *Christian Science Monitor,* January 12, 1993, p. 11. This article traces the anti-environmental wise use movement from its roots in the Sagebrush Rebellion of the 1970s and 1980s to its rise in power during the early 1990s. The anonymous author cites leaders of several organizations within the movement, as well as spokespersons for a few of the environmental groups that oppose them.

Ortega, Bob. "To Barry Clausen, The Woods Are Full of Eco Terrorists: Media Go to Him for Analysis of Environmental Violence the FBI Hasn't Spotted." *Wall Street Journal,* March 2, 1999, p. A1. Ortega profiles Barry Clausen, author of *Walking on the Edge: How I Infiltrated Earth First!* and self-styled leading authority on ecoterrorism. When Earth Liberation Front (ELF) took credit for burning ski-resort buildings in Vail, Colorado, in 1998, CBS News had Clausen on television three times in a day. Many, however, have criticized him for exaggeration, such as including pie throwings on his list of ecoterrorism acts. The list also includes many incidents that law enforcement officials do not know who committed, such as a 1993 arson at a U.S. Bureau of Land Management building in Nevada that many federal officials believe could just as likely be the work of antigovernment right-wing activists. In 1995, Clausen gained national attention when he told reporters he could connect Theodore Kaczynski to Earth First!, although he refused to disclose his proof, which consisted of the contention that Kaczynski had attended a forestry conference in 1994. Federal investigators never verified his presence, and conference organizers say Kaczynski was not there.

Annotated Bibliography

INTERNET DOCUMENTS

Arnold, Ron. "Overcoming Ideology." Center for the Defense of Free Enterprise. Available online. URL: http://www.cdfe.org/wiseuse.htm. Downloaded September 1, 2003. In this essay, Arnold debunks environmental ideology, suggesting it be replaced by the ideology at the core of the wise use movement.

Pendley, William Perry. "The Continuing Role for Public Interest Litigation During the Administration of President George W. Bush." Mountain States Legal Foundation. Available online. URL: http://www.mountainstateslegal.org/articles_speeches.cfm?articleid=12. Downloaded on September 1, 2003. Pendley uses two examples of the Mountain States Legal Foundation (MSLF) defending individuals against government regulation as the point of departure for a discussion on the Clinton administration's "war on the West." Among Clinton's abuses were attempting to draft a compromise solution to the timber wars in the Pacific Northwest in 1993, creating the Grand-Staircase-Escalante National Monument, and closing federal land considered to be sacred to Native Americans to recreational and economic activity. Pendley writes that although President George W. Bush and Vice President Dick Cheney appear to be in accord with the MSLF's views on how the West should be managed, disappointing court decisions, staffing delays, and problems in Congress indicate that the MSLF must continue to fight for its version of the American way of life.

CHAPTER 8

ORGANIZATIONS AND AGENCIES

This chapter provides contact information for organizations and agencies involved with ecoterrorism-related issues. Among these are government agencies, academic research institutes, public policy organizations, anti-environmentalist groups, and environmentalist groups, both mainstream and radical.

American Civil Liberties Union (ACLU)
URL: http://www.aclu.org
E-mail: aclu@aclu.org
Phone: (212) 944-9800
Fax: (212) 869-9065
125 Broad Street
18th Floor
New York, NY 10004
The ACLU provides legal advice and support for people whose civil rights guaranteed by the Constitution are endangered, an increasing concern among radical activists since passage of the USA PATRIOT Act. The web site includes information on recent court cases dealing with civil liberties issues. Relevant links will lead researchers to additional information on criminal justice, free speech, and national security. The union publishes

ACLU Online and the semiannual *Civil Liberties Alert.*

Americans for Medical Progress (AMP)
URL: http://www.ampef.org
E-mail: info@amprogress.org
Phone: (703) 836-9595
Fax: (703) 836-9594
908 King Street
Suite 301
Alexandria, VA 22314
AMP's mission is to protect society's investment in medical research by promoting public understanding of and support for the appropriate role of animals in biomedical research. In addition to news about medical research, the web site provides updated news stories about opposition to animal testing and information about the

philosophy and tactics of animal rights activists.

Animal Liberation Front (ALF)
URL: http://www.
  animalliberationfront.com
P.O. Box 950
Camarillo, CA 93011
This radical animal rights group, which operates in sympathy with the Earth Liberation Front, promotes vegetarianism while condemning vivisection, animal testing, wearing leather and furs, and hunting. It advocates destroying the property (primarily through arson) of individuals and businesses involved with these activities. The ALF does not keep membership lists, collect annual fees, or publish a magazine; advocates operate in secrecy while following no identifiable leader. According to the web site, people "join" the ALF simply by committing actions condoned by the ALF. The web site also includes information on planning actions, living a "cruelty-free" lifestyle, animal rights education and philosophy, and the organization's history.

Bay Area Coalition for
  Headwaters Forest (BACH)
URL: http://www.
  headwaterspreserve.org
E-mail: bach@igc.org
Phone: (510) 835-6303
2530 San Pablo Avenue
Berkeley, CA 94702
BACH formed in 1993 in response to logging activity in Humboldt County in Northern California. The group's purpose is to mobilize people in the San Francisco Bay Area to preserve a biologically viable redwood forest system in Northern California. BACH publishes an occasional newsletter and press releases.

BlueRibbon Coalition (BRC)
URL: http://www.sharetrails.org
E-mail: broffice@sharetrails.org
Phone: (208) 237-1008
Fax: (208) 237-9424
4555 Burley Drive
Suite A
Pocatello, ID 83202-1921
The coalition works to keep public lands open to motorized recreational vehicles, such as trail motorcycles, snowmobiles, and four-wheel-drive trucks. The BRC's *BlueRibbon* magazine, available online, features news items, editorial essays, and updates on relevant court cases.

Bureau of Land Management
  (BLM)
U.S. Department of the Interior
URL: http://www.blm.gov
E-mail: woinfo@blm.gov
Phone: (202) 452-5125
Fax: (202) 452-5124
Office of Public Affairs
1849 C Street, NW
Room 406-LS
Washington, DC 20240
The BLM administers more than 260 million acres of public lands, primarily in the 12 western states, balancing conservation, environmental management, recreation, and tourism. From the main web

site, browsers can link to the BLM's numerous field offices for detailed information on local issues, including resource management, recreation, law enforcement, land titles, hazardous materials management, and public health and safety.

Cato Institute
URL: http://www.cato.org
Phone: (202) 842-0200
Fax: (202) 842-3490
1000 Massachusetts Avenue, NW
Washington, DC 20001-5403
Founded in 1977, the Cato Institute is a nonprofit public policy research foundation dedicated to such conservative ideals as limited government and a free market economy. As such, members see environmentalism as an attack on reason and personal freedom. The web site includes links to sections on terrorism and civil liberties that may yield useful information to those researching domestic terrorism. The institute hosts conferences and publishes books, monographs, and briefing papers, as well as the *Cato Journal* and *Regulation* magazine.

Center for the Defense of Free Enterprise (CDFE)
URL: http://www.cdfe.org
E-mail: contact@cdfe.org
Phone: (425) 455-5038
Fax: (425) 451-3959
12500 NE 10th Place
Bellevue, WA 98005
The CDFE, founded by Alan Gottlieb in 1976, is an education and research organization that works on

free enterprise studies and public policy research. Executive vice president Ron Arnold has been credited with founding the wise use movement and has been a longtime critic of environmentalism. The organization spreads its message through book publishing, conferences, white papers, and media outreach. The web site has an extensive section on ecoterrorism, with news reports, articles, profiles of radical environmental groups, and a database of crimes committed by environmental activists.

Center for Democracy and Technology (CDT)
URL: http://www.cdt.org
E-mail: feedback@cdt.org
Phone: (202) 637-9800
Fax: (202) 637-0968
1634 I Street, NW
Suite 1100
Washington, DC 20006
This civil liberties group works to "promote democratic values and constitutional liberties in the digital age." Issues relating to free speech and government surveillance are explored on its web site.

Competitive Enterprise Institute (CEI)
URL: http://www.cei.org
E-mail: info@cei.org
Phone: (202) 331-1010
Fax: (202) 331-0640
1001 Connecticut Avenue, NW
Suite 1250
Washington, DC 20036
This nonprofit public policy organization encourages the removal of

government regulation in order to establish a system in which private incentives and property rights would be used to protect the environment. Among the CEI's concerns are federal land management and species protection. Publications include *The Environmental Source 2002.*

Council on Environmental Quality (CEQ)
URL: http://www.whitehouse. gov/ceq/
Phone: (202) 395-5750
Fax: (202) 456-6546
722 Jackson Place, NW
Washington, DC 20503
The CEQ coordinates federal environmental efforts and works to develop environmental policies. Visitors to the web site will find information on current federal environmental initiatives, news releases, and links to federal agencies involved with environmental issues, such as the Department of the Interior and the Environmental Protection Agency.

Defenders of Property Rights (DPR)
URL: http://www. yourpropertyrights.org
Phone: (202) 822-6770
Fax: (202) 822-6774
1350 Connecticut Avenue, NW
Suite 410
Washington, DC 20036
DPR was founded in 1991 by former Reagan administration Justice Department officials Roger and Nancie Marzulla to fight a broad

range of federal regulations, including environmental laws, that they feel infringe on the freedoms of private property owners. One of their primary tactics is to fight such regulations in court. The web site has news briefs, court reports, and more.

Defenders of Wildlife
URL: http://www.defenders.org
E-mail: info@defenders.org
Phone: (202) 682-9400
1130 17th Street, NW
Washington, DC 20030
Defenders of Wildlife focuses on protecting native plants and animals in their natural environments by working to curtail the accelerating rate of species and biodiversity loss, as well as habitat alteration and destruction. It advocates protecting entire ecosystems and exploring new approaches to conservation. The web site provides news, details about programs, links to online publications, and information about wildlife viewing tours.

Earth First!
URLs: http://www.earthfirst.org, http://www.earthfirstjournal. org/efj (Earth First! Journal)
E-mail: collective@ earthfirstjournal.com
Phone: (520) 620-6900
Fax: (413) 254-0057
P.O. Box 3023
Tucson, AZ 85702
EF! Media Center
E-mail: efmc@asis.com
P.O. Box 324
Redway, CA 95560

This radical environmental group was founded in 1980, and its tactics are reflected in the slogan "No Compromise in Defense of Mother Earth." Earth First! activists helped pioneer such direct-action tactics as tree spiking, tree sitting, human blockades, and the destruction of heavy equipment. Since the group maintains no central office, the *EF! Journal* is the best source of information for articles, upcoming events, and reports about recent actions.

Earth Island Institute
URL: http://www.earthisland.
 org
Phone: (415) 788-3666
Fax: (415) 788-7324
300 Broadway
Suite 28
San Francisco, CA 94133
Formed in 1982 by David Brower, Earth Island Institute is dedicated to the conservation, preservation, and restoration of the global environment. The institute acts as a cooperative enterprise that centralizes certain administrative and organizational services while urging individual members to create and foster their own local environmental projects. The group publishes the quarterly *Earth Island Journal.*

Earth Liberation Front (ELF)
URL: http://www.
 earthliberationfront.com
E-mail: elfpress@resist.ca
Although it has no central headquarters or identifiable leaders, the ELF does maintain a web site with press releases, how-to guides, security advice for activists, and an online handbook with information on how to deal with an FBI investigation.

Electronic Frontier Foundation
 (EFF)
URL: http://www.eff.org
E-mail: eff@eff.org
Phone: (415) 436-9333
Fax: (415) 436-9993
454 Shotwell Street
San Francisco, CA 94110
Formed in 1990 to protect fundamental rights of free speech in electronic media, the EFF opposes legislation that it considers threatening to these rights and provides defense in civil liberties court cases. The "Anti-Terrorism" and "USA PATRIOT Act" links on its web page provide access to articles on federal legislation intended to curtail terrorist activity. The EFF also publishes an online newsletter and Internet guidebooks.

Electronic Privacy Information
 Center (EPIC)
URL: http://www.epic.org
E-mail: info@epic.org
Phone: (202) 483-1140
Fax: (202) 483-1248
1718 Connecticut Avenue, NW
Suite 200
Washington, DC 20009
EPIC was established in 1994 to focus public attention on privacy, First Amendment, and constitutional issues relating to emerging electronic media and communication systems. The group litigates

civil liberties issues and publishes several books, including *Privacy Law Sourcebook, Consumer Law Sourcebook, Technology and Privacy,* and *Information Privacy Law.*

Environmental Defense
URL: http://www.
    environmentaldefense.org/
    home.cfm
E-mail: members@
    environmentaldefense.org
Phone: (212) 505-2100
Fax: (212) 505-2375
257 Park Avenue South
New York, NY 10010
This environmental organization tackles a wide range of environmental issues using the advice of experts from the fields of science, economics, and law. The group's 750,000-member Action Network is an online community that responds to environmental alerts by sending e-mails and faxes on timely issues to policymakers. Environmental Defense publishes newsletters, fact sheets, educational materials, and an annual report on the state of the environment.

**Environmental Protection
    Information Center (EPIC)**
URL: http://www.wildcalifornia.
    org
E-mail: epic@wildcalifornia.org
Phone: (707) 923-2931
Fax: (707) 923-4210
P.O. Box 397
Garberville, CA 95542
Since 1977, EPIC has used education and strategic litigation to de-fend the redwood forests and endangered species of coastal Northern California. Much of its work between 1986 and 1998 focused on protecting the Headwaters Forest area. Since then, it has shifted its attention to the protection and recovery of salmon habitat and clean water throughout the region. The web site maintains an archive of press releases, news updates, activist resources, and links to other web sites of interest.

**Federal Bureau of Investigation
    (FBI)**
U.S. Department of Justice
URL: http://www.fbi.gov
Phone: (202) 324-3000
935 Pennsylvania Avenue, NW
Washington, DC 20535
The FBI investigates and compiles data on domestic terrorism. The web site includes a link to Domestic Terrorism Section Chief James F. Jarboe's 2002 statement on the threat of ecoterrorism before the House Resources Committee.

**First Amendment Foundation
    (FAF)**
URL: http://www.floridafaf.org
E-mail: foi@vashti.net
Phone: (800) 337-3518
336 East College Avenue
Suite 101
Tallahassee, FL 32301
Founded in 1984 by the Florida Press Association, the Florida Society of Newspaper Editors, and the Florida Association of Broadcasters, the First Amendment Foundation

seeks to protect the public's constitutional right to an open government by providing education and training, legal aid, and information services.

Forests Forever
URL: http://www.forestsforever.
 org
E-mail: mail@forestsforever.org
Phone: (415) 974-3636
Fax: (415) 974-3664
50 First Street
Suite 401
San Francisco, CA 94105
This organization uses citizen education and grassroots organizing to defend and restore California's 17 million acres of diverse woodland ecosystems. Like many of the organizations formed for this purpose, Forests Forever coalesced around efforts to save Headwaters Forest from logging by Maxxam/Pacific Lumber Company in the 1990s. The web site features a newsletter, action alerts, and links to like-minded organizations.

Friends of the Earth (FoE)
URL: http://www.foe.org
E-mail: foe@foe.org
Phone: (202) 783-7400
Fax: (202) 783-0444
1025 Vermont Avenue, NW
Third Floor
Washington, DC 20005-6303
Founded in 1969 by David Brower, this international environmental organization has affiliates in 70 countries. Over the past several decades, members have helped stop questionable dams and water projects, ban international whaling, oust James Watt from his position as secretary of the interior, press for increased regulation of strip mines and oil tankers, reform the World Bank, and eliminate billions in taxpayer subsidies to corporate polluters. Publications include the *Friends of the Earth Annual Report* and the annual *Green Scissors*, which reveals environmentally harmful government programs that the organization believes should be cut.

George C. Marshall Institute
 (GMI)
URL: http://www.marshall.org
E-mail: info@marshall.org
Phone: (202) 296-9655
Fax: (202) 296-9714
1625 K Street, NW
Suite 1050
Washington, DC 20006
Founded in 1984, this nonprofit research group provides technical advice on scientific issues that have an impact on public policy, particularly those related to the environment and national security. The institute advocates "civic environmentalism," which would allow "a role for government in setting national standards, but would leave the work of actual environmental protection up to collaborative efforts between industry and local governments." Publications dealing with environmental and national security issues are accessible through the web site.

Organizations and Agencies

Greenpeace International
URL: http://www.greenpeace.
org/homepage
E-mail: supporter.services@ams.
greenpeace.org
Phone: (31) 20 523 6222
Fax: (31) 20 523 6200
Keizersgracht 176
1016 DW Amsterdam
The Netherlands

Greenpeace USA
URL: http://www.greenpeaceusa.
org
Phone: (800) 326-0959
702 H Street, NW
Suite 300
Washington, DC 20021
This global environmental organization is dedicated to peaceful direct
action with the aim of curbing global
warming, genetic engineering, nuclear testing, whaling, and deforesta-
tion. Publications include fact sheets,
reports, and briefings, as well as the
quarterly *Greenpeace Magazine*.

The Heritage Foundation
URL: http://www.heritage.org
E-mail: info@heritage.org
Phone: (202) 546-4400
Fax: (202) 546-8328
214 Massachusetts Avenue, NE
Washington, DC 20002-4999
This conservative think tank supports free enterprise and limited
government in environmental matters, standing in opposition to
many views taken by mainstream
environmentalists. Publications include scholarly journals, reviews,
and books.

**International Association for
Counterterrorism and Security
Professionals (IACSP)**
URL: http://www.iacsp.com
E-mail: iacsp@erols.com
The association was founded in
1992 to educate people about ter-
rorism with the aim of developing
innovative and effective counterter-
rorism measures. It publishes *The
Journal of Counterterrorism and Se-
curity International*.

J. N. "Ding" Darling Foundation
URL: http://www.ding-darling.
org
E-mail: kipkoss@hotmail.com
Phone: (305) 361-9788
785 Crandon Boulevard
Suite 1206
Key Biscayne, FL 33149
Named after a political cartoonist
who in the 1930s helped lay the
foundation for the current National
Wildlife Reserve system, the foundation has worked since 1963 to
support Florida's J. N. "Ding" Darling National Wildlife Refuge and
to produce teaching materials for
conservation education. Among its
founding trustees were former
presidents Harry S. Truman and
Dwight D. Eisenhower.

**Mountain States Legal
Foundation (MSLF)**
URL: http://www.
mountainstateslegal.org/
index.cfm
E-mail: info@
mountainstateslegal.org
Phone: (303) 292-2021

2596 South Lewis Way
Lakewood, CO 80227
MSLF offers pro bono (free of
charge) legal counsel to people who
feel that government regulations
(such as those mandated by the Endangered Species Act) have limited
their personal freedoms or their
right to use private property in the
way they desire. The web site has
press releases, articles, speeches, information on court cases, and an
online version of the quarterly
newsletter *The Litigator.*

National Audubon Society
URL: http://www.audubon.org
E-mail: education@audubon.org
Phone: (212) 979-3000
Fax: (212) 979-3188
700 Broadway
New York, NY 10003
Named after American naturalist
and wildlife painter John James
Audubon, the society was created
in 1886 to conserve and restore
natural ecosystems vital to the
health of bird populations. It has
since grown into a national network of community-based nature
centers and chapters that run scientific and educational programs,
and also advocates the protection
of birds and other wildlife. Publications include *Audubon Magazine*
and annual reports.

National Coalition Against
  Censorship (NCAC)
URL: http://www.ncac.org
E-mail: ncac@ncac.org
Phone: (212) 807-6222

Fax: (212) 807-6245
275 Seventh Avenue
New York, NY 10001
This alliance of 50 national nonprofit organizations—including library, artistic, religious, educational,
professional, labor, and civil liberties
groups—is dedicated to fighting for
freedom of thought and expression.
Among its concerns is analyzing the
impact of the Homeland Security
Act and the USA PATRIOT Act.
The coalition publishes flyers, essays, magazine article reprints, and
the quarterly *Censorship News.*

National Committee Against
  Repressive Legislation
  (NCARL)
URL: http://www.ncarl.org
E-mail: ncarl@aol.com
Phone: (213) 484-6661
Fax: (213) 484-0266
1313 West Eighth Street
Suite 313
Los Angeles, CA 90017
This civil liberties organization
works to defend the right of politi-
cal expression in the United States.
It has signed letters urging mem-
bers of Congress to oppose the Do-
mestic Security Enhancement Act
(PATRIOT Act II).

National Park Service (NPS)
U.S. Department of the Interior
URL: http://www.nps.gov
Phone: 202-208-6843
1849 C Street, NW
Washington, DC 20240
This agency within the Interior
Department oversees the preserva-

tion of national parks and monuments. The web site provides access to a wide array of information, from NPS policies and programs to educational, historical, and cultural materials. Each park and monument within the system has its own detailed web site, all of which are accessible from the main site.

National Parks Conservation Association (NPCA)
URL: http://www.npca.org/ home.html
E-mail: npca@npca.org
Phone: (800) 628-7275
Fax: (202) 659-0650
1300 19th Street, NW
Suite 300
Washington, DC 20036
Founded in 1919, the NPCA works to preserve the U.S. national park system by mobilizing citizens, businesses, and politicians to protect resources; lobbying Congress to promote park legislation; and using the court system to establish safeguards to protect the parks from abuse. The web site provides information on specific preservation programs. A list of the 10 most endangered national parks enumerates the specific threats to each park, the solutions to the problems, and suggestions for what citizens can do to help realize the solutions.

National Wildlife Federation (NWF)
URL: http://www.nwf.org
Phone: (703) 438-6000

11100 Wildlife Center Drive
Reston, VA 20190-5362
This organization seeks to protect wildlife and the environments they live in by bringing together individuals, organizations, businesses, and government officials to fight for conservation issues. Efforts include returning gray wolves to their native habitat in Yellowstone National Park and Idaho, restoring the Florida Everglades, and protecting threatened wetlands and coastal areas. Publications include an annual report and *National Wildlife* magazine.

Natural Resources Conservation Service (NRCS)
U.S. Department of Agriculture
URL: http://www.nrcs.usda.gov
P.O. Box 2890
Washington, DC 20013
The NRCS is responsible for assisting private landowners—as well as local, state, and federal agencies—in efforts to conserve, maintain, and improve soil, water, and other natural resources. The web site maintains a database of news releases, fact sheets, and speech transcripts. A number of publications on a variety of conservation issues can also be downloaded.

Natural Resources Defense Council (NRDC)
URL: h@ADD:ttp://www.nrdc. org
E-mail: nrdcinfo@nrdc.org
Phone: (212) 727-2700
Fax: (212) 727-1773

40 West 20th Street
New York, NY 10011
The NRDC relies on law, science, and member support to protect wildlife and wilderness areas around the world. Among its areas of concern are clean air and energy; clean water and oceans; global warming; wildlife and fish; toxic chemicals and health; nuclear weapons and waste; and parks, forests, and wildlands. A number of publications, including the quarterly magazine *OnEarth*, are available online.

The Nature Conservancy (TNC)
URL: http://nature.org
E-mail: comment@tnc.org
Phone: (703) 841-5300
4245 North Fairfax Drive
Suite 100
Arlington, VA 22203-1606
Founded in 1951, the Nature Conservancy takes a nonconfrontational approach to its work of protecting land with the purpose of preserving plants, animals, and natural communities. The organization has created approximately 1,400 preserves that protect 15 million acres of land in the United States and 101 million acres in other countries. Publications include *Nature Conservancy* magazine, an e-newsletter, and a number of science-based books on environmental issues.

Pacific Legal Foundation (PLF)
URL: http://www.pacificlegal.org
E-mail: plf@pacificlegal.org
Phone: (916) 362-2833

Fax: (916) 362-2932
10360 Old Placerville Road
Suite 100
Sacramento, CA 95827
PLF provides legal representation for U.S. citizens who believe their personal freedoms have been infringed upon by "a form of tyranny engendered by overzealous bureaucracies, government red tape, ignorance or indifference of our courts and elected officials, and a complex maze of laws and regulations that are strangling our personal and professional lives." The web site allows access to an index of court cases, as well as media kits, press releases, and editorials. The PLF also publishes several periodicals, including the quarterly newsletter *Guidepost* and the biweekly bulletin *Action Report*.

**People for the Ethical
   Treatment of Animals (PETA)**
URL: http://www.peta.org
E-mail: info@peta-online.org
Phone: (757) 622-7382
Fax: (757) 622-0457
501 Front Street
Norfolk, VA 23510
PETA was founded in 1980 on the principle that "animals are not ours to eat, wear, experiment on, or use for entertainment." Tactics range from direct action to confrontational advertising campaigns, some of which have been banned from billboards and television. The organization also works to educate the public and policymakers on animal rights issues.

The web site provides access to news, fact sheets, a vegetarian starter kit, vegetarian recipes, a nonleather shopping guide, and videos on investigations into animal cruelty issues, vivisection, and more. PETA also publishes the quarterly magazine *Animal Times.*

Rachel Carson Council, Inc. (RCC)
URL: http://members.aol.com/ rccouncil/ourpage/index.htm
E-mail: rccouncil@aol.com
Phone: (301) 593-7507
Fax: (301) 593-6251
P.O. Box 10779
Silver Spring, MD 20914
Founded in 1965, the RCC seeks to educate and advise institutions and individuals about the negative effects that pesticides have on the health of living organisms and biological systems. It espouses "alternative, environmentally benign pest management" to promote healthier living. The web site includes short reports about pesticides in the news, alerts about new research findings, feature articles, and a catalog of videos and publications.

Rainforest Action Network (RAN)
URL: http://www.ran.org
E-mail: rainforest@ran.org
Phone: (415) 398-4404
Fax: (415) 398-2732
221 Pine Street
Suite 500
San Francisco, CA 94104

Since its founding in 1985, RAN has worked to preserve tropical rain forests around the world by addressing problems associated with the logging and importation of tropical lumber, cattle ranching in rain forests, and the human rights of those living in and around rain forests. Publications include the *RAN Annual Report.*

Rainforest Alliance
URL: http://www.rainforest-alliance.org
E-mail: canopy@ra.org
Phone: (212) 677-1900
Fax: (212) 677-2187
665 Broadway
Suite 500
New York, NY 10012
This environmental organization is concerned with promoting sustainable business practices that will protect ecosystems and the people and wildlife that live within them. Programs include Adopt-a-Rainforest and the Sustainable Agriculture Network. The Rainforest Alliance also publishes the bimonthly newsletter *The Canopy.*

Reason Foundation
URL: http://www.reason.org
E-mail: gpassantino@reason.org
Phone: (310) 391-2245
Fax: (310) 391-4395
3414 South Sepulveda Boulevard
Suite 400
Los Angeles, CA 90034-6064
This national public policy research organization promotes economic

and individual liberty, and therefore tends to oppose strict environmental regulation imposed from the federal level. Web site links will take researchers to essays on private approaches to conservation and competitive sourcing of concessions in national parks. Publications include the monthly *Reason Magazine*.

Ruckus Society
URL: http://www.ruckus.org
E-mail: info@ruckus.org
Phone: (510) 763-7078
Fax: (510) 763-7068
369 15th Street
Oakland, CA 94612
The Ruckus Society holds weeklong camps during which it trains activists in the use of nonviolent direct action, the planning of strategy, the establishment of coalitions, and the use of effective media outreach. The web site lists upcoming camps with information on how to apply.

Sea Shepherd Conservation
Society (SSCS)
URL: http://www.seashepherd.
org
E-mail: seashepherd@
seashepherd.org
Phone: (360) 370-5650
Fax: (360) 370-5651
P.O. Box 2670
Malibu, CA 90265
This organization, which split from Greenpeace in 1977, is dedicated to the preservation of marine ecosystems and species via two principal means: public education, and "investigation, documentation, and where appropriate and where legal authority exists under international law or under agreement with national governments, enforcement of violations of national treaties, laws and conventions designed to protect oceans." This has, at times, meant participating in direct action confrontations in the effort to eradicate illegal fishing and whaling. The web site features a log of recent activity, descriptions and photographs of the vessels used by the Sea Shepherds, and profiles of crew members.

Sierra Club
URL: http://www.sierraclub.org
E-mail: information@sierraclub.
org
Phone: (415) 977-5500
Fax: (415) 977-5799
85 Second Street
2nd Floor
San Francisco, CA 94105-3441
The Sierra Club was founded by John Muir in 1892 to promote the protection and preservation of natural resources. It has since become one of the largest and most powerful mainstream environmental organizations in the world. Issues of concern include clean water, global population, energy, human rights, protection of national forests, global warming, and preservation of wildlands. The main web site provides news of national interest and has links to Sierra Club chapters in all 50 states, as well as Canada. Publications include the bimonthly magazine *Sierra* and the monthly activist resource *The Planet*.

Stop Eco-Violence (SEV)
URL: http://www.
stopecoviolence.org
E-mail: info@stopecoviolence.
com
Phone: (503) 570-2848
Fax: (503) 570-2863
P.O. Box 2118
Wilson, OR 97070
SEV seeks to raise public awareness about ecoterrorism with the goal of convincing policy makers to pass legislation aimed at stopping such activities. The web site has breaking news, ecoterror alerts, and a summary of recent attacks. Although mostly concerned with actions that involve property destruction, the web site also reports on some instances of nonviolent civil disobedience.

**Stop Huntingdon Animal
  Cruelty (SHAC)**
URL: http://www.shac.net
E-mail: info@shac.net
Phone: (44) 845 458 0630
6 Boat Lane
Evesham, Worcestershire WR11
  4BP
United Kingdom
Although based in England, SHAC has been active in the United States with the support of the Animal Liberation Front (ALF). The group was founded in 1999 "with the sole aim" of closing down Huntingdon Life Science, a Europe-based testing lab accused by SHAC of killing 500 animals each day in medical and product tests. Toward that end, SHAC uses direct action tactics,

some of which have been called terrorist acts by opponents.

**Terrorism Research Center
  (TRC)**
URL: http://www.terrorism.com
E-mail: trc@terrorism.com
The center provides information on terrorism and information warfare. The web site features essays on current issues, as well as links to other documents, research, and resources concerned with terrorism.

Trees Foundation
URL: http://www.
  treesfoundation.org
E-mail: trees@treesfoundation.
  org
Phone: (707) 923-4377
Fax: (707) 923-4427
P.O. Box 2202
Redway, CA 95542
Trees Foundation was formed in 1991 by a group of local business owners to determine the best way to support environmental activists who were working to protect the redwood forest of coastal Northern California. The organization publishes the quarterly newsletter *Branching Out*, the *Headwaters Forest Update*, and the *Headwaters Forest Stewardship Plan*.

**U.S. Department of Homeland
  Security (DHS)**
URL: http://www.dhs.gov/
  dhspublic
Washington, DC 20528
The DHS is a government agency created in the wake of the September

251

11, 2001, terrorist attacks on the United States. It coordinates 22 previously separate federal agencies into one department in an effort to more efficiently protect the nation against terrorist threats.

U.S. Environmental Protection
Agency (EPA)
URL: http://www.epa.gov
E-mail: public-access@epa.gov
Phone: (202) 260-2090
401 M Street, SW
Washington, DC 20460
The mission of the EPA is to protect human health and to safeguard the natural environment. Part of the agency's mandate is to oversee the Endangered Species Act and evaluate environmental impact statements.

U.S. Forest Service (USFS)
U.S. Department of Agriculture
URL: http://www.fs.fed.us
E-mail: webmaster@fs.fed.us
Phone: (202) 205-8333
P.O. Box 96090
Washington, DC 20090-6090
This agency of the U.S. Department of Agriculture manages national forests and grasslands. The web site provides access to national forest fire information, timber harvesting policies and practices, guides to recreation, links for submitting public comments for management plans, and links to web sites covering all national forest and grassland areas under its jurisdiction. Each of these sites has detailed local management, policy, and recreation information.

USFS publications (which include annual reports, "facts and figures" brochures, and land area reports) fall into three categories: administrative, general, and research. Many are available online.

U.S. Public Interest Research
Group (U.S. PIRG)
URL: http://www.pirg.org/
uspirg
E-mail: uspirg@pirg.org
Phone: (202) 546-9707
Fax: (202) 546-2461
218 D Street, SE
Washington, DC 20003
U.S. PIRG was created in 1983 by a coalition of state public interest research groups to act as a watchdog for the public interest in the nation's capital. Among the environmental issues on the organization's agenda are Arctic wilderness, clean air and water, endangered species, energy, forest protection, global warming, and toxics. The web site provides access to information on these and other issues, as well as links to current news articles, reports, and congressional scorecards that rate whether members of the Senate and the House of Representatives have voted for or against the public interest.

The Wilderness Society
URL: http://www.wilderness.org
Phone: (800) 843-9453
1615 M Street, NW
Washington, DC 20036
The Wilderness Society, founded in 1935, works to protect roadless

and wilderness areas in the United States. Among its concerns are saving the Arctic National Wildlife Refuge from oil and gas drilling, stopping logging and road building on 58 million acres of roadless land, and curbing abuse of public land by off-road vehicles. The organization publishes reports and scientific papers, policy and science briefs, maps, fact sheets, legal documents, and activist handbooks and guides.

The Wildlands Project
URL: http://www.
wildlandsproject.org
E-mail: info@wildlandsproject.
org
Phone: (802) 434-4077
Fax: (802) 434-5980
P.O. Box 455
Richmond, VT 05477
This organization was cofounded by Dave Foreman and John Davis with the ambitious purpose of establishing a vast, interconnected system of wildlands to better preserve and restore natural areas in the United States. The project publishes the quarterly conservation journal *Wild Earth*.

Worldwatch Institute
URL: http://www.worldwatch.org
E-mail: worldwatch@worldwatch.
org

Phone: (202) 452-1999
Fax: (202) 296-7365
1776 Massachusetts Avenue, NW
Washington, DC 20036-1904
This nonprofit public policy research organization works to focus the attention of policy makers and the public on global problems, including environmental concerns such as global warming and the relationship between the world economy and the environment. The institute publishes the Vital Signs report and State of the World report (both annual), the bimonthly magazine *World Watch*, and numerous papers, books, and CD-ROMs.

World Wildlife Fund (WWF)
URL: http://www.panda.org
Phone: (202) 293-4800
Fax: (202) 293-9211
1250 24th Street, NW
Washington, DC 20037-1175
This global environmental organization works to conserve biological diversity, ensure that natural resources are utilized in a sustainable manner, and reduce pollution and wasteful consumption. Among its priorities are protecting endangered species and preserving forests around the world.

PART III

APPENDICES

APPENDIX A

STATEMENT OF JAMES F. JARBOE, FEBRUARY 12, 2002

(*Note:* James F. Jarboe was Domestic Terrorism Section Chief, Counterterrorism Division, Federal Bureau of Investigation. This statement, supplied to the U.S. House Subcommittee on Forests and Forests Health, was made at a hearing on ecoterrorism.)

Good morning Chairman McInnis, Vice-Chairman Peterson, Congressman Inslee and Members of the Subcommittee. I am pleased to have the opportunity to appear before you and discuss the threat posed by eco-terrorism, as well as the measures being taken by the FBI and our law enforcement partners to address this threat.

The FBI divides the terrorist threat facing the United States into two broad categories, international and domestic. International terrorism involves violent acts or acts dangerous to human life that are a violation of the criminal laws of the United States or any state, or that would be a criminal violation if committed within the jurisdiction of the United States or any state. Acts of international terrorism are intended to intimidate or coerce a civilian population, influence the policy of a government, or affect the conduct of a government. These acts transcend national boundaries in terms of the means by which they are accomplished, the persons they appear intended to intimidate, or the locale in which perpetrators operate.

Domestic terrorism is the unlawful use, or threatened use, of violence by a group or individual based and operating entirely within the United States (or its territories) without foreign direction, committed against persons or property to intimidate or coerce a government, the civilian population, or any segment thereof, in furtherance of political or social objectives.

During the past decade we have witnessed dramatic changes in the nature of the terrorist threat. In the 1990s, right-wing extremism overtook left-wing terrorism as the most dangerous domestic terrorist threat to the country. During the past several years, special interest extremism, as characterized by the Animal Liberation Front (ALF) and the Earth Liberation Front (ELF), has emerged as a serious terrorist threat. Generally, extremist groups engage in much activity that is protected by constitutional guarantees of free speech and assembly. Law enforcement becomes involved when the volatile talk of these groups transgresses into unlawful action. The FBI estimates that the ALF/ELF have committed more than 600 criminal acts in the United States since 1996, resulting in damages in excess of 43 million dollars.

Special interest terrorism differs from traditional right-wing and left-wing terrorism in that extremist special interest groups seek to resolve specific issues, rather than effect widespread political change. Special interest extremists continue to conduct acts of politically motivated violence to force segments of society, including the general public, to change attitudes about issues considered important to their causes. These groups occupy the extreme fringes of animal rights, pro-life, environmental, antinuclear, and other movements. Some special interest extremists—most notably within the animal rights and environmental movements—have turned increasingly toward vandalism and terrorist activity in attempts to further their causes.

Since 1977, when disaffected members of the ecological preservation group Greenpeace formed the Sea Shepherd Conservation Society and attacked commercial fishing operations by cutting drift nets, acts of "eco-terrorism" have occurred around the globe. The FBI defines eco-terrorism as the use or threatened use of violence of a criminal nature against innocent victims or property by an environmentally-oriented, subnational group for environmental-political reasons, or aimed at an audience beyond the target, often of a symbolic nature.

In recent years, the Animal Liberation Front (ALF) has become one of the most active extremist elements in the United States. Despite the destructive aspects of ALF's operations, its operational philosophy discourages acts that harm "any animal, human and nonhuman." Animal rights groups in the United States, including the ALF, have generally adhered to this mandate. The ALF, established in Great Britain in the mid-1970s, is a loosely organized movement committed to ending the abuse and exploitation of animals. The American branch of the ALF began its operations in the late 1970s. Individuals become members of the ALF not by filing paperwork or paying dues, but simply by engaging in "direct action" against companies or individuals who utilize animals for research or economic gain. "Direct action" generally occurs in the form of criminal activity to cause economic loss or to destroy the victims' company operations. The ALF activists have engaged in a steadily growing campaign of illegal activity against fur companies, mink farms, restaurants, and animal research laboratories.

Appendix A

Estimates of damage and destruction in the United States claimed by the ALF during the past ten years, as compiled by national organizations such as the Fur Commission and the National Association for Biomedical Research (NABR), put the fur industry and medical research losses at more than 45 million dollars. The ALF is considered a terrorist group, whose purpose is to bring about social and political change through the use of force and violence.

Disaffected environmentalists, in 1980, formed a radical group called "Earth First!" and engaged in a series of protests and civil disobedience events. In 1984, however, members introduced "tree spiking" (insertion of metal or ceramic spikes in trees in an effort to damage saws) as a tactic to thwart logging. In 1992, the ELF was founded in Brighton, England, by Earth First! members who refused to abandon criminal acts as a tactic when others wished to mainstream Earth First!. In 1993, the ELF was listed for the first time along with the ALF in a communiqué declaring solidarity in actions between the two groups. This unity continues today with a crossover of leadership and membership. It is not uncommon for the ALF and the ELF to post joint declarations of responsibility for criminal actions on their web sites. In 1994, founders of the San Francisco branch of Earth First! published in the *Earth First! Journal* a recommendation that Earth First! mainstream itself in the United States, leaving criminal acts other than unlawful protests to the ELF.

The ELF advocates "monkeywrenching," a euphemism for acts of sabotage and property destruction against industries and other entities perceived to be damaging to the natural environment. "Monkeywrenching" includes tree spiking, arson, sabotage of logging or construction equipment, and other types of property destruction. Speeches given by Jonathan Paul and Craig Rosebraugh at the 1998 National Animal Rights Conference held at the University of Oregon, promoted the unity of both the ELF and the ALF movements. The ELF posted information on the ALF website until it began its own website in January 2001, and is listed in the same underground activist publications as the ALF.

The most destructive practice of the ALF/ELF is arson. The ALF/ELF members consistently use improvised incendiary devices equipped with crude but effective timing mechanisms. These incendiary devices are often constructed based upon instructions found on the ALF/ELF web sites. The ALF/ELF criminal incidents often involve pre-activity surveillance and well-planned operations. Members are believed to engage in significant intelligence gathering against potential targets, including the review of industry/trade publications, photographic/video surveillance of potential targets, and posting details about potential targets on the Internet.

The ALF and the ELF have jointly claimed credit for several raids including a November 1997 attack of the Bureau of Land Management wild

259

horse corrals near Burns, Oregon, where arson destroyed the entire complex resulting in damages in excess of four hundred and fifty thousand dollars and the June 1998 arson attack of a U.S. Department of Agriculture Animal Damage Control Building near Olympia, Washington, in which damages exceeded two million dollars. The ELF claimed sole credit for the October 1998 arson of a Vail, Colorado, ski facility in which four ski lifts, a restaurant, a picnic facility, and a utility building were destroyed. Damage exceeded $12 million. On 12/27/1998, the ELF claimed responsibility for the arson at the U.S. Forest Industries Office in Medford, Oregon, where damages exceeded five hundred thousand dollars. Other arsons in Oregon, New York, Washington, Michigan, and Indiana have been claimed by the ELF. Recently, the ELF has also claimed attacks on genetically engineered crops and trees. The ELF claims these attacks have totaled close to $40 million in damages.

The name of a group called the Coalition to Save the Preserves (CSP) surfaced in relation to a series of arsons that occurred in the Phoenix, Arizona, area. These arsons targeted several new homes under construction near the North Phoenix Mountain Preserves. No direct connection was established between the CSP and ALF/ELF. However, the stated goal of CSP to stop development of previously undeveloped lands is similar to that of the ELF. The property damage associated with the arsons has been estimated to be in excess of $5 million.

The FBI has developed a strong response to the threats posed by domestic and international terrorism. Between fiscal years 1993 and 2003, the number of Special Agents dedicated to the FBI's counterterrorism programs grew by approximately 224 percent to 1,669—nearly 16 percent of all FBI Special Agents. In recent years, the FBI has strengthened its counterterrorism program to enhance its abilities to carry out these objectives.

Cooperation among law enforcement agencies at all levels represents an important component of a comprehensive response to terrorism. This cooperation assumes its most tangible operational form in the Joint Terrorism Task Forces (JTTFs) that are established in 44 cities across the nation. These task forces are particularly well-suited to responding to terrorism because they combine the national and international investigative resources of the FBI with the street-level expertise of local law enforcement agencies. Given the success of the JTTF concept, the FBI has established 15 new JTTFs since the end of 1999. By the end of 2003 the FBI plans to have established JTTFs in each of its 56 field offices. By integrating the investigative abilities of the FBI and local law enforcement agencies, these task forces represent an effective response to the threats posed to U.S. communities by domestic and international terrorists.

The FBI and our law enforcement partners have made a number of arrests of individuals alleged to have perpetrated acts of eco-terrorism. Several of these individuals have been successfully prosecuted. Following the investigation of the Phoenix, Arizona, arsons noted earlier, Mark Warren Sands was indicted and arrested on 6/14/2001. On 11/07/2001, Sands pleaded guilty to ten counts of extortion and using fire in the commission of a federal felony.

In February 2001, teenagers Jared McIntyre, Matthew Rammelkamp, and George Mashkow all pleaded guilty, as adults, to title 18 U.S.C. 844(i), Arson, and 844(n), Arson Conspiracy. These charges pertain to a series of arsons and attempted arsons of new home construction sites in Long Island, New York. An adult, Connor Cash, was also arrested on February 15, 2001, and charged under the same federal statutes. Jared McIntyre stated that these acts were committed in sympathy of the ELF movement. The New York Joint Terrorism Task Force played a significant role in the arrest and prosecution of these individuals.

On 1/23/2001, Frank Ambrose was arrested by officers of the Department of Natural Resources with assistance from the Indianapolis JTTF, on a local warrant out of Monroe County Circuit Court, Bloomington, Indiana, charging Ambrose with timber spiking. Ambrose is suspected of involvement in the spiking of approximately 150 trees in Indiana state forests. The ELF claimed responsibility for these incidents.

On September 16, 1998, a federal grand jury in the Western District of Wisconsin indicted Peter Young and Justin Samuel for Hobbs Act violations as well as for animal enterprise terrorism. Samuel was apprehended in Belgium and was subsequently extradited to the United States. On August 30, 2000, Samuel pleaded guilty to two counts of animal enterprise terrorism and was sentenced on November 3, 2000, to two years in prison, two years probation, and ordered to pay $364,106 in restitution. Samuel's prosecution arose out of his involvement in mink releases in Wisconsin in 1997. This incident was claimed by the ALF. The investigation and arrest of Justin Samuel were the result of a joint effort by federal, state, and local agencies.

On April 20, 1997, Douglas Joshua Ellerman turned himself in and admitted on videotape to purchasing, constructing, and transporting five pipe bombs to the scene of the March 11, 1997, arson at the Fur Breeders Agricultural co-op in Sandy, Utah. Ellerman also admitted setting fire to the facility. Ellerman was indicted on June 19, 1997, on 16 counts and eventually pleaded guilty to three. He was sentenced to seven years in prison and restitution of approximately $750,000. Though this incident was not officially claimed by ALF, Ellerman indicated during an interview subsequent to his arrest that he was a member of ALF. This incident was investigated jointly by the FBI and the Bureau of Alcohol, Tobacco and Firearms (ATF).

Rodney Adam Coronado was convicted for his role in the February 2, 1992, arson at an animal research laboratory on the campus of Michigan

State University. Damage estimates, according to public sources, approached $200,000 and included the destruction of research records. On July 3, 1995, Coronado pled guilty for his role in the arson and was sentenced to 57 months in federal prison, three years probation, and restitution of more than $2 million. This incident was claimed by ALF. The FBI, ATF, and the Michigan State University police played a significant role in the investigation, arrest, and prosecution.

Marc Leslie Davis, Margaret Katherine Millet, Marc Andre Baker, and Ilse Washington Asplund were all members of the self-proclaimed "Evan Mecham Eco-Terrorist International Conspiracy" (EMETIC). EMETIC was formed to engage in eco-terrorism against nuclear power plants and ski resorts in the southwestern United States. In November 1987, the group claimed responsibility for damage to a chairlift at the Fairfield Snow Bowl Ski Resort near Flagstaff, Arizona. Davis, Millet, and Baker were arrested in May 1989 on charges relating to the Fairfield Snow Bowl incident and planned incidents at the Central Arizona Project and Palo Verde nuclear generating stations in Arizona; the Diablo Canyon Nuclear Facility in California; and the Rocky Flats Nuclear Facility in Colorado. All pleaded guilty and were sentenced in September 1991. Davis was sentenced to six years in federal prison and restitution to the Fairfield Snow Bowl Ski Resort in the amount of $19,821. Millet was sentenced to three years in federal prison and restitution to Fairfield in the amount of $19,821. Baker was sentenced to one year in federal prison, five months probation, a $5,000 fine, and 100 hours of community service. Asplund was also charged and was sentenced to one year in federal prison, five years probation, a $2,000 fine, and 100 hours of community service.

Currently, more than 26 FBI field offices have pending investigations associated with ALF/ELF activities. Despite all of our efforts (increased resources allocated, JTTFs, successful arrests and prosecutions), law enforcement has a long way to go to adequately address the problem of eco-terrorism. Groups such as the ALF and the ELF present unique challenges. There is little if any hierarchal structure to such entities. Eco-terrorists are unlike traditional criminal enterprises which are often structured and organized.

The difficulty investigating such groups is demonstrated by the fact that law enforcement has thus far been unable to effect the arrests of anyone for some recent criminal activity directed at federal land managers or their offices. However, there are several ongoing investigations regarding such acts. Current investigations include the 10/14/2001 arson at the Bureau of Land Management Wild Horse and Burro Corral in Litchfield, California, the 7/20/2000 destruction of trees and damage to vehicles at the U.S. Forestry Science Laboratory in Rhinelander, Wisconsin, and the 11/29/1997 arson at the Bureau of Land Management Corral in Burns, Oregon.

Appendix A

Before closing, I would like to acknowledge the cooperation and assistance rendered by the U.S. Forest Service in investigating incidents of eco-terrorism. Specifically, I would like to recognize the assistance that the Forest Service is providing with regard to the ongoing investigation of the 7/20/2000 incident of vandalism and destruction that occurred at the U.S. Forestry Science Laboratory in Rhinelander, Wisconsin.

The FBI and all of our federal, state, and local law enforcement partners will continue to strive to address the difficult and unique challenges posed by eco-terrorists. Despite the recent focus on international terrorism, we remain fully cognizant of the full range of threats that confront the United States.

Chairman McInnis and Members of the Subcommittee, this concludes my prepared remarks. I would like to express appreciation for your concentration on the issue of eco-terrorism and I look forward to responding to any questions.

APPENDIX B

WRITTEN TESTIMONY OF CRAIG ROSEBRAUGH, FEBRUARY 7, 2002

(*Note:* Craig Rosebraugh was a former spokesperson for the Earth Liberation Front. This statement, supplied to the U.S. House Subcommittee on Forests and Forests Health, was submitted for the February 12, 2002, hearing on ecoterrorism.)

"When a long train of abuses and usurpations, pursuing invariably the same object, evinces a design to reduce [the people] under absolute despotism, it is their right, it is their duty, to throw off such government, and to provide new guards for their future security. The oppressed should rebel, and they will continue to rebel and raise disturbance until their civil rights are fully restored to them and all partial distinctions, exclusions and incapacitations are removed." ———Thomas Jefferson, 1776

On April 15, 1972, I came into this world as a child of two wonderful parents living in Portland, Oregon. Growing up in the Pacific Northwestern region of the United States, I had the privilege of easy access to the natural world. Much of my childhood was spent in the fields and forested areas behind our home, playing and experiencing life in my time of innocence. I had no knowledge of societal problems, especially those pertaining to the natural environment.

Throughout my childhood and adolescent years, the education I received from my parents, schools, popular media and culture instilled in me a pride for my country, for my government, and everything the United States represented. I was taught about the great American history, our Constitution, Bill of Rights, and our legacy of being at the forefront of democracy and freedom. I considered myself to be just an average boy taking an active part in the popular American pastimes of competitive sports, consumer culture, and existing within a classic representation of the standard, middle-class suburban lifestyle.

Upon graduating from high school, I became exposed to new forms of education and ideas. Resulting from my exposure to people from differing socio-economic backgrounds and beginning college, I found my horizons beginning to widen. For the first time in my life, I was presented with the notion of political and social conflict coupled with the various issues contained within both categories. It was alarming yet, at the same time, invigorating as I began to feel passion burn within me.

George Bush, Sr. had just thrust the United States into what became known as the Gulf War. Now, as I was raised with a certain absolutist support of my country and government, my first inclination was to wave the stars and stripes and support unconditionally this noble pursuit of "promoting democracy and freedom" in the "less fortunate" and "uncivilized" lands. Yet, as I began to look further into the matter, I found myself asking questions such as why are we there? Why are we killing civilians? What is the true motive behind the conflict? After extensive research, I came to the logical and truthful conclusion that natural resources and regional power were the primary motives.

As news from independent sources slowly filtered out, I became increasingly horrified at the slaughter of Iraqi civilians by the U.S. military. With NO WAR FOR OIL as my personal guiding statement, I joined the local anti-war protests and movement existing in Portland, Oregon. Little did I realize that this first political activity would lead me to a life of devotion to true justice and real freedom.

While my anti-war involvement progressed, I also began to understand the disastrous relationship our modern society has with the many animal nations. Out of an interest inspired both by independent reading and through early college courses, I became involved with a local animal advocacy organization. At first, I attended meetings to hear the numerous arguments for the rights of animals and further my own education. The more I learned, the more compelled I felt to involve myself fully in working for animal protection. My activities went from merely attending meetings, rallies, and protests to organizing them. Of all the issues I had learned about during the six years I spent with that organization, I focused the majority of my time, research, and interest on fighting against the use of animals in biomedical and scientific experimentation.

While a great percentage of the public in the United States had been convinced that animal research progressed and continues to improve human health, I soon realized that this myth was not only untruthful and single sided, but the work of a slick public relations campaign by the pharmaceutical industry in coordination with federal agencies such as the National Institutes of

Health. I also learned that just like the factory farm industry, the use of animals for human entertainment and for the fashion industry, animal experimentation was motivated first and foremost by profits. Furthermore, I learned how the government of the United States not only economically supports these various institutions of exploitation and slaughter, but how it continues to perpetuate and politically support the dangerous lie that animal research saves human lives. My support for various governmental policies was slowly fading.

And then memories of innocence were torn away. In the early 1990s, I learned that the lush natural acreage I used to play in as a child had been sold to a development firm. It intended to bulldoze the entire area and create a virtual community of homes for the upper middle class to wealthy. Within two years, the land as I knew it was no more. The visual reminder I used to appreciate, the one that would take me back to the years when the fields and trees were my playground, was stolen by a development corporation who saw more value in the land as luxurious houses than for its natural beauty and life.

I remember asking myself, what would happen to the various wildlife who made the area their home for so many years? Where would the deer, coyotes, skunks, wild cats, mice, raccoons, opossums, and others go? It was obvious that the developers had not even considered these questions. Rather, it appeared, the main pursuit of the corporation was working towards building incredibly large homes as close as possible to one another for maximum financial gain.

As the 1990s progressed, I became increasingly aware of the relationship between social and political problems in the United States. No single issue was truly independent but rather was affected by many others. In my work with the local animal advocacy organization, I realized that exploitation and destruction at the hands of human domination over animals also involved much more. Economics, politics, sociology, psychology, anthropology, science, religion, and other disciplines all played a significant role in understanding this unhealthy and unbalanced relationship between humans and other animals. But, by far the most important realization I made was that the problems facing animals, the problems facing the natural environment, and those affecting humans all came from a primary source. Understanding this crucial connection, I co-founded a non-profit organization in 1996 dedicated to educating the public on this fundamental realization.

During the mid-1990s, through continued formal and informal education, I also began to understand that the history I had learned growing up was only one story of many. I gained insight into the fact that everything I had learned about the origins of the United States of America had been purely from the viewpoint of the colonists and European settlers. Thus, the history I was taught was from the perspective of the privileged white man, which not only told a mere fraction of the story, but also provided an extreme amount of misinformation as well.

I was never taught that the origins of this country were based upon murder, exploitation, and ultimate genocide. My teachers neglected to mention the fact that the white European settlers nearly annihilated the various indigenous peoples who had existed on this land for ages. Instead, I was taught about Thanksgiving and Columbus Day. I bought into this version of American history so much that I vividly recall my excitement over creating a paper model of one of Columbus' ships years ago.

No one ever seemed to provide the insight to me that the settlers, immediately upon their arrival, immediately enslaved the natives, and forced them to work and assist the European powers in their quest for gold and spices. Likewise, I failed to ever have access to a true African-American history that began when blacks were captured and shipped as property to this land to work as slaves for white men.

While I was taught about the so-called "Great American Revolution," it was never mentioned that this war for independence against the European powers only served and benefited the privileged white male. Of course, all white men were privileged to some degree; however, many were enslaved initially just like the natives and blacks. Women, natives, blacks, and, to a limited degree, poor whites were considered property, bought, sold, and owned by the affluent white hierarchy.

In school, my teachers did explain to me the importance of the U.S. Constitution and the Bill of Rights and how our forefathers drew up these documents to serve the people. This, I learned, was the foundation of our supposed great democracy. Yet, in reality, these items were created by the white power structure and only served to benefit the privileged members of white society. Women, blacks, natives, and poor white men still were not enfranchised nor had any accessibility to self-determination and freedom. Land ownership—a notion completely foreign and absurd to most of the indigenous—became a deciding factor of power and privilege for white men. Those without land lacked the opportunity for the vote, for ultimate power and respect.

As more and more settlers pushed westward through the country, the government committed endless treaty breaches and violations, stealing land that whites had allotted to the indigenous. Perhaps one of the most disturbing facts was that these original agreements made between various indigenous nations and the United States government were supposed to have international standing. Each of the indigenous populations was recognized at the time each document was signed as being a sovereign nation and, yet, the U.S. government still exerted its power and domination to steal land for eventual development and drainage of resources. This genocide against the varied Native American nations by the United States continues today with innocent people such as Leonard Peltier being imprisoned for years simply due to the government's perception of him as a political threat. Free Leonard Peltier!

On July 4 annually, U.S. citizens celebrate the founding of our country, most either blatantly forgetting or ignorant of the true issues surrounding that date. The fact that the United States as a nation systematically committed mass genocide against the indigenous of these lands, to catastrophic extremities, is certainly no cause for celebration. Rather, it should be a time for mourning, for remembrance, and, most of all for education of our children so we are not doomed to repeat the mistakes of the past.

The plight of blacks and women throughout U.S. history, although perhaps not as overtly catastrophic, still constituted outright mass murder, enslavement, exploitation, and objectification. Early on, white European settlers found that natives were much more difficult to enslave and manage due to their ability to maintain at least partial elements of their cultures. When blacks began to first arrive on slave ships, chained in the darkness below the decks, white settlers theorized they would make better slaves because they would be further removed from their cultures. Thus, the enslavement of blacks began in this land and would, in its overt form, last for a couple hundred years. During this time and well beyond, blacks were considered property to be bought, sold, traded, used, and disposed of at will.

Even after the abolitionist movement, which began in the 1820s, blacks continued to be considered second-rate citizens, restricted from voting and experiencing the free life which whites were accustomed. When the modern U.S. civil rights movement began in the 1940s, it took some twenty years of constant hardship and struggle to achieve some reform in the fascist policies of the United States. Even though blacks "won" the right to vote and exist in desegregated zones, there still was an absence of overall freedom, never any actual resemblance of equality. Today, the saga continues. While African Americans have made incredible progress in obtaining certain rights and privileges, there continues to be a more hidden, underlying discrimination that is every bit as potent. We can see a clear example by taking an honest look at the prison industrial complex and understanding who continues to be enslaved in mass to make that industry financially viable. Free Mumia Abu Jamal! Free the Move 9! Free all the political prisoners in the United States!

A similar and equally unfortunate history has and continues to haunt women in U.S. society. Also once considered property, women were not even able to vote in this country until the 1920s. Even after, they continued to be faced with a patriarchal society consisting of white men in power. While women have made many wonderful advances for themselves, they still exist today in the United States under that same sexist and patriarchal society. A quick glance at the profiles of the federal government as well as top CEOs from U.S. corporations fully illustrates this reality.

Appendix B

When I co-founded the non-profit organization in Portland, Oregon, in 1996, I was becoming more aware that the similarities in the human, environmental, and animal advocacy movements stemmed from this rich U.S. history, not of glory, freedom and democracy, but of oppression in its sickest forms. I began to also realize that just as the U.S. white male power structure put itself on a pedestal above everyone else, it also maintained that attitude toward the natural environment and the various animal nations existing within it. As a society, we have continuously acted towards these natural life forms as though we owned them, therefore giving us the right to do whatever we wanted and could do to them.

Particularly, with the advent of the industrial revolution in the United States, the destruction of the natural world took a sharp turn for the worse. The attitude, more so than ever, turned to one of profits at any cost and a major shift from sustainable living to stockpiling for economic benefit. This focus on stockpiling and industrial productivity caused hardship on communities, forcing local crafters and laborers to be driven out of business by overly competitive industries. Additionally, with this new focus on sacrificing sustainable living for financial gain, natural resources were in greater demand than ever. Semi-automatic to automatic machinery, production lines, the automobile, the roadway system, suburbs, and the breakup of small, fairly self-sufficient communities all came about, at least in part, due to the industrial revolution. This unhealthy and deadly transgression of course was supported and promoted by the U.S. government, always eager to see growth in the domestic economy.

All of this set the stage for the threatening shortage of natural resources and the massive environmental pollution and destruction present today in the United States. In cities such as Los Angeles, Detroit, and Houston, the air and soil pollution levels are so extreme people have suffered and continue to face deadly health problems. Waterways throughout the country, including the Columbia Slough in my backyard, are so polluted from industries it is recommended that humans don't even expose themselves to the moisture let alone drink unfiltered, unbottled water. The necessary and crucial forests of the Pacific Northwestern region of the country have been systematically destroyed by corporations such as Boise Cascade, Willamette Industries, and others within the timber industry whose sole motive is profits regardless of the expense to the health of an ecosystem. In Northern California, the sacred old growths, dreamlike in appearance, taking your breath away at first glance, have been continuously threatened and cut by greedy corporations such as Maxxam/Pacific Lumber Company. The same has occurred and still is a reality in states including Washington, Oregon, Idaho, and Colorado.

The first National Forests were established in the United States more than a century ago. One hundred fifty-five of them exist today spread across

191 million acres. Over the years, the forest products industry has decimated publicly owned National Forests in this country, leaving a horrendous trail of clear cuts and logging roads. Commercial logging has been responsible for annihilating nearly all of the nation's old growth forests, draining nutrients from the soil, washing topsoil into streams, destroying wildlife habitat, and creating an increase in the incidence and severity of forest fires. Only an estimated 4 percent of old growth forests in the United States are remaining.

The National Forests in the United States contain far more than just trees. In fact, more than 3,000 species of fish and wildlife, in addition to 10,000 plant species, have their habitat within the National Forests. This includes at least 230 endangered plant and animal species. All of these life forms co-exist symbiotically to naturally create the rich and healthy ecosystems needed for life to exist on this planet.

The benefits of a healthy forest cannot be overrated. Healthy forests purify drinking water, provide fresh clean air to breathe, stabilize hillsides, and prevent floods. Hillsides clear cut or destroyed by logging roads lose their ability to absorb heavy rainfall. If no trees exist to soak up moisture with roots to hold the soil, water flows freely down slopes, creating muddy streams, polluting drinking water, strengthening floods, and causing dangerous mudslides. Instead of valuing trees and forests for being necessary providers of life, the U.S. Forest Service and commercial logging interests have decimated these precious ecosystems.

The timber corporations argue that today in the United States more forests exist than perhaps at any time in the last century or more. It doesn't take a forestry specialist to realize that monoculture tree farms—in which one species of tree, often times non-native to the area, is grown in mass in a small area for maximum production—do not equate to a healthy forest. Healthy forests are made up of diverse ecosystems consisting of many native plant and animal species. These healthy ecosystems are what grant humans and all other life forms on the planet with the ability to live. Without clean air, clean water, and healthy soil, life on this planet will cease to exist. There is an overwhelming battery of evidence that conclusively shows that we are already well on our path toward massive planetary destruction.

The popular environmental movement in the United States, which arguably began in the 1960s, has failed to produce the necessary protection needed to ensure that life on this planet will continue to survive. This is largely due to the fact that the movement has primarily consisted of tactics sanctioned by the very power structure that is benefiting economically from the destruction of the natural world. While a few minor successes in this country should be noted, the overwhelming constant trend has been the increasingly speedy liquidation of natural resources and annihilation of the environment.

The state sanctioned tactics, that is, those approved by the U.S. government and the status quo and predominantly legal in nature, rarely, if ever, actually challenge or positively change the very entities that are responsible for oppression, exploitation, and, in this case, environmental destruction. Throughout the history of the United States, a striking amount of evidence indicates that it wasn't until efforts strayed beyond the state sanctioned that social change ever progressed. In the abolitionist movement, the Underground Railroad, public educational campaigns, in addition to slave revolts, forced the federal government to act. With the Suffragettes in the United States, individuals such as Alice Paul acting with various forms of civil disobedience added to the more mainstream efforts to successfully demand the vote for women. Any labor historian will assert that in addition to the organizing of the workplace, strikes, riots, and protests dramatically assisted in producing more tolerable work standards. The progress of the civil rights movement was primarily founded upon the massive illegal civil disobedience campaigns against segregation and disenfranchisement. Likewise, the true pressure from the Vietnam anti-war movement in this country only came after illegal activities such as civil disobedience and beyond were implemented. Perhaps the most obvious, yet often overlooked, historical example of this notion supporting the importance of illegal activity as a tool for positive, lasting change, came just prior to our war for independence. Our educational systems in the United States glorify the Boston Tea Party while simultaneously failing to recognize and admit that the dumping of tea was perhaps one of the most famous early examples of politically motivated property destruction.

In the mid-1990s, individuals angry and disillusioned with the failing efforts to protect the natural environment through state sanctioned means, began taking illegal action. At first, nonviolent civil disobedience was implemented, followed by sporadic cases of nonviolent property destruction. In November 1997, an anonymous communiqué was issued by a group called the Earth Liberation Front claiming responsibility for their first-ever action in North America.

Immediately, the label of ecoterrorism appeared in news stories describing the actions of the Earth Liberation Front. Where exactly this label originated is open for debate, but all indications point to the federal government of the United States in coordination with industry and sympathetic mass media. Whatever the truth may be regarding the source of this term, one thing is for certain—the decision to attach this label to illegal actions taken for environmental protection was very conscious and deliberate. Why? The need for the U.S. federal government to control and mold public opinion through the power of propaganda to ensure an absence of threat is crucial. If information about illegal actions taken to protect the natural environment were presented openly to the public without biased interpretation, the opportunity would exist for citizens to make up their own minds about the legitimacy of the tactic, target, and movement. By attaching a label such as "terrorism" to the activities of groups such as the Earth Liberation Front, the public is left with little choice but to give into their preconceived notions negatively associated with that term. For many in this country, including myself, information about terrorism came from schools and popular culture. Most often times, the definition of terrorism was overtly racist associated frequently in movies and on television shows with Arabs and the others our government told us were threatening. Terrorism usually is connected with violence, with politically motivated physical harm to humans.

Yet, in the history of the Earth Liberation Front, both in North America and abroad in Europe, no one has ever been injured by the group's many actions. This is not a mere coincidence, but rather a deliberate decision that illustrates the true motivation behind the covert organization. Simply put and most fundamentally, the goal of the Earth Liberation Front is to save life. The group takes actions directly against the property of those who are engaged in massive planetary destruction in order for all of us to survive. This noble pursuit does not constitute terrorism, but rather seeks to abolish it.

A major hypocrisy exists when the U.S. government labels an organization such as the Earth Liberation Front a terrorist group while simultaneously failing to acknowledge its own terrorist history. In fact, the U.S. government by far has been the most extreme terrorist organization in planetary history. Some, but nowhere near all, of the examples of domestic terrorism were discussed earlier in this writing. Yet, further proof can be found by taking a glimpse at the foreign policy record of the United States even as recently as from the 1950s.

In Guatemala (1953–1990s) the CIA organized a coup that overthrew the democratically elected government led by Jacobo Arbenz. This began some 40 years of death squads, torture, disappearances, mass executions, totaling well over 100,000 victims. The U.S. government apparently didn't want Guatemala's social democracy spreading to other countries in Latin America.

In the Middle East (1956–1958) the United States twice tried to overthrow the Syrian government. Additionally, the U.S. government landed 14,000 troops to purportedly keep the peace in Lebanon and to stop any opposition to the U.S. supported Lebanese government. The U.S. government also conspired to overthrow or assassinate Nasser of Egypt.

During the same time, in Indonesia (1957–1958), the CIA tried to manipulate elections and plotted the assassination of Sukarno, then the Indonesian leader. The CIA also assisted in waging a full-scale war against the government of Indonesia. All of this action was taken because Sukarno refused to take a hard-line stand against communism.

Appendix B

From 1953 to 1964, the U.S. government targeted Cheddi Jagan, then the leader of British Guiana, out of a fear he might have built a successful example of an alternative model to the capitalist society. The U.S. government, aided by Britain, organized general strikes and spread misinformation, finally forcing Jagan out of power in 1964.

In Cambodia (1955–1973), Prince Sihanouk was severely targeted by the U.S. government. This targeting included assassination attempts and the unpublicized carpet bombings of 1969 to 1970. The U.S. government finally succeeded in overthrowing Sihanouk in a 1970 coup.

The examples continue. From 1960 through 1965, the United States intervened in Congo/Zaire. After Patrice Lumumba became Congo's first Prime Minister following independence gained from Belgium, he was assassinated in 1961 at the request of Dwight Eisenhower. During the same time in Brazil (1961–1964), President Joao Goulart was overthrown in a military coup, which involved the United States. Again, the alleged reasoning for U.S. participation amounted to a fear of communism or, more importantly, anything that threatened this country's way of life. In the Dominican Republic (1963–1966), the United States sent in 23,000 troops to help stop a coup which aimed at restoring power to Juan Bosch, an individual the U.S. government feared had socialist leanings.

Of course, no one should forget about Cuba. When Fidel Castro came to power in 1959, the United States immediately sought to put another government in place, prompting some 40 years of terrorist attacks, bombings, a full-scale military invasion, sanctions, embargoes, isolations, and assassinations.

In Chile, the U.S. government sabotaged Salvador Allende's electoral campaign in 1964. In 1970, the U.S. government failed to do so and tried for years later to destabilize the Allende government particularly by building up military hostility. In September 1973, the U.S. supported military overthrew the government with Allende dying in the process. Some 3,000 people were executed and thousands more were tortured or disappeared. In Greece during the same period (1964–1974), the United States backed a military coup that led to martial law, censorship, arrests, beatings, torture, and killings. In the first month, more than 8,000 people died. All of this was executed with equipment supplied by the United States.

Back in Indonesia in 1965, fears of communism led the United States to back multiple coup attempts, which resulted in a horrendous massacre against communists. During this time the U.S. embassy compiled lists of communist operatives, as many as 5,000 names, and turned them over to the Army. The Army would then hunt down and kill those on the list.

The U.S. government also has had its dirty hands connected to East Timor (1975 to present). In December 1975, Indonesia invaded East Timor

---

using U.S. weapons. By 1989, Indonesia had slaughtered 200,000 people out of a population between 600,000 and 700,000.

In Nicaragua (1978–1989), when the Sandinistas overthrew the Somoza dictatorship in 1978, the U.S. government immediately became involved. President Carter attempted diplomatic and economic forms of sabotage while President Reagan put the Contras to work. For eight years, backed by the United States, the Contras waged war on the people of Nicaragua.

Continuing on with Grenada (1979–1984), the United States intervened to stop a 1979 coup led by Maurice Bishop and his followers. The United States invaded Grenada in October 1983, killing 400 citizens of Grenada and 84 Cubans. Of course the Libya example (1981–1989) must be mentioned. In the 1980s, the United States shot down two Libyan planes in what Libya regarded as its air space. The United States also dropped bombs on the country killing more than [missing number] people including Qaddafi's daughter. Yet that wasn't enough as the U.S. government engaged in other attempts to eradicate Qaddafi. This included a fierce misinformation campaign, economic sanctions, and blaming Libya for being responsible for the Pan Am flight 103 bombing without any sound evidence. The U.S. government, also in 1989, bombed Panama, leaving some 15,000 people homeless in Panama City. Thousands of people died and even more were wounded.

Prior to the October 7, 2001, invasion of Afghanistan by the United States, the U.S. government had intervened there from 1979 to 1992. During the late 1970s and most of the 1980s, the U.S. government spent billions of dollars waging a war on a progressive Afghani government, merely because that government was backed by the Soviet Union. More than one million people died, three million were disabled, and five million became refugees.

In El Salvador (1980–1992), the United States supported the government, which engaged in electoral fraud and the murder of hundreds of protesters and strikers. These dissidents, who had been trying to work within the system, took to using guns and declared a civil war in 1980. The U.S. government played an active role in trying to stop the uprising. When it was over in 1992, 75,000 civilians had been killed and the United States had spent six billion dollars.

In Haiti, from 1987 through 1994, the United States supported the Duvalier family dictatorship. During this time, the CIA worked intimately with death squads, torturers, and drug traffickers. Yugoslavia must also be mentioned, as no one should ever forget the United States' responsibility for bombing that country into annihilation.

In the early 1990s, the U.S. government continuously bombed Iraq for more than 40 days and nights. One hundred seventy-seven million pounds of bombs fell during this time on the people of Iraq. The remaining uranium deposits from weapons resulted in massive birth defects and incidences of cancer. Between 1990 and 1995, the United States was directly responsible for killing more than 500,000 Iraqi children under the age of five due to economic sanctions. Additionally, due to these sanctions, coupled with the continuous U.S. bombing that has occurred on Iraq since the Gulf War, more than 1.5 million innocent Iraqi people have been killed.

These few examples since 1950 of U.S.-sponsored and organized terrorism are horrendous, and, unfortunately, these massive murderous tactics continue today. On October 7, 2001, the U.S. government began a full-scale military invasion of Afghanistan without even providing a shred of factual evidence linking Osama Bin Laden or Al Qaida to the attacks in this country on September 11. To date, well over 4,000 innocent Afghani civilians have been killed by the U.S. government in this massive genocidal campaign. All along, U.S. government officials have claimed to possess concrete evidence proving the guilt of both Bin Laden and Al Qaida, but repeatedly said they cannot release this "proof" as doing so may endanger the lives of U.S. military personnel. This simply makes no sense, as there could not be any justifiable threat to U.S. personnel if they weren't already in inexcusable positions, violating the sovereignty of internationally recognized nations.

The Taliban, which the United States help put into power in 1994, have stated repeatedly to the U.S. government and the world that it would hand over Bin Laden to an international court if the United States provided proof of his guilt. The United States refused and instead claimed the Taliban was not cooperating and was therefore harboring terrorists.

Can you imagine what would have happened if, prior to September 11, 2001, a structure in Kabul were bombed and the Taliban immediately suspected CIA director George Tenet as the prime suspect? Would the United States hand over Tenet to the Taliban if requested if there was not substantial evidence provided of his guilt? Even if the Taliban supplied any shred of evidence, the United States still would refuse to hand over Tenet or any privileged citizen to an international court because the United States does not abide by them or agree to them. Regardless, the U.S. government believes that it has the right to provide no evidence of Bin Laden's or Al Qaida's guilt to the Taliban or the world before launching a massive genocidal campaign against Afghanistan civilians.

The true motives and the identities of those involved both in September 11, 2001, and October 7, 2001, are known only to a select few in power. However, evidence does exist in media sources as mainstream as the BBC (reported on September 18, 2001) that suggests the U.S. government was planning a military invasion of Afghanistan to oust the Taliban as early as March 2001. Furthermore, the intended deadline for the invasion was set for not later than October of the same year. The October 7, 2001, invasion by the United States into Afghanistan appears to have been right on schedule.

Ecoterrorism

This war against terrorism, otherwise known as Operation Enduring Freedom, is the latest example of U.S. based terrorism and imperialism. It is clear that the events of September 11, 2001, were used as a chance for the U.S. government to invade Afghanistan, to attempt to increase U.S. regional and global power in addition to open up the much-sought-after oil reserves in the Middle East and Central Asia. The bonus, of course, was that this mission has given the United States the opportunity to target and attempt to annihilate any anti-U.S. sentiment within that region. As the war against terrorism expands, so does the possibility of more U.S. military bases and more security for the global economic powers.

If the U.S. government is truly concerned with eradicating terrorism in the world, then that effort must begin with abolishing U.S. imperialism. Members of this governing body, both in the House and Senate as well as those who hold positions in the executive branch, constitute the largest group of terrorists and terrorist representatives currently threatening life on this planet. The only true service this horrific organization supplies is to the upper classes and corporate elite.

As an innocent child, I used to have faith in my government and pride in my country. Today I have no pride, no faith, only embarrassment, anger, and frustration. There are definite and substantiated reasons why the U.S. government is not only disliked but hated by populations in many nations around the globe. The outrage and anger is justified due to the history of U.S. domestic and foreign policies.

Here in the United States, the growth of the empire, of capitalism, and of industry, has meant greater discrepancies between the wealthy and poor, a continued rise in the number of those considered to be a threat to the system, as well as irreversible harm done to the environment and life on the planet. Corporations in the United States literally get away with murder, facing little or no repercussions due to their legal structures. The U.S. government, which sleeps in the same bed as U.S. corporations, serves to ensure that the "business as usual" policies of imperialism can continue with as little friction as possible. Anyone questioning the mere logic of this genocidal culture and governing policy is considered a dissident and, more often than not, shipped off to one of the fastest growing industries of all, the prison industrial complex.

Internationally, U.S. policies have amounted to the same, often times worse, forms of violence. As I demonstrated herein with examples since 1950, the foreign policy track record has included genocide, assassinations, exploitation, military action, and destruction. Disguised as promoting or protecting freedom and democracy, U.S. foreign policies aim to directly control and conquer, while gaining power, finances, and resources.

U.S. imperialism is a disease, one that continues to grow and become more powerful and dangerous. It needs to be stopped. One of the chief weapons

276

used by those protecting the imperialist policies of the United States is a slick, believable propaganda campaign designed to ensure U.S. citizens do not question or threaten the "American way of life." Perhaps the strongest factor in this campaign is the phenomenon of capitalism. By creating a consumer demand for products, corporations, greatly aided by the U.S. government, can effectively influence people's dreams, desires, wants, and life plans. The very American Dream promoted throughout the world is that anyone can come to the United States, work hard, and become happy and financially secure. Through the use of the propaganda campaign designed, promoted, and transmitted by the U.S. ruling class, people are nearly coerced into adopting unhealthy desires for, often times, unreachable, unneeded, and dangerous consumer goods. Through impressive societal mind control, the belief that obtaining consumer products will equal security and happiness has spread across the United States, and much of the planet at this point, like some extreme plague. The fact that the policies of the United States murder people on a daily basis is unseen, forgotten, or ignored, as every effort is made by people to fit into the artificial model life manufactured by the ruling elite.

A universal effort needs to be made to understand the importance and execution of abolishing U.S. imperialism. This by no way refers to simply engaging in reformist efforts, rather, a complete societal and political revolution will need to occur before real justice and freedom become a reality. The answer does not lie in trying to fix one specific problem or work on one individual issue, but rather the entire pie needs to be targeted, every last piece looked upon as a mere representation of the whole.

If the people of the United States, who the government is supposed to represent, are actually serious about creating a nation of peace, freedom, and justice, then there must be a serious effort made, by any means necessary, to abolish imperialism and U.S. governmental terrorism. The daily murder and destruction caused by this political organization is very real, and so the campaign by the people to stop it must be equally as potent.

I have been told by many people in the United States to love America or leave it. I love this land and the truly compassionate people within it. I therefore feel I not only have a right, but also an obligation, to stay within this land and work for positive societal and political change for all.

I was asked originally if I would voluntarily testify before the House Subcommittee on Forests and Forest Health at a hearing focused on "ecoterrorism." I declined in a written statement. U.S. Marshals then subpoenaed me on October 31, 2001, to testify at this hearing on February 12, 2002, against my will. Is this hearing a forum to discuss the threats facing the health of the natural environment, specifically the forests? No, clearly there is not even the remotest interest in this subject from the U.S. government or industry. The goal of this hearing is to discuss methodologies to improve the failed attempts law enforcement have made since the mid-1990s in catching and prosecuting individuals and organizations who take nonviolent, illegal direct action to stop the destruction of the natural environment. I have no interest in this cause or this hearing. In fact, I consider it a farce.

Since 1997, the U.S. government has issued me seven grand jury subpoenas, raided my home and work twice, stealing hundreds of items of property, and, on many occasions, sent federal agents to follow and question me. After this effort, which has lasted nearly five years, federal agents have yet to obtain any information from me to aid their investigations. As I have never been charged with one crime related to these so-called ecoterrorist organizations or their activities, the constant harassment by the federal government constitutes a serious infringement on my Constitutional right to freedom of speech. This congressional subcommittee hearing appears to be no different, harassing and targeting me for simply voicing my ideological support for those involved in environmental protection.

I fully praise those individuals who take direct action, by any means necessary, to stop the destruction of the natural world and threats to all life. They are the heroes, risking their freedom and lives so that we as a species as well as all life forms can continue to exist on the planet. In a country so fixated on monetary wealth and power, these brave environmental advocates are engaging in some of the most selfless activities possible.

It is my sincere desire that organizations such as the Earth Liberation Front continue to grow and prosper in the United States. In fact, more organizations, using similar tactics and strategies, need to be established to directly focus on U.S. imperialism and the U.S. government itself. For, as long as the quest for monetary gain continues to be the predominant value within U.S. society, human, animal, and environmental exploitation, destruction, and murder will continue to be a reality. This drive for profits at any cost needs to be fiercely targeted, and those responsible for the massive injustices punished. If there is any real concern for justice, freedom, and, at least, a resemblance of a true democracy, this revolutionary ideal must become a reality. ALL POWER TO THE PEOPLE. LONG LIVE THE EARTH LIBERATION FRONT. LONG LIVE THE ANIMAL LIBERATION FRONT. LONG LIVE ALL THE SPARKS ATTEMPTING TO IGNITE THE REVOLUTION. SOONER OR LATER THE SPARKS WILL TURN INTO A FLAME!

APPENDIX C

TESTIMONY OF RON ARNOLD, JUNE 9, 1998

(*Note:* Ron Arnold is the author of the book *Ecoterror: The Violent Agenda to Save Nature.* This statement, supplied to the U.S. House Committee on the Judiciary, was made at a hearing on ecoterrorism held by the Subcommittee on Crime.)

Mr. Chairman and Members of the Committee, my name is Ron Arnold. I am testifying as the executive vice president of the Center for the Defense of Free Enterprise, a nonprofit citizen organization based in Bellevue, Washington. The Center has approximately 10,000 members nationwide, most of them in rural natural resource industries.

Mr. Chairman, the Center does not accept government grants and is in full compliance with House Rule XI, clause 2(g).

Mr. Chairman, I would like to thank you on behalf of our members for holding this hearing today. It is long overdue. For the past five years our members have routinely contacted our headquarters to report crimes committed against them of a type we have come to call ecoterrorism, that is, a crime committed to save nature. These crimes generally take the form of equipment vandalism, but may include package bombs, blockades using physical force to obstruct workers from going where they have a right to go, and invasions of private or government offices to commit the crime of civil disobedience. So you can see, Mr. Chairman, the range of ecoterror crimes ranges from the most violent felonies of attempted murder to misdemeanor offenses such as criminal trespass. But they are all crimes. I am not here to discuss noncriminal actions that do not result in arrests and convictions.

My organization's membership is nationwide. There is no region of the United States where I have not received complaints from members about being victimized by ecoterrorists. It is a broad and pervasive crime that is seriously under-reported because the victims are terrorized and fear reprisals, copycat crimes, or in the case of corporations, loss of customer confidence and resulting drops in share prices.

I am the author of a book on the subject of this hearing, titled, *EcoTerror.* In this book I have reported the tactics of organized vandalism called by environmentalists "monkeywrenching," which means sabotage against goods producers and their equipment in order to save nature. Ecoterrorism has been studied by social scientists with illuminating results. In particular, the tactics of the group known as Earth First! have been described in the *Academy of Management Journal* in a study titled Acquired Organizational Legitimacy Through Illegitimate Actions. I request that pages 699, 715, 716, and 717 of this study be made a part of the record. I interviewed the lead author of this study to verify its contents. Kimberly Elsbach told me that the data were gathered directly from Earth Firsters who allowed her to witness criminal acts on condition that she destroy her notes as soon as her scholarship no longer needed them. One of the most pertinent tactics she discovered was called "decoupling," which is a set of techniques denying the crime while deploring the conditions that caused the perpetrators to become so frustrated they committed the crime. Thus decoupling throws blame for the crime on the victim while it denies guilt. However, law enforcement officers have concluded that in fact Earth Firsters were the perpetrators, a conclusion drawn as a result of several arrests and convictions in which the defendant admitted connection to Earth First.

As Earth First in recent years has tried to mainstream itself, ecoterror crimes have become more destructive to their wishes for a good public image. Therefore, Judi Bari, an Earth First leader, wrote an article in the *Earth First Journal* recommending that a decoupling group call itself Earth Liberation Front in order to create deniability for Earth Firsters crimes. I document this in my book *EcoTerror* on page 270, which I respectfully request be made part of the record. In fact, the Earth Liberation Front has subsequently become a well-known entity to law enforcement.

Furthermore, Mr. Chairman, the Earth Liberation Front and the Animal Liberation Front signed a joint communiqué stating their solidarity and blending. I have been able to determine that certain criminal Earth Firsters, Earth Liberation Front members and the Animal Liberation Front members are the same people. Examples are David Barbarash and Darren Thurston, convicted felons now under indictment in Canada for attempted murder by pipe bombs, were at one time Earth Firsters. I am stating that there is no difference between ecoterrorism and animal rights terrorism. The perpetrators are in large part the same, and the solidarity of action is openly declared.

These crimes to save nature are difficult to solve for law enforcement. The solution is to extend federal protection to loggers, miners, fishermen, farmers and ranchers, and others who are the most frequent targets of ecoterrorist attack. A simple way to accomplish that would be to add those classes of people to the list of persons protected by the Animal Enterprise Protection Act of 1993. That law federalized crimes of property damage over $10,000 or that resulted in dismemberment or death to a human being as a result of attacks on animal enterprises.

A simple amendment would create the Resource Enterprise Protection Amendment of 1998 by adding to the list of protected persons loggers, miners, fishermen, farmers, trappers, ranchers, food outlets and processors and all resource enterprises subject to ecoterror crimes. This law also needs a citizen attorneys general clause to allow harmed parties to seek relief in federal court, and it needs a periodic report to Congress. The existing Animal Enterprise Protection Act also needs to be reviewed because its enforcement has proven to be lax and virtually ineffectual. Congressional oversight of its enforcement is badly needed.

I feel that this modest proposal would meet with congressional approval and would go far to protecting the interests of all natural resource producers in America.

Thank you again, Mr. Chairman, for holding this hearing.

APPENDIX D

TESTIMONY OF BARRY R. CLAUSEN, JUNE 9, 1998

(*Note:* Barry R. Clausen is the author of the book *Walking on the Edge: How I Infiltrated Earth First!* This statement, supplied to the U.S. House Committee on the Judiciary, was made at a hearing on ecoterrorism held by the Subcommittee on Crime.)

Mr. Chairman, members of the committee, I thank you for this opportunity to speak to you today.

My name is Barry Clausen, I represent North American Research of Port Ludlow, Washington. For over nine years myself and others have monitored the actions of many extremist groups throughout the United States and several countries.

In December of 1989, as a licensed private investigator in the state of Montana, I was hired by timber workers, mining and ranching interests to investigate acts of sabotage against their industries.

This particular investigation led to Earth First!. Earth First! is an organization which the FBI has labeled "A militant environmental group." In 1990, with the knowledge of two federal agencies, the FBI and the United States Forest Service, I infiltrated the group and spent the entire year as one of them. During that time I discovered how militant and violent this group was. It still is. Mr. Chairman, this group advocates anarchy, revolution and terrorism to the youth of our country. Not only must this be addressed, this must stop.

Since 1990 North American Research has worked with many organizations nation wide to monitor the actions of Earth First!. We monitor their publications, the sabotage attributed to them, their ideologies, their supporters, their financial supporters as well as their connections and crossover to other groups. Some of those groups include the Earth Liberation Front, which has taken credit for several arson fires (some against government facilities), the Animal Liberation Front (ALF), who, according to an article in the February 18, 1998, edition of the *Dallas Morning News* the FBI labeled ALF as a terrorist organization.

Starting in March of 1997 radical extremists began using new tactics against public officials and law enforcement agencies in order to intimidate officers, thwart the law, and achieve their desired goals. Even those working in the offices of elected officials have been harassed and terrorized by Earth First! as you have heard. In 1997 Delyla Wilson, an Earth Firster from Bozeman, Montana, was convicted in both State and Federal court of assault on Senator Burns, Secretary of Agriculture Dan Glickman and Montana's Governor Mark Racioct after having thrown bison entrails on the men during a public meeting.

In an attempt to hamstring law enforcement by removing some of their tools to force compliance with the laws, the Sheriff and deputies of Humboldt County in California and the Chief of Police in Eureka, California, are being sued by protestors. Police officers in Eugene, Oregon, are also being sued as are deputy sheriffs in Okanogan County, Washington. The goals are to intimidate law enforcement officials into reluctance to make arrests for fear of reprisals through additional lawsuits, to limit law enforcement's ability to take those arrested into custody, and deplete county court resources.

There are federal law enforcement officers within federal agencies known to myself who would have welcomed the opportunity to testify before this committee today regarding the violence and magnitude of the crimes they have documented involving Earth First! and other radical environmental and Animal Rights activist groups. However, they are concerned about testifying for fear of reprisals by their supervisors and heads of their respective agencies should they testify and their identities become known.

Actions by persons connected to these extremist groups have led to millions of dollars lost due to sabotage committed against an increasing number of industries within our country. There have also been an as of yet unknown number of death threats to American citizens and families, including myself as well as actual incidents of attempted murder and murder itself. There have been numerous arson fires and bombings, including one the FBI labeled as "The second worst terrorist attack against a government facility in the history of our country." These acts have not only been advocated in the literature published by these groups, but have also in some cases been committed. North American Research, in conjunction with other organizations have documented over 1400 acts of sabotage against industry, homes and American citizens ranging from smashed windows to attempted murder and deaths, which have understandably impacted tens of thousands of lives.

Rodney Adam Coronado, a member of the Animal Liberation Front who has acknowledged publicly his connection to Earth First!, and other extremist groups, was arrested and convicted in 1995 for a 1992 arson fire at Michigan State University. He was quoted on the front page of the February 15, 1998, addition of the *Dallas Morning News*, "I see a trend toward actions that do more destruction."

As an American citizen and a six year military veteran who believes in our country, our freedoms and our rights, I would like to ask this committee to please listen, please consider what you hear today and please act to preserve those freedoms and rights.

APPENDIX E

EXCERPTS FROM THE "UNABOMBER MANIFESTO," SEPTEMBER 19, 1995

(*Note:* The "Unabomber Manifesto" was originally published as "Industrial Society and Its Future" in the *Washington Post* and attributed to "FC." These excerpts were reproduced from a non-copyrighted edition of the manifesto published by Jolly Roger Press. The manifesto in its entirety consists of 232 numbered paragraphs, plus 36 endnotes. The paragraph numbers and subheadings supplied here are consistent with those in the manifesto as it was originally published.)

INTRODUCTION

1. The Industrial Revolution and its consequences have been a disaster for the human race. They have greatly increased the life-expectancy of those of us who live in "advanced" countries, but they have destabilized society, have made life unfulfilling, have subjected human beings to indignities, have led to widespread psychological suffering (in the Third World to physical suffering as well) and have inflicted severe damage on the natural world. The continued development of technology will worsen the situation. It will certainly subject human beings to greater indignities and inflict greater damage on the natural world, it will probably lead to greater social disruption and psychological suffering, and it may lead to increased physical suffering even in "advanced" countries.

. . .

3. If the system breaks down the consequences will still be very painful. But the bigger the system grows the more disastrous the results of its

breakdown will be, so if it is to break down it had best break down sooner rather than later.

4. We therefore advocate a revolution against the industrial system. This revolution may or may not make use of violence: it may be sudden or it may be a relatively gradual process spanning a few decades. We can't predict any of that. But we do outline in a very general way the measures that those who hate the industrial system should take in order to prepare the way for a revolution against that form of society. This is not to be a POLITICAL revolution. Its object will be to overthrow not governments but the economic and technological basis of the present society . . . .

THE NATURE OF FREEDOM

93. We are going to argue that industrial-technological society cannot be reformed in such a way as to prevent it from progressively narrowing the sphere of human freedom. But because "freedom" is a word that can be interpreted in many ways, we must first make clear what kind of freedom we are concerned with.

94. By "freedom" we mean the opportunity to go through the power process, with real goals not the artificial goals of surrogate activities, and without interference, manipulation or supervision from anyone, especially from any large organization. Freedom means being in control (either as an individual or as a member of a SMALL group) of the life-and-death issues of one's existence; food, clothing, shelter and defense against whatever threats there may be in one's environment. Freedom means having power; not the power to control other people but the power to control the circumstances of one's own life. One does not have freedom if anyone else (especially a large organization) has power over one, no matter how benevolently, tolerantly and permissively that power may be exercised. It is important not to confuse freedom with mere permissiveness . . . .

TECHNOLOGY IS A MORE POWERFUL SOCIAL FORCE THAN THE ASPIRATION FOR FREEDOM

125. It is not possible to make a LASTING compromise between technology and freedom, because technology is by far the more powerful social force and continually encroaches on freedom through

REPEATED compromises. Imagine the case of two neighbors, each of whom at the outset owns the same amount of land, but one of whom is more powerful than the other. The powerful one demands a piece of the other's land. The weak one refuses. The powerful one says, "OK, let's compromise. Give me half of what I asked." The weak one has little choice but to give in. Some time later the powerful neighbor demands another piece of land, again there is a compromise, and so forth. By forcing a long series of compromises on the weaker man, the powerful one eventually gets all of his land. So it goes in the conflict between technology and freedom . . . .

REVOLUTION IS EASIER THAN REFORM

140. We hope we have convinced the reader that the system cannot be reformed in a such a way as to reconcile freedom with technology. The only way out is to dispense with the industrial-technological system altogether. This implies revolution, not necessarily an armed uprising, but certainly a radical and fundamental change in the nature of society . . . .

STRATEGY

183. . . . [A]n ideology, in order to gain enthusiastic support, must have a positive ideals as well as a negative one; it must be FOR something as well as AGAINST something. The positive ideal that we propose is Nature. That is, WILD nature; those aspects of the functioning of the Earth and its living things that are independent of human management and free of human interference and control. And with wild nature we include human nature, by which we mean those aspects of the functioning of the human individual that are not subject to regulation by organized society but are products of chance, or free will, or God (depending on your religious or philosophical opinions).

184. Nature makes a perfect counter-ideal to technology for several reasons. Nature (that which is outside the power of the system) is the opposite of technology (which seeks to expand indefinitely the power of the system). Most people will agree that nature is beautiful; certainly it has tremendous popular appeal. The radical environmentalists ALREADY hold an ideology that exalts nature and opposes technology. It is not necessary for the sake of nature to set up some chimerical utopia or any new kind of social order. Nature takes care of itself: It

was a spontaneous creation that existed long before any human society, and for countless centuries many different kinds of human societies coexisted with nature without doing it an excessive amount of damage. Only with the Industrial Revolution did the effect of human society on nature become really devastating. To relieve the pressure on nature it is not necessary to create a special kind of social system, it is only necessary to get rid of industrial society. Granted, this will not solve all problems. Industrial society has already done tremendous damage to nature and it will take a very long time for the scars to heal. Besides, even pre-industrial societies can do significant damage to nature. Nevertheless, getting rid of industrial society will accomplish a great deal. It will relieve the worst of the pressure on nature so that the scars can begin to heal. It will remove the capacity of organized society to keep increasing its control over nature (including human nature). Whatever kind of society may exist after the demise of the industrial system, it is certain that most people will live close to nature, because in the absence of advanced technology there is no other way that people CAN live. To feed themselves they must be peasants or herdsmen or fishermen or hunter, etc. And, generally speaking, local autonomy should tend to increase, because lack of advanced technology and rapid communications will limit the capacity of governments or other large organizations to control local communities . . . .

193. The kind of revolution we have in mind will not necessarily involve an armed uprising against any government. It may or may not involve physical violence, but it will not be a POLITICAL revolution. Its focus will be on technology and economics, not politics . . . .

200. Until the industrial system has been thoroughly wrecked, the destruction of that system must be the revolutionaries' ONLY goal. Other goals would distract attention and energy from the main goal. More importantly, if the revolutionaries permit themselves to have any other goal than the destruction of technology, they will be tempted to use technology as a tool for reaching that other goal. If they give in to that temptation, they will fall right back into the technological trap, because modern technology is a unified, tightly organized system, so that, in order to retain SOME technology, one finds oneself obliged to retain MOST technology, hence one ends up sacrificing only token amounts of technology.

INDEX

Locators in **boldface** indicate main topics. Locators followed by *g* indicate glossary entries. Locators followed by *b* indicate biographical entries. Locators followed by *c* indicate chronology entries.

A

Abbey, Edward **27–29**, 99*c*,
  127*b*–128*b*
  and anarchism 148
  Glen Canyon Dam protest
    31, 101*c*
  introduction to *Ecodefense*
    33
  and monkeywrenching 151
  New Mexico billboard
    destruction 18
  on terrorism/sabotage
    distinction 7
ACLU. *See* American Civil
  Liberties Union
Adams, Ansel 131
Administration Procedure Act
  (APA) 74
AEDPA. *See* Antiterrorism and
  Effective Death Penalty Act
  of 1996
agribusiness 14
AIDS 32–33, 106*c*
Alaskan pipeline 16, 96*c*, 98*c*
Aleutian Islands nuclear tests
  24, 94*c*–97*c*
Alexander, George 34, 106*c*
ALF. *See* Animal Liberation
  Front
alienation, ecofeminism and 22
Ambrose, Frank 48, 116*c*, 128*b*
Amchitka Island nuclear tests
  24, 97*c*
American Civil Liberties Union
  (ACLU) 73, 238
American Freedom Coalition
  129
American Lands Alliance 48,
  128
American Library Association
  63
Americans for Medical Progress
  (AMP) 238–239
Ammons, A. E. 40, 113*c*

Amory, Cleveland 26
AMP (Americans for Medical
  Progress) 238–239
anarchism 22, 28, 130–131,
  148*g*
Angelakos, Diogenes 102*c*, 104*c*
Animal Enterprise Protection
  Act of 1992 **61–62**
animal enterprise terrorism 145
Animal Liberation Front (ALF)
  45–49, 109*c*, 112*c*, 113*c*,
  119*c*–125*c*, 239. *See also* Earth
  Liberation Front
  David Barbarash and 129
  bibliography 215–222
  Rod Coronado and 134
  Douglas Ellerman and
    112*c*, 135
  al-Qaeda comparisons 8
  University of Arizona
    action 107*c*
animal liberationist 148*g*
animal rights
  ALF and 45
  bibliography 186–190
  Rod Coronado and 134
  Douglas Ellerman 135
  Ingrid Newkirk and 142
  Craig Rosebraugh and 144
  Justin Samuel and 145
  Daniel San Diego 145
animals, value of humans vs.
  21, 28, 32
animal testing/experimentation
  45, 61, 129, 134, 142
anthropocentrism 20, 148*g*
anti-environmentalism **40–45**
  bibliography 234–237
  Sagebrush Rebellion
    40–42, 152–153
  and Unabomber 54
  James Watt and 146–147
  wise use movement 42–45,
    155

Antiquities Act. *See* Lacey
  Antiquities Act of 1906
Antiterrorism and Effective
  Death Penalty Act of 1996
  (AEDPA) **62**, 85, 86
APA (Administration Procedure
  Act) 74
appropriate technology 22,
  148*g*–149*g*
Arches National Monument
  (Utah) 27
Arctic National Wildlife
  Refuge 42, 128, 132
Arissa Media Group 47,
  142–144
Arizona Five **35–37**, 149*g*
  arrest of 107*c*
  Ilse Asplund and 129
  Marc Baker 129
  Mark Davis and 134
  Peg Millett and 140
Arizona Phantom 4, 18–19, 95*c*
Armentrout, Forrest 75
Army Corps of Engineers 100*c*
Arnold, Ron 6, 21, 42–43,
  107*c*, 128*b*–129*b*, 279–281
arson 111*c*, 112*c*, 114*c*–117*c*,
  133, 139–140, 143
  ALF and 45
  and ELF/ALF 46
  Long Island developments
    48
  Michigan State animal lab
    47–48
  as monkeywrenching 6
  al-Qaeda attacks vs. 8
  Mark Sands and 145
  Tre Arrow and 145
Ashcroft, John 63, 125*c*
Asian philosophy 10
Asplund, Ilse Washington
  107*c*, 129*b*
  and Arizona Five 36, 149
  Mark Davis and 134

Asplund, Ilse Washington
(*continued*)
Mike Fain and 135
Peg Millett and 140
Atlantic Ocean 18
atomic age 14
Auckland, New Zealand 25
Audubon Society. *See* National
Audubon Society
Aulerich, Richard 109*c*, 134

B
BACH (Bay Area Coalition for
Headwaters Forest) 239
Baker, Marc 36, 107*c*, 129*b*,
134, 135, 140, 149
Bald Mountain Road (Oregon)
103*c*–104*c*
Band of Mercy 45
Barbarash, David 119*c*, 121*c*,
129*b*
Bari, Judi 119*c*, 129*b*–130*b*
bombing of car 38–39, 108*c*
Darryl Cherney and 133,
134
and Earth First!/ELF split
40, 109*c*–110*c*
Redwood Summer
campaign 38
Bay Area Coalition for
Headwaters Forest (BACH)
239
Bay Area Institute 17, 95*c*, 147
Bearnson, Leroy Wood 102*c*
Beck, Thomas 92*c*, 138
Beneville, Craig 55
Berman, Richard 8
Best, Steve 121*c*
bibliography 170–237
animal rights (general)
186–190
Earth First! 207–214
ELF/ALF 215–222
environmentalism (general)
174–185
Greenpeace/SSCS
200–207
radical environmentalism
(general) 190–200
terrorism (general)
171–174
Unabomber 223–234
wise use/anti-
environmentalism
234–237
Big Wild Adventures 147
Billboard Bandits 18
billboards, destruction of
by Edward Abbey 93*c*
by Billboard Bandits 18

Ecotage!'s advocacy of 17
in New Mexico 18
Mike Roselle and 144
by Tucson Eco-Raiders
19, 97*c*
biocentrism. *See* deep ecology
biological diversity
(biodiversity) 149*g*
"biological pollution" 25
bioregionalism **22–23**, 149*g*
biosphere 149*g*
biotechnology industry 55
Bitterroot Valley (Montana) 147
Black, Calvin 42
Black Mesa (Arizona) 4, 18–19,
29, 94*c*, 95*c*, 139
Black Mesa Defense Fund 19,
135, 139
Blackmun, Harry A. 75
Blaine, Washington 24, 96*c*
Blewett, Don 111*c*
BLM. *See* Bureau of Land
Management
BlueRibbon Coalition (BRC)
239
Boeing Aircraft 104*c*–105*c*
Boise Cascade office arson 114*c*
Bolton Institute for a
Sustainable Future 136
Bolt Weevils 18
bombs 135, 145. *See also*
Unabomber
Bookchin, Murray 22, 23, 98*c*,
130*b*–131*b*, 144, 153
BP Amoco 25
Bradshaw, Toby 117*c*
Bratton, William J. 8
BRC (BlueRibbon Coalition)
239
Brennan, William J. 75
Bridger-Teton National Forest
100*c*, 144, 147
British Columbia Hydro
Substation 102*c*
Brower, David 14, 15, 93*c*, 94*c*,
102*c*, 131*b*–132*b*, 147
Bryan, Robert 120*c*
Bureau of Biological Survey 92*c*
Bureau of Land Management
(BLM) 15, 99*c*, 100*c*,
239–240
intimidation by wise use
radicals 44
and RARE II 30
and *Robertson v. Seattle
Audubon Society* 83, 84
Burford, Ann Gorsuch 30
Burson-Marsteller 51, 55, 110*c*
Bush, George W. 25, 41
Butz, Earl 76

C
California Department of
Forestry (CDF) 79
California Forestry Association
(CFA) 51, 55
California v. Bergland 78–79
California v. Block **77–79**, 103*c*
capitalism 20, 22, 47, 56
Cargill 115*c*, 119*c*
Carhart, Arthur 138
Carson, Rachel 14–15, 20, 93*c*,
132*b*–133*b*
Carson National Forest (New
Mexico) 138
Carter, Jimmy 29–30, 67, 84
Carver, Dick 45
Cash, Connor 48, 117*c*, 133*b*,
139, 143
Cato Institute 240
Cavel West 112*c*
CCR. *See* Center for
Constitutional Rights
CDF (California Department
of Forestry) 79
CDFE. *See* Center for the
Defense of Free Enterprise
CDT (Center for Democracy
and Technology) 240
CEI (Competitive Enterprise
Institute) 240–241
cells (organizational units) 45
Center for Constitutional
Rights (CCR) 85, 86
Center for Democracy and
Technology (CDT) 240
Center for the Defense of Free
Enterprise (CDFE) 128, 240
Century magazine 141
CEQ (Council on
Environmental Quality) 241
CFA. *See* California Forestry
Association
Chain, David "Gypsy" 40, 113*c*
Chase, Alston 54
Cherney, Darryl 38–39, 108*c*,
119*c*, 130, 133*b*–134*b*
Chevron 41, 105*c*
Chicago Daily News 18, 136
Chiron Corporation 124*c*, 145
Chocola, Chris 125*c*
CITES (Convention on
International Trade in
Endangered Species of Wild
Fauna and Flora) 70
civil disobedience **5, 6**, 97*c*,
149*g*
Judi Bari and 129–130
and Bolt Weevils campaign
18
and bombing/sabotage 6

Index

and Earth First! 39, 40
and environmental
  legislation 66
equating of terrorism with
  6
Greenpeace and 23
and road blockade 152
Mike Roselle and 144
Thoreau's acts of 11
tree sitting 154
"Civil Disobedience" (Henry
  David Thoreau) 11
civil libertarians 8, 56, 63
civil liberties 62
Civil Rights movement 4
Clarke, Judy 52
Clausen, Barry R. 54, 282–284
Clean Air Act of 1963 15, 93*c*
Clean Air Act Revisions of
  1970 16, 95*c*
Clean Water Act of 1972 16, 97*c*
Clear Creek Legal Defense
  Fund 77
clear cutting 99*c*, 150*g*
Judi Bari and 130
and *EPIC v. Maxxam* 79,
  80
and *Izaak Walton League v.
  Butz* 76, 77
and National Forest
  Management Act 70
Cleary, Robert 52
Cleveland, Grover 12, 90*c*
Clinton, Bill 25
Close, Elaine 119*c*
Cloverdale, California 34, 106*c*
Coalition to Save the Preserves
  (CSP) 118*c*, 145
coal mining 18–19
cold war 14, 56
Collins, Audrey 85–87,
  125*c*–126*c*
colonial America 6, 9
Colorado Public Radio 3
Colorado River 29
Colville National Forest 104*c*
Competitive Enterprise
  Institute (CEI) 240–241
conservation **11–14**, 150*g*
  and Forest Reserve Act of
    1891 67
  Franklin Roosevelt's
    sympathy for 14
  George Perkins Marsh and
    139
  Gifford Pinchot and
    90*c*–91*c*, 143
  preservation vs. 12–13
  Theodore Roosevelt and
    143

Conservation Conference
  (1908) 12, 91*c*, 143
constitutionality, of antiterror
  laws 62, 63
Convention on International
  Trade in Endangered Species
  of Wild Fauna and Flora
  (CITES) 70
cooperation 22
Coronado, Rodney 110*c*, 121*c*,
  134*b*
  David Barbarash and 129
  Michigan State animal lab
    arson 47–48, 109*c*
  whaling sabotage 27
Cottrell, William 126*c*
Council on Environmental
  Quality (CEQ) 241
counterculture 19
court cases 72–87
  California v. Block **77–79**,
    103*c*
  EPIC v. Maxxam **79–80**,
    106*c*, 108*c*
  *Humanitarian Law Project
    v. Ashcroft* **85–87**
  Izaak Walton League v. Butz
    75–77
  *Northern Spotted Owl v.
    Manuel Lujan* **80–82**
  research resources 168–169
  *Robertson v. Seattle Audubon
    Society* **82–84**
  Sierra Club v. Morton
    73–75
Cove Mallard (Nez Perce
  National Forest) 39,
  109*c*–111*c*
Cravens, Jay H. 76
Crist, Buckley, Jr. 49
critical habitat 80–82
CSP. *See* Coalition to Save the
  Preserves
Cutler, Rupert 100*c*
Cuyahoga River (Ohio) 15, 95*c*

D

dams
  David Brower and 93*c*,
    131–132
  Dinosaur National
    Monument 14
  Glen Canyon. *See* Glen
    Canyon Dam
  Grand Canyon 15
  Hetch Hetchy Valley 13,
    91*c*
  John Muir and 141
  Stanislaus River 100*c*–101*c*
  Tellico 84

Darling, Jay Norwood 92*c*, 138
Davis, John 37
Davis, Mark 106*c*, 107*c*, 134*b*
  and Arizona Five 36, 37,
    149
  Mike Fain and 135
  Peg Millett and 140
DDT (dichloro-diphenyl-
  trichloro-ethane) 97*c*, 133
death, from ecoterrorism
  attacks 49–51
The Death of Nature (Carolyn
  Merchant) 22, 140
decentralization 22
"Declaration of
  Interdependence"
  (Greenpeace) 24
deep ecology **20–21**, 150*g*
  anthropocentrism vs. 148
  Bill Devall and 134–135
  ecofeminist critique of
    21–22
  Dave Foreman and 31, 32
  and Leopold's "Land
    Ethic" 13
  Arne Naess and 98*c*, 141
  social ecology vs. 22,
    31–32, 37
  and transcendental
    movement 10
  and Unabomber's ideology
    49
Deep Ecology (Bill Devall and
  George Sessions) 135
Defenders of Property Rights
  (DPR) 241
Defenders of Wildlife 241
democracy 7–8, 28
Democratic National
  Convention (Chicago, 1968)
  144
Dennison, William 51, 110*c*
Denvir, Quin 52
Department of Fish and Game
  (DFG) 79, 80
Department of Homeland
  Security (DHS). *See* U.S.
  Department of Homeland
  Security
Desert Land Act of 1877 10,
  90*c*
Desert Solitaire (Edward Abbey)
  27–28
destruction of property. *See*
  property, destruction of
Details magazine 144
Devall, Bill 20, 134*b*–135*b*
development/developers 19,
  97*c*, 115*c*, 116*c*, 120*c*,
  122*c*–124*c*, 145

Devils Tower (Wyoming) 68
DFG. *See* Department of Fish
and Game
DHS. *See* U.S. Department of
Homeland Security
Diablo Canyon Nuclear Facility
94*c*, 129, 132, 134, 140
Dial soap 136
Dinosaur National Monument
(Colorado) 14, 93*c*, 131–132
Direct Action 102*c*
direct action 5, 99*c*. *See also
specific actions, e.g.:*
monkeywrenching
and Earth Day (1970) 15
Earth First! and 33
and *Earth Tool Kit* 17, 97*c*
and ELF/ALF 46
Mike Roselle and 145
SSCS rules concerning 26
Paul Watson and 146
Distefano, Lisa 113*c*
diversity, of ecosystems 24
Dodge, Jim 23
Dominy, Floyd E. 28
Donora, Pennsylvania, smog
attack 14, 92*c*
Don't Make a Wave
Committee (Greenpeace)
24, 94*c*–95*c*
Douglas, William O. 74–75
Dow Chemical 129
Doyle, Frank 39
DPR (Defenders of Property
Rights) 241
drift-net fishing 26, 108*c*, 146
Drug Act of 1988 35, 70
Dubois, Mark 100*c*–101*c*
due process 62
Dulles Airport 50, 101*c*
DuPont 41

E

Earth Day (1970) 15–16, 96*c*
Earth First! 29–40, 32, 101*c*,
103*c*–108*c*, 110*c*, 111*c*, 137,
241–242
Edward Abbey and 127,
128
after Dave Foreman's
departure 37–40
Frank Ambrose and 128
and anarchism 148
Arizona Five 35–37, 107*c*
Ilse Asplund and 129
Marc Baker 129
Judi Bari and 129, 130
bibliography 207–214
Darryl Cherney and 133,
134

Mark Davis and 134
and deep ecology 21
Dave Foreman and 135
foundation of 4, 101*c*
Ron Kezar and 137
Bart Koehler and 137
and Law Against Tree
Spiking (1988) 70
Ned Ludd as inspiration to
139
Peg Millett and 140
and *The Monkey Wrench
Gang* 29, 99*c*
monkeywrenching 33–35,
151
origins and ideas 30–33
and RARE 152
Mike Roselle and 144
SSCS as naval arm of 26
and terrorism 154
and tree spiking 154
and Unabomber
connection 54–56
wise-use threats against 43
Howie Wolke and 147
Earth First! Journal 32, 55,
101*c*, 106*c*, 109*c*–110*c*, 134
Earth in the Balance (Al Gore)
54
Earth Island Institute 102*c*,
132, 242
Earth Liberation Front (ELF)
3–5, 45–49, 109*c*, 111*c*,
113*c*–121*c*, 125*c*, 242
Frank Ambrose and 128
bibliography 215–222
Connor Cash and 133
ideology of 7
as liability to movement 9
George Mashkow and 139
Jared McIntyre and 140
Leslie Pickering and 142
al-Qaeda comparisons 8
Matthew Rammelkamp
and 143
Craig Rosebraugh and
143–144
solidarity with ALF 45
split with Earth First! 40
and terrorism 4–5, 154
Tre Arrow and 145
Earth Tool Kit 17, 97*c*
Eastern philosophy, deep
ecology and 20
Eaubonne, Françoise d' 21
Eco-Commando Force '70 18,
96*c*–97*c*
*Ecodefense: A Field Guide to
Monkeywrenching* (Dave
Foreman) 33–34, 104*c*, 136

ecofeminism 21–22, 23, 136,
140, 146, 150*g*
Ecofeminist Philosophy (Karen J.
Warren) 146
"ecological preserves" 32
ecology 150*g*
*Ecology, Community, and
Lifestyle: Outline of an Ecosophy*
(Arne Naess) 20
economic interests,
environmental law vs. 84
ecosabotage 6. *See also*
monkeywrenching
ecosystem 151*g*
ecotage 6, 17, 18, 102*c*. *See also*
monkeywrenching
Ecotage! 17, 97*c*
ecoterrorism (definition) 3–4
EIS. *See* environmental impact
statement
Electronic Frontier Foundation
(EFF) 242
Electronic Privacy Information
Center (EPIC) 242–243
electronic surveillance 63
ELF. *See* Earth Liberation
Front
Ellerman, Douglas Joshua
112*c*, 135*b*
El Salvadoran war 130
Emerson, Ralph Waldo 10
EMETIC. *See* Evan Mecham
Eco Terrorist International
Conspiracy
emissions standards 16, 95*c*
endangered species 80–82, 108*c*
Endangered Species
Committee 82
Endangered Species
Preservation Act of 1973
(ESA) 16, 69–70, 73, 80–82,
84, 98*c*
energy conservation 98*c*–99*c*
the Enlightenment 9, 10
entrapment 36–37
Environmental Action 17–18,
97*c*
Environmental Defense 243
environmental ethic. *See* ethics,
environmental
environmental impact
statement (EIS) 69, 78, 79,
96*c*, 103*c*, 104*c*, 151*g*
environmental legislation
66–72
environmental movement in
the United States 9–16
Environmental Protection
Information Center (EPIC)
72–73, 79, 106*c*, 133, 243

Index

EPA. *See* U.S. Environmental
Protection Agency
EPIC. *See* Electronic Privacy
Information Center;
Environmental Protection
Information Center
EPIC v. Maxxam **79–80**, 106*c*,
108*c*
Epstein, Charles J. 50, 109*c*
equal protection 62
Ervin, William Joseph 34–35,
106*c*
E.S.A. *See* Endangered Species
Preservation Act of 1973
ethics, environmental 11, 12,
146
*An Evaluation of Roadless Areas
in the Medicine Bow National
Forest* (Bart Koehler) 137
Evan Mecham Eco Terrorist
International Conspiracy
(EMETIC) 36, 37, 106*c*, 107*c*
Everhart, Kevin 103*c*
Exxon Corporation 55
Exxon Valdez oil spill 51, 107*c*

F

FAF (First Amendment
Foundation) 243–244
Fain, Mike 36, 37, 135*b*
Fairfield ski resort 36, 106*c*,
129, 134, 140
Farrell, Mike 26, 103*c*
FBI. *See* Federal Bureau of
Investigation
FC (Freedom Club) 51, 52
federal antiterrorism legislation
61–66
Federal Bureau of Investigation
(FBI) 243
Edward Abbey and 127
and Arizona Five 35–37
Judi Bari and 130
Bari/Cherney car explosion
38–39, 119*c*
Darryl Cherney and 134
Mark Davis and 134
and ELF/ALF 3–4, 46
Mike Fain and 135
Daniel San Diego 145
and special interest
extremists 4
and terrorism 154
Tre Arrow and 146
Unabomber and 50–52,
137
and USA PATRIOT Act
8, 62
Federal Land Policy and
Management Act of 1976 15

Federal Water Quality
Administration 18
feminism. *See* ecofeminism
Fifth Amendment 47, 87, 144
First Amendment 39, 56,
85–87, 119*c*, 130, 134
First Amendment Foundation
(FAF) 243–244
FISA (Foreign Intelligence
Surveillance Act) 64
Fischer, Patrick 102*c*
fishing, drift-net. *See* drift-net
fishing
Flora, Gloria 44
Ford, Gerald 98*c*
Foreign Intelligence
Surveillance Act (FISA) 64
Foreman, Dave 100*c*, 103*c*,
104*c*, 108*c*, 110*c*, 135*b*–136*b*
Edward Abbey and 128
Arizona Five and 36, 37,
149
arrest of 36, 107*c*
and Black Mesa Defense
Fund 19
and *California v. Block* 79
condemnation of
vandalism 34
Mark Davis and 134
and deep ecology 21
and Earth First! 4, 30, 31,
37, 101*c*
and ELF ideology 47–48
Mike Fain and 135
Ron Kezar and 137
Bart Koehler and 137
Peg Millett and 140
and *The Monkey Wrench
Gang* 29, 99*c*
on monkeywrenching 7
Mike Roselle and 144
and Sagebrush Rebellion
42
Gerry Spence and 146
Howie Wolke and 147
Forest and Rangeland
Renewable Resources
Planning Act 70
Forest Practices Act of 1973 79
Forest Reserve Act of 1891 **67**
forest reserves. *See* national
forests
forestry 142–143, 147
Forests Forever 244
Fourth Amendment 39, 56, 64,
119*c*, 130, 134
The Fox 4, 18, 97*c*, 136*b*
Freedom to Read Protection
Act 63
Free Enterprise Press 128

free speech 62. *See also* First
Amendment
Friends of the Earth (FoE) 94*c*,
132, 147, 244
frontier, settling of 10
fuel efficiency standards 99*c*
Fund for Animals 26
Fur Breeders Agricultural Co-
op 112*c*, 135
FWS (U.S. Fish and Wildlife
Service) 14

G

Gaede, Marc 19
gag orders 65
Gail, Maxwell 26
Game Management (Aldo
Leopold) 138
Gandhi, Mohandas K. 4, 7, 23,
127
GE foods. *See* genetically
engineered foods
Gelernter, David 50–51, 109*c*
genetically engineered (GE)
foods 25, 114*c*, 115*c*, 119*c*,
123*c*, 126*c*
George C. Marshall Institute
(GMI) 244
George Washington National
Forest (Virginia) 34
Getty Oil 100*c*, 102*c*, 144, 147
Gila National Forest (New
Mexico) 91*c*–92*c*, 138
Glen Canyon Dam (Arizona)
14
Edward Abbey and 27–28,
127–128
David Brower and 132
Darryl Cherney and 133
Earth First! gathering 31,
101*c*
Dave Foreman and
135–136
The Monkey Wrench Gang
and 29
Glick, Daniel 46
GMI (George C. Marshall
Institute) 244
Goldwater, Barry 135
Gore, Al 54
Grand Canyon dam project 15,
93*c*, 94*c*, 132
Gray, Elizabeth Dodson 22,
136*b*
Gray Whale Campaign
Expedition 113*c*
Great Depression 14, 131
Green Anarchist magazine 55
"green anarchist" movement
55, 56

Green Paradise Lost (Elizabeth Dodson Gray) 22, 136
Greenpeace **23–25,** 94*c*–95*c*, 98*c*, 99*c*, 105*c*, 115*c*, 118*c*, 126*c*, 245
 bibliography 200–207
 first protests 4
 founding of 24
 David McTaggart and 140
 Mike Roselle and 145
 and saboteurs 6
 SSCS's defection from 25–26
 view of destruction of property 7
 Paul Watson and 146
Greenpeace (boat) 24, 97*c*
Greenpeace III (boat) 25, 98*c*, 99*c*, 140
Greenpeace Too (boat) 24, 97*c*
Gros Ventre 100*c*, 102*c*, 144, 147
guerrilla theater 31
Gutierrez, Mary 49, 100*c*

H

Haeckel, Ernst 150
Hardesty Mountain (Oregon) 34
Harris, John 50, 100*c*
Harrison, Benjamin 12, 67, 90*c*
Harvard Divinity School 136
Hatch, Orrin 41, 100*c*
Hatfield, Mark 35, 107*c*, 154
Hayes, Denis 15
Headwaters Forest 40, 72, 79, 80, 106*c*, 108*c*, 111*c*
health, human 12, 91*c*
Helvarg, David 42, 43
Hemstreet, Leslie 55
The Heritage Foundation 245
Hetch Hetchy Valley 13, 91*c*, 141
Hickel, Walter 16, 96*c*
Hicks, Michael 47
hierarchical structures 22
high-voltage power lines 18
Hill, Julia Butterfly 40, 112*c*, 136*b*–137*b*
HLS. *See* Huntingdon Life Sciences
Hodel, Donald 30
Holmes, William 43
Homestead Act of 1862 10, 88*c*
homesteading 10
House Committee on Forests and Forests Health 119*c*, 257–278
House Committee on the Judiciary 6, 279–284

Humanitarian Law Project v. Ashcroft **85–87**
humans, injury to 49
Humphrey, Hubert 147
Humvee 124*c*, 125*c*
hunting, in 19th-century America 10
Huntingdon Life Sciences (HLS) 45, 118*c*, 120*c*, 122*c*, 124*c*, 125*c*

I

IACSP (International Association for Counterterrorism and Security Professionals) 245
Ickes, Harold L. 14
illegal immigrants 28
immigration 28
Imperial Valley (California) 44
inanimate objects 7, 26
Industrial Revolution 10–12, 49
industrial smog. *See* smog
"Industrial Society and Its Future" (Unabomber Manifesto) 52
Industrial Workers of the World (IWW) 38, 128
Ingram, Nigel 25, 98*c*, 140
Inquiry (journal) 20, 98*c*, 141
insanity defense, Unabomber trial and 52–53
Institute for Social Ecology 22, 98*c*, 131, 144
interconnectedness, of life 20, 22, 24, 150
Interior Board of Land Appeals 102*c*
Internal Revenue Service (IRS) 93*c*, 132
International Association for Counterterrorism and Security Professionals (IACSP) 245
International Whaling Commission (IWC) 26, 105*c*
Iraq War (2003) 47, 56, 122*c*–123*c*, 144
irrigation 10
IRS. *See* Internal Revenue Service
Ives, Catherine 114*c*
IWC. *See* International Whaling Commission

J

Jakubel, Mike 104*c*, 137*b*
Jarboe, James F. 7, 25–26, 46, 257–263

J. N. "Ding" Darling Foundation 245
Johansen, Hank 24
John Muir Award 132
John Muir Institute 132
Johnson, Huey 79
Johnson, Lyndon 94*c*, 147
Johnson, Robert Underwood 141
Johnson, Sally 53
Judeo-Christian tradition 20

K

Kaczynski, David 52, 111*c*, 137
Kaczynski, Theodore. *See* Unabomber
Kalil Company 19
Katz, Michael 53
Kennedy, John F. 14–15, 93*c*, 133
Kerr-McGee Corporation 146
Kettle Planning Unit timber sales 104*c*
Kezar, Ron 30, 101*c*, 137, 137*b*, 144, 147
King, Martin Luther, Jr. 6
King, Ynestra 22
Kintz, Theresa 55
Kirk Timber Sale 120*c*
Kline, Benjamin 9
Koehler, Bart 30, 101*c*, 102*c*, 137*b*, 144, 147
Korman, Harvey 26
Kropotkin, Peter 22, 153
Kurdistan Workers' Party (PKK) 85, 86
Kyoto Protocol 25

L

Lacey Antiquities Act of 1906 12, **67–68,** 91*c*, 143
land ethic 151*g*
"The Land Ethic" (Aldo Leopold) 13, 92*c*, 138–139
land management system 68–69
land ownership, in colonial America 9
Law Against Tree Spiking (1988) 35, **70–72,** 107*c*, 154
lawsuits 19, 66, 72–73, 139, 153. *See also* court cases
The Legacy of Luna (Hill) 137
Legacy Trading 123*c*
legal issues **61–87.** *See also* specific court cases; specific laws
 and civil disobedience 5
 court cases 72–87
 environmental legislation 66–72

Index

federal antiterrorism
legislation 61–66
research resources
167–169
Leopold, Aldo 13, 14, 20,
91c–92c, 137b–139b, 151
Liberation Collective 46, 114c,
142
Liberation Tigers of Tamil
Eelam (LTTE) 85, 86
life-forms, interdependence of
24
List, Peter C. 23
Live Wild or Die 55
Loeffler, Jack 19, 95c, 139b
logging industry 108c, 109c
    Darryl Cherney and 133
    and clear cutting 150
    and *Izaak Walton League v.
    Butz* 77
    and RARE 152
    Redwood Summer 38
    and *Robertson v. Seattle
    Audubon Society* 82–84
    SLAPP as legal strategy
    153
    Tre Arrow and 145–146
    and tree spiking 34, 35,
    154
Long Island, New York 48,
117c, 133, 139, 140, 143
Louisiana-Pacific 34, 55, 106c
LTTE (Liberation Tigers of
Tamil Eelam) 85
Ludd, Ned 33, 88c, 139b, 151
Luddite 88c, 139, 151g
Lujan, Manuel 82
Lyon, Leslie 32

M
mainstream environmentalism
20, 130
Makah Indians 27, 113c
Malecky Mink Ranch 109c
Malthus, Thomas 139b, 151
Malthusian 151g
Man and Nature (George
Perkins Marsh) 11, 89c, 139
Manes, Christopher 32–33, 48
Manifest Destiny 9–10
Marker, Terry 49, 100c
Mars Bars 104c
Marsden, Steve 103c
Marsh, George Perkins 11,
89c, 139b
Marshall, Robert 14
Martin State Forest 115c
Mashkow, George 48, 117c,
133, 139b, 143
material support 85, 86

maturity (of trees) 76
Maxxam/Pacific Lumber
Company 40, 80, 104c, 108c,
133
MBTA. *See* Migratory Bird
Treaty Act
McClure, James 35, 107c, 154
McConnell, James V. 105c
McDonald's 116c, 122c
McGuire, John R. 76
McInnis, Scott 8, 47, 119c
McIntyre, Jared 48, 117c, 133,
139b–140b, 143
McTaggart, David 25, 98c, 99c,
140b
Meese, Edwin 35
Mello, Michael 53
Melo's Construction Company
116c
Merchant, Carolyn 22, 140b
Merlo, Harry 35
Mexican consulate (Boston,
Massachusetts) 113c
Michigan State University
47–48, 134
Migratory Bird Treaty Act
(MBTA) 82, 84
Millett, Peg 36–37, 106c, 107c,
134, 135, 140b, 149
Mineral King Valley project
73–75
Mirror Worlds (David
Gelernter) 51
misanthropy 28, 32–33
Moab, Utah 42, 101c
The Monkey Wrench Gang
(Edward Abbey) 28–29, 99c,
128, 144, 151
monkeywrenching
(ecosabotage) 33–35, 151g
    Edward Abbey and 27–28
    and Earth First! 4, 40
    Dave Foreman and 7, 37,
    136
    and Luddites 151
    Mike Roselle and 144
    and terrorism 153–154
    tree spiking. *See* tree
    spiking
Monongahela National Forest
(West Virginia) 75–77, 98c
Monsanto Corporation 114c
monuments, national. *See*
national monuments
Mosser, Thomas 51, 55, 110c
Mountain States Legal
Foundation (MSLF) 41,
245–246
MSLF. *See* Mountain States
Legal Foundation

Muir, John 12–13, 89c–91c,
140b–141b
multiple use 12–13
Multiple Use Strategy
Conference 42, 107c, 128
Multiple-Use Sustained-Yield
Act of 1960 (MUSY) **68**, 77,
78, 99c
Murkowski, Lisa 63
Murray, Gilbert 51, 55, 110c
Mururoa Atoll tests 25, 98c,
140
MUSY. *See* Multiple-Use
Sustained-Yield Act of 1960

N
NAELFPO. *See* North
American Earth Liberation
Front Press Office
Naess, Arne 20–21, 98c, 141b,
150
National Audubon Society 82,
84, 246
National Coalition Against
Censorship (NCAC) 246
National Committee Against
Repressive Legislation
(NCARL) 246
National Environmental Policy
Act of 1969 (NEPA) **69**, 98c,
99c
    and *California v. Block*
    77–78
    and EISs 151
    and lawsuits 73
    passage of 16, 95c–96c
    and *Robertson v. Seattle
    Audubon Society* 82, 84
    and *Sierra Club v. Morton*
    75
National Federal Lands
Conference 129
National Forest Management
Act of 1976 (NFMA) **70**, 77,
78, 82, 84
national forests 12, 67, 68, 90c,
141
national monuments 12,
67–68, 91c, 143
national park movement
11–12, 132
National Parks Conservation
Association (NPCA) 247
National Park Service (NPS)
18, 30, 68, 91c, 246–247
National Park Service Organic
Act of 1916 **68**, 76–77, 98c
National Parks Reform Act 42,
128
national park system 14

295

National Resources Defense
Council 77
National Wilderness
Conference 55
National Wildlife Federation
(NWF) 92*c*, 247
Native Americans 10
natural objects, legal standing
of 75
natural resources, wasting of 11
Natural Resources
Conservation Service
(NRCS) 247
Natural Resources Defense
Council (NRDC) 75,
247–248
nature, conquest of 9
nature, oppression of 21
nature, rights of 74–75
The Nature Conservancy
(TNC) 248
Navajo Generating Station 94*c*
Naval Recruiting Office
(Montgomery, Alabama) 47
NCAC (National Coalition
Against Censorship) 246
NCARL (National Committee
Against Repressive
Legislation) 246
Nelson, Gaylord 15, 94*c*
neo-paganism 151*g*
NEPA. *See* National
Environmental Policy Act of
1969
Nevada Access and Multiple Use
Stewardship Coalition 41
New Deal 14
Newkirk, Ingrid 45, 142*b*
New Mexico Game Protective
Association (NMGPA) 138
New Mexico Wilderness Study
Committee 135
New York Times 51, 52, 110*c*,
137
Nez Perce National Forest 39,
109*c*–111*c*
NFMA. *See* National Forest
Management Act of 1976
Nicaraguan war 130
Nike outlet store (Albertville,
Minnesota) 48, 117*c*
Nixon, Richard 16, 69, 95*c*, 96*c*
NMGPA (New Mexico Game
Protective Association) 138
nonviolence 7, 38, 130, 145, 149
North American Earth
Liberation Front Press Office
(NAELFPO) 46, 47, 142
northern spotted owl 82–84,
107*c*, 108*c*

Northern Spotted Owl v. Hodel
80, 82
*Northern Spotted Owl v. Manuel
Lujan* **80–82**
North Phoenix Mountain
Preserve 118*c*, 145
Northstar oil pipeline 25
Northwest Timber
Compromise of 1990 83, 84
Norton, Gale 41
Norway 26
NPCA (National Parks
Conservation Association)
247
NPS. *See* National Park Service
NRCS (Natural Resources
Conservation Service) 247
NRDC. *See* Natural Resources
Defense Council
nuclear plant sabotage 136
nuclear tests 24, 25, 94*c*–97*c*
NWF. *See* National Wildlife
Federation

O
Oakland Police Department
38, 39, 130
Oakridge Ranger Station 111*c*
oil embargo 98*c*
oil refinery (Honolulu, Hawaii)
16, 96*c*
oil spills 15, 95*c*, 107*c*
Oklahoma City bombing
(1995) 62
old-growth forest (ancient
forest) 81, 152*g*
old-growth redwood 79, 133
On the Duty of Civil Disobedience
(Henry David Thoreau) 6
OPEC (Organization of
Petroleum Exporting
Countries) 98*c*
oppression, of nature and
women 21–22
Oregon Natural Resources
Council 103*c*
Organic Act. *See* National
Park Service Organic Act of
1916
Organization of Petroleum
Exporting Countries (OPEC)
98*c*
Otter, C. L. "Butch" 63
Otter Wing Timber Sale 118*c*
Oversoul 10, 20

P
Pacheco, Alex 142
Pacific Legal Foundation (PLF)
248

Pacific Lumber 79, 106*c*, 111*c*,
113*c*. *See also* Maxxam/Pacific
Lumber Company
package bombs. *See*
Unabomber
Palo Verde nuclear plant 35,
105*c*, 129, 134, 140
Passacantando, John 25
passive resistance, Greenpeace
and 23
patriarchal systems 20–22
Peabody Coal Company 95*c*,
139
Pease, Dave 35
Pence, Guy 44–45
Pendleton, Michael Roy 44
Penthouse magazine 52, 110*c*
People for the Ethical
Treatment of Animals
(PETA) 45, 125*c*, 142,
248–249
People's Brigade for a Healthy
Genetic Future 102*c*
Pereira, Fernando 25, 105*c*
Perm, Arthur 125*c*
Persian Gulf War (1991) 144
pesticides 14–15, 93*c*, 94*c*, 102*c*
PETA. *See* People for the
Ethical Treatment of Animals
philosophies, of radical
environmentalism **19–23**
Pickering, Leslie James 46–47,
117*c*, 118*c*, 142*b*
Pinacate Desert (Mexico) 30,
101*c*
Pinchot, Gifford 12–13, 67,
90*c*–91*c*, 142*b*–143*b*
pipeline, Alaskan. *See* Alaskan
pipeline
PKK. *See* Kurdistan Workers'
Party
Plant, Judith 23
PLF (Pacific Legal Foundation)
248
Plumley 103*c*
Portland Audubon Society 82,
83
postwar economic boom 14
preservation **13**, 89*c*, 90*c*, 152*g*
conservation vs. 12–13
and deep ecology 20
and Earth First! 31
and Forest Reserve Act of
1891 67
President's Committee on
Wild-Life Restoration 92*c*,
138
President's Science Advisory
Committee 14–15, 93*c*, 94*c*,
133

Index

"primitive" areas 77
Progressive Era 12
Project Ahab 99c
property, destruction of 102c.
    See also monkeywrenching;
    sabotage; vandalism, petty
    and ELF/ALF 45, 47
    Dave Foreman and 136
    as liability to movement 9
    philosophical views of 7
    Craig Rosebraugh on 47,
        144
Protecting the Rights of
    Individuals Act 63

Q
al-Qaeda 8, 47

R
racism 28
radical environmentalism
    16–40, 45–56. *See also specific*
    organizations, e.g.: Earth
    First!
    Edward Abbey and 27–29
    and anarchism 148
    anti-environmentalism
        40–45
    bibliography 190–234
    bioregionalism 22–23
    and conservation 91c, 150
    deep ecology 20–21
    disavowal of Unabomber's
        methods 49
    early militant actions
        17–19
    ecofeminism 21–22
    neo-paganism and 151
    and old-growth forest 152
    philosophies of 19–23
    and RARE 152
    social ecology 22
    and transcendental
        movement 10
    and tribalism 154
    Unabomber. *See*
        Unabomber
    Barry Weisberg and 95c
Rainbow Warrior 25, 105c
Rainforest Action Network
    (RAN) 249
Rainforest Alliance 249
Rammelkamp, Matthew 48,
    117c, 133, 139, 143b
RAN (Rainforest Action
    Network) 249
rape, ecofeminist view of 21,
    150
RARE. *See* Roadless Area
    Review and Evaluation

rationality, rejection of 10
RCC (Rachel Carson Council,
    Inc.) 249
Reader's Digest 15
Reagan, Ronald 29–30, 41,
    100c, 146–147
Reason Foundation 249–250
Reclamation Bureau 28
Redden, James 103c–104c
Redwood Summer 38–40,
    108c, 130, 133
Reforestation Trust Fund 70, 77
Reiland, Ralph 54
Reinhardt, Stephen 116c
Reno, Janet 52, 110c
Rensselaer Polytechnic
    Institute 49, 50
Rentech 105c
researching ecoterrorism,
    resources for 159–169
    academic and
        environmental news sites
        164
    bibliographic resources
        165–167
    bookstore catalogs 166
    civil liberties web sites 165
    court decisions 168–169
    government web sites
        163–164
    Internet 159–165
    laws 167
    legal research 167–169
    legislative news 167
    library catalogs 165–166
    organizations/people 163
    periodical databases
        166–167
    radical web sites 165
    search engines 161–163
    web indexes 160–161
responsibility, and natural
    resources 11
restoration ecology 152g
revolution, as part of
    environmental rhetoric 16
Revolutionary Cells 124c
Reykjavík, Iceland 27, 105c,
    134
Ridge, Tom 125c
rights, of nature 74–75
road blockade 152g
Roadless Area Review and
    Evaluation (RARE and
    RARE II) 104c, 152g
    and *California v. Block*
        77–79
    Dave Foreman and 135
    as impetus for Earth First!
        30, 100c

Bart Koehler and 137
Mike Roselle and 144
Howie Wolke and 147
roadless areas 77, 79, 103c
Robertson, Dale 83
Robertson v. Seattle Audubon
    Society **82–84**
Robinson-Scott 112c
Rocky Flats Nuclear Facility
    129, 134, 140
Romanticism 10
Ronay, Chris 50
Roosevelt, Franklin D. 14, 92c,
    138
Roosevelt, Theodore 143b
    and conservation 12
    and Conservation
        Conference 91c
    and Hetch Hetchy
        (Yosemite) dam 13, 91c
    and Lacey Antiquities Act
        of 1906 67–68, 91c
    John Muir and 90c, 141
    Gifford Pinchot and 143
Rosebraugh, Craig 117c, 118c,
    121c–123c, 143b–144b
    at ecoterrorism hearings
        47, 264–278
    and ELF/ALF 46, 47
    Leslie Pickering and 142
    Unabomber and 56
Roselle, Mike 103c, 106c,
    144b–145b
    and Earth First! 30, 31,
        37, 101c
    Ron Kezar and 137
    Bart Koehler and 137
    on tree-spiking 35
    Howie Wolke and 147
Ross, Brian 54
Round River Rendezvous 140
Royko, Mike 18, 136
Ruckus Society 37, 145, 250

S
sabotage **5–8,** 88c, 95c. *See also*
    monkeywrenching
    Edward Abbey and 128
    Ilse Asplund and 129
    David Barbarash and 129
    Bolt Weevils campaign 18
    Earth First! and 33–35
    Dave Foreman and 136
    The Fox and 136
    militant environmentalism
        17
    The Monkey Wrench Gang
        and 29
    in 1970s 4
    terrorism vs. 7

sabotage *(continued)*
  Thoreau's contemplation
    of 11
  Tre Arrow and 145–146
  Barry Weisberg and 147
Sagebrush Rebellion **40–42,**
  100*c*, 101*c*, 146, 152*g*–153*g*,
  155
Sagebrush Rebellion Act 41
Sahara Club 43
Sallinger, Rick 56
Samuel, Justin 145*b*
A Sand Country Almanac (Aldo
  Leopold) 13, 92*c*, 138
Sanders, Bernie 63
San Diego, Daniel Andreas
  145*b*
Sands, Mark 118*c*, 145*b*
Santa Barbara, California, oil
  spills 15
Saylor, John 147
Scarpitti, Michael James (Tre
  Arrow) 126*c*, 145*b*–146*b*
Schurz, Carl 11, 89*c*
scientific revolution 9, 22, 140
Scrutton, Hugh 50, 105*c*
seal hunt protests 26, 103*c*, 146
sealing (seal hunting) 26
sea mammals 23
search and seizure 8, 65
Sea Shepherd Conservation
  Society (SSCS) **25–27,** 105*c*,
  113*c*, 250
  bibliography 200–207
  Rod Coronado and 134
  forming of 4, 7, 99*c*
  stance on harm to
    humans/animals 7
  Paul Watson and 146
Sea Shepherd II (boat) 108*c*, 146
Seattle anti-globalization
  protests 55–56
Seattle Audubon Society 82,
  83
Seattle Weekly 43
self-sufficiency 23
September 11, 2001, terrorist
  attacks 5, 8, 62
Sequoia National Forest 73, 74
Sessions, George 20, 134
SEV (Stop Eco-Violence) 251
sewage, tracking of 18, 96*c*–97*c*
SHAC. *See* Stop Huntingdon
  Animal Cruelty
Shaklee Corporation 125*c*, 145
"shallow ecology," vs. deep
  ecology 20
shareholder actions 25
Shee Atika 153
Shell Oil Company 25

"Should Trees Have Standing?"
  (Christopher Stone) 75
Sieman, Rick 43
Sierra Club 250
  David Brower and 15, 93*c*,
    94*c*, 131, 132
  and *California v. Bergland*
    79
  and *EPIC v. Maxxam* 108*c*
  expansion of focus in 1950s
    14
  Dave Foreman and 110*c*,
    136
  founding of 90*c*
  growth after Earth Day 16
  and Hetch Hetchy dam
    91*c*
  and *Izaak Walton League v.*
    Butz 75
  Ron Kezar and 137
  John Muir and 12, 140,
    141
  and RARE II 30
  SLAPP 153
  Howie Wolke and 147
Sierra Club Legal Defense
  Fund 72
Sierra Club v. Morton **73–75**
Sierra Nevada 12, 89*c*, 90*c*,
  131, 141
Silent Spring (Rachel Carson)
  14–15, 93*c*, 133
Silkwood, Karen 146
Sirenian (boat) 27, 113*c*
Siskiyou National Forest 103*c*,
  104*c*
60 Minutes 133
ski resort. *See* Fairfield ski
  resort; *Sierra Club v. Morton*
SLAPP (strategic lawsuit
  against public participation)
  153*g*
Smith, Janet 102*c*
Smith, Robert 35
smog 14, 16, 92*c*, 95*c*
snail darter 84
"sneak and peek" searches 63,
  65
Snow, Tony 54
Snyder, Gary 23
social ecology **22,** 153*g*
  and bioregionalism 23
  Murray Bookchin and 98*c*,
    131
  deep ecology vs. 31–32, 37
  and ELF ideology 47
soft drink bottles 19
Sonora Desert 147
southwestern United States
  18–19, 67

Soviet Union 99*c*
Spanish Civil War 130
Speak Out for Animals 128
special interest extremism 4
speculators, 19th century 10
speed limit 99*c*
Spence, Gerry 37, 146*b*
spiking. *See* tree spiking
Sport Utility Vehicle Owners of
  America (SUVOA) 125*c*
sport utility vehicles (SUVs)
  120*c*, 121*c*, 123*c*, 124*c*, 126*c*
SSCS. *See* Sea Shepherd
  Conservation Society
Stanislaus River (California)
  100*c*–101*c*
states' rights 40–41
Stegner, Wallace 127
Sterling Woods Development
  114*c*–115*c*
Stewart, Potter 74
Stone, Christopher D. 75
Stop Eco-Violence (SEV) 251
Stop Huntingdon Animal
  Cruelty (SHAC) 45, 121*c*,
  123*c*, 251
Stop Terrorism of Property Act
  of 2003 125*c*
strategic lawsuit against public
  participation (SLAPP) 153*g*
strip mining 19, 29, 95*c*, 139
subduing of nature 9
Suino, Nick 105*c*
sunset clause 66
Superior Lumber Company
  116*c*
surveillance, electronic 63,
  65–66
survey stakes 97*c*, 102*c*, 105*c*
  Edward Abbey and 27
  Ecotage! and 17
  The Monkey Wrench Gang
    and 29
  National Park Service road
    18
  Tucson Eco-Raiders 19
SUVOA (Sport Utility Vehicle
  Owners of America) 125*c*
SUVs. *See* sport utility vehicles
sweatshop labor 47
symbolic action 5
Synar, Mike 55

T
TAC. *See* Timber Association
  of California
tactical philosophies 5, 23
Taft, William Howard 13
"Tait, Mike." *See* Fain, Mike
Tama, Pedro 103*c*

Index

Taylor, Bob 51
Taylor Grazing Act 92c
"teach-in" 15
technological advancement, conquest of nature and 9
technology, appropriate. See appropriate technology
Tellico Dam 84
Tennessee Valley Authority v. Hill 84
terminology, debate over 5–9
terrorism **7–9**, 153g–154g
  antiterrorism legislation **61–66**
  bibliography 171–174
  effects of 9/11 attacks on debate 8
  and ELF/ALF 46, 47, 49
  equating of civil disobedience with 6
  and *Humanitarian Law Project v. Ashcroft* 85–87
  sabotage vs. 7
  and tree-spiking 35
  Unabomber as genuine terrorist 56
  and USA PATRIOT Act 62
  and wise use radicals 43–44
Terrorism Research Center (TRC) 251
THERMCON 135, 149
This is Dinosaur (David Brower) 131
Thoreau, Henry David 6, 10, 11, 88c, 146b
THPs (timber harvest plans) 79
Three Laws of Ecology 24
Tiburon, California 50
Timber and Stone Act of 1878 10, 90c
Timber Association of California (TAC) 51, 55
Timber Culture Act of 1873 10, 67, 89c
timber harvest plans (THPs) 79
timber industry. See logging industry
timber sales 75–77, 104c, 118c, 120c
Title II (of USA PATRIOT Act) 62
TNC (The Nature Conservancy) 248
Toiyabe National Forest (Nevada) 44
Tolstoy, Leo 127
Trans-Alaska Pipeline 98c

transcendentalism 10, 146
TRC (Terrorism Research Center) 251
Tre Arrow. *See* Scarpitti, Michael James
Trees Foundation 251
tree sitting 154g
  Cove Mallard action 110c
  as direct action 5
  Headwaters Forest protest 40
  Hill and 112c, 136–137
  Mike Jakubel and 104c, 137
tree spiking 104c, 106c, 112c, 118c, 120c, 154g
  Frank Ambrose and 116c, 128
  Judi Bari's denunciation of 130
  Darryl Cherney and 133
  as direct action 5
  Earth First! campaigns 34
  and ELF 48
  William Ervin and 34–35
  Dave Foreman and 136
  law against (1988) 35, 70–72, 107c, 154
  and Redwood Summer 38
  and sabotage 5–6
tribalism 154g
Troutt, Alfred H. 76
Trudeau, Pierre 24, 97c
Tucson Eco-Raiders 19, 97c

U

Udall, Stewart 94c
Unabomber (Theodore Kaczynski) **49–56**, 95c, 100c–102c, 104c–105c, 109c–114c, 116c, 119c, 137b
  beginning of campaign 4
  bibliography 223–234
  and ecoterrorist philosophy 5
  manifesto 52–54, 110c, 137, 285–288
Unification Church 129
United States v. Klein 83
United Vaccines 113c
University of California at Berkeley 102c, 137, 140
University of Michigan 15, 105c, 137
University of New Mexico 127, 135
University of Wisconsin 138, 141
uranium mine power sabotage 36

urbanization, in 19th-century America 10
U.S. Atomic Energy Commission 24, 96c
U.S. Bureau of Fisheries 132
U.S. Chamber of Commerce 17
U.S. Coast Guard 24, 97c
U.S. Department of Agriculture 100c, 113c, 143
U.S. Department of Commerce 16
U.S. Department of Homeland Security (DHS) 251–252
U.S. Department of Justice 7, 46, 53, 63
U.S. Department of the Interior 41
U.S. Environmental Protection Agency (EPA) 16, 30, 97c, 252
U.S. Fish and Wildlife Service (FWS) 14, 17, 30, 80–82, 92c, 132–133
U.S. Forest Industry headquarters arson 114c
U.S. Forest Service (USFS) 90c–91c, 103c–104c, 109c, 252
  and *California v. Block* 77, 78
  and conservation 150
  and Cove Mallard 39
  creation by Theodore Roosevelt 12
  intimidation by wise-use radicals 44
  and *Izaak Walton League v. Butz* 75
  Bart Koehler and 137
  Aldo Leopold and 13, 137, 138
  Gifford Pinchot and 142, 143
  and RARE/RARE II 30, 152
  and *Robertson v. Seattle Audubon Society* 82–84
  and *Sierra Club v. Morton* 73
  and tree spiking 34, 154
  Howie Wolke and 147
U.S. Public Interest Research Group (U.S. PIRG) 252
U.S. Steel 18, 136
U.S. Supreme Court
  Amchitka Island nuclear test decision 24, 97c
  and *Humanitarian Law Project v. Ashcroft* 86
  and *Robertson v. Seattle Audubon Society* 83–84

U.S. Supreme Court *(continued)*
and *Sierra Club v. Morton*
74
and *Tennessee Valley
Authority v. Hill* 84
and Unabomber appeal 53
USA PATRIOT Act of 2001
62–66, 125*c*–126*c*
effect on civil liberties 8
and *Humanitarian Law
Project v. Ashcroft* 86–87
and lawsuits 73
Leslie Pickering and 47,
142
potential for creating
radicals 56
and terrorism 153
USFS. *See* U.S. Forest Service

V
Vail, Colorado 3, 114*c*
Vail Trail 3
Vancouver, British Columbia
24
vandalism, petty 34, 37, 49,
110*c*, 114*c*
veganism 47, 154*g*
Veneman, Ann 41
Vernadsky, Vladimir 149
Vietnam War 129, 135, 144
vigilantism 42
violence 7, 43–45, 47, 54, 66
vivisection 154*g*

W
Walden (Henry David Thoreau)
11
Walden Pond 146
Wal-Mart 119*c*, 125*c*
Walt Disney Enterprises 73–75
war on terrorism 46–47, 56,
124*c*, 142
Warren, Karen J. 22, 146*b*
Washington Contract Loggers
Association 82, 83
Washington Post 52, 110*c*, 137
Watson, Paul 103*c*, 108*c*, 146*b*
anti-whaling efforts 26–27
expulsion from
Greenpeace 7, 26
and SSCS 4, 26, 99*c*
Watt, James 30, 41, 43, 103*c*,
108*c*, 146*b*–147*b*

web sites, of ELF/ALF 46, 47
*A Week on the Concord and
Merrimack Rivers* (Henry
David Thoreau) 11, 88*c*
Weisberg, Barry 17, 95*c*, 147*b*
Wenatchee National Forest
(Washington) 34
Wenden, Arizona 36, 107*c*
*West Virginia Division of the
Izaak Walton League of
America v. Butz* **75–77**
West Virginia Highlands
Conservancy 75
westward expansion 10
Weyerhaeuser 55
whaling 99*c*, 105*c*
Rod Coronado and 134
Project Ahab 99*c*
sabotage of Reykjavík plant
27
and SSCS 26–27
Paul Watson and 146
White Mountains (Arizona)
137–138
Wild Earth (journal) 37, 136
wilderness 89*c*, 152, 154*g*–155*g*
Wilderness Act of 1964 **68–69,**
92*c*, 94*c*, 99*c*
David Brower and 132
and *California v. Block* 77
Aldo Leopold and 138
passage of 15
and preservation 152
and RARE 152
and wilderness 154
Howard Zahniser and 147
wilderness designation 15, 102*c*
"wilderness fundamentalism" 31
wilderness management,
conservation vs. preservation
in 12–13
Wilderness Society 252–253
and *California v. Bergland*
79
Dave Foreman and 135
foundation of 14
growth after Earth Day 16
Bart Koehler and 137
and RARE II 30
Howard Zahniser and 147
Wilderness System 77
The Wildlands Project 38,
108*c*, 136, 253

wildlife refuges 90*c*, 92*c*, 138,
143
Willamette National Forest
112*c*
Willis, Dave 103*c*
The Winning of the West
(Theodore Roosevelt) 90*c*
wiretapping 64
"Wise Use Agenda" 42, 107*c*,
128
Wise Use Leadership
Conference 42
wise use movement **42–45,**
128, 153, 155*g*, 234–237
wolf protection 13, 138
Wolke, Howie 100*c*, 105*c*, 147*b*
forming of Earth First!
30, 101*c*
Ron Kezar and 137
Bart Koehler and 137
Mike Roselle and 144
women's movement,
ecofeminism and 21, 22
Wood, Percy 101*c*
World Trade Center bombing
(1993) 62
World War II 14, 130, 131
Worldwatch Institute 253
World Wildlife Fund (WWF)
253
Wright, Gary 50, 105*c*
WWF (World Wildlife Fund)
253

Y
Yale School of Forestry 137
Yellowstone National Park 11,
67, 89*c*
Yellowstone Protective Act of
1894 **67**
Yosemite National Park 90*c*, 91*c*
David Brower and 131
Hetch Hetchy dam 13
John Muir and 141
Theodore Roosevelt and
143
Yosemite Valley 12, 141, 143
Young Americans for Freedom
135

Z
Zahniser, Howard 94*c*, 147
Zerzan, John 55, 56